Running a Successful Construction Company

Completely Revised and Updated

DAVID GERSTEL

The Taunton Press

 **The Taunton Press**
Inspiration for hands-on living®

The Taunton Press, Inc., 63 South Main Street, PO Box 5506, Newtown, CT 06470-5506

e-mail: tp@taunton.com

Editor: Jackie Parente

Jacket/Cover design: Cathy Cassidy

Interior design and layout: Jeff Potter/Potter Publishing Studio

Illustrator: Ron Carboni

Photographer: Ken Gutmaker, except where noted

For Pros/By Pros® is a trademark of The Taunton Press, Inc., registered in the U.S. Patent and Trademark Office.

Library of Congress Cataloging-in-Publication Data

Gerstel, David U., 1945-

    Running a successful construction company / David Gerstel.—completely rev. and updated.

      p.   cm.—(For pros, by pros)

    New ed. of: The builder's guide to running a successful construction company / David Gerstel. 1991

    Includes index.

     ISBN-13: 978-1-56158-530-4

     ISBN-10: 1-56158-530-0

     1. Construction industry—Management. I. Gerstel, David U., 1945- Builder's guide to running a successful construction company. II. Title. III. Series.

   HD9715.A2 G46 2002

  690'.068—dc21   2002010520

Printed in the United States of America

10 9 8 7

The following manufacturer appearing in *Running a Successful Construction Company* is a trademark: Skilsaw

An Important Note to the Reader: *Legal issues and dollar figures*

Running a Successful Construction Company covers several topics including accounting, taxes, insurance, contracts, and labor relations that are subject to federal and other laws. The text is intended as a guide to the subjects from a builder's perspective, not as a substitute for expert counsel. In all matters that involve local, state, and federal laws, builders should seek additional help from government agencies, attorneys, accountants, brokers, or other appropriate professional sources.

    In writing this book, along with relating on my own experiences I have described the experiences of others to illustrate ideas in the text. Where appropriate, I have given their real identity, but occasionally, I have taken the liberty of changing place, name, and time to maintain anonymity.

    All dollar figures cited have been adjusted for inflation to year 2001 values.

For Sandra with love.

ACKNOWLEDGMENTS

Years ago, I learned that every writer needs a good editor. Without a capable editor giving you feedback, you lose a clear sense of your own prose. You think you are being precise, but you are being vague. You think you're being funny; you are being silly. You worry that certain of your ideas are too obvious or boring. You are ready to toss them. Your editor stops you, letting you know that you are giving just the sort of practical advice that your readers want. For this book I was fortunate to have a superb editor—Jackie Parente of Editorial Services, LLC (www.editorial-services.com). She constantly coached me to clarify my ideas and steadily suggested ways of presenting material that I never would have thought of. Jackie worked on this book way beyond the call of duty. She put her heart into it. I am greatly indebted to her, as is every reader who takes away something useful from *Running a Successful Construction Company*.

Many other people have made substantial contributions to this book. They include the editors and artists with The Taunton Press, builders, specialty contractors, developers, designers, engineers, construction industry consultants and journalists, friends, and other writers. I would like to include a paragraph of thanks to each and every one of them. Space constraints prevent that. I must limit myself to listing them in alphabetical order, with apologies to anyone I might have left out inadvertently.

Sal Alfano, Keith Alward, Barbara Antel, Anneliese Armstrong, Roger Bash, Chris Benton, Fred Blodgett, Moses Brown, Curt Burbick, Bryant Byrnes, Barb Kam, Chris Catlett, Linda Case, Greg Casorso, Peter Chapman, Gene Clements, Paul Conrado, Whitney Collins, Mercedes Corbell, Phil Coombs, Tory Courtney, Les Cunningham, Eric Danysh, Paul Deffenbaugh, Theresa de Valence, Clayton DeKorne, Paul Eldrenkamp, Phil Emminger, Lance Farina, Laura Ferrell, Tom Frainier, Blake Gilmore, David Haight, Rick Harper, Devon Hartman, Iris Harrell, Steve Harvey, John Hausman, Larry Hayden, Randy Hellstern, Ann Hollingsworth, Peggy Hosmer, Tom Jackson, Josh Kardon, Steve Kendall, George Kiskaddon, John Kraft, Bob and Rose Kroll, Leslie Lacko, Dan Larsen, John Larson, David Lassman, Gary Lazar, Jordan Lourie, Jim Lunt, David Lupberger, Robert Malone, Leigh Marymor, Harold Martin, John McLean, Bob and Debbie McNeil, Mike McCutcheon, Seth Melchert, David Meiland, Charles Miller, Judith Miller, Karen Mitchell, Richard Morrison, Lee Moulton, Mike Muscardini, Steve Nicholls, Bill Olin, Satya Palani, Andy Pauley, Mark Pearsall, Tek Pei, Ken Perry, Mark Phillips, Daniel Ramirez, Linda Randolph, Deva Rajan, Ron Roberts, Howard Robbins, Daryl Rush, Craig Savage, Janet Scoll, Donna Schlachman, Claire Schooley, Steven and Lisa Schliff, Pam Seifert, Chuck Seliger, John Seuss, Steve Shambaugh, Denia Shields, George Skaates, Joan Skolnick, Carole Swain, Robert Swatt, Roland Turk, David Turner, Kurtis Trieu, Laura Tringali, Megan Twadell, Peter Vandersterre, Mimi and John Ward, Donald Wardlaw, Anida Weyl, Joe Wilkinson, Les Williams, Lon Williams, Gary Wilson, Paul Winans, and Peter Witti.

Contents

Introduction   2

PART ONE

Getting Ready   4

1 A Builder's Career   5

What It Takes   5

Opportunities and Challenges   12

Making a Plan   17

2 A Builder's Tools   23

Office and Shop   23

Computers in Construction   30

Policy Statement   36

Operating Capital   41

Insurance   45

3 A Builder's Numbers   51

Knowing Your Numbers   51

Starting with a Shoebox   60

Moving Up to a One-Write System   69

Keeping Job Cost Records   77

Adding Payroll   83

Leaping to a Computer Program   87

Going Deeper into Your Numbers   95

PART TWO

Getting the Right Jobs   100

4 Entering the Marketplace   101

Marketing   101

Connecting with Design Professionals   110

Evaluating Projects   115

Competitive Bidding   121

Design/Build   127

Cost Planning   133

5 Estimating and Bidding   142

Nailing Your Numbers   142

Gathering Information   152

Calculating Direct Costs   158

Figuring Overhead   163

Figuring Profit   169

Alternative Methods   172

6 Construction Contracts   177

Why and Which One   177

The Agreement   183

The Conditions   189

Two Critical Conditions:
Change Orders and Dispute Resolution   193

Subcontracts   197

PART THREE

Getting the Jobs Done Right   200

7 Labor, Materials, and Subcontractors   201

Hiring and Firing   201

Crew   210

Project Leads and Delegation   215

Pay   221

Subcontractors and Suppliers   228

8 Project Management   235

Safety First   235

Job Setup   238

Running Projects   244

Working with Clients   252

Resources   258

Glossary   260

Index   263

Introduction

When the first edition of this book was published in 1991 and the reviews began to come in, one reader commented that sitting down with it was "like having a conversation with a dozen other builders who are sharing their hard-won experience." In fact, the ideas in that first edition flowed from the generosity not only of a dozen, but of many dozens of construction professionals who had shared their knowledge and experience with me. Together we were offering a comprehensive guide to the fundamentals of organizing and running a construction company.

In the decade that has followed, my education has gone on nonstop, as I have continued to learn from fellow builders and from the experience, now spanning over 25 years, of running my own construction business. My understanding of every one of the issues that I write about has expanded and sharpened. At the same time, there have been major changes in the construction industry. Computers were just nudging their way into builders' offices when I wrote the first edition. Now they are as commonplace as telephones and file cabinets. Construction technology has been evolving at a blistering pace with tools, materials, and specialty trades all proliferating and building codes becoming more complex. The changes in technology have brought on changes in the way builders run their companies and organize projects.

When I set out to write this second edition, my intent was simply to put into play my increased knowledge and to reflect the impact of new technology. What I ended up producing, however, is far more than a revision. There are entire new chapters and subchapters—on computers, on delegation, on design/build, and on many other subjects. The chapter on cost planning, the alternative to competitive bidding that I have developed, has been completely reworked. Every chapter includes new concepts and examples and makes use of new ways of presenting information. In fact, few paragraphs or sentences have survived intact from the first edition. For all practical purposes, what you hold in your hand is a new book.

Even so, readers of the first edition will, I believe, feel at home with this new book. It uses the same logical, three-part organization of material—Getting Ready, Getting the Right Jobs, Getting the Jobs Done Right. It remains a "what-and-why" book as well as a "how-to" book. While focusing on *what* you must do to succeed as a builder and explaining *why*, it provides plenty of *how-to* advice. You will find ample suggestions and even detailed checklists for creating procedures for key tasks from marketing to estimating and bidding right on through to creating contracts, producing change orders, and running jobs. Finally, this new book comes back again and again to the same core ideas as the first edition. It urges adherence to the same basic principles:

- *Plan and focus.* To succeed as a builder you must organize and prioritize relentlessly.
- *Travel light. Run lean. Operate economically.* To prosper over the long run, make careful use of money, material, and equipment. Don't fool yourself into thinking of that fully loaded new pickup as a cost-effective investment in your business when it is really just excessive personal consumption.
- *Act with integrity.* Easy to say, hard to do. To achieve integrity, work at it nail-by-nail at your projects, encounter-by-encounter with your clients, workers, subs, and suppliers. Integrity is its own reward, but in the building business it is also rewarded with client and employee loyalty—and by freedom from lawsuits over corner-cutting construction.
- *Be fair to everyone, including yourself.* Being fair to clients includes seeing to it that they receive good value and responsive service. Being fair to workers includes compensating them fully and treating them with respect. Being fair to yourself includes commanding respect and collecting your due pay—a reasonable salary for managing your company as well as a wage for any hands-on work you do and a moderate profit. For many builders, being fair to themselves is the far harder part of maintaining the balance. When they don't, we lose them. They can't stay in business.

Adhere to your own versions of such principles, and you will build a successful construction company. The qualities

During my building career, I have enjoyed jobs from retaining walls and garden fences to the construction of new buildings...

of such a company were neatly summed up by a stone mason I met in Ireland a while back. I was walking along a country lane when I came upon him repairing a rough stone wall enclosing a pasture. I stopped to watch, we struck up a conversation, and I explained to him that I was a builder from America and wanted to learn about his craft. "Then don't pay this much heed, lad," he said, gesturing at the wall he was patching. "It's junk, this is. If you want to see a good wall of mine, go on down the lane there, and look at the wall behind the schoolhouse." I told him I would and inquired how I would be able to tell it was a good wall. "What should I look for?" I asked. He thought for a moment, and then he said, "Well, I tell you, it's the same as with a person. It's got character and stability. That's what marks a good wall." I walked on, stopping behind the schoolhouse to admire the stonemason's work. It was some time later that it hit me—his words describing a good wall also fit a well-run construction company. Like the wall, a good company has character and stability. I hope that my book will help you in building your own company with just those qualities. Good luck to you.

David Gerstel
January 2002

... as well as the complete overhaul and remodeling of old homes such as the one shown here.

PART ONE

Getting Ready

1 A Builder's Career

What It Takes

Opportunities and Challenges

Making a Plan

2 A Builder's Tools

Office and Shop

Computers in Construction

Policy Statement

Operating Capital

Insurance

3 A Builder's Numbers

Knowing Your Numbers

Starting with a Shoebox

Moving Up to a One-Write System

Keeping Job Cost Records

Adding Payroll

Leaping to a Computer Program

Going Deeper into Your Numbers

CHAPTER 1

A Builder's Career

What It Takes

BUILDERS I have known come from a variety of backgrounds: Homemaker. Sculptor. Professor. Cop. Pinball machine vendor. Schoolteacher. Whatever their past experience, they have developed an impressive range of capabilities in achieving success as builders. Whatever size company they have chosen to organize—whether it's an artisan operation in which the owner works with only an occasional helper, or a chamber of commerce company with 30 carpenters on the payroll—they have established competency in four broad areas:

- *Clarity of purpose*—They know why they have chosen a career in construction, the values they will uphold in their work, and what services they want to offer.
- *Construction*—Successful builders almost always have at least journey-level skills in the trades, usually at carpentry. They understand how buildings are put together.
- *Communication*—They know how to listen effectively. They know how to

clearly and convincingly convey information to workers, clients, and other construction professionals.
- *Controls*—They have mastered the management systems necessary for making sure legal and insurance protections are in place, for knowing where money is coming from and where it is going, and for using time and material resources effectively.

Glancing over these capabilities quickly, it's easy to breezily reassure yourself about each one—"Oh, yeah, I've got that covered"—when, in fact, you don't.

I've made the mistake myself and often have seen other builders delude themselves into thinking they can get by without one or another of the "four Cs," or that they are better at it than they really are. Then they find themselves in a situation like that of the general contractor who is now staggering at the edge of bankruptcy, even though his loyal clients have booked him solid for the next two years. He is superb at construction. He is a master of communication. For years, however, he has rationalized his resistance to establishing controls. His accounting systems are so weak he recently found him-

COMING UP

Clarity of Purpose

Three More "Cs": Construction, Communication, and Controls

The Three Rs: Reading, Writing, and Arithmetic

Trade Knowledge

Entrepreneurial Ability

Time Management

Financial Discipline

Standardized Operating Procedures

Delegation

One Step at a Time

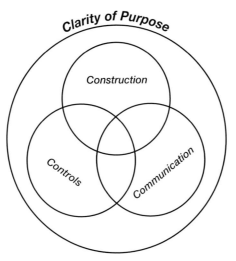

In order to get where you want to go as a builder you need to develop the appropriate capabilities in construction, communication, and controls.

self reaching the midpoint of the year unable to tell whether he was making or losing money on his projects. He was unable even to figure how much tax he owed. Still worse, when one of his employees drove a company truck into another vehicle, he discovered he had only the legally required minimum insurance in place. It is not nearly enough to cover his potential medical and legal liabilities. As a result, the lawsuit he now faces could clean out his life savings.

Construction has become an information-age business.

A Mission Statement

Some so-called mission statements run on forever, giving you an overcooked, flavorless minestrone of good intentions. Some mission statements, like the following, are beautifully simple and direct. They hit home:

"Allied Building Products will strive to be the leading building materials distributor in the West by hiring and keeping the best employees, meeting their needs as well as their families', promoting high-quality products at a competitive level, and providing uncompromising service to our customers."

It is a tall order, building a business with clarity of purpose, plus capability at construction, communication, and controls. If you are just starting out or are struggling and wondering whether to continue, you would do well to take inventory of yourself and decide whether you really *do* have what it takes. You can begin by checking up on your clarity of purpose—or, to use a term currently fashionable in the business world, by writing out a "mission statement."

Many mission statements I have seen are nothing more than a string of high-sounding clichés. On the other hand, if you can write in a *few* honest words that state clearly what you want to accomplish as a builder, then you know what you are about. You have a starting point. You have a direction. You are ready to evaluate your level of competence at or willingness to acquire the specific skills you will need to carry out your responsibilities in construction, communication, and controls.

The Three Rs

To achieve competence at the four Cs you need your three Rs: reading, writing, and arithmetic. You must be able to read and write well, and you must be able to handle numbers.

Construction has become an information-age business. Builders are constantly dealing with complex specifications, with reams of product information, and with changing laws. We are, in addition, experiencing a nonstop revolution in technology—in both construction materials and tools and in so-called "information technology," not only computers and software but a host of other devices. As a builder, to understand and cope with all the information and change, you must be able to read with speed and comprehension. To be a bit blunt, if you barely got through high school and struggled to get through your books, while you may be able to succeed at a career in the trade, you are heading for a miserable experience if you try to become a general building contractor. You need to build up your literacy first. You can do so by reading magazines about the construction work you love (see Resources on p. 258) and by taking courses in construction management at your local junior or technical college.

You will need to learn to take in written information and to put it out— to write policy statements, contracts, and a variety of documents for effectively and profitably running jobs. Likewise, you must be fluent with basic business math (also taught at community colleges) so you can achieve precision at your estimating and bidding. You will be able to stay atop the accounting of money taken in and money spent so that you understand and can manage the financial side of your business. With your three Rs in place, you will be able to support the work of your company in the field.

Trade knowledge

Before starting their own companies, successful builders usually acquire trade skills by working for other contractors. There are exceptions. Occasionally, I meet a builder who first entered construction as a salesperson, administrator, or designer. But for the most part, successful builders—at least at the level of the small- to medium-volume companies that dominate our industry—have placed concrete and framed walls. They have hung and cased doors and flashed windows. Because they have put in years on the job site themselves, they can quickly recognize the moves of a skilled carpenter or of an uncertain one. They can hire and fire tradespeople effectively. The can reject work likely to fail and convincingly promote good craftsmanship.

If you try to become a builder without sufficient trade experience, you can

put yourself and your clients in harm's way. As one former builder explained to me, "You must have the trade knowledge so that you can worry about management without struggling with building itself." He had attempted to transform his painting company into a general contracting operation before gaining experience in construction. As a result: On his first sizable job, a residential remodel, he lost so much money that he went bankrupt, leaving his client with his house torn apart.

Letter to an Aspiring Builder

After reading an article I wrote about project management, a young man with a couple of years' job site and trade school experience wrote to ask for advice on setting up a construction company. I responded with the letter excerpted below. Some years later, the young man called to say that he had taken my advice and delayed starting his business. Now he is operating his own company. With a thorough knowledge of his trade, he had gotten off to a strong start.

April 10, 1988

Dear Steve,

Thank you for your nice remarks about my article. You ask if I have any suggestions for you. Yes, I do. DON'T START YOUR OWN BUSINESS YET. Master your trade first. Do whatever it takes. Work for lower wages. Commute great distances. Move to another state. But get yourself a job in a well-organized company where you will learn sound construction techniques and be exposed to good project management.

Work for that company (or companies) for three to four years. In your last year of employment, set up all the systems you need to manage a construction company. Once you have them in place, not before, begin seeking your first projects…

Construction companies fail because people who start them don't know their trade well or they don't know business management. If you start your own company now, you will know neither. It takes more than two years in the field to learn a trade… You do not want to be still unsure of the trade when you take on the challenge of management.

Good Luck,

David Gerstel

Resisting the Job of Running Your Company

Early in their careers, especially, builders resist hanging up their tools, even for part of their work week, and giving priority to running their companies for a variety of reasons.

- They feel that the hands-on work is the fun part of being a contractor.
- Having made their living with their tools for years, they can't imagine they will be able to support themselves if they put them down. They don't notice that, all around them, other builders are swinging a briefcase instead of a hammer and are prospering.
- They scorn "business types." They are proud to be wearing those tools, may even brag to clients, "I do the work myself" (unlike those slick characters who take their customers' money for just shuffling paper).
- They don't see that even on quite small projects, management is the work most crucial to success—that every other element of the project depends upon it.
- They fail to understand that if they want to have a career as a builder of good buildings, they must also build a strong business.

Taking off the tool belt to run your own company

Ironically, after working hard to learn your trade, you probably will have to hang up your tools to become a builder. You do have the option of becoming what I call an "artisan builder." You can limit yourself to relatively small projects and build them one at a time, doing most of the hands-on work yourself, and occasionally hiring temporary help or subcontractors. Working as an independent artisan builder can make for a satisfying way of life, at least until your body begins to give out sometime during middle age.

But if you want to take on larger projects, especially if you want to handle more than one at a time, you will find yourself up against this compelling logic: On-schedule, on-budget construction of multiple, larger projects requires a stable group of carpenters and subcontractors who have worked together often enough to work as a team. For the team to be stable, it must have a steady stream of work. Providing that work—marketing, estimating, bidding, and developing contracts—is a full-time job. It is *your* job.

For a variety of reasons many builders, including myself in my early days, resist taking off the tool belt and dedicating ourselves to running our companies. But once having made the change, we often have found our new job as rewarding as hands-on construction. We take pride in our well-kept job sites, the high morale and loyalty of our crew, the efficient organization of our projects, the financial discipline that allows us to provide good pay and benefits to everyone in our company, including ourselves. We enjoy our role as teachers and leaders. And we find the continual development of our general-contracting skills challenging.

The best place for an aspiring builder to learn trade skills is in a well-run, small-volume company. As an employee of a big company that builds large projects, you may find yourself doing the same task over and over. I have known carpenters who put in years with large companies and can execute only a few phases of their trade—though I will say they're mighty fast at running joists or laying subfloor. With a small-volume company, you can get the opportunity to work through the whole sequence from deconstruction to setting trim over and over. Over and over, you see the meshing of all the sub trades with rough and finish carpentry. You learn thoroughly the sequence in which all the many components that make up a structure are laced together. That experience is invaluable, because when you become a builder in your own right, your contractual responsibility is to see that the parts do come together.

We take satisfaction, also, in honing our entrepreneurial instincts—that talent for finding and winning or creating viable projects in a competitive marketplace. Entrepreneurial instinct distinguishes people who lead companies from those who simply manage one or another business process. Builders must have the instinct. It's not only that you must create a marketing strategy and sales technique. You must develop a "nose for business," a capability that, regrettably, is not quite teachable but that you must somehow discover and encourage in yourself. In the concrete business, they say, "We find a hole and fill it." That's what you have to do as a builder. You must relentlessly search out the right holes for your company to fill, and then get the job of filling them.

Time management and financial discipline

To operate successfully, builders need to make economical, effective use of all their resources—time, material, and finances. A great deal has been written about time management (see Resources on p. 258), and there are various planners and even electronic devices on the market designed to help you navigate through your days efficiently. Some builders who struggle with procrastination and do not use their time well find it helpful to actually log their use of time. They maintain a diary of what they do with each quarter hour of each day. When they see how much time they fritter away, they are shocked into making more disciplined use of their hours. If you are a procrastinator, you could benefit from keeping a time log.

In my own work as a builder, I have found that time management boils down to a simple process repeated over and over:

■ *Prioritize relentlessly.* Distinguish what you really need to take care of—both long-term development tasks and daily and weekly management and production responsibilities—from the unimportant distractions.
■ *Organize the important tasks on calendars and charts.* Block out time for

---

Time Management

Effective use of time results from steadily prioritizing and organizing tasks.

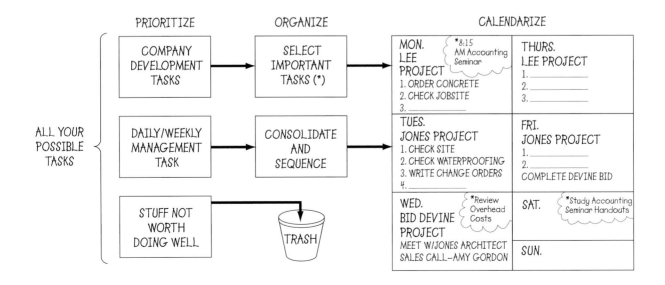

the development tasks—like attending a seminar on accounting or marketing—that fuel your company's long-term growth and stability. Group the daily and weekly nuts-and-bolts tasks into efficient sequences. As my first carpentry teacher taught, consolidate your motions.

■ *Push the unimportant stuff off your desk entirely.* Don't just hurry through it. Get *rid* of it. If it is not worth doing well, it is not worth doing, so don't do it!

The same disciplined approach necessary to effective use of time must be brought to the use of financial resources. *Builders who are financially successful in the long run are those who make necessary investments in services and equipment, but at the same time rigorously control the costs of running their businesses.* Financial discipline will be a recurring theme in coming chapters. For now, it is enough to say that to make effective use of financial resources you must do something similar to what you do with time. Figure out what you really need. Invest in it. Resist investing in all the other stuff that is pushed at you. Concentrate on getting maximum benefit from the tools and services in which you have invested.

Standard operating procedures

Often I hear other builders speak of time as well as financial management as "getting organized." But to be really organized, to use time as well as financial resources efficiently, you need to go a step further. You must develop standard procedures for doing the tasks that actually take up your time and use your money. You must create procedures for every routine task that your company handles—from taking a prospective customer's first phone call, to bidding

on a project and signing a contract for it, to scheduling subcontractors for a job, and completing punch lists at its end.

If you are inventing a procedure from scratch for each task, if you are reaching for scrap paper and a pencil instead of a form or checklist, you are going miss a lot of steps in these tasks. You are going to work awfully long hours making up for your oversights. One veteran educator of contractors points out that in the poorly run company, the answer to every question that comes up is, "We'll play it by ear," or "We'll work it out." The competent builder says, "Let me make a note of that," and knows on just what form, list, or schedule to place the note.

This book should get you a long way toward creating your standard operating procedures (SOPs). Once in place they will greatly increase your personal efficiency. But they will do more than that. They will enable you to effectively hand off tasks to other people. In the parlance of the business world, they enable you to successfully "delegate" functions so you don't get stuck in a permanent spread eagle trying to cover every base yourself.

With SOPs in place, when you hire someone to handle a facet of your company's business that you have been handling, you will be able to coach them in executing it with a well worked out set of procedures. When, for example, you ask carpenters to step up to running jobs, you will be able to introduce them to your procedures for project management progressively. You won't just be dumping a wad of tasks in their lap, then wondering why they bumbled them.

As your business grows, delegation can become the core of your work. In the classical scenario, first you hand off job site production, next, clerical work and bookkeeping, then project and office management, and finally, estimating and sales. Eventually, you find you have

---

E

ventually, you find you have moved entirely from working with things to working with people.

moved entirely from working with things to working with people. Of course, not all builders complete the sequence. Some—including myself—prefer to run smaller operations, keeping some of the job site or office production in their own hands.

Builders have differing theories about delegation. Some say, "Hire to your weakness"—hire someone to do the thing you are not good at. Others share my preference for "hiring to strength"—becoming skilled at a task and then handing it off carefully. But regardless of the angle they take or the size of their operations, every builder I have ever talked to about the subject finds delegating a challenge.

In Part 3 we will look into delegation in some detail. For here it is enough to say that the challenge is to give your employees space to do things in their own way but at the same time get reasonable adherence to your standard procedures. You have to avoid micromanaging, yet maintain your controls.

You must walk a fine line between delegation and abdication. If you maintain too much control, you will destroy the initiative of people, even as you are asking them to take responsibility. If you go over it into abdication, you can find yourself in the shoes of a former subcontractor of mine bent on expanding his business at too fast a rate. He hired an experienced estimator and, so that he could concentrate on marketing, quickly extended to the man complete and unchecked responsibility for estimating and bidding even large projects. The estimator so badly underbid two of the first jobs entrusted to him that he put the company into bankruptcy.

A demanding program

And that is my overview of what it takes to successfully run a construction company. Along with clarity of purpose, you need strength at all the many skills required for competent execution of your overlapping responsibilities in construction, communication, and controls. Working from a strong base in the three "Rs" and the trades, you will need to develop entrepreneurial savvy, disciplined intelligence in the allocation of time and financial resources, a willingness to create and hone procedures, and skill at delegation.

You will need something else, too, and that is a deep reservoir of patience. No matter how honed your purpose, how sharp your time management skills, and how precise your operating procedures, your applecart *will* get knocked over. Like every successful, seasoned builder you will need to absorb the hits, to rigorously organize with the expectation that your plans will be blown apart regularly by weather, project changes, economic recession, loss of key people, and hot opportunities. You will learn to take a deep breath, tip the cart back onto its wheels, and keep going. A mentor of mine once lost his office manager, estimator, and three top lead carpenters over a short period of time. Still a little new to the building business, I expressed my concern for his survival. "Oh," he responded smilingly, "your best people build your company, David. But they also define and limit it. When they leave, you have the opportunity to stride off into new directions with new people." And that is exactly what he did.

All in all, it is a lot to ask of oneself, all this cultivation of purpose, skills, and patience. It is a lot for me to ask of you. In truth, my book lays out a demanding program. Probably more than one reader has felt what an acquaintance did tell me. "After I read your book," he said, "I figured if this is what I have to do to be a builder, I will never make it." So that you not feel overwhelmed, I would like to

t is not necessary to acquire all the capabilities by next Tuesday. You can take them on incrementally.

emphasize to you, valued reader, it is not necessary to acquire all the capabilities by next Tuesday. You can take them on incrementally, in small and manageable chunks. You can steadily build your knowledge, ability, and systems one step at a time, even as you operate your company. That, in fact, is what most of us who have enjoyed success as builders have done. And that is what we continue to do, even after decades of experience.

O f course, lean years punctuate the lucrative ones.

COMING UP

High Demand for
Capable Builders

Rewards, Financial and Beyond

Getting Going Gets Tough

Stress of a
Boom and Bust Business

Bucking the Public's Demand
for Quantity over Quality

Low Status and Lowballers

Promising Developments

Opportunities and Challenges

The needs for shelter of a growing population, changing technology, and the toll of time on existing structures combine to generate tremendous demand for construction services. During periods of economic boom, such as much of the 1980s and most of the 1990s, builders who have the skills at construction, communication, and controls are deluged with calls from prospective clients. They can readily book work a year and more in advance. Even during slower periods, builders with a reputation for reliability generally enjoy enough call for their services to get by. In fact, I was able to get my own business under way during the deep recession of the early 1970s.

Of the demand for construction work, roughly half to two-thirds (estimates vary) is for repair and remodeling. Therein lies especially great opportunity for builders at the beginning of their careers. Repair and remodeling projects of limited scope—siding and window replacements, decks and fences, structural repairs, and interior renovations—provide the startup guy a chance to build management systems and business skills while limiting financial risk. If you underbid a bathroom renovation, at least you will

be through it in a few weeks—likely escaping with a modest wage for your hands-on work, though with nothing to cover the overhead costs of running your company, never mind a profit.

Established builders in built-up urban areas, find great opportunity in remodeling—kitchens, baths, additions, renovations. In fact, remodeling, held in contempt by "real builders" when I started out 30 years ago, is a growing field attracting first-class operations. Along with new construction and traditional remodeling jobs, there are increasing numbers of what, for lack of a better term, can be called "reuse" projects. While incorporating some components of an existing structure, they result in essentially new buildings. Reuse projects require the skills of both the consummate remodeler and the builder of new custom structures, and can be especially satisfying, if challenging, to build.

Rewards, financial and beyond

Even small-volume builders—those with one to three crews and total sales of a few hundred thousand to a million dollars or so annually—can earn incomes ranging well up into six figures. Of course, lean years punctuate the lucrative ones. As one builder quips, "The buck stops with you, and sometimes it stops in your pocket." But running your own building company offers opportunities even greater than a shot at financial prosperity. Do you cherish well-crafted work? You can embrace practices that produce enduring and architecturally delightful exteriors and interiors. Have you come to understand the urgent importance of creating a sustainable economy? You can model the best of what veteran remodeler Larry Hayden has aptly named "environmentally considerate" (also called "green") construction practices. You can turn your projects into virtual recycling centers, like the builder I admire who takes pride in running a job so tightly that nothing "but a little sawdust and sheetrock scrap ends up in the dump."

Among the greatest of rewards is clients' appreciation for work well done. Among my favorite moments in construction is a chance encounter in a coffee shop with a client whose home I had expanded and renovated. A single mom, she had been surviving in a cramped, dilapidated, badly laid out space with her two teenagers. "I want you to know," she said quietly, "I'm happy in my house now. I like being there. I hated being there before."

While opportunity and reward for builders are abundant, they are not often attained. Not many builders stay in business long enough to enjoy them. Like restaurants, construction companies come and go in multitudes.

Getting going gets tough

Builders go out of business for numerous reasons—and not all are bad, as explained in the top sidebar on p. 14. But too many men and women who try their hand at running their own construction companies do struggle at the job. Often it is because they have not been adequately prepared. They find it difficult to get decent, much less really good, training in the necessary trade skills and more so in construction management.

Even when you do find employment as an apprentice carpenter with a relatively capable company, it can be grueling. The work is hard, and you are often clumsy at it. You're bruised. You bleed. Often, you feel humiliated. Said one builder who knows he set up in business for himself before he really had his trade skills down, "I got tired of being treated like a Skilsaw®, like a disposable resource.

My only way out was to start my own operation."

As for management, there are not many well-run construction companies to begin with, especially at the small-volume level, and those that are offer few managerial positions. It's a rare builder who has enjoyed on-the-job training in the sound procedures needed to start and run a construction company properly. Most who enter the construction business find themselves under-developed not only at the trade but naive about business management. They find themselves cobbling together operational procedures at night after tiring days on their job sites, and, too often, that effort

Since adding a second story to this home 20 years ago, I have become friends with two of the families who have lived in it. Such connection to community is one of the best things about being a builder.

"The buck stops with you, and sometimes it stops in your pocket."

Shelter Builders

As your career lengthens, your projects dot your town. You see them as you go about your business. They anchor you in your community. You have provided the community's shelter. "That's why I like building," Ann Hollingsworth, a carpenter and general contractor, once told me. "I like making something. I like imagining it in my mind, then figuring it out and doing it, and then it's there. Ten years later you come back, and it's still there doing its job."

"Failure" Can Lead to Opportunity

"Nine out of ten contractors fail within a couple of years." If you enter the building business, you will see that sad statistic regularly in the construction industry publications. Don't let it discourage you. The numbers don't mean quite what they seem to say. Counted in the failure rates are the innumerable men and women who try contracting and decide it is not for them but who have not "*failed*" in the usual business meaning of the word—i.e., gone bankrupt. They have simply shelved their businesses. Often, they go on to use their contracting experience as a springboard to new opportunities. For example, an ace lead carpenter I know got his license and started his own company. After a couple of years, he realized that, with his big heart, he was never able to charge enough to make the effort financially worthwhile. He closed up shop, then used his experience to win a good job managing large projects for a development firm. Another builder chose not to continue in construction at all. He became a schoolteacher. His contracting experience proved invaluable as a source of lesson ideas and for classroom management. He knew how to take charge.

Blindsided

As challenging as the roller-coaster ride on the business cycle can be, at least it is predictable. "This too shall end," applies equally to lean and lucrative years, even if you do not know exactly when the end will come. But builders must take other jolts that come out of nowhere. During cleanup on a high-end kitchen remodel, a conscientious apprentice carefully scrubs away crayon marks on the plastic laminate cabinet doors with a nylon pad. It dulls their glossy surface permanently. Replacements cost the builder his entire margin for overhead and profit on the three-month project. On a different job, an equipment operator inadvertently loosens a large boulder. It rolls down the hillside and crashes not into the siding of the house below but—with just inches to spare all around—through a window, breaking the owner's arm as he sits at his computer and knocking him out. Then there's the legendary experience of the paving contractor whose crew performs a superb job of installing a semicircular drive to a handsome home on the historic registry. Regrettably, as the owners of the home indicate when they return from vacation just at final cleanup, it was actually not themselves but their next-door neighbors who had contracted for the drive.

is made only in response to disastrous experiences. You get clobbered in an IRS audit, so you organize your accounting and set up a legitimate payroll. A client refuses to pay you for many thousands of dollars worth of extras they ordered, and you realize you have to put into place a good contract and change order procedure. You find yourself repeatedly going from being swamped with work to scrambling to keep busy. Grudgingly, you invest in a basic marketing program.

The roller-coaster ride on the business cycle

Even if you have been lucky enough to receive good training in the trades and to acquire management and business capabilities before you open your company, no smooth path to success lies before you. As a builder, you are especially subject to the often steep accelerations and plunges of the free enterprise system. An up and then down ride, such as dot.com businesses experienced during the 1990s, has always been business as usual for builders.

Both the up and the down sides of the cycle pose challenges. When business is booming, you can pick and choose from among prospective clients and have a chance to earn good markups for overhead and profit on the projects you take. On the other hand, it is dangerously easy during boom times to get overextended. You find yourself unable to take care of requests from even your favorite past clients. You can't recruit the talent needed to build the projects you do commit to. Your management systems buckle under workloads larger than they were designed to handle.

When the economy slows, and businesses in general experience a drop-off in revenue, construction often pitches over the edge of a cliff. I have worked through periods when 8 out of 10 carpenters in my area were without work while unemployment was at roughly 10 percent in the general population. I have known builders who earned a large income one year and could not pay their mortgage the next.

Low status, low standards, lowballers

Along with economic stress comes an emotional burden. One highly regarded builder summed it up bluntly: "It really fries me that engineers and architects are seen as professionals, and we are seen as sleaze." Unfortunately, however, the public's disdain for contractors is, to a degree, rooted in truth. The unhappy fact is that the bar for entry into the construction business is set very low. Even California standards, reputed to be relatively tough, long have offered a contractor's license to anyone who can manage a couple of baby steps.

All that is required is "proof" (not closely checked, often fabricated) of several years' supervisory or journey-level experience in the trades and a low passing score on a superficial test about building codes, laws, and business practices.

Once out in the marketplace, newly minted contractors who *do* want to conduct business and build with a high standard of care, face entrenched forces pushing them in the reverse direction. To begin with, there's the cynicism that runs through the industry. You've got the "Slapstick Framers" (as an apprentice of mine with a gift for malaprops once called them), the guys whose slogan is "can't see it from my house." Then you have the contractors for whom a project means nothing but a chance to "get in, get out, and get my money." Worst of

The Perils of Apprenticeship

Inspired by a love of beautiful buildings, Tom decided to become a general contractor. To begin learning carpentry, he hustled an apprentice's job with a builder constructing a greenhouse. Tom soon discovered, however, that the clients requested half the greenhouse be built on a public park adjacent to their property and that the builder, loaded on cocaine much of the day, could not care less. Tom gave notice and quickly found employment at a different site. There, the builder paired him with another young carpenter of equal inexperience, gave them a few sketches of a deck, a pile of lumber, and instructions on how to reach him aboard his sailboat if they needed direction. Tom moved on. At his next job, when the builder discovered Tom could read a set of plans, he put him in charge of the carpentry crew, a gang of unskilled adolescents whose wild antics, Tom realized, were endangering his life. He moved on.

He then found work with an architect/builder in a sylvan setting meant for the cover of *Fine Homebuilding*. Tom's hopes soared. On his first day on the job, however, the builder dropped a 2×12 on his own head, and upon returning to the project with his scalp stitched together,

announced that while thinking things over at the hospital he had realized the project was going too slowly. He decided, therefore, to institute a bonus system intended to encourage productivity. Instead, it produced an amputated finger, cut off by an apprentice rushing to rip a 2×4 with his Skilsaw, holding it out in front of himself without support.

Tom moved on again, and again, and finally found work with a remodeler whom I will call Prokovich. When the fiberglass tub/shower Prokovich had specified for an upstairs bathroom would not fit through the front door of the house, Tom suggested ordering a knock-down unit. But Prokovich dismissed the idea, and two days later the tub/shower *was* in the bathroom—Prokovich and his crew had built a ramp to the second story, broken out a stucco wall, and cut through studs and wiring and water supply lines and plaster, only to find that the tub/shower unit was too big. As Prokovich took out a saber saw to cut it down to size, Tom decided to head down the road once more—this time to a different career.

Lowballed

For months, I worked with a likeable young couple who wanted to build a new home on a very tight budget. Finally, rather than cut back the size of the project, they elected to terminate our relationship and go with a builder whose prior experience was entirely as a painter and small-scale remodeler. He agreed to give them what they wanted for 15 percent less than I would have charged. When construction got under way, it moved slowly, with the project taking more than twice as long as normal. Quality was, to put it kindly, "uneven." Both builder and owner were lucky to avoid worse problems—namely the builder going bust and leaving the client with a partially built house. The builder later confided to me that she ran out of money long before the job was done, was able to complete it only after putting her life savings in hock, and even then walked a financial razor's edge to the end. It's not the first, nor will it be the last, time I lose a good project to a contractor unable to accurately project the costs of building it.

Out in the marketplace, while gluttony *is* rampant, there are many customers who believe that if something is worth doing, it is worth doing well.

all, you have the self-declared "educators" in the construction industry who glorify profit margins virtually to the exclusion of other values.

But while the public's frustration with the dismal standard of performance embraced by too many builders is justified and understandable, it is also true that in good part it is the public that perpetuates those low standards. As an article in *Forbes* magazine pointed out, "Americans crave bigger and more lavishly equipped homes than any other people on earth or in history." Their appetite often cannot be met without compromising quality at every step of the building process, from design through painting. An architect once told me, "Americans want the sizzle, not the steak." He may have had it only partly right. Too many of our potential customers want steak at sizzle prices. The upshot for builders committed to construction done skillfully and with care is a perpetual dilemma. They must regularly compete against the lowballers and

incompetents who promise clients all they want for whatever they wish to pay.

Help and hope

For all the challenges, over the years many builders have acquired the skills they need and have gone on to organize strong companies that do good work, and can survive the ride on the business roller coaster. For those readers now at an early point in their career, opportunity for success is greater than for builders of an earlier time. You have vastly better resources available for education in the trades and in business management (see Resources on p. 258). While there may not be more good trade apprenticeships, there are several good magazines, books, and videos that can help you understand how to build quality structures. If you study them, they will greatly expand the knowledge you pick up in the field.

As for help with learning how to run a company, the abundance of information is stunning. When I started out, there was virtually nothing available. A book such as the one you are holding, which takes you all the way through the fundamentals, did not exist. The various groups and conventions where you can associate with other builders and trade hard-won lessons were even far less numerous. Computer software for accounting and estimating, which helps you understand the tasks as well as helps you do them, had not yet been invented.

Out in the marketplace, while gluttony *is* rampant, there are many customers who believe that if something is worth doing, it is worth doing well. They appreciate well-designed, carefully crafted buildings. They will choose quality over quantity. They are willing to pay a premium for reliably managed construction and are leery of lowball contractors, if only because they have naively hired one in the past and gone through a nightmare.

Especially hope inspiring is the publication in the late '90s of a book called *The Not So Big House* by Sarah Susanka (see Resources on p. 258). At first glance, it might strike you as another nice coffee-table adornment for architecture buffs. But inside it contains a surprising, uncompromising, and persuasively delivered message. If you want to build or remodel a house, you have a choice: Put up one of those pretentious, cavernous, soulless, slapped together "custom homes," or, for the same budget, build a place that is only half the size but thoughtfully designed, richly crafted, and a joy to live in. When I first read the book, I fell in love with it, but I assumed it would interest only a tiny audience. I was wrong. In its first two years in print, *The Not So Big House* sold a quarter of a million copies. There is in America a consciousness of the false promise of quantity and a thirst for quality.

The message in *The Not So Big House* is one that good builders have been carrying to clients for years: "Build less but build well." In the language of the marketplace, the message is "value, not price." Do you want to join their ranks? Then my advice, as laid out in the next chapter, is first make a plan for setting up the systems you will need to run a good company, then act on your plan.

Making a Plan

When I urge would-be builders to make a plan before starting up, or encourage established builders to plan their growth before ratcheting up volume, I often meet resistance. One construction journal, while recommending my book, urged its readers to ignore the chapter on making a plan. No builder, said the journal (now out of business), would have

ever gotten under way if he or she had planned so carefully.

When I worried to a friend that one of our builder buddies was operating with a dangerously seat-of-the-pants approach, the friend scoffed, "You can't wait until you've got your ducks in a row. You may have nothing more than your truck and a few tools. But when opportunity comes, you pull together the resources you need, and you do the job." Brave words. A few years later our buddy got in so far over his head he would have lost not only his business but his home if it had not been for a big loan from Mom. Now he carefully maps and monitors his company's growth. He even invests thousands of dollars a year to get guidance from consultants. Today he operates a thriving company.

Only a few readers will make use of planning, but they will be among the most successful. They will not be constantly expending resources to shore up weak spots in their operation. They will have in place the systems they need to profit from their work.

Not so big a deal

I am not suggesting anything fancy here. I am not suggesting you put together a spiral-bound presentation complete with market analyses, revenue growth projections, and profitability targets. That's the kind of thing you might need to woo a banker for a loan. You don't need a loan to start a construction company.

What I propose in the way of planning is a simple step-by-step program. Before you open the doors to your company, put into place the basic and inexpensive business tools and procedures you will need to serve your clients ably. If you are already in business and struggling, make a plan to retrofit your operation with the needed systems.

The rest of this chapter will explain the sample plan laid out across the bot-

COMING UP

The Resistance to Planning

A Bare Bones Approach

Defining Your Market

Choosing a Legal Form for Your Business

Setting Up Headquarters

Creating Controls

Taking On Projects

tom of these pages. The following chapters will provide you with the detailed information necessary to carry it out. Your plan may be different. You may choose to focus on somewhat different issues. Your circumstances may suggest a different sequence or a longer or shorter time line. But whatever your plan, keep it simple, so that you'll be able to accomplish it.

Defining your market and other essential first steps

Successful entrepreneurs know that no amount of hard work will lead to business success if there are no customers. If you intend to start a building business, you need first to determine if there are potential customers within reach. You need to define the services you will offer and check out the market for them in your area. Do you want to do tenant improvements? If so, is there room for another contractor or is the market saturated? To find out, ask builders in your area. Walk onto their job sites and ask how they are doing. Is business good? If there is plenty of work, maybe you can crack the market. If established people are barely working, you will have to redefine or broaden your services or service area.

Once you are clear about your market, you can then open a business checking account. Open it at a bank that functions as a "federal depository," namely one that will be able to handle your payroll taxes when you begin hiring employees. For both accounting purposes and to get tax write-offs, *run all your start-up costs through that business account.* As soon as you have the minimum required amount in your checking account, open a higher-interest account in which to build operating capital, an absolute must. Businesses constantly fail for lack of cash in the bank. As a builder you must project your needs for operating capital, and stick to a program for putting it in place.

While you will not call on their services just yet, locate and become acquainted with an attorney, an accountant, and an insurance broker. All must meet two requirements. They must be thoroughly acquainted with the construction business. They must be able to answer your questions in language you can understand.

Selecting your form of business

Many builders slide into business naturally as "sole proprietors." You automatically become a sole proprietor when you contract for your first project. You are now in business, and you are the sole owner, or proprietor, of the business. It's that simple.

What is important to realize is that if you are operating as a sole proprietor, legally speaking, you *are* the business.

A Sample Start-up Plan

Month 1	Month 2	Month 3	Month 4	Months 5 and 6
Define your purpose	Select a business form	Set up an office	Write a company policy statement	Choose and set up an accounting system
Decide what services you will offer	Open a business checking account	Purchase a computer	Choose an accountant, attorney, and insurance broker	
Determine market opportunities	Set up a program to build operating capital	Start a professional library and join a builders' association		

The business' earnings are considered your earnings for tax purposes. You pay social security and income tax on the entire earnings of the business, not just the portion you take for personal use. Moreover, you and your business are one and the same before the law. *You can be held personally liable for any of its obligations.* Say you leave an oily rag wadded up on a pile of sawdust at the end of a workday. The rag ignites and starts a fire, which immolates the owners' music parlor and antique grand piano. Your insurance policy, it turns out, excludes coverage of grand pianos. Guess what? Your client can lay claim to your personal assets—your savings, investments, and even your home to cover the loss of the piano which, without doubt, will turn out to have once been Beethoven's personal piano and be worth roughly as much as your entire neighborhood.

Instead of going it alone as sole proprietors, some builders team up with a friend and form a legal partnership. Partnering up can be tempting. Construction is a turbulent business, and it may appear that it would be comforting to head into it arm-in-arm with someone else. Unfortunately, while *partnership* may be just a legal form, the *partnering* that goes along with it involves a serious emotional entanglement with a steep downside, as I have described in the bottom sidebar at right.

A Choice of Business Forms
- Sole Proprietorship
- Partnership
- Limited Liability Company (LLC)
- "S" Corporation
- "C" Corporation

Partnering, a Rough Road

Partnership is a legal form. But the *partnering* that goes with it is an intense personal relationship that can blow out at the seams, blowing up the business when it does. As their business matures, partners develop differing ideas about where to go with it, what roles they should play, and the value of their respective contributions. Often their disagreements lead to a breakup, with both sides suffering losses. All three of the partnerships that I alluded to in the last edition of my book as exceptions to the rule that partnering is doomed to failure have since come apart. The breakups have ranged from tense to bitter, and the financial losses from considerable to devastating. Meanwhile, my accountant, who has had an even longer business career than I, says she has *never* seen a partnership that did not eventually come to grief. "Tell your readers not to go the partnership route under any circumstances," she instructed me. Another old-timer advises, "Don't take on a partner to do what you could hire done"—and, of course, there is *nothing* you cannot hire done, or learn to do yourself.

Months 7 and 8	Month 9	Month 10	Month 11	Month 12
Set up an estimating system	Create a low-cost marketing program	Develop contracts for preconstruction services	Buy insurance	Form a relationship with temporary labor pool
	Begin marketing	Develop a construction contract	Set up a shop	Purchase insurance
		Develop a change order form		Sign the contract for your first job!

Whether you elect to go into business alone or to partner up, you can "incorporate" your company. If you do, so far as the law is concerned, you and your company are no longer one and the same entity. Oddly enough, for legal purposes, your incorporated company, or "corporation," has become a separate "person" or entity of which you (or you and a partner or even other investors you've recruited) are the owner(s). As a result, if you were incorporated at the time you reduced Beethoven's piano to ashes, the aggrieved client could have gone after the corporation and its assets—computer, truck, operating capital. Your personal savings and other holdings, however, *may* have been safe.

"May" is a pivotal word here. Just how much protection for your personal assets incorporation will provide is a matter of some dispute. Some attorneys insist that a properly maintained corporation is virtually impregnable. Others will say something like "the corporate veil can be quite readily pierced"— meaning that a smart lawyer might be able to push it aside and lay hands on your personal assets after all. But when all is said and done, there seems to be

general agreement that, as one veteran builder puts it, incorporating will at least "set up an additional barrier between your life savings and litigious clients who think they should take everything you have because you made a real or fancied mistake on their project."

Setting up headquarters

After defining your market and choosing a business form, you are ready to establish a "headquarters," namely an office, for your company. Like your business plan itself, your headquarters need not be fancy. But it doesn't do—as the usual caricature of contractors has it—to run our operations out of a glove compartment stuffed with wads of invoices, used chewing gum, and yesterday's sports page, or even from the kitchen table. A compact, well-lighted, well-organized office is a necessity. It is the place from where you will communicate with the many people who your business will involve—clients, subcontractors, suppliers, designers and engineers, employees, and fellow builders. If you don't have an office from which you can operate efficiently, your communication, and therefore your business, will suffer.

It is feasible, especially at the start-up stage, to organize an office without a computer. You can take care of all your documentation using preprinted forms and a typewriter or even pencil and pen. But a computer with printer, if properly used, can greatly increase your office productivity. So if you can afford one without digging too deeply into operating capital, you should get a computer and learn how to use basic business software before you take on your first construction project. Learning to use a computer requires time. It is best to have it under your belt before you open for business and are swamped with pressing office and field tasks.

---

t is feasible, especially at the start-up stage, to organize an office without a computer. You can take care of all your documentation using preprinted forms and a typewriter or even pencil and pen. But…

Costs of Incorporating

One builder I know says, "If your are a sole proprietor and do not change to an LLC (to protect yourself), you are an idiot." He may be right. Incorporating does, however, entail costs as well as benefits. The costs can include:

■ Time to understand the pros and cons of LLCs, "S" Corps, and "C" Corps, and to choose the option that is right for you
■ Legal and filing costs for setup
■ Retooling your stationery
■ Additional paperwork at tax time
■ Monitoring your corporate procedures to make sure you are always in compliance with the requirements
■ Tax consequences

As part of setting up headquarters, start building a construction library (see Resources on p. 258). Buy a few really good books that you can refer to when you have questions about construction technology and methods or business procedures. Subscribe to magazines that service your niche in the industry. Also, though it *is* a bold step for builders just starting out or struggling, join a builders' association. You may feel self-conscious, as I surely was, when you first sit down with the members. Here are these guys who are running multimillion-dollar operations while you are still grappling with the meaning of "overhead" and "gross margins." But you will soon discover that they daily pound away at the same problems you do, just on a larger scale. And you will meet individuals who will generously answer your questions and offer guidance. You will, as I did, find mentors.

Putting controls into place

If you do the hard work of acquiring computer fluency, it will pay off as soon as you begin to develop your controls—the procedures you use to keep a handle on every aspect of your company's performance, from project schedules to accounting. If you have acquired word-processing skills, you will be able to use the computer to write and print out your company policy statement. Writing it is an excellent way to clarify your purpose for being in business and the values by which you want to operate. By providing a copy to each of your prospective employees and subcontractors, you will make sure they are on the same page as you regarding key issues such as job site safety.

You may want to first take on the crucial number-crunching tasks of accounting and estimating, using precomputer technology. In chapter 3, I will suggest pencil-and-paper systems you can start

with. But when you are ready to move up to the computer, you will be impressed with its speed at even such simple tasks as writing checks. You will be pleased at its power to bring you information about your company's financial performance and how it speeds up the grueling chore of estimating.

In my sample start-up plan, I have suggested a span of five months to set up controls including policies, accounting, estimating, and contracts. It is impossible to overstate how important they are. Without controls, you will never have control of your business. Once they are in place, you are ready to begin marketing your services and to take the last steps to ready your company for projects.

Getting projects, getting ready, getting paid

You will notice in my sample start-up business plan that I suggest you start marketing in the ninth, not the final, month. It takes time to get even small projects up and running—to go from a "lead" on a job to actually contracting for

> have suggested a span of five months to set up controls including policies, accounting, estimating, and contracts. It is impossible to overstate how important they are.

SAMPLE LETTERS AND FORMS Business Card

A business card does not have to be expensive. Mine came from a copy shop and cost me only $20 per thousand. Though inexpensive, it's nice to look at and gives a potential clients the information they need to reach me.

David Gerstel
Builder

Bonded 268 Coventry
Insured Kensington, CA 94707
Lic. #325650 510/524-1039

Developing Your Company

Once you have begun contracting for projects, you can choose from among many different paths. One natural series of steps:

1. Do very small side jobs while continuing as an employee in someone else's company. Though it may seem like overkill, use your full business systems to gain fluency with them.

2. Give up life as an employee. Go to work full time as an independent contractor doing small projects. Continue honing your controls as well as your communication and construction skills.

3. Begin building a team of subcontractors.

4. When you are ready, develop a crew, then a lead person.

5. Steadily remove yourself from field operations, delegating increasing responsibility to your lead(s).

6. Put your tool belt down and move full time to running and developing your company.

Getting Paid for *All* the Work You Do

At the beginning of your career you may not be able to charge for your preconstruction services. You may have to provide estimating, and even design and planning, to clients for free in the hope of being selected to build their projects. Giving away estimating and planning time is a real drag. It is the single most demoralizing aspect of being in the construction business. The earlier you learn to charge for your preconstruction services, and develop a contract under which you will be paid for them, the better. You can do it! In San Francisco, legend has it, there is an old pickup truck contractors occasionally spot ghosting through the fog. Some believe it to be a messenger from the patron saint of builders. They remember it for the inspirational words painted on its doors: "*No free estimates since 1971!*" I have gone nearly as long without working for free myself.

As you come closer to actually starting construction on your first projects, you can tune up your systems and put a few last pieces in place, such as purchasing your insurance policies and setting up a shop. You may be surprised—or maybe disgusted if you love the trades—to see setting up a shop among the last steps in the sample plan. It's there for a reason. Most of us who become builders come from the trades. When we go into business for ourselves, we naturally gravitate toward the familiar and comfortable—the tools and the materials. There we get stuck, never putting into place the business systems even a one-person construction company needs. When setting up a business, we need to give priority to the management tasks and not to our beloved construction equipment.

If you are just starting out, you probably will not have employees yet, but you will occasionally need help at your job site, especially for lower-skilled workers. Sign a contract with a temporary labor pool, one that specializes in construction work. You will find it invaluable when you need extra hands to dig trenches or get some heavy timber into place—and not just at the beginning of your career but also as your company does increasing volumes of work.

Once you are up and running, you will find that you are not managing a static operation. Changes in the economy, in technology, in your market area, and your own desire to change and grow will force constant adjustment in your business practices. You should pause occasionally—many builders make it a yearly ritual—to make a new plan to suit your evolving enterprise. Reclarify your purposes. Review and revise your policy statement. Sharpen and strengthen all your systems and procedures for construction, communication, and controls.

and building it. You don't want to leave marketing till the weekend before you need work. While you are generating leads and planning projects, you can develop your contracts, not only for construction but also for preconstruction services, as the bottom sidebar above emphasizes.

CHAPTER 2

A Builder's Tools

Office and Shop

A WELL-EQUIPPED carpenter needs a reliable pickup stocked with construction tools. Likewise, a builder needs an office fitted with business tools. If your office (and an adjacent "shop" for storing construction equipment when it is not in use) is well designed for comfort and efficiency, it will enhance the satisfaction of your daily work. If it is designed for economy as well, it will help keep down overhead (general and administrative) costs of running your company, leaving that much more for you to set aside for operating capital or to put in your pocket.

Your office

What you need in the way of an office, to build on the title of Ernest Hemingway's famous reminiscence about the writer's life in Paris, is a *clean, well-lighted, well-organized place of your own.* You need a private area where you can take phone calls and do your paperwork without disturbing or being disturbed by your family. That place of your own—though it can be modest in size—must be comfortable. If it is not, you will be less willing to go to it and take care of essential management tasks such as evaluating prospective jobs, estimating project costs, and analyzing your accounting records.

Often overlooked in the creation of a comfortable office is the installation of good lighting. Studies indicate great increases in productivity when the lighting in work areas is improved. Make sure your office is well lit. Also, provide yourself with a comfortable, ergonomically correct desk chair. Office work can be harder on the back than carpentry!

With some luck and ingenuity you will be able to create an office in your home that will serve for at least the start-up phase of your company, and maybe for your whole career. I have never felt a need to move my office from my home, even when my company was building several large projects simultaneously. Of the several home offices I have enjoyed, the two best are illustrated on p. 24 and p. 25). If you do not happen to have a windowed walk-in closet or a spare room, you may find another good spot. I have seen inviting offices built into backyard sheds, basements, and even under stairwells. As a builder you can carve out a good office almost anywhere.

Office organization

Wherever you maintain your office, you will want to organize it for efficiency so that every unnecessary movement and effort is eliminated. The benefits of time and motion engineering can be huge.

COMING UP

A Comfortable, Well-lit Place of Your Own

The Efficient Office

A Compact Storage Area

Mobile Equipment and Hardware Storage

The Warehouse Syndrome

An Office in a Closet

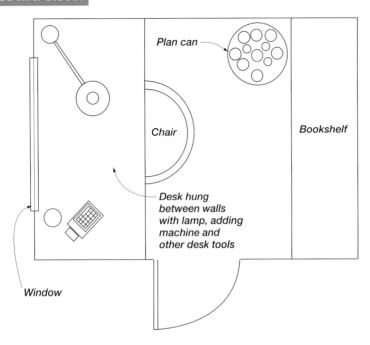

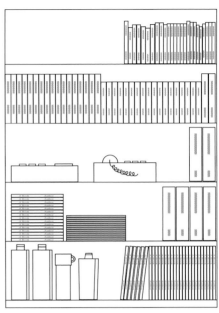

Floor-to-ceiling bookshelves with reference books, back copies of magazines, files, adding machine, phone/answering machine, briefcases

At the beginning of my career as a builder, when my family and I were living in a rented apartment, I set up my office in a walk-in closet with a large window. While tiny, the office was well-lit. It was comfortable—it contained everything I needed to plan projects, estimate their costs, do my bookkeeping, and dispatch miscellaneous office work during my start-up years.

Any single efficiency you introduce—such as placing your stapler and tape dispenser right on your desktop and within reach so that you do not have to hunt for them—may save you only a minute a day on average. But those minutes add up. Invent a few dozen such savings, and you have rescued the better part of an hour a day from office tedium. That's 150 hours or the equivalent of four work weeks a year. You can go even further, as I have. By constantly increasing efficiency in my office work and project management, I was a able to reduce the time it took me to run my company to about 20 hours a week.

My current office has contributed enormously to my efficiency. Its central feature is an L-shaped workstation. Built from solid-core doors trimmed with redwood and supported by file cabinets, it measures 15 ft. along the outside length of its legs. The station is organized as a miniature processing line, with an "in" end and an "out" end, and each component of the station is likewise organized logically. For example, at the "in" end file cabinet, forms are sequenced in the order I would typically use them in contracting for and managing a project. At the out end, receipts and other records are stored by category and chronologically.

Your own arrangement of forms and records will be different than mine. We all have differing ideas as to what makes for logical and efficient organization. My wife believes dishes should be washed and sorted after each meal; I lean toward stockpiling them until there's no room left in the sink. And our son, in his heyday as family dishwasher, favored heaping them up till not a single clean platter or cup was left in the cupboards. You should organize your office in a pattern that seems efficient and logical to you. The logic will be easy to hold in your mind and will guide you to any needed tool, form, or record.

A portable office

As an extension to your logically organized main office, you will find it worthwhile to create a portable office, which you can carry out into the field. A laptop computer can be programmed to serve as a very advanced sort of portable office. But if you are still in the start-up phase of your career, concentrating (wisely) on building up operating capital and not yet ready to spring for a laptop, you will want an old-fashioned portable office. To create one, all you need do is purchase a

Desktop Materials and Tools

Included among the tools and materials on the worktable and in the file cabinets:

- Tickler (a set of 12 file folders, one per month, with reminder notes of coming tasks)
- Three-hole punch
- Stapler
- Tape dispenser
- Postage scale
- Heavy-duty calculator with paper tape
- A canister for pencils and another for pens
- Storage containers with rubber bands, paper clips, staples, and postage stamps
- Basic stationery supplies
- Checks
- Frequently used forms

Office in the Corner of a Spare Room

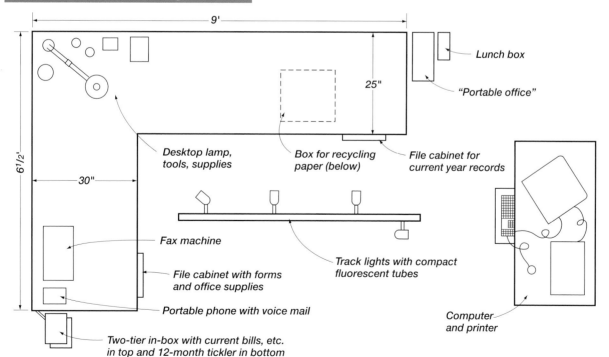

9'

25"

61/2'

30"

Lunch box

"Portable office"

Desktop lamp, tools, supplies

Box for recycling paper (below)

File cabinet for current year records

Fax machine

Track lights with compact fluorescent tubes

File cabinet with forms and office supplies

Portable phone with voice mail

Computer and printer

Two-tier in-box with current bills, etc. in top and 12-month tickler in bottom

Plan can

Since moving from my closet, I have graduated to an office occupying about 80 sq. ft. in a small spare room. Its L-shaped worktable is organized so that work flows logically from one end to the other. Incoming materials—letters, bills, payments, plans for new projects, and messages—enter at one end. They are then processed across the ample work area, or at the computer. Finally, they exit into file cabinets, field briefcases, the mail, or the recycling box.

The Old-fashioned, Portable Office

The first time I walked onto a job site lugging my big briefcase full of project records and office supplies a carpenter called out laughingly, "Hey! What's that, a portable office?" The name stuck. Over the years, the portable office often has been the subject of friendly jokes. "What's next," a client asked as I pulled out project records, a hole punch, and a couple of forms, "a canned ham?" But the old portable office has greatly enhanced my efficiency. I expect I will have use for it even as more of my business communication and control functions are done via a laptop computer and other high-tech devices.

Costs of Moving from a Home Office

Ongoing costs
- Rent or ownership costs
- Time and vehicle use for commute
- Additional insurance
- Security
- Cleaning and maintenance

One-time costs
- Renting a moving van
- Moving
- Reorganizing furniture, equipment, and records in the new space
- Purchasing and installing different or additional furniture and equipment
- Installing additional lighting
- Installing new electrical, Fax, phone, and computer wiring
- Ordering new business cards and stationery
- Ordering new signs with updated information for the office, job site, and trucks
- Notifying all past clients, subcontractors, designers, and engineers of new location (repeatedly)

spacious briefcase. Among key items to include in it:

- *Project records.* A heavy-duty, tabbed, three-ring binder to hold the documentation for ongoing jobs.
- *Forms and stationery supplies.* Change orders, invoices, letterheads, and envelopes.
- *Other office supplies.* Stamps, paper clips, rubber bands, and tape.
- *Office tools.* Compact versions of desktop tools, including a stapler, three-hole punch, an adding machine, and a supply of pens and pencils.
- *A field checkbook.*
- *Contact list.* A three-ring binder holding a printout of the names, phone and Fax numbers, E-mail addresses, and addresses of your business associates and other contacts.

I have used such a portable office for years. With it in hand, I always have the information and tools I need to do business in the field. I do not have the problem of a builder friend who says he is always slapping his forehead at his job sites, groaning, "Oh, I forgot to bring..." I do not have to remember to bring anything. It is already in my portable office, which I grab automatically every time I go out the door.

Moving out of the home office

You may have worked successfully from your home but now feel it is time to move out. Several builders I know moved simply because they wanted greater separation between their work and family life. Others had hired several office workers and could not fit them all into a home office.

If you are in a similar situation and thinking of making the move from a home office, first make a realistic projection of the costs. An office away from home carries with it the burden of increased rent or costs of ownership. Your home office was not free; you pay to rent or purchase and maintain the space you use in your home. *But it's likely to be space that you were and will be paying for whether it contains your office or not.* When you take space outside the home, you add a new and substantial rental or ownership cost that must be paid from your company's earnings every month—including times when business is slow, which is when you really feel the pain.

An office away from home will bring other costs as well. Your change of address may lead to increases for insurance, company vehicles, and office equipment. You may have to pay for security that was not necessary at your home. You will likely be incurring new commuting costs, and they can be substantial. Take the case of the builder who moved out of his home office because he found himself pining, as he put it, "to go off to work in the morning" like all the other men in his neighborhood. He now spends an hour or more a day driving about 30 miles to his office and back through thick traffic. On an annual basis, that's roughly 15,000 miles of vehicle use and 250 hours—*better than six full work weeks*—in commuting time.

You will also shoulder the one-time cost of making the move, and it may be much greater than a casual glance up the road reveals. A builder friend of mine recently constructed a small office on a piece of land he purchased. Though he had carefully figured the costs of his improvements and of his ongoing costs, he was taken by surprise, once he had built his new place, at the costs of moving into it. Moving costs are substantial, as the bottom sidebar on the facing page indicates.

All these costs may be worth incurring, whether to enhance the satisfaction you get from your work or to support the growth of your company. But you should

On Office and Image...

Builders often justify fancy office space as necessary to maintain a professional image that will attract good projects. Some building businesses—such as design/build firms that cater to wealthy clients in posh areas—may need impressive offices. Most construction companies do not. For the most part, clients are impressed by competence. There are much better ways to demonstrate it—references and past work for example—than with excessive office space you can pay for only by padding their bill. I have always worked from a compact and low-cost home office. During boom times, I have been equally swamped with projects as builders who operate from much fancier digs. When work slows, I have been free of the anxiety and pressure of footing the monthly bill for a trophy space. I will take the cost benefits to my clients and my peace of mind over a fancier "image" any time.

take them on with an understanding of their true extent. Figure carefully, "Will the new office enable my company to increase earnings enough to cover its costs and to make a profit as well? Especially, will I be able to handle the costs if we get into a steep recession and my volume drops by two-thirds?" If the answer is "yes," you may want to go for it. If you see that the office is merely a trophy you covet for its own sake or to enhance some nebulous image, you may decide to forego it.

Your shop

Just as they are tempted by the trophy office, builders are drawn by the well-equipped shop. With the sculpted steel of its saws and planers and drill presses, the shop seduces you with promises of prominence and prowess. You step into the large shop of a friend, and suddenly he seems a baron of the industry at ease in his throne room, diminishing your own significance. Instantly, you crave a bigger shop of your own, as if the horsepower of all the machinery within will somehow become your power.

> ncreasingly, our job is to manage the assembly of components that have been prebuilt elsewhere.

For some, the shop is irresistible. You may decide that you must have one. But before you do, ask yourself a few hard-nosed questions: Will you actually be putting into place a needed building block for your company? Or will you instead be engaging in gluttonous personal consumption while pretending it is a business investment?

I urge these questions because as construction industry technology evolves, builders have less and less *economic* reason for owning their own shop. Cabinetmakers need a shop. Millwrights and custom stair builders need a shop. Hairdressers need a shop. Builders do not. For the sake of our financial viability, we are better off getting the things that are made in shops from the people who specialize in making them, who do so over and over, who spread the cost of their equipment across many jobs.

You can't compete with the specialists. As technology develops, your hope of competing grows ever dimmer. Specialty shops and manufacturers are installing remarkably efficient equipment—such as the computerized saws that will automatically slice 4×8 sheets into the components for an entire kitchen's worth of cabinet carcasses in a couple of hours. How can a small-volume builder, who needs a few kitchens' worth of cabinets a year go up against that? You cannot! Either you will be using inferior equipment and taking 10 times as long to do the job, or you will be making a huge investment in higher-quality equipment, resulting in astronomical costs per unit of cabinetry. Whichever way you go, you will subsidize your inefficient operation with hour upon hour of your own unpaid labor.

Rather than attempt to go up against such specialists, builders can treat them as resources. If we are interested in making a reasonably good living, we need to appreciate that, increasingly, our job is to manage the assembly of components that have been prebuilt elsewhere. That includes not only finish items such as cabinets and windows, but also structural assemblies like roof frames, wall systems, and even foundation components.

As with any generalization, there will be exceptions. But I suspect most small-volume builders who think their shops are, financially speaking, anything other than a drain would experience a severe shock if they subjected it to a rigorous audit. Some builders insist their shops (like trophy offices) enhance image and thereby indirectly contribute to profitability. One maintains that by producing his own millwork and cabinets, he cultivates a certain *cache* with his clients, so that even though his shop only breaks even, it allows his company "to do the other things it does" that are profitable. Perhaps so, but to me the justification seems a bit vague. I suspect the builder hangs onto his large shop primarily because he loves it and owns a business successful enough to afford him such a splendid hobby.

Beware the warehouse

For some builders, as they slowly accept the economic unreality of producing their own millwork and cabinets and subcontract the work, their shop gradually

Move It On

Builders have better options for disposing of valuable leftover materials than embalming them in an expensive piece of real estate, euphemistically called a "warehouse" or "shop":

■ Send them back to the supplier, preferably on the return trip of a truck making a delivery, for a credit against future purchases.

■ Reward an apprentice by inviting him or her to take them to a used building materials yard and to spend the proceeds on a new tool.

■ Haul them to a recycling center.

■ Put them at curbside with a sign that says "free materials."

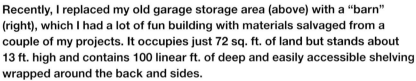

Recently, I replaced my old garage storage area (above) with a "barn" (right), which I had a lot of fun building with materials salvaged from a couple of my projects. It occupies just 72 sq. ft. of land but stands about 13 ft. high and contains 100 linear ft. of deep and easily accessible shelving wrapped around the back and sides.

morphs into a warehouse. It becomes the place where they keep all that delicious material left over at the end of projects—the misordered doors that they hope will work out in some future project.

The builder's warehouse—astutely defined by one construction consultant as "a place where you put something and never take it out"—is even more devoutly to be avoided than the trophy office or overambitious shop. The costs of such a building material burial tomb are, over the long haul, huge. Steadily you dribble away money and time to own it or rent it, to insure it, to maintain and clean it, to warm and illuminate it, to place materials inside it, and to move that material around to make room for yet more stuff. There are much better things builders can do with leftover materials.

As a builder, you can work out of a surprisingly compact space, for your job site is your shop and storage area. For years, I operated from a 10-ft. by 10-ft. staging area in my garage. These days I use an even less costly space, one I have named "the barn," which I built in a corner of my yard. In the barn, as previously in the garage, I maintain a system of buckets and bins (see Resources on p. 258), which allow me to store, in an organized and accessible fashion, a selection of hardware and tools sufficient to support three crews in the field. But usually, of course, my staging areas are empty. The tools and materials are at job sites, which, to my way of thinking, is where a builder's equipment really should be, for it if is not in use most of the time, why own it?

COMING UP

The Surge of Computers
into the Construction World

New Technology,
Traditional Tasks

The Real Cost of Computers

A Strategy for Bringing
Computers into Your Business

Computers in Construction

Over the last 15 years of the 20th century, computers—and other so-called "business information technology" like Fax machines and cell phones—swept into the construction industry as forcefully as worm drive saws, the electric drill, and tool belts earlier took over from handsaws, the brace and bit, and overalls. In the late 1980s, when I began to plan the first edition of this book, about the only business technology that builders needed was paper, pens and pencils, a phone and answering machine, access to a copy service, and a calculator. Fax machines were about as frequently seen in builders' offices as orchids. Computers were even more rare. I did not recommend them. The potential benefits did not seem to justify the cost, and a number of builders I knew who had computerized in an attempt to get a handle on their estimating and accounting had gotten even more snarled.

But a few years later, as I was completing the book, the cost of computers and software was plummeting. More builders were investing in a computer system, at first as automated typewriters for creating documents like contracts and then increasingly for estimating and accounting.

Now, only a decade later, established builders—even those who do quite small volumes of work—use computers routinely for virtually all their paperwork. Use of other technology such as Fax machines, cell phones, and digital cameras is as taken for granted as use of chop saws and cordless tools. Many builders equip not only their offices, but also their job sites with high-tech business information devices.

Using information technology

The tide of computers and related technology that has surged through the construction industry has changed *how* builders do their work. But it has not changed *what* they do. Suppose a veteran builder had gone to sleep at his desk in 1961 and reawakened 40 years later to find his grandson, Russell, running the company. Would the Old Man be staggered by the technology he saw the younger man deploy? Sure. But after he got over his dazzlement, he would note that it was being applied to *exactly* the same tasks he had attended to before his long nap.

On the way up the steps to his office in the morning, Russell turns on his cell phone and dials up his voice-mail service. He listens to a message from the owner of a printing company who wants to talk to him about a project. Reaching his desk, he dials back. While the owner describes her plans to reconstruct an old firehouse into offices for her firm, Russell turns on his computer and opens his contact management program—the computerized version of an address book. He creates a space for the caller and types in information she is giving him about herself and her project. At the end of the conversation, Russell pulls another high-tech device from his shirt pocket, and holding it in his palm, records in it the time and place of the appointment he makes to further discuss the project. Russell has started his day doing exactly the things his grandfather would have done—taking messages, answering calls, recording information about a prospective customer, and making a sales appointment. The pattern—same tasks, different tools—will continue.

Still at the computer, Russell clicks his mouse a few times, connects to the service that links him to the Internet and

An Overview of Computers and Other Business Information Technology

Hardware

Computer—Builders use personal computers, usually with a Windows operating system. Computers are used by builders primarily for writing, accounting, estimating and E-mail communication over the Internet. Many builders also maintain a Web site as part of their marketing. Some are experimenting with setting up Web sites as project communication centers.

Phone—So that they are always available to their customers and crew, builders increasingly carry cell phones or phones that can function as two-way radios and as telephones.

Fax machine—Nearly every construction professional uses a Fax to send and receive documents. Some clients, designers, and subcontractors will be very frustrated working with you if you do not have one.

Personal digital assistant—These palm-size computers are an expensive, but stylish, way to keep track of appointments and phone numbers. As they come down in price and evolve into all-in-one pocket computers incorporating phones, E-mail, Web browsing, and digital cameras, they may be cost effective as well as cool.

Digital camera—Because they let you store photos in your computer and view them on the screen, they save you the cost of film and development. They are cost-effective for maintaining project records and collecting architectural and construction details.

Software

Word processing—Builders use it for creating many types of documents from letterheads and contracts through change orders to invoices. If you learn to touch-type, and can write reasonably well, word processing software will save you a lot of time.

Electronic spreadsheet—For years, builders have been using paper versions to "spread out"—record and organize—and total their numbers for accounting and estimating. The electronic versions do the addition automatically. They save a lot of tedious labor.

Database—One computer expert compares database software to a file cabinet. Many software programs can pull information from such an electronic file cabinet. For example, an estimating program could pull from its database the cost of hanging a door just as you would take the cost from your paper records if you were doing a handwritten estimate. Building a database tailored to your operation takes a lot of time, but once it is up and running, it can save you time in the long run.

Estimating and bidding—Programs designed specifically for construction, combining spreadsheets with databases, have the potential to save much labor.

Accounting—Generic small-business programs and specialized construction programs can tie you in knots. But if you learn to use them properly, they can be real labor savers and give you accounting information you probably would not otherwise have time to produce yourself.

Job costing—Used to record the costs of building each of your projects and compare them to your estimates of the costs.

Scheduling—Charts the steps in building a project.

Construction management—Combines many of the functions of estimating, bidding, accounting, job costing, and scheduling in one package. While the all-in-one format is appealing, it is expensive, and you have to be doing a sizable volume of work before the investment will pay off.

Browsing and E-mail—Available from an Internet service provider (ISP), much the way phone service is available from a phone company. Once you have subscribed to an ISP you will be able to connect to the Internet and use software to send and receive E-mail or to browse the World Wide Web in search of information and services.

Uses of Computers and Other Information Technology Products

Computers and other business information technology have not changed what builders produce in the management of their business, only how they produce it.

Conversation—Formerly, you went to the phone. Now it goes with you.

Messages—Once recorded on paper, now left in voice-mail "boxes" or as E-mail.

Documents—Formerly typed and filed or mailed, now word-processed and saved on the computer, Faxed, E-mailed, or posted at Web sites.

Contact records—Contacts, once called "people" and recorded alphabetically in an address book, now are stored on a computer and organized by software.

Accounting records—Once written out on paper forms, now stored in accounting programs on the computer.

Estimates—Previously penciled onto a form and totaled on an adding machine, now keyed into and totaled on a computer.

Portfolios—Once kept in photo albums, now posted on Web sites.

Project schedules—Formerly charted on paper with a pencil, now charted on a computer screen with a mouse.

Drawing and drafting—Once done with paper and pencil, now done on a computer screen.

reviews his E-mail. He sees he has received an application for the bookkeeper's job he had advertised in both the print and Web versions of his local newspaper. He responds to the applicant with a return E-mail, suggesting possible times for an interview.

Next, he clicks to a Web site, one he has leased as a "meeting place" for all the people involved in the remodeling of Taqueria Extremo, the largest of the projects he has under construction. He checks to see if there are any messages from the project clients, architect, subcontractors, or the lead carpenter. Still at the Web site, he writes up a change order for a bank of skylights not included in the original plans, then posts it for his clients and the architect to review.

After standing for a couple of minutes to stretch, Russell sits down again in front of the computer, opening a file that his lawyer sent him as an attachment to an E-mail and reads it carefully. He likes what he sees—a set of clauses for his construction contract that require that he and the client enter into nonbinding mediation as a first step to settle disputes rather than jumping right into a lawsuit. With a few clicks of the mouse and taps on the keyboard he opens his contract and adds the mediation clause. Now, every time he prints out a contract for a new client, the clause will be included. Looking over Russell's shoulder, the Old Man nods approvingly. "That maneuver," he thinks to himself, "was very impressive."

Next, Russell opens his accounting program and clicks on the folder labeled "Taqueria Extremo." He wants to review how labor and material costs on the job are running in comparison to his estimate. He opens up the job cost report and studies the numbers on the screen. They look good. With the job halfway complete, for every phase of work with the exception of framing, where he had been a couple of hundred dollars low on his estimate of material costs, he is within budget. For the project as a whole, the report tells him, he is running 1.3 percent under his estimated costs. Seeing the figure, the Old Man exults inwardly, "The kid has the stuff. He's got the genes."

Russell will continue wielding his high-tech devices till the end of his workday, wrapping it up with a stop at a new job where he will use his digital camera to take "before" pictures for storing in his computer later. While continuing to be impressed, the Old Man does find himself asking a question: The technology looks very expensive, and he wonders whether it's really worth buying simply to do the things he managed to do successfully for decades with paper, pencils, an adding machine, a rotary phone, and a tough, old Kodak box. In my opinion, the Old Man asks a very good question.

The costs of information technology

To answer that question, first you need to recognize the costs, which are considerable, as the list at right indicates. There are the initial costs of purchase. Even an economical desktop personal computer and printer, together with basic software, will run you about as much as a dozen or more good power tools. And that's just the beginning. The computer is not like a biscuit joiner. You do not just buy it, pull it out of the box, make a few test cuts, and then use it effectively on job after job for many years without further outlay, except an occasional fresh blade. With information technology, the costs stretch on and on. Of the costs, the out-of-pocket dollars are the lesser. The greater cost is the time it takes to learn and manage the technology.

When you are just starting out, it is advisable to resist getting sucked too far into technology. You are likely better off using paper and pencil at first and putting your money into building up your operating capital account. You will find, too, that it is possible to run and grow your business profitably for years with minimal adoption of technology. Others may tell you differently. The people I call "information technology evangelists" insist with religious fervor that if you do not go heavily into computers, you will never be able to compete with your more geared-up competitors. That's utter nonsense. You can effectively perform the time-honored tasks of running a construction company with very little of the

Footing the Bill for Information Technology

Initial purchases
- Computer with basic software
- Printer
- Accounting software
- Estimating and bidding software
- Contact management software
- Backup device
- Fax machine, copier, scanner
- Portable and/or cell phones
- Personal digital assistant
- Design and setup of Web site

Operating costs
- Accessories and supplies
- On-site service warranty on computer
- Monthly fees for cell phone
- Monthly fees for voice-mail service
- Monthly fees for Internet service provider
- Fees for maintaining Web site
- Electricity

Maintenance costs
- Replacement of computer and other hardware
- Regular upgrades of software
- Updating of Web site
- Initial training in the use of the software
- Continuing education in use of software
- Technical support for hardware and software
- Recovery from data losses
- Time lost to distractions built into computer
- Other costs including those not yet invented

Inevitabilities
"I have learned that three things are inevitable: Death. Taxes. And Upgrades."
—Words of wisdom from a contractor who disconnected his computer and sailed away toward the South Pacific.

new business technology, should that be your preference.

At the same time, it is quite clear that deeper into his or her career, *a well-organized* builder can get a solid return on an investment in computers. The technology is expensive, but you can get a lot back for the money and time you put in. Here is an example: You value your time

One Possible Path into Information Technology

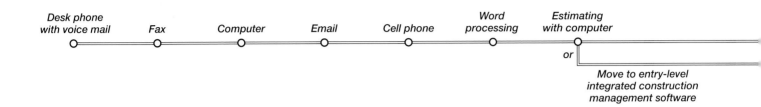

Desk phone with voice mail — Fax — Computer — Email — Cell phone — Word processing — Estimating with computer

or

Move to entry-level integrated construction management software

F or many of his builder-clients, computers serve as nothing more than an "expensive hobby."

at $50 an hour. By computerizing your estimating, you figure to cut the time it takes you to do estimates by one-third, a reasonable goal. If you average 15 hours a week at estimating, and cut it to 10 using a computer, you free up 5 hours to spend at other money-making tasks (or reading to your children). In dollar terms, the computer saves you $250 a week, or about $13,000 annually in labor.

These savings, it is crucial to note, are not net savings. To realize them, you have to make a considerable investment—in hardware, software, and especially in time and effort. If you talk with other builders about computers, it will not be long before you will meet one who has been tied in knots by a software program, lost thousands of dollars by using it incorrectly, and then spent many more hours and a great deal of additional money for expert help to get straightened out.

For builders who move from off-the-shelf software to the more powerful, specialized, construction management programs, the labor and consulting costs of dealing with their technology can go through the roof. As even one of the information technology evangelists admits, the construction management programs require a "dedication bordering on fanaticism." You have to gain a lot of efficiency to justify the investment.

The sad truth seems to be many builders get involved with computers, pour time and money into them, and never reap the benefits. Two nationally known construction consultants—both of whom earn part of their living selling computer software—are emphatic on the point. One says that for many of his builder clients, computers serve as nothing more than an "expensive hobby." Another reports that after spending thousands of dollars on software, her clients frequently realize less than 10 percent of its potential value, instead using the computer as a "fancy adding machine."

In the end, it's difficult to predict how much of that potential five-hour-a-week savings will be netted by any given individual. For some, the net gain will be modest or negligible. Others may actually register a loss. But if you have the discipline and aptitude to master word processing, estimating, and accounting software, the gains can be substantial. Once you are up and running, you will save yourself much grueling work and gain better control of your business.

Strategies for adopting computers and other information technology

Given the costs, it is important to adopt information technology, IT for short, in a reasonably businesslike fashion. Take

Accounting with computer	Scheduling with computer	Contact management with computer	Website for marketing	Website for project management	Into the future

it on not merely because you think it is really nifty (we builders do have a tendency to go nuts over tools) but because it increases your effectiveness. Bring the technology into your business in a way that will bring benefit proportionate to the investment required.

There is no one-size-fits-all strategy. Your best strategy will be rooted in your individual aptitudes, emotions about the technology, and particular business needs. Do you enjoy it? Fear it? What programs will you be able to learn effectively with reasonable effort? Which ones might strangle you? Which parts of your business might benefit from conversion from paper-and-pencil systems to off-the-shelf software and then to specialized construction management programs? Which not?

With that said, there are several principles for IT adoption that you should consider:

- If you are struggling with an aspect of running your construction business such as accounting, a computer program is not going to bail you out. It will make matters worse. You'll find yourself tangled up in the software even as you continue to battle with the task. Get a handle on the task first, then determine whether software might help you do it better.

- Steadily take time to learn about information technology so you can make informed choices. Read articles. Talk to vendors. Talk to other builders about costs versus benefits.
- Don't be pennywise when buying IT. The value of the labor you have invested in the technology will soon far exceed its purchase price. Leverage your labor with good-quality technology—just as you buy professional-grade tools, not hobbyist's toys, for building your projects.
- Adopt IT one step at a time. Adopt it at a pace that allows you to get a handle on each new electronic tool without investing so many hours you neglect the usual work of running your business.
- Regardless of when you decide to adopt other technologies, do equip your office with communication technology as soon as you can afford it. Buy a good portable phone. Sign up for voice mail. Install a fax machine. If you do not have fax and voice mail, many clients, designers, and subcontractors will grow frustrated doing business with you. You may lose them. For similar reasons, you may feel compelled to get on-line with E-mail and to carry a cell phone. It fact, some builders would say, and reasonably so, that a cell phone is the technology to buy first.

f you are struggling with an aspect of running your construction business such as accounting, a computer program is not going to bail you out. It will make matters worse.

■ Before purchasing other IT— accounting software, for example— make as good an estimate as you can of all its costs, including training yourself to use it and ongoing support. Ask yourself if the potential benefits justify the investment.

■ When evaluating computers for creating estimates and other documents, factor in the marketing benefits. The computer will produce much crisper, more easily readable documents than you will be able to crank out by hand. The quality inspires confidence in clients. I once lost a three-quarter of a million dollar job to a builder who does lower-quality work, partly because his estimate was computer generated and mine was hand scrawled.

If you do invest in a computer, cultivate a few important habits for using it effectively. Learn to 10-finger type, i.e. "touch-type." Otherwise, as my editor neatly puts it, "You have accomplished the equivalent of purchasing a powerful pickup truck and then electing to pole it along like a barge." Once you have begun storing information on the computer, train yourself to back it up regularly to avoid losing documents that took you many hours to create. Learn how to say no to your phones, especially your cell phone. Do not let it constantly interrupt and distract you. Make sure your employees do not become overreliant on the fact that you have that phone hooked to your belt, calling you for input on every decision rather than taking responsibility. *You own the technology. Do not let it own you.*

Going forward

Once you have integrated computers and other business information technology into your business, you will continue to face choices. You will need to decide

just how to carve a path for yourself into whatever technological future is to come. Again, builders differ widely in their approaches.

At one end of the spectrum are those who try to stay on the cutting edge, figuring the technology will increase their productivity more than enough to offset cost. They replace their computers every two years, upgrade software annually, and try out new devices and applications soon after they come on the market. At the other end are builders who minimize their investment and push their hardware and software as far as they can. They hold onto computers until they break down. They squeeze everything they can get from one generation of software before they upgrade.

Others stake out a middle ground. Your choice should depend on a rational analysis of how effectively you can make use of technology in light of what it will cost you. Use your own sense of your aptitudes and opportunities to decide which route you take rather than merely following the crowd, obeying the summons of the IT evangelists, or giving in to gadget infatuation. As one builder says, "It is easy to be romanced by the technology." There are better places to look for romance than in a plastic box filled with lead and processed silicone.

Policy Statement

To run even a small construction company with only occasional temporary employees and subcontractors, you should have a clear, written statement of the company's values and practices— a "policy statement" as it is commonly called. You need it to protect yourself legally and to efficiently and effectively setting out the ground rules by which

COMING UP

Why You Need a
Policy Statement

Starting with a
Statement of Purpose

Specific Policies

A Tool Policy

Other Key Policies

How to Write
a Policy Statement

Review by an Expert

you, your employees, and your subs work together.

Without a clear policy statement, you may find yourself in the position I was in early in my career. I found myself repeatedly going over the same issues with my crew and subs. "Sorry, Pete, out of consideration for the neighbors, we don't play loud music on our jobs," and, "Guys, if you want to have a beer after work, we ought to head over to the pub. We can't drink on our clients' property." Or, as the frustration finally overflowed, "I'm not going to tell you again. Get to work on time or go get another job!"

Having a policy statement in place is of great help when you hire new employees or negotiate with new subcontractors. You ask them to review it, to raise concerns or questions they may have, and otherwise to agree to the policies—or to seek work elsewhere. Peering back to the beginning of my career, I can appreciate that the miserable experience I had with a couple of carpenters arose in part because we had different ideas about appropriate job site conduct. If I'd had a policy statement for them to read and discuss at the time I interviewed them, perhaps we would have realized we were not a good match.

Starting with a statement of purpose

Your policy statement should flow, not only in specifics, but in tone and attitude, from the statement of purpose (mission statement) you put together at the very start of your business (see What It Takes on p. 6). If your statement of purpose emphasizes values such as service and concern for the needs of others, your actual policies should back up those values. A policy statement can read like a declaration of respect and concern for the people who work in a construction company and the community it serves. Or, at

the other end of the spectrum it, can read as a threat. I have seen both. In fact, I have encountered companies whose statements of purpose wax eloquent about respect, concern, excellence, even compassion. They bring a smile to your face. Then you turn the page to the actual policies, and you feel like you're being dressed down by a boot camp sergeant. When you read the purpose and policies one after the other, you feel as if you have encountered evidence of a seriously split personality. You don't want that. You want policies that are at one with your purposes.

If I were starting out as a builder today and writing my first policy statement, I would introduce it something like this: *Our company succeeds because of the integrity of the people who work in our office and on our projects, our commitment to working with respect and consideration for our clients and for one another, and our passion for building structures that are beautiful, durable, and constructed with consideration for the environment.* I would go on to explain that the specific policies that follow were intended as guidelines to help us achieve our purposes.

In writing the specific policies, I would minimize phrases like (and I quote from an actual policy statement) "if you fail to …," and "result in disciplinary action," and "shall be penalized by …" Instead, I would use language such as, "For the health and safety of workers, clients, and others we adhere to the following safety practices …," "So that projects go forward efficiently, we agree that all those working at job sites …," "Out of consideration for the environment we all share, we commit ourselves to …"

A tool policy

Of all the concerns covered in a good policy statement, the one that is likely to prove thorniest at the beginning of

A policy statement can read like a declaration of respect and concern for the people who work in a construction company and the community it serves.

Important Policy Issues

Policy development
- Crew involvement
- Periodic changes

Hiring
- Tryout period

Pay and benefits
- Pay period
- Payday
- Raises
- Vacations
- Paid holidays
- Medical coverage
- Pension
- Profit sharing
- Tuition assistance
- Use of company equipment for side work

Days and hours
- Workdays
- Hours
- Lunch and other breaks
- Overtime requirements
- Sick call-in
- Leaves of absence

Job site behavior and appearance
- Dress
- Appearance of vehicles
- Smoking, alcohol, and drugs
- Obscene language, sexual harassment, ethnic slurs
- Playing radios and music loudly
- Site care and cleanup

Tool requirements
- Tools provided by company
- Tools owned by employees
- Tool maintenance
- Tool allowance

Safety
- Site protection
- Personal safety gear— footwear, hard hats, kneepads, ear protection
- Equipment use
- Running on job sites

Environmental considerations
- Choice of materials
- Use of materials
- Deconstruction not demolition
- Toxic materials

Insurance
- Workers' compensation
- Reporting injuries
- Disability and unemployment

Relationships with clients
- Communication with clients
- Protecting clients' property
- Use of clients' property

Discipline and termination
- Reasons for
- Procedures

your career is that concerning tools. With an ever-increasing number of power tools available to builders, the matter of who—the company or the employee—provides what has developed into an issue with big financial consequences. Builders, worried that employees treat company tools with less care than their own, hesitate to provide them. On the other side, workers don't want to see too big a chunk of their paycheck go for tools used on company jobs.

You need a policy that supports both cost control and morale. It should set out clearly what tools you provide, what tools employees are expected to bring to work, and how they are to be compensated for the use of their tools on company projects. In my own company, I provide three levels of tools: First, small power tools used by apprentices. Second, utility tools such as safety equipment, ladders, power cords, and wheelbarrows—in other words the stuff that is not that much fun to buy and own. And finally, larger pieces of power equipment such as concrete saws, table saws, and compressors with nail guns.

At the same time, I ask crew members to bring to their projects a selection of tools appropriate to their skill levels. For apprentices, that's a gun belt, hammer, tape measure, and other basic manual hand tools. For basic, midrange, journey-level, and lead carpenters the list includes the manual tools plus increasing numbers of power hand tools as they ascend the skill, responsibility, and pay ladder.

At the upper end, the tools can be worth several thousands of dollars. Employees bringing in that amount of equipment need to be compensated for the use of their tools on company projects. My policy has been to pay for all maintenance of the tools, including replacements for those worn out or stolen, and to offer use of company equipment for side or home projects. Other builders with similar requirements provide a cash tool allowance. Whatever compensation you offer, make sure to stay atop the tax consequences. Above all, make sure that your employees feel fairly treated. If they feel ripped off, if they feel you are asking them to subsidize your profits by providing the equipment for company projects, you will lose in the long run. Your employees will leave when they have the chance, and the costs of replacing them will greatly exceed whatever savings you made by chiseling on tool use.

Other critical policies

If there is an issue that comes up as often as tools, it is *safety practice* at job sites. You cannot negligently expose your workers to dangerous working conditions. If you do, you can open yourself to fines, escalating insurance costs, civil lawsuits, and even criminal prosecution.

Equally, employees do not have the right to work recklessly. Those who do endanger others at the job site. They put at risk the financial security of everyone in the company. When they get hurt, workers' compensation insurance costs can soar, making it difficult for the company to compete, and thereby undermining its ability to provide employees with steady work and its owner with an income. You and your employees need a thorough and agreed upon safety policy that protects them, you, and your company. Among other things, the policy should require the use of protective gear—hard hats, ear protection, kneepads, work boots—to prevent both traumatic and gradual injury.

Other issues a policy statement must cover will be taken up in later chapters. Among issues meriting extra comment here are those grouped under "Job Site Behavior and Appearance." Too many

Traveling in Ireland, Gerstel saw this sign at the entry to a construction site.

construction sites look like public dumps. Strewn about materials and piles of trash are hazardous and express disrespect for valuable resources and for the people who work at the site. Your policy should provide that each job site be maintained as if it were the work environment of valued professionals—*because it is.*

Other policies regarding appearance and behavior are more debatable, and your position on each will depend upon the preferences of you, your crew, and the niche you occupy within the construction industry. In my company, we have not been uncomfortable with occasional cussing—so long as it did not demean anyone. But we have never permitted loud music or radios. Never has smoking, alcohol, or drug use been okay. You and your crew will strike your own balance—*excepting that sexual harassment or racist comments, even uttered in jest, are not to be tolerated.* Such degradation is genuinely abusive and it's illegal. Allow it and you can find yourself buried in a well-deserved lawsuit.

Increasingly, along with policies requiring respect of people, companies of all kinds are developing environmentally considerate practices, both to conform to law and to capitalize on business opportunity. I am convinced there is money to be made in construction by paying atten-

am increasingly convinced there is money to be made in construction by paying attention to environmental issues. I call it getting rich by doing good.

Flubbing It

Because you are the one liable for the results of your company's policies, you have final call as to what they will be. But you can do damage if you hand down policies without taking your crew's and subcontractors' feelings into account. I found that out firsthand. When I revised my company's policies to require that employees bring a more complete set of tools to work, my employees were enraged—as much because I had changed a policy of vital interest to them without asking for their input as by the changes I had made. Had I not been steered into backing off by my senior lead carpenter, I might have lost the whole crew. Since then, whenever a policy change seems necessary, I first ask the crew for their ideas.

tion to environmental issues. I call it getting rich by doing good. Keeping toxic materials out of the project carries weight in marketing to clients and in the recruitment of employees. Recycling job site scrap and salvage saves dump fees and can even be a source of income. Products made from recycled materials can be cheaper and of superior quality. For example, concrete made with fly ash, in place of Portland cement, will cure virtually crack-free and is nearly impenetrable by water. Using it can save you costly callbacks for failing foundations—and impress prospective customers with your quality control.

With even the best, most respectful company practices and thorough hiring procedures (see "Hiring and Firing" on p. 201), you will occasionally need to discipline or terminate a worker. You need to provide for that eventuality in your policy statement. Some personnel experts emphasize that you must preserve the right to terminate an employee at will. They make an important point. But it is also true that if a policy statement is to be part of your process of building a team of people who treat each other with consideration, it should provide for a termination process that is more than a gun to the head. It should provide for progressive discipline—steps like a friendly letter outlining problems and suggesting solutions intended to foster the employee's turnaround and success instead of dismissal.

How to write a policy statement

When you are ready to put together a policy statement, you could use the checklist on p. 38 and simply write out a user-friendly position on each issue that will be of concern in your company. However, you should do some reading to deepen your understanding of the issues before you write out your policies. Plentiful magazine articles and books dealing with policies for construction companies have been published. If you have joined a builders' association, you will probably find that other members will share their policy statements with you. One caution here. If you do take content from other builders' policy statements, be careful to not take on board any adversarial or dictatorial language they use.

Expect your policy to evolve. As you interview prospective employees and subcontractors and ask them to read your policies, make notes of their feedback. Periodically make use of it to improve your statement. Make it clear, even as an introduction to your statement, that you welcome input and ideas for improvement. When you revise your statement, pass out the draft to your crew and key subs and ask for their opinions. If the statement is reasonable, rooted in a continuing attitude of respect and concern for the welfare of all in the company, the likelihood is you will get little feedback. (At least that is my experience. "Looks fine," the guys say.) But even then they will appreciate the respect you have shown, and they are more likely to feel the policies are theirs, not only yours.

Avoid dropping changes in policy—especially those having to do with the sensitive issues like tools—on your crew and subs without warning. You will find yourself in hot water as I once did (see "Flubbing It" on the facing page).

Once your policy statement is drafted, have it *reviewed by an expert.* Many of the issues you will deal with in your statement are covered by labor relations law. Sometimes the law is not what you'd expect it to be. A policy might seem common sense to you, but, in fact, violates the rights of your employees.

Operating Capital

A supply of cash stashed in a business checking account and a backup money market fund is among the most important and the most neglected of the builders' tools. Such "operating capital," or "working capital," to use business-world lingo, strengthens your hand in many areas of your operation. It will enable you to make sounder decisions, especially about what work to take and what to turn away. It will allow you to operate more efficiently. It will position you to build stable business relationships.

The power of operating capital

With cash in the bank, you will be better able to resist the tendency to produce dangerously low estimates when work is slow. If you see your accounts nearly empty and realize that soon you will be unable to pay for your company's insurance or pay yourself enough to take care of your family, you can grow desperate. Your desperation leads to delusions about what it will really cost to build that project you are bidding. You need it so badly.

You've got to make some money. You want to believe the project can be built for what the owners have said they are willing to pay, and that's the number you give them. When construction gets under way and the real costs begin piling up, you find that not only are you not making money, but you are sinking deeper in the hole. On the other hand, if you'd had a cushion in the bank, you would have been better positioned to resist your wishful thinking and hold out for a more reasonable project.

Ample operating capital can save you time. Builders who are chronically short of cash in the bank get deeply involved in what the accountants call "cash flow projections"—figuring out if they will have enough money coming in over the next weeks to cover what they must pay out—and in scrambling around to cover shortfalls. With ample operating capital, you avoid that laborious, anxiety-inducing process. An occasional timely glance at your account balances and a rough calculation of upcoming collections and payments assures you that you are, as usual, maintaining a prudent margin of safety.

COMING UP

The Benefits
of Cash in the Bank

Problems Arising from
Undercapitalization

Deciding How Much
Operating Capital You Need

Using a Line of Credit

Building Up Your
Operating Capital

Managing Your Capital

Ample Operating Capital Helps You

Ample operating capital helps:

- Resist overoptimistic estimating
- Save time
- Foster employee security
- Build subcontractor trust and loyalty
- Earn supplier discounts and support
- Develop bonding capacity
- Take on projects with retainage provisions
- Maintain client confidence
- Replace exhausted equipment promptly
- Sleep (more) soundly

Adequate operating funds support you in fostering the trusting relationships with employees, subcontractors, and suppliers that are the soul of a successful construction company. You never have to say to your employees, "Guys, our client has not paid us yet. Can you wait an extra few days for your paychecks?" Do that a few times, and your employees will be looking for a more reliable boss. Likewise, you don't have to stall your subs when they request payment. You can pay promptly, earning their loyalty so that they will welcome working with you not only when jobs are scarce but also during boom periods—when good subs can be hard to find. Checks due to your suppliers can go in the mail immediately so that you capture their discounts for prompt payment and earn their trust sufficiently to get an extension of credit if you do eventually hit a cash crisis.

An ample operating capital reserve will help you qualify for performance bonding—a necessity for many commercial and public projects. With adequate operating capital, you will also have the financial strength to take on projects for which a percentage of each payment will be retained until the project reaches completion, as illustrated in the sidebar

below. Finally, operating capital supports the crucial core of your marketing program, namely the confident referrals of satisfied clients. One builder who poured her profits into a large shop instead of building a reserve in her operating account said, "I find myself worrying about money instead of the job. It sets a bad tone with clients because I have to worry after them, asking 'When can you pay me?'" Those clients, made uneasy by her cash flow problems, are less likely to refer her to new projects. Who wants to recommend a builder teetering on the edge of insolvency? Thus, the builder's lack of operating capital is costing her not only on current projects but is costing her future work.

How much capital is enough?

With the benefits of plentiful cash in the bank so extensive, the question is not whether to build up operating capital, but just how much to maintain in your account. I have seen a range of recommendations:

- At the low end, The National Association of Home Builders (NAHB), with its focus on builders of new homes to be offered for sale, recommends 5 percent of sales. If you built three homes a year with sale prices totaling $600,000, NAHB would suggest $30,000 in your operating account.
- Next up the ladder of recommendations is that of construction author Michael Stone, who writes primarily for custom remodelers and builders. Stone recommends that both builders and remodelers keep enough cash on hand to cover four months' worth of the costs of running a company (i.e., overhead as opposed to direct construction costs), *including their own pay.*

Operating Reserves and Growth

You are ready to move up. You are sure you can profitably build that $68,000 architect-designed project, though it is twice the size of anything you have built previously. Then you discover the contract the architect insists upon stipulates 10 percent of each payment—a total of $6,800, your entire projected profit—be retained by the owners until you've got the new space ready for their use. You can live with the condition (whether or not you should is a topic of a later chapter). Your operating capital account is full, and you are confident it will allow you to pay your bills promptly until you can collect the retainage.

▪ Further along are my recommendations for small-volume builders. *For slow times*, I like to see enough capital in reserve to cover a year's worth of sharply restrained overhead including subsistence pay for the owner. With that level of cash in the bank, a company can take on a project paying just enough to cover the cost of labor and materials to keep a seasoned crew—an asset replaceable only at great cost—intact during the bad period. *For times when business is strong*, I like to see 10 percent of a company's projected 12 months' sales in reserve. With that amount, a company is positioned to take on good projects even when they involve retainage that will slow cash flow. Using my guideline, if you are heading into a good year in which you expect to do $600,000 volume, you will have $60,000 in reserve.

▪ Bonding companies, which serve primarily commercial and larger-volume builders, can be even more conservative. They understand, as *The Basic Bond Book* points out, that "it takes money to start up a job, to carry a company over a period in which there might be a dispute with an owner, to pay overhead, and to finance slow receivables"—namely to cover your bills when money you are owed has not been paid. Bonding companies ask for as much as 10 percent of the value of backlogged work in the operating capital account—and that can amount to a great deal more than 10 percent of the projected next year's sales when work is under contract far into the future.

It is a lot that I (never mind the bonding companies) ask for, but I have worked through several long and deep

How Much Operating Capital?

A hierarchy of recommendations:
▪ Five percent of total sales
▪ Four months' coverage of overhead, including owner's pay
▪ Ten percent of projected 12 months' sales
▪ Ten percent of dollar value of work under contract

recessions. I have learned that work can dry up for longer than a few months—*a lot longer*. I have seen builders with shallow reserves give in to the temptation to lowball projects during those scarce times to get cash pulsing through their company. The result for some has been bankruptcy. For others it has meant rushing the job or bringing in cheap, marginal subcontractors and carpenters who leave them with liabilities hanging over their heads. Readers of the first edition of this book have told me that they survived hard periods because they followed my conservative recommendation on operating capital. Others have told me they wished they had followed it.

Better a saver than a borrower be

Whichever guideline for operating capital balance you adopt, you are looking at a lot of money. With my guideline, if you are at the start-up stage of your career and anticipate doing $100,000 worth of work (a small addition and two modest kitchen renovations), you will want $10,000 capital in reserve. A few years along, with $500,000 worth of work planned (one large remodel/addition and three custom kitchens) your target rises to $50,000. Another step up, to a custom home and a couple of sizable commercial remodels, and you will need $100,000 or more. That's cash in the bank!

They speak of their "relationship" with their banker as if they were now dating the first violinist from the city symphony.

To sidestep the effort needed to build such reserves, contractors often set up a line of credit with a bank and draw short-term loans against it when their capital accounts are low. I have met builders who seemed to believe that by acquiring a line of credit and *putting themselves in the position of borrowers,* they have ascended the ladder of business world prestige. They speak of their "relationship" with their banker as if they were now dating the first violinist from the city symphony. In fact, they have only added another cost of doing business. It is a cost that can be painful when incurred during a project already in financial difficulty. One builder, after totaling the charges on a credit line he had used to see himself through a badly underestimated job, groaned "I did not have the bank's interest and fees in my bid either."

A line of credit *can* be an asset. If it involves only a modest maintenance charge and does not become a temptation to relax financial discipline, it can be a prudent last ditch protection against an unforeseen but always possible cash crunch. A credit line, however, is no substitute for operating capital.

Building up and managing your cash reserves

Other than finding it in a dumpster, winning it at gambling, or receiving a gift from a rich benefactor, there is only one way to build your own operating capital. Save it out of earnings, one step at a time.

Once you have built up your capital, manage it for earnings. Keep only the necessary minimum in your business checking account. Put the rest in your higher-interest money market account. You can move money back and forth between the two accounts in minutes a month. The additional interest will handsomely reward you for your effort. You do the math: $20,000 in a business bank account at three-tenths of a percent interest versus a money market fund at 5 percent, compounded annually for 10 years. (Pssst! The difference in interest earned is $11,969.72.)

Building up operating capital is a test of (and training in) financial discipline. In our ardently consumerist society, the pressure to acquire business trophies—new trucks and tools, cool computers, fancy offices, etc.—hits as relentlessly as the pressure to stuff our personal lives with material goods. But to succeed as a builder, you must resist. William Mitchell, author of *Contractor's Survival Manual,* makes the point with unvarnished bluntness: "Ignore that urge to buy the latest luxury car. Salt that cash away. Someday you will need the money in reserve. If you can't stand the thought of driving an old truck and answering your own phone, turn directly to chapter four, which deals with bankruptcy, because you are going to need it."

Building Up Your Capital Account

- Open a business checking account.
- In the year before going into business for yourself and while you are still an employee, discipline yourself to put 5 to 10 percent *off the top of each paycheck* in your capital account.
- Fill your checking account to the point that you will not need to pay a monthly fee.
- Open a higher-interest account such as a money market account, and put additional operating capital into it.
- When you are doing side jobs en route to becoming a full-time contractor, place into your capital account all earnings not needed to outfit an office or acquire business tools.
- When you begin contracting full time, put a percentage of profits on each project in the capital account.
- If you find you are not earning enough to build up your operating capital, especially during times when business is strong, take steps to increase markups on your projects. Any properly run construction business can pay its owner a reasonable salary and earn a profit to build up operating capital as well.

Insurance

To succeed financially as a builder you need to not only earn a fair salary and profit job after job, but you also need to avoid having money go back out the door in big chunks on completed jobs as a result of sloppy practices, errors, and accidents. Your best protection against losses is the disciplined use of the procedures for construction, communication, and controls we will be discussing throughout this book. You need a comprehensive and clear construction contract. You need to incorporate excellent moisture control details in your buildings and to comply rigorously with building codes. You need a strong safety program to prevent job site injuries.

As a final measure of protection, you also need insurance. Not only does the law require certain coverages, but without insurance you can lose your life savings in a lawsuit by an injured worker or client as a result of one bad accident or mistake. Without insurance you risk devastating lives irreversibly; with it, you can repair damage. Here's an illustration from the recent past. The painting subcontractor of a respected builder in my area left an oily rag wadded up at a job site when he left for the day. The rag ignited, starting a fire that burned down the clients' nearly completed home. The painter had no insurance to build them a new one. The builder, fortunately, did.

Who Sells You What

You can purchase insurance through a number of channels. It is sold by salespeople who work for large companies, by agents who represent a company, and by brokers who can sell you insurance products of many different companies. Of the three, brokers are typically the most independent and knowledgeable. Find yourself a good one. Insurance is a complicated matter, and the complications vary from state to state. Here I will be able to give you only a broad overview, and *that from a builder's, not an expert's, perspective*. You are not likely to become expert yourself, for you will need to deal with insurance rarely, perhaps only when you pay your annual premiums and give your policy a quick riffle.

You will need an independent professional to guide you. A good broker can play that role. She can assess your needs and let you know what policies with exactly which provisions and levels of coverage you should carry. She can find you policies offered at competitive rates by strong companies and steer you away from second-rate operations. She can advise you how to cut your insurance costs by adjusting coverage or by adding detail to your accounting records.

To locate a broker, ask other builders for recommendations, stressing that you want someone who really knows *construction* insurance. Talk with several brokers. Pose a few open-ended questions:

- How do I determine what policies I need?
- How much coverage do you think is prudent, and why?
- Can you recommend ways to control costs without losing quality?
- How do I select a company that is likely to be responsive if I have a major claim?

Be suspicious of a broker who breezily offers easy solutions to every question. Insurance is treacherous territory. The broker you want is the one who will tell you candidly there are difficulties and where they lie, as well as offer you solutions.

Once you have selected a broker, stick with her (though you may want to shop your business around occasionally to make sure she is offering a competitive

COMING UP

Why You Buy Insurance

Who You Buy It From

What Policies You Need

How Much Coverage to Buy

What You Do and Do Not Get for Your Money

How You Control Cost

Y ou will need an independent professional to guide you in the right direction. A good broker can play that role.

Insurance Policies for Contractors

Liability

- Commercial general liability (CGL)
- Business vehicle
- Nonowned vehicle
- Equipment theft

Employee

- Workers' compensation
- Unemployment
- Disability

Claims Made versus Occurrence Coverage

A *claims made* policy covers claims made while the policy is in effect. For example, a skylight you installed in 1997 leaks, resulting in severe rot in the roof frame. In 2001, the owner discovers the rot. The claims made policy you have purchased for 2001 will apply to your liabilities. So far, so good. But in the future you may have a problem. If at any point you stop buying claims made, you may have no insurance that applies to the years for which you did buy claims made. So, if you run your construction company for 10 years, buying claims made every year during that time, then become a Web designer and stop buying insurance, you may have no insurance that applies to all those structures you put up during your years as a builder. (There are ways to extend a claims made policy, but they can be expensive and complex.)

An *occurrence* policy covers problems with work that "occurred" when the policy was in effect. Using the example above, if you had an occurrence policy in 1997, the year you put in the skylight, it would apply to damage caused by the skylight leak whenever that damage was discovered (unless the occurrence policy had a time limit). If you have a 10-year run as a builder, buy occurrence insurance every year, then switch careers, you will leave behind insurance that applies to all the work you did. The problem with the occurrence policy is that building costs increase. For a large claim, an occurrence policy bought years earlier, when building costs were lower, might not have a high enough limit to cover the claim when it occurs.

rate). A good, long-term relationship should pay dividends. An insurance-industry expert told me that he has seen small-volume builders enjoy extraordinary service from brokers simply because they were loyal and expressed appreciation for what they were given.

You will want your broker to provide you with policies that fall into two broad divisions: liability coverage, including general liability coverage and vehicle insurance, and employee coverage, including workers' compensation insurance.

Liability Insurance

In the liability area, your biggest cost will be for a commercial general liability (CGL) policy. CGL covers a bewildering range of liabilities. What is most important to appreciate about it is this: *We must carry it because it compensates clients (and others) for injury or damage we might inflict on them or their property in the course of doing our work. In addition, it covers the legal fees we run up in the course of settling claims for such injury or damage. Thereby, CGL protects people we might harm and ourselves.*

CGL is a *must* for contractors. You have to cover yourself and your clients against accidents as well as against failures in your work. But just what kind of CGL, providing exactly which coverage, is a matter for discussion with your broker. To begin with, you will need to choose between two types of liability coverage: Do you want a "claims made" policy, or do you want "occurrence" coverage? The distinction between the two is a bit mind-numbing (see the bottom sidebar at left for a highly simplified explanation). Your broker will likely recommend an occurrence policy, but you should discuss the choice so that you understand what you are getting and what you are giving up.

Additionally, you must tell your broker exactly what kind of construction you do. It's tempting to blur the outlines a bit to qualify for lower rates ("Who? Me? Work on roofs? On no, never been on a roof in my life! I leave that strictly to the roofer, and he has his own insurance."), but you must resist. Otherwise, you might end up with a policy that does not cover what you actually do. After all, you concealed it from the insurance company, and as a result, you may find your insurer with justification for denying responsibility if a large claim against you occurs.

Together with your CGL, you will need a couple of companion liability coverages. You need to cover your own business vehicle. And, *very importantly,* you need coverage for what the insurance industry calls "nonowned" vehicles—rentals, employee cars and trucks—used in the course of your operation. Your nonowned coverage takes care of *your* liability, though not the employee's, if he rams his pickup into a competitor's brand new 4×4 during a run to the lumberyard. Finally, you want to consider tool theft coverage, especially if you are new in business and still building operating capital.

Exclusions

Along with making certain that the policy you purchase includes the coverage you need, you will want to acquaint yourself with its exclusions. Some are a matter of course. Assume, for example, the hotdog shipping center you built for the local start-up, Pooches-in-a-Pocket.com., gets wasted in a nuclear attack. Your insurance company is not going to pay for replacing the building. "No," they will point out, "if you will just turn to page 22 of your policy and reference clause 654.321 you will see that our policy specifically excludes coverage of building failure due to hydrogen bombs going off in the parking lot next door." No injustice or surprise there. But

Tool Theft Insurance

I have been hit by tool thieves half a dozen times in my career. My tool theft insurance has covered the full cost of the replacements. But has it paid me back more than I have paid out in premiums? Yes and no. The answer is "no" if I include the return I could have earned on the money had I invested it. But I sure was glad to have the coverage each time I was ripped off. If you buy coverage and your tools are stolen when you are short of cash, the coverage may be the difference between your being able to stay in business or not.

some exclusions can be a bit unsettling when you first come upon them, especially the "work-product exclusion." It excuses the insurance company from paying for replacement or repair of a "particular" and "faulty" item installed by you and/or your crew. If you improperly flash a window, for example, your policy will not pay for a proper reinstallation when the window leaks. "What?!" you might exclaim, "Then why bother to buy insurance?" The answer: The work-product exclusion is limited. While you may be responsible for reinstalling the "particular faulty" item—the window flashing—the insurance company still picks up the tab for the damage (soaked walls, insulation, and drywall), resulting from the leak.

A tricky area, falling somewhere between inclusions and exclusions, has to do with coverage of building failures due to improper design. In a given CGL policy, design coverage may be neither explicitly included nor excluded. But the reality is that while insurance companies do not want to cover builders for design under CGL policies, we almost inevitably are drawn into design in the course of projects. Plans from designers and architects are often so sketchy that "design completion"—designing how things really are to be built—becomes unavoidable; and, of course it is how they are *built,* not how they *look,* that determines

How to Control Liability Insurance Costs

■ *Overtime payroll*—Make sure you are paying premium on the base pay only, not the overtime pay.

■ *Subcontractor insurance certificates*—Get certificates of liability coverage from all your subs, and make sure they fulfill the requirements of your insurance company, such as naming you as an "additional insured."

■ *Business vehicle*—Ask for the lowest cost category applicable to your business.

■ *Umbrella policy*—Sometimes buying an umbrella is a cheaper way to expand coverage than by upping the base policy limit. But watch out for the exclusions.

■ *Shop in advance*—Call your broker well before your policy expires to make sure he will have a new policy available at a competitive price. Sometimes insurance companies abruptly exit the business of writing CGL coverage for contractors, and you do not want to have go hustling after a new policy under emergency pressure.

whether or not they fail. As a result, when you build, you risk taking on liabilities for failure due to design, even though your policy does not explicitly cover it.

Given the situation, what's the best you can do? So that you know where you stand, discuss with your broker any design coverage or exclusion under your policy. Find out as best you can where your boundaries are under your CGL policy and do what you can to stay within them. However, expect lack of clarity. You are in a gray area. I have heard it often discussed by construction professionals, but I've never seen it resolved clearly.

Setting limits and controlling costs

Just how much coverage you decide to carry, just what "limits"—to use insurance industry language—you select for your CGL and other policies will be largely determined by the volume and type of work you do. There are, however, a couple of further guidelines worth bearing in mind:

■ Your goal should be to protect your clients, others affected by your operations, and yourself against catastrophic loss.

■ The additional costs of pushing your limits up to the catastrophe level may be relatively low. When I increased my CGL coverage more than 300 percent, to $1 million, my premium increased by only 33 percent—from 4.6 percent to 6.1 percent of payroll.

■ When you choose your limit, do so with an eye to whether it is *per claim* or an *aggregate* for the life of the policy. A $300,000 per claim limit will cover two claims, one for $280,000 and one for $210,000. The aggregate policy will pay the first claim and $20,000 of the second, but leave you holding the bag for the balance. Ouch!

Whatever combination of policies you do choose, liability insurance is going to be among the major expenses of running your business. Control the expense to the extent you can. The sidebar above suggests effective cost control measures.

Employee Insurances

Just as with liability insurance, both enlightened self-interest and your moral obligations to the people you work with dictate that you carry workers' compensation, unemployment, and disability insurance for employees. The insurance for employees, however, is also required by law. Where I work, you can not even get a building permit without carrying workers' compensation insurance.

In my state, unemployment insurance and disability insurance are provided by the government, and you make payments for them along with submitting other payroll taxes. In your state, you may have the option of purchasing them through a private insurer. Rather than going into the options, however, I'll recommend you talk them over with your broker and here will concentrate on the gorilla of employee insurance—namely, workers' compensation.

The key to workers' comp insurance is its "no fault" design. When an employee gets hurt on one of your projects, he is entitled to benefits regardless of whether he is "at fault" for the injury. He is entitled to benefits—including medical care, rehabilitation, compensation to take the place of lost wages, and/or a lump sum settlement if the injury results in permanent disability—even if his own carelessness caused the injury. If a carpenter falls off scaffolding because you neglected to provide a safety rail, that carpenter is entitled to workers' comp benefits. If the carpenter falls because she removed the rail, then she is still entitled to benefits. The no-fault arrangement protects both workers and employer from the nobody-wins-but-the-lawyers mire of litigation.

No-fault is helpful, but do not let it lure you into thinking that, with it, workers' comp sets up a "win-win" situation that substitutes for a strong safety program. It does not. Any serious accident still results in heavy losses all around. The employee suffers pain, fear, loss of income, maybe even loss of a career. If the builder's negligence caused the accident, he suffers guilt. He loses an employee, and replacing employees is extremely expensive. He suffers additional financial loss because the accident will crank up his insurance rates by raising his "experience modification factor."

Here's how experience modification will work for your business. You purchase a workers' comp policy. The industry then monitors the claims you make under that policy. If you make no significant claims, they assign you a factor that modifies your insurance rate downward. If they have a bad experience with you, the reverse happens. For example, your first few years holding the policy you pay the base rate of 10 percent of wages, or $10 per hundred of wages. Then the industry sees you've had no claims and it

> No-fault is helpful, but do not let it lure you into thinking that, with it, workers' comp sets up a "win-win" situation that substitutes for a strong safety program.

How to Control Workers' Compensation Insurance Costs

- *Overtime*—Pay premium on the base pay only, not the overtime pay.
- *Subcontractor insurance certificates*—Make sure you have one from every sub and that it meets your insurance company's requirements.
- *Experience modification*—Make sure your rate is lowered when it should be.
- *Handling claims*—If a worker is injured, support the worker in claiming benefits so that he or she does not feel a need to go outside the no-fault system and to an attorney.

- *Classifications*—When reporting your employees' pay, divide it into categories. Your insurance rate for the pay your crew earns cleaning up the site will be much lower than for the time they spend on the roof.
- *Group policy*—You may get lower and more stable rates if you join a group.
- *Dividend*—Your broker may be able to find you a carrier with a history of returning a large percentage of premium to clients as a year-end dividend (though past performance is never a guarantee of the future results).

assigns you a modification factor of 70 percent. Now you are paying only $7 per hundred.

The next year bad luck strikes. A couple of your workers are hurt, one injuring his back so badly he has to give up construction work completely. Workers' comp insurance takes care of him, and you are spared a lawsuit. But your experience mod factor zooms to 150 percent. Now you are paying $15 per hundred in wages for insurance.

We are talking big bucks here. For just one carpenter making $30 an hour the leap can be $2.40 an hour, or about $5,000 a year in insurance costs. I've heard of worse. I have heard of a builder's rates going to several hundred percent. In other words, their insurance was cost-ing them three times what they paid in wages. Clearly, even with no-fault, a strong job site safety program is key to controlling your insurance costs.

As the sidebar on p. 49 suggests, there are additional measures, as well, that you can take to control workers' comp costs. Once you get the hang of it, managing insurance costs will take you relatively little time to earn potentially huge rewards. Over the course of your career as a builder, even if you remain a small-volume contractor, you will spend enough on insurance to buy a fair-sized yacht. Save a percent of that total through attentive management, invest it prudently, and by the time you retire you'll have enough stashed away to buy the yacht anyhow.

CHAPTER 3

A Builder's Numbers

Knowing Your Numbers

A FEW YEARS AGO while taking my morning break at Semi-Freddi's, my favorite neighborhood bakery and caffeine dispensary, I ran into Semi's chief executive officer, Tom Franier. Tom is one of the most capable small-business owners I know. Starting a decade ago with a six-person operation, he has, together with his sister and brother-in-law, built Semi's into a 100-person company while keeping it virtually debt-free and providing good pay and a supportive environment for its workers. Tom and I got to talking about business education, and I asked him a question I'd been thinking about for a while. Of all the courses he'd taken during his MBA program, I wondered which did he consider the most valuable? Without hesitation, he answered, "Accounting. I hated it at the time, but now I'm thankful for it. You've got to understand *your* numbers. Where's the money coming from? Where's it going? That's *survival* information."

Accounting avoidance

Builders as much as bakers need to know where the money is coming from and where it is going. If you are to run a construction company, you must have accounting systems for recording and analyzing your income and expenses in an organized way. Only then will you be able to understand your company's financial performance and get it up to par.

Unfortunately, many builders neglect or avoid their accounting responsibilities. During their start-up years, some simply do not yet grasp the importance of accounting as a tool for managing their business and do not give the task the priority it deserves. One builder says of his early years, "I was so busy out in the field 'making money,' I didn't take time to keep accurate records and make sure I really *was* making money." When he finally did analyze his numbers, he found that his remodeling operation was subsidizing thousands per month in losses by his cabinet shop. Because cabinetmaking was his first love, he closed out remodeling and, with the help of systematic accounting, turned his shop into a sound business.

COMING UP

Accounting, a Survival Skill

Accounting Avoidance

Taking On the Challenge

A Map of Accounting Responsibilities

Tools and Concepts, Basic and Advanced

A Ladder of Accounting Systems

More seasoned builders, while glimpsing the truth that accounting is integral to business management, slough the task off to others. "The wife takes care of that," they say. Or they declare, "As a builder you're much better off doing what you know how to do out in the field and leaving the accounting stuff to the experts."

That last rationalization is mouthed even by self-appointed construction industry educators. So I need to tell you loud and clear what I think of it. *It is utter, dangerous nonsense.* True, you can hand off the *bookkeeping*—namely, the clerical work of recording and totaling your income and expenses, but you must still understand your accounting system and what must go into it in order to get the needed output. You need to be involved in setting it up and in developing it. And you must pay attention to and analyze the summaries of income and expenses it produces. The idea that you can be in business but oblivious to accounting is like thinking you can sail across the ocean without using navigational instruments. Try it and you will end up in a financial shipwreck.

What accounting gives you

With attention to accounting you will know such things as:

- How close the actual costs of construction on your projects are to estimated costs.
- What percentage of your revenue is going for new equipment.
- What percentage of revenue is spent on callbacks.
- What percentage of income goes right back out to pay for the labor and material of building projects and for general expenses like truck insurance, and what percentage is left over to pay yourself and as profit for your company.

Based on what you see, you can determine for what phases of construction your estimates are sound and for what phases you need to improve. You can tell whether you are overindulging a love of tools or investing reasonable amounts in new equipment. You'll know whether the quality of your work is as it should be or whether you are seeing too many failures and need to bear down on your construction details. Finally, you will know your bottom line—whether you are making a profit for the risks and responsibilities of being in business as well as paying yourself for the hard work of running your company.

Your accounting system will, additionally, provide you with the income and expense figures required for tax returns, both the end-of-year return and the quarterly returns for estimated taxes you must file when you go into business for yourself. Regardless of whether you think it is ethical or not to evade taxes, paying taxes is a business necessity for builders. Because so many do attempt to evade taxes, contractors are a prime target for the tax authorities. When the IRS catches an evader or even someone who has simply made an error on his return, there can be devastating penalties. A specialty contractor who operates a one-person company in my area got caught. The IRS discovered he had neglected to report payments from general contractors, so they hit him with a bill for $70,000, three-quarters of it interest and fines, and the state piled on additional charges. No sensible businessperson will let such potential liabilities arise and destroy his future. To avoid them, you need not only to make up your mind to pay taxes but also to do the accounting that allows you to calculate them accurately.

I should emphasize, however, that I will be focusing not on tax accounting but on management accounting—the kind you must do to run your company. In "Resources" (see p. 258), I have listed a good book and an IRS publication, both of which give you understandable instructions on tax requirements for small businesses. Otherwise, I will, for the most part, leave tax issues to you and your accountant. Please note that I will be introducing management accounting as a builder with experience and training in accounting, but not as an accounting specialist. I am aiming to give you a hands-on, practical take on management accounting. When you take up the same issues with your accountant, she may make more technical use of terms and concepts.

Taking on the challenge of accounting

If you are new in business, accounting may seem a little intimidating at first glance. It's not an easy subject. But with persistent effort it's learnable. The essential goals of construction accounting are pretty much common sense. They break out into a logical pattern, as illustrated in the "map" on p. 54. Some of the words may be new to you, but you will quickly learn their meanings as you read on. The math needed to accomplish your responsibilities is elementary-school stuff—addition, subtraction, multiplication, and division, maybe a bit of graphing. What's more, accountants have evolved a set of marvelous tools and concepts for doing the work. In the next few pages, we will first take a look at the basic goals of accounting, then at certain of the key accounting tools and ideas. With that introduction to the subject of accounting accomplished, we will be able to move on to a discussion of specific accounting systems from a start-up to high octane.

Our discussion does assume a bit of prior knowledge. In particular, you need to know how to reconcile, or balance,

your checkbook and checking account statement. If you need to learn how, see "Resources" on p. 258 for help. If you know how to reconcile a checking account statement you are ready to move ahead.

The overall goals of construction accounting, as you see at the top of the map, are to record and analyze your income and expenses. In other works, as Tom of Sem-Freddi's says, you need to know how much money is coming in, and you need to know where it is going. There are tasks for income. There are tasks for expenses. Of the two, tracking income is the less complex. So let's start there.

Accounting for income

Your first task on the income side has to do with keeping track of the money that you have earned. You need to stay on top of what your clients owe you, when you bill them for what they owe (as agreed in your contracts), and when you collect it. That may seem pretty obvious. But the fact is small businesses, including builders, can easily lose track of what they are owed and forget to collect it. Just as bad, they overcollect, thereby cheating and angering clients. With some embarrassment, I will tell you that I once overcollected enough from a client to buy a new top-of-the-line pickup. Fortunately, I caught my mistake, managed to resist the pickup, and returned the money to the client before she noticed my error. (She forgave me.)

If you take a few more steps down the map, you will see that I have suggested you record your income separately for construction work and for preconstruction services like design and estimating. As a builder, you spend a great deal of your time planning projects. It is important to monitor your progress at learning to get paid for that work.

A s a builder, you spend a great deal of your time planning projects. It is important to monitor your progress at learning to get paid for that work.

A Map of Essential Accounting Responsibilities

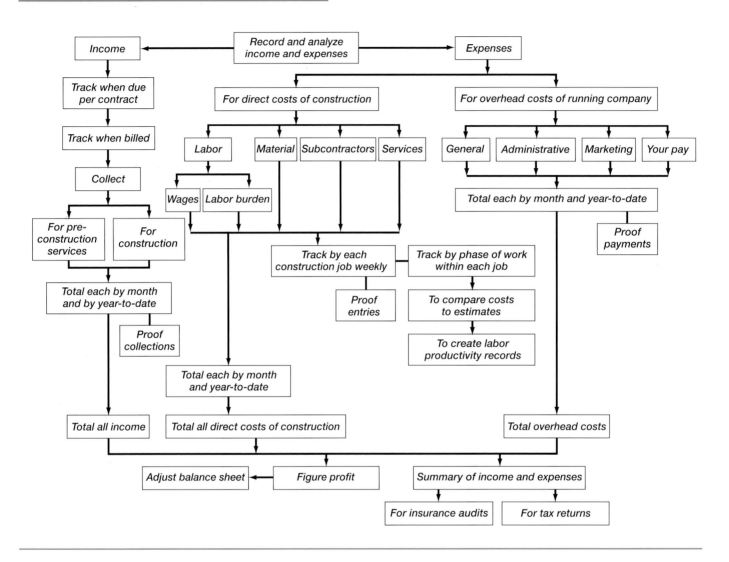

Keeping track of your income for preconstruction services separately will help you see how well you are doing.

Finally, on the income side of the map, you want to know how much you've collected in total. Once you have the total, you have half the picture of financial performance that you need. The other half comes from tracking expenses.

Accounting for expenses

Accounting for expenses breaks down into two broad areas—tracking your costs to build each of your projects and tracking what it costs to run your company.

The costs of running the company— your "overhead" in accounting language— in turn divide into three categories: general, administrative, and marketing. General expenses include rent for office or storage space, the costs of your pickup and other equipment, and of office supplies. Administrative could include your payments to a bookkeeper when you are ready to subcontract that work. Marketing includes all the costs of bringing in work. For some outfits marketing is a big expense. One window replacement company reportedly spends roughly ½ million dollars on marketing to bring in $3 million worth of work annually. On the other hand, for a small-volume remodeler with satisfied clients recommending him or her regularly, outlay for marketing hardly may be necessary. In fact, your main reason for tracking marketing expenses may be to make certain you are putting *something* into marketing, not neglecting it entirely.

When you have a small-volume operation, by far the biggest expense of running your company will be to pay yourself for all your hard work at general, administrative, and marketing tasks. For simplicity's sake, in the diagram on the facing page, I have shown accounting for pay to yourself as a separate task. In a more complex map, "your pay" would be shown as subdivisions of general, administrative, and selling costs because your work as manager of your company is divided among these three areas.

Along with, but separately from, tracking costs for general, administrative, and marketing overhead, you need to track the costs of actually constructing your projects out in the field. As you will see by working your way down the middle area of the map, construction costs—called "direct costs" or "job costs" (and sometimes "cost of goods sold" in accounting lingo)—divide into four areas. From your years on job sites you know what they are: labor (the costs of having employees), material, subcontractors, and services such as inspections. The labor breaks down into two more groups—wages and labor burden—the additional employee costs like workers' compensation insurance incurred on top of wages. All this is straightforward enough so far, but as you take the next steps down the map you come to the area of accounting that probably gives builders the most fits. And that is keeping up with those direct construction costs on a job-by-job basis at several different levels.

In this photo you see several direct costs of construction—lumber, concrete, and two carpenters at work. Just out of the picture are a couple of overhead costs—the company pickup and the contractor taking the picture for his marketing portfolio.

Accounting for direct construction costs

As the map indicates, you must keep track of the direct costs of construction for each job overall. You must also keep track of costs for the phases of work such as foundation and framing within each job. You must track the phase costs for two pur-

Labor Productivity

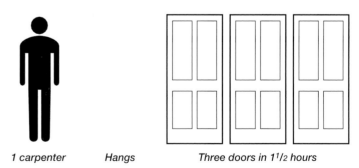

1 carpenter　　*Hangs*　　*Three doors in 1¹/2 hours*

Labor Productivity
Material: 3 × $60 per door = $180
Labor: 1.5 hours × $50 per hour = $75
　Note: $50 includes $27-per-hour wage plus $23-per-hour labor burden (27 + 23 = 50)
Labor Productivity: One-half hour to hang one door (1.5 hours divided by 3 doors equals 0.5 hours per door)

poses: to compare how the actual costs are stacking up against your estimates of what the costs would be and to build labor productivity records for future estimates.

Let's look at each of these tasks and purposes in somewhat more detail. To begin with, you need to know the costs of constructing each of your jobs. You will want to know what it is costing you to build the Smith addition over on Canyon Road, and at the same time you want to know just what it is costing you to do the restaurant renovation down on Eleventh Avenue.

In addition, you need to track the costs for each phase of work on each project so that you can see how those costs are running in comparison to your estimate. In other words, to use the language of construction accounting, you need to do job costing. For the Smith addition you want to know how much is going out for foundation work and how those costs stack up against your estimate. Over at the restaurant, you want to know how the costs of plumbing and electrical are running compared with what you had allowed. You need that information so that if you are running high, you can either do something to control costs or, in the worst case, recognize you have made an estimating error and take steps to avoid repeating it in the future.

For your job costing to be of full value in helping you control costs and creating future estimates, you need to break down phase costs—at least for work done by your own employees, though not necessarily for subs—into material and labor costs. For framing, you want to know the costs of the carpenters' labor and of the lumber. By job costing materials separately, you learn whether your estimating of material quantities is accurate. You see whether your method for figuring lumber in floor frames is giving you the board footage of joists and blocking you need

or whether it is resulting in an undercount so that you are throwing material into your jobs without getting paid for it.

On the labor side, you determine not only whether your estimates for ongoing jobs have been accurate, but also get the information you need to make accurate estimates in the future. You steadily build up records of how long it takes your crew to frame a foot of wall, install a sheet of roof decking, or hang a door, or do the myriad other items of work they *produce* on each project. Without such *labor productivity* records, you will never be able to create accurate estimates for employees' work. You will produce "guesstimates." That is not good enough.

With your accounting complete for direct construction costs, overhead, and income, you have what you need to accomplish the tasks given at the bottom of the map. You can determine your profits (or losses). You have the income and expense figures needed to fill out your tax returns. Not incidentally, you have all the necessary figures to satisfy your insurance auditors (your insurance company *is* going to send someone over to look at your books and make sure you are not underpaying them). Finally, you will be able to update something called your balance sheet, which we will discuss next along with other accounting tools.

Basic accounting tools and concepts

Now that we have made our way through the map of essential accounting responsibilities, let's look at certain key tools and concepts accountants have created for accomplishing the goals. Some have already come up in our discussion of the map. But it is worth your while to look at them from a different angle as a way of getting ready to take on the actual accounting systems we will discuss in coming chapters.

KEEPING THE BOOKS In the old days bookkeepers recorded income and expenses in cloth-bound books. They called their work "keeping the books." We still use the phrase, though now when accounting is done with computers, instead of literal "books" we have "files" stored in the computer.

SPREADSHEET The pages in the old-fashioned books were typically spreadsheets, which are nothing more than sheets divided into columns and rows—much like a piece of graph paper—on which you can spread, categorize, and total numbers. Today's computer files feature screens that mimic the look of old-fashioned spreadsheets. To get a clear picture of how spreadsheets work, turn to the illustration on pp. 64–65.

GENERAL LEDGER The old-fashioned accounting books were often called ledgers, and the main ledger was called the general ledger. Computer systems have a file called "general ledger." A general ledger includes spreadsheets on which all income and expenses—both for direct job costs and for the general, administrative, and marketing expenses—are recorded. Because it is so inclusive, the general ledger gives you an overview of the financial experience of the company.

CHART OF ACCOUNTS In the general ledger, income and expenses are grouped by categories called accounts. These accounts are summarized on a chart of accounts. When doing bookkeeping you refer to the chart to make sure you are consistently entering the same type of expenses in the same account. Using your chart, you will enter the cost of a new computer program under I.T. every time, not under computer one time and in the office supplies category the next.

OVERHEAD AND DIRECT JOB COSTS A chart of accounts for builders includes two primary groups of accounts for expenses. *Overhead* costs include the general, administrative, and marketing costs of running your company and bringing in work. *Direct costs* are the costs for labor, material, subcontractors, and miscellaneous services such as permits and inspections that you incur in the actual construction of your projects.

JOB COST RECORDS Using a separate spreadsheet for each project, you can record the project's costs by phase of work in order to compare the costs to your estimates. (For an illustration of a job cost record, see p. 78 and p. 94.)

LABOR PRODUCTIVITY RECORD A labor productivity record is a more detailed kind of job cost, one that shows how much time your crew needed to produce a particular item of work. Over the years you can build up labor records, ranging from those for a small item, like hanging a door, to those for complex assemblies, like a floor frame including

Accounting Tools and Concepts

- Keeping the books
- Spreadsheet
- Payables journal
- Receivables journal
- General ledger
- Chart of accounts
- Job cost records
- Invoices
- Profit and loss statement
- Gross profit margin
- Net profit
- Balance sheet
- Cash and accrual

Two Levels of Profit

Total revenue (money collected)	
Direct costs of construction for labor, material, subs, and services including your wages for work on your construction jobs	Gross Profit
	Overhead costs including your pay for running your company / Net Profit

Gross profit really includes not only profit but certain expenses. Net profit is what is left after all expenses have been subtracted from income.

all blocks, joists, and subfloor. See p. 81 for an illustration.

INVOICES, STATEMENTS, AND RECEIPTS An invoice is a form that you can use to notify your clients that they owe you money. A statement is a summary of invoices and receipts (payments) showing the contract price of a job, how much has been paid, and how much more will be invoiced as the job goes along. See p. 62 for an illustration of an invoice.

PROOFS (LAST, BUT BY NO MEANS LEAST) Accounting systems must incorporate proofs—built-in checks and balances—for making certain income collection, bill payment, and, in general, all entered and totaled numbers are complete and correct. Unproofed numbers are worthless.

Early in your career, with invoices, a checkbook, a general ledger and chart of accounts, job cost records, and labor productivity records, you will be able to collect your income, pay your bills, and attend to your most basic accounting responsibilities. As you grow your company, you will want to make use of other tools.

Advanced accounting tools and concepts

The more advanced tools and concepts will do two things for you. They will give you a more detailed view of your company's overall financial performance. They will give you a more up-to-date view. They include:

PROFIT AND LOSS STATEMENT
"P and L" statements show you whether you are making or losing money for a

The Accounting Equation

If you start with what you own (assets) and take away what you owe (liabilities), you get your net worth (equity). In other words, assets minus liabilities equal equity. (A – L = E). Therefore, as the classic accounting equation states, assets equal liability plus equity (A = L + E).

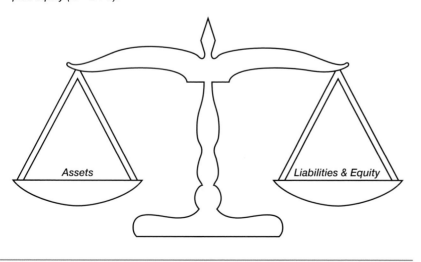

Assets

Liabilities & Equity

given period of time—such as January, or January through March, i.e. the first quarter of the year.

GROSS PROFIT MARGIN   Profit is looked at two ways in the accounting world. Gross profit margin, or GPM, is what is left over after the subtraction of direct job costs from income. GPM is not profit as we think of it in everyday terms, because overhead costs have not yet been taken out.

NET PROFIT   Here we are talking about the real thing—the money left over after you subtract all expenses, both direct job and overhead costs, from the money you take in.

BALANCE SHEET   You can think of a balance sheet as an old-fashioned scale with two trays placed on opposite ends of a balance arm. On one side are the assets of your company such as your truck, tools, operating capital, and money that is owed you. On the other are liabilities such as money you owe on a line of credit (heaven forbid!) or a bill you have not paid. If the assets are greater than the liabilities, you have a positive balance.

NET WORTH   To get the net worth of your company, you subtract its liabilities from its assets. If assets are greater than liabilities, you have a positive net worth.

EQUITY   Another term for the net worth of a company is equity.

THE ACCOUNTING EQUATION   Assets minus liabilities equals equity. If you run a very compact operation with minimal assets and debt, the balance sheet and the accounting equation will not be of much concern to you. But if your company acquires serious assets and/or assumes significant loans, it is worth keeping an

eye on the balance sheet. If equity drops rapidly, that can be a red flag. Your company may be taking on too much debt.

As your company grows—or even before if you are eager to produce the highest-quality accounting—you will want to upgrade not only the tools you use, but also the *timing* of your accounting. In accounting language, you will want to move from "cash" to "accrual" accounting. You can think of cash accounting as commonsense accounting.

Ladder of Accounting Systems

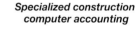

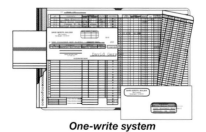

Specialized construction computer accounting

Generic small business computer accounting

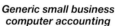

Accounting systems range from the homemade to sophisticated computer programs.

One-write system

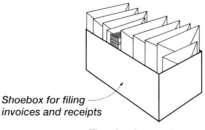

Receipts and invoices

Shoebox for filing invoices and receipts

The shoebox system

The gross pile system

Accounting is really nothing more than sorting income and expenses into groups, totaling the items in the groups, then combining and looking at the totals in different ways.

COMING UP

The Gross Pile System

Using a Shoebox System

Collecting from
Your Customers

Accounting for Income,
Overhead, and Job Costs

Guarding against
the Cash Flow Fallacy

Tale of a Tax Audit

Limits to the Shoebox System

You enter your income and expenses when money actually moves in and out of your checking account. You receive and deposit a payment from a customer, you enter the amount in your books. You pay a bill from a supplier or sub, you enter it in your books.

Accrual accounting is more subtle. On the income side, you enter money earned as soon as you have "accrued" it—that is, given your customer an invoice for it—*even if you have not collected it!* Likewise, on the expense side, *you enter a bill when you incur it.* When you buy lumber, you enter the amount it will cost you in your books, even if it will be a couple of weeks till you pay the lumberyard.

Accrual accounting gives you a more up-to-date picture of where you stand financially. You see not only what you've got but also what you have coming in and what you owe. To do accrual accounting, you need a couple of additional books—or "journals" as they are called. Use a *payables journal* to record bills you owe but have not yet paid. Use a *receivables journal* to keep track of the income that is receivable by you but that has not yet come in. If you consider moving from cash to accrual accounting, first talk to your accountant about the tax implications—which can be major.

A ladder of accounting systems

If you are just starting out in the building business and are new to accounting, you may be sweating oak splinters by now. "Good grief," you may be thinking, "this is just too much. If this is what I have to do to have a nice, little construction company and be my own boss, forget it." But let me tell you two things. First, if you want a satisfying career as a builder, you do have to stay on top of the accounting responsibilities outlined in the map. Otherwise, you will not be in control of

your company's finances and will experience an enormous amount of anxiety. Second, you don't have to master accounting in one fell swoop. You can build up your accounting system and your understanding of accounting one step at a time, beginning with a virtually homemade system that fits in a shoebox.

From a shoebox system you can, for surprisingly little additional cost, move up to a professional-grade paper-and-pencil system, then to a basic computer system. Next, if your company reaches the size that justifies more powerful accounting controls and can sustain the added overhead, you can move into the world of specialized construction accounting software.

Starting with a Shoebox

Most builders, even when they are just starting out in the business, realize instinctively that they have to do *some* sort of accounting. You recognize that you've got to keep track of your income and expenses. So you set aside a drawer or a box or a sack and into it you toss your bank deposit slips and receipts for business purchases. At the end of the first year, you hand the bundle to your accountant. She hands it right back to you with a peeved expression on her face and instructs you to sort the deposit slips and receipts into categories such as "income," "materials," and "office supplies," to total the amounts in each category, and to summarize the totals on a sheet of paper. When you bring back the totals, she will use them to fill out your tax return.

Such "systems" of accounting are so widespread among small-business owners that accountants even have a name for them—the "gross pile" method. Using the gross pile, you actually can attend to basic management accounting goals outlined in our map (see p. 54). At any point in the year, for example, you can add up your deposit slips and expense receipts, subtract expenses from deposits, and see what your company has produced in the way of earnings. The fact is, you can use the gross pile method to accomplish just about every one of the accounting goals. Whatever system you use, accounting is really nothing more than sorting income and expenses into groups, totaling the items in the groups, then combining and looking at the totals in different ways.

Obviously, however, digging through a heap of deposit slips and receipts is a very inefficient way to get your accounting numbers. The gross pile system has other deficiencies too numerous to go into here. You are best off, even at the start of your business, moving at least one step up the ladder of accounting systems.

The shoebox system and accounting for income

If you feel you have a handle on the basic accounting responsibilities mapped out and explained in the previous chapter, you might want to jump right to "Moving up to a One-Write System" on p. 69. Otherwise, you can take a big step beyond the gross pile by starting out with a shoebox system. All that's needed for a shoebox system is a cardboard box, some manila envelopes, a checkbook, and an invoice pad. On the income side, you can bill clients and monitor collection of receivables—i.e. payment due for work done. On the expense side, you can control your payments to subs and suppliers. You can also break out and track your overhead, the costs of running your company, from the direct costs of building each of your projects.

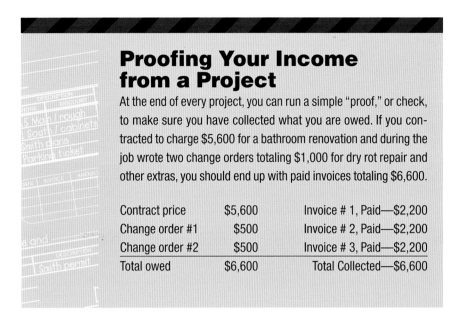

Proofing Your Income from a Project

At the end of every project, you can run a simple "proof," or check, to make sure you have collected what you are owed. If you contracted to charge $5,600 for a bathroom renovation and during the job wrote two change orders totaling $1,000 for dry rot repair and other extras, you should end up with paid invoices totaling $6,600.

Contract price	$5,600	Invoice # 1, Paid—$2,200
Change order #1	$500	Invoice # 2, Paid—$2,200
Change order #2	$500	Invoice # 3, Paid—$2,200
Total owed	$6,600	Total Collected—$6,600

Shoebox Accounting System

Your shoebox accounting system will work best if you get an invoice pad that includes triplicate invoices and a checkbook that includes checks with duplicates so that you can keep copies on file. Invoices are available from office supply stores. Your bank should be able to provide you with duplicate checks.

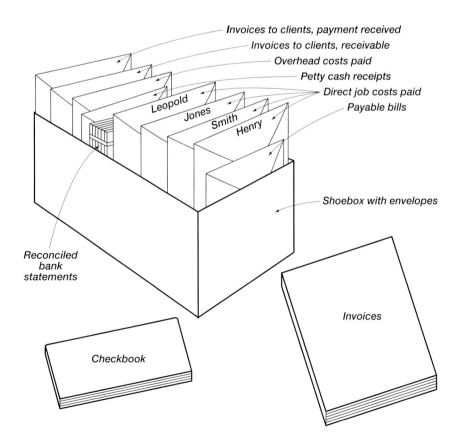

For each of your construction projects, you will set up a payment schedule in the contract and then, during construction, write invoices as the schedule requires. Make sure to bill for extras as the job goes along. Don't delay those billings till the end of the project. That's the surest way in the construction world to end up in a dispute with your customer.

David Gerstel/Builder
Lic. #325650
268 Coventry Road
Kensington, CA 94707

Date: 4/19/2001
Number: #2

To: Everett Jones

Terms: Due now, please $2,130.00

- - - - - - - - - - - - - - PLEASE DETACH AND RETURN WITH YOUR REMITTANCE - - - - - - - - - - - - - -

Due: Payment #2, per Construction Agreement, for completion of deck frame   1,900.00

Change order #1 for repair of rot in existing wall   230.00

2,130.00

Pay last amount in this column

Thank You

To stay on top of your receivables, use the following procedure:

1. In each construction contract include a payment schedule. For the construction of a deck you might set up four payments, each to be made after completion of a phase of work.
2. When you reach the end of a phase, write up a triplicate invoice and present one copy to the client. (Presenting invoices is an art form in itself, and we will discuss it in later

chapters on running projects.) What is critical, for accounting purposes, is that you keep two copies of the invoice for yourself and place them in a "receivables" envelope.
3. During your weekly paperwork session, check the receivables envelope to make sure that due payments are coming in on schedule.
4. When you receive a payment, write the check number on one of your copies of the invoice and place it in the "received" envelope.
5. Deposit the payment; staple the last invoice copy to the deposit slip and file it with your bank records.
6. At completion of the project, add up the total of the paid invoices, and make sure it equals the total of the contract price plus any change orders—orders for extras that were not included in the original contract.

It is really important to proof your collection of receivables. It is very easy to make a mistake in collections. The most likely mistake is undercollecting, overlooking a payment that is due, rather than overcollecting. If you don't proof your receivables, you will probably shortchange yourself.

The shoebox system and accounting for expenses

For tracking expenses, use a procedure parallel to that used on the income side of shoebox accounting:

1. When a bill comes in, place it in a "payables" envelope.
2. When you sit down to do your end-of-week paperwork (and I strongly advise clearing out your in-box, including paying bills, weekly), empty the payables envelope.
3. Check the bills to make sure they are legitimate. Check carefully!

Suppliers make mistakes and charge you for materials you never ordered. Subcontractors, because their own accounting controls are weak, frequently double bill. If you are not vigilant, you will end up paying a plumber or electrician twice for their rough work, or three times for a change order.

4. Using duplicate checks, the type with carbon copies, write a check for each legitimate bill.
5. Mail the original check and fasten the copy to the invoice.
6. File the invoice in the relevant envelope for overhead or direct job cost.

At the end of each project, run a final check, similar to the proof run for income, for payments made to subs. Total the payments made to each sub. Then check the result against the total of that sub's original contract and change order charges.

To mine additional information from your shoebox system, you can use the same procedure as that used with the gross pile. You can sort receipts and deposit slips into piles and total them up. But you can also do much better than that. Adding one more inexpensive tool to your shoebox system will enable you to keep running totals as you make deposits and pay bills. With the totals handy, you can more easily gain insight into your business' financial performance. The tool is called a spreadsheet. It is a humdinger, the business management equivalent of the lever, a device of tremendous power that couldn't be simpler to use.

The spreadsheet

I can recall from my early days as a builder, when I was quite intimidated by accounting and its specialized vocabulary, that the term "spreadsheet" seemed especially impregnable. Soon, however,

---

SAMPLE LETTERS AND FORMS P&L

When you put together a P&L statement, just how much you allow yourself as pay for your office work, estimating, marketing, and other work of running your company is your call. Early in your career, you are probably worth less than you would pay an apprentice carpenter. Later, if you hone your management skills, they will be valuable.

Do the Right Thing Construction Company
Profit & Loss Statement for 2002

Income from all jobs	$110,000
Market value of owner's labor on jobs	($40,000)
Costs of other labor, material, subs, and services for jobs	(<u>$30,000</u>)
Gross profit margin	$40,000
Costs for truck, tools, office, and other overhead expenses	($12,000)
Owner's salary for estimating and other costs of running the company (75 hours a month at $20 an hour)	(<u>$18,000</u>)
Net margin (profit)	$10,000

Note: In accounting parentheses are used to indicate negative numbers.

I realized that a spreadsheet is exactly what it says it is. As the illustration on pp. 64–65 shows, it's nothing more than a sheet of paper on which numbers can be spread into labeled columns—in a word, categories—which, in accounting lingo, are called accounts. The spreadsheet in the illustration is a simple one such as might be used by a builder with no employees doing small jobs. As we shall see later, spreadsheets can incorporate many more accounts than provided for here.

To use a spreadsheet, when you collect income and deposit it, simply enter the amount in the appropriate income account. When you pay a bill, enter the amount in the appropriate expense account. At the end of each month total

▪ SAMPLE LETTERS AND FORMS Spreadsheet

A general ledger, consisting of a one-page spreadsheet, can provide a basic breakdown of income and expenses for a very small company.

Week/Date		Income			Direct Job Costs		
		1	2	3	4	5	6
		Preconstruction	Construction		Material	Subs	Services
01 1/1	1						$100.00
02 1/3	2				$512.19		
03 1/3	3					$1,200.00	
04 1/4	4				$1,114.11		
05 1/5	5						
Deposit 1/7		$200.00	$4,213.00				
		$200.00					
Deposit 1/18	##	$280.00	$4,000.00				
23 1/19	##						
24 1/19	##				$21.60		
25 1/21	##						
26 1/24	##					$400.00	
27 1/24	##						$50.00
28 1/27	##				$144.98		
	##						
	##						
Month total	##	$480.00	$8,213.00				
Year-to-date total		$900.00	$17,419.00		$3,712.29	$2,400.00	$210.00

up your accounts and figure your year-to-date totals.

Now you have useful information about where your money is coming from and where it is going. It is now "accounted" for; you are doing "accounting"! You can see whether you are spending excessively on equipment, what proportion of your income is from preconstruction services, whether the costs of operating your old truck are running so high you should consider getting a new one, and whether you are subcontracting such a high proportion of your work your insurance company may be unwilling to continue your policy.

A few of the accounts in the spreadsheet illustrated above deserve extra comment:

▪ *Income is recorded in two accounts, one for construction work and the other for preconstruction services.* It is important to learn how to get paid for the immense amount of estimating, design, and other preconstruction services you provide as a builder. By recording income for preconstruction services separately, you can prod yourself to learn the lesson. If by the end of June you have accumulated only $390 in your preconstruction services column and have been

Overhead

Office	Vehicle	Equipment	Marketing	Other
$9.21				
	$52.00			$1.12
			$41.00	
$6.45				
	$61.00			
$52.00			$22.62	$0.63
		$363.41		
$198.16	$249.72	$363.41	$104.91	$2.09

My Tax Audit

Back in the '80s, heading down to the IRS building for my first audit, I repeated my accountant's advice to myself: "Be courteous. Answer questions concisely. Hand over documents briskly. Volunteer nothing. *Nothing!*"

I felt ready. My confidence was high…until I took a seat in the waiting room. I was hit with premonitions of huge bills for unpaid taxes, penalties for late tax payments, interest on the late taxes, for general negligence and incompetence. Around the room were seated a dozen people armed with cartloads of files and stacks of cloth-bound ledgers, all looking as if they were about to be taken by some sort of green death. If they felt vulnerable, what sort of target would I make, with just my shoebox of envelopes and check registers?

My turn came, I was shown to a small cubicle, and was greeted by my auditor, a pale man who gave the impression—a trout leapt from the blue stream of a necktie flowing down his shirt front—that he'd rather be fishing. (Good idea. Me too. Let's go!) I relaxed a bit and performed just as my accountant had advised, volunteering not a thing. Three-quarters of an hour later, the auditor declared our session over. "No charges," he wrote across my file, and complimented me on the orderliness of my records. The shoebox had passed muster.

The Cash Flow Fallacy

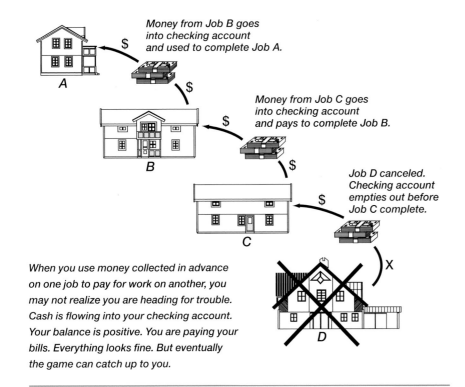

Money from Job B goes into checking account and used to complete Job A.

Money from Job C goes into checking account and pays to complete Job B.

Job D canceled. Checking account empties out before Job C complete.

When you use money collected in advance on one job to pay for work on another, you may not realize you are heading for trouble. Cash is flowing into your checking account. Your balance is positive. You are paying your bills. Everything looks fine. But eventually the game can catch up to you.

averaging 15 hours a week on estimating and other preconstruction work, you will know you aren't making much progress learning to get paid for the work. You are averaging only a buck an hour.

■ *Direct job costs are divided into the three categories of most concern to a one-person company.* The spreadsheet is not adequate for a company with employees.

■ *Overhead accounts are provided only for office, vehicle, equipment, marketing and miscellaneous other costs.* If you are a small-volume operator, the biggest of your overhead costs will be your own time—the labor you put in at general, marketing, and administrative work. In this simple spreadsheet, your pay for running your company, your wages for hands-on work on your job sites,

and company profit are not broken out. You can, however, give yourself a look at your two levels of pay and at profit by running a profit and loss report such as that shown on p. 63. Doing so is quite a leap forward from typical shoebox accounting. But it is an important leap. The sooner you begin to recognize the difference between wages for the work you do on your jobs, salary for running your company, and actual company profit the better.

One final feature you will want to add to your shoebox system is accounting for petty cash expenditure—that is, the small purchases you make by pulling cash out of your wallet rather than writing a check. You should use cash as rarely as possible, partly because the IRS likes to see canceled checks to back up expense claims. When you must use cash, simply stick the receipts in an envelope, and when they amount to more than $100 or so, total them into categories and enter the totals in the appropriate columns on your spreadsheet. Then staple the receipts together, label them "entered," and put them back in the envelope.

Avoiding the cash flow fallacy

The shoebox and a simple spreadsheet give you a good start toward handling your essential accounting responsibilities. They will even give you the numbers you need to do a solid job of tax reporting, as my personal story of a tax audit on p. 65 illustrates. The system, however, has deficiencies. One of them, the cash flow fallacy, is downright dangerous.

You enter the danger zone by asking a simple, entirely reasonable question: "Am I making money or losing it?" To reassure yourself, you give your checking account a quick look. If you see that you have a nice, fat positive balance you think, "Great." Now you have a problem, because too often the positive balance disguises one of several variants of trouble and you are not seeing it:

- The positive balance exists only because *you have deposited money collected* from clients for work completed but have not yet paid out the *money you owe* employees, subcontractors, or suppliers involved in the work. If they had been paid, the balance might be very different, maybe negative.

- The positive balance exists only because money has been *collected* from clients, call them the Smiths, *in advance* of work being done on the Smiths' project. If the work had been done and the labor and material involved paid for, the balance would have been negative. In other words, you have really been taking a "loan" from the Smiths—possibly without either yourself or the Smiths realizing it.

- The positive balance exists because you have taken a "loan" from a new job to pay bills from an old project. For example, you are using a large advance from the Valdez kitchen project, which has just begun, to pay subcontractors for work over at the Druther addition, which is just being completed.

Taking such "loans" can get builders into real trouble, as in this scenario: You complete the Druther addition using advance payments from Valdez. Deep into the Valdez kitchen you realize the money they still owe you is enough to complete only two-thirds of their project. Just as the truth dawns, the economy slows and future projects from which you might have "borrowed" money to complete Valdez are canceled. Your

checking account empties out. Bills pile up on your desk from your subs and suppliers. You cannot pay them. They file liens on the Valdez place rather than show up to complete the kitchen. Then Maria and Juan Valdez sue you.

Your momentarily positive checking account balance concealed from you the hole into which you were falling. You were in the black not because you had earned more than you had spent but because your account had been filled with cash received for work not yet done. You have fallen victim to the cash flow fallacy.

To avoid the cash flow fallacy, do not calculate your earnings picture right from your checkbook. Even when it is current, it gives you the result merely of your *cash accounting*—money you have

SAMPLE LETTERS AND FORMS   Cash Flow Analysis

So long as you are alert to your unrecorded income and expenses, you can readily adjust your checkbook balance to determine your cash flow situation. In the example below, John Petri can see that his checkbook balance, as of 1/10, actually gives him much too positive a take on his situation going into the last half of January. To keep a reasonable reserve in his checking account as the month progresses, he might need to either reduce his draw or transfer cash into his checking account, or both.

Cash Flow Analysis for John Petri Construction

Balance from spreadsheet and/or checkbook on 1/10/2001	$7,876
Insur. payment due 1/20/2001	($1,119)
Owner's draw 1/20/2001	($3,000)
Payments due subcontractors by 1/31/2001	($4,357)
Payments due suppliers by 1/31/2001	($3,214)
Miscellaneous office and other overhead expenses through 1/31/2001	($150)
Due from clients by 1/31/2001	*$4,456*
Projected cash in checking account 1/31/2001	$492

received and recorded, and bills you have paid and recorded. It fails to take into account money that you have coming or owe that might radically change your picture. To get a more up-to-the-minute take, you must take into account money you have earned but not received and money owed but not paid. (In other words, you must supplement your cash accounting with a rudimentary bit of what is technically known as *accrual accounting*. To do so and get an up-to-date picture of your position, you can take the following steps:

1. Bring your checkbook up to date and figure your balance.
2. Figure the income you have earned but not yet received.
3. Figure the bills you have incurred but not yet paid.
4. Add the earnings and subtract the bills from the checkbook balance.

Along with making the adjustments to your checkbook balance, avoid the cash flow fallacy by strictly refusing to take advances on work not yet done or "loans" from one project to complete another. Not only can this contribute to distortion of your cash picture, but it can also get you into really serious trouble with a client.

Limits of the shoebox system

Other deficiencies of the shoebox system are equally deadly but are more difficult to solve. The system doesn't easily lend

One-Write System

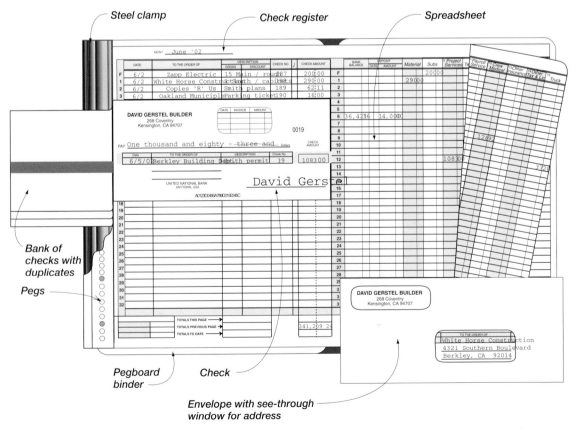

Steel clamp

Check register

Spreadsheet

Bank of checks with duplicates

Pegs

Pegboard binder

Check

Envelope with see-through window for address

The one-write system consists of three parts: a binder with a clamp and a column of small steel pegs at the left edge, a foldout sheet of paper with a check register printed on the left side and a spreadsheet printed to the right and continuing on the back, a deck of duplicate checks. Both the register/spreadsheet and the deck of checks are perforated with holes—the holes fit over the steel pegs so that the checks can be aligned atop the register, then pinned in place by the clamp.

itself to job costing—neither to tracking costs and comparing them to estimates on individual projects nor to building up labor productivity records.

There are "work arounds" you can use to accomplish job costing. You can regress to the gross pile system and add up receipts to compare actual to estimated costs. Or you can set up separate spreadsheets for job costing (look ahead to p. 78 if you want to see an example of a job cost sheet). Likewise, you can make up a time card for recording how long it takes you to produce different items and assemblies—hanging a door, casing a window, framing a bay window— and from them produce labor productivity records.

With all these add-ons, however, your shoebox/spreadsheet system develops a jury-rigged feel and becomes cumbersome to use. Moreover, its lack of built-in proofs and checks can cause costly errors. If, for example, you write out a check and drop your copy of the bill with a check duplicate in an expense envelope but forget to enter the check amount in your spreadsheet, the oversight can cost you in two ways. Because the expense is not shown on your spreadsheet, you'll get an exaggerated idea of how well you are doing when you create a profit and loss statement. At tax time, when you take numbers from your spreadsheet, expenses will be understated, your taxable income thereby exaggerated, and you will pay more tax than you owe. As with the other deficiencies, there are ways around these problems. But you have better options than trying to extend your shoebox system and force it to do tasks that are beyond its natural reach. You can move up to the professional quality—though still manual, not computerized—system we will discuss in the next section.

Moving Up to a One-Write System

By stepping up the ladder of systems from shoebox to one-write, you will be moving from the realm of a "homemade" system to a professional system. It is still, however, a *manual* system. Moving to it, unlike conversion to a computer system (which can be daunting), is quite straightforward.

I personally used a one-write system for years. I loved it and believe that manual one-write systems are superior to computer accounting for many small businesses, even today with computers and software having become relatively inexpensive.

A one-write system will cost you only about as much as a small power tool. Even so, it will give you a much more detailed picture of your numbers than a shoebox system. At the same time it will increase your efficiency at and control over your accounting. It incorporates proofs and checks to catch the sort of errors that can so easily slip by when you use a shoebox system. It can be readily expanded to include job costing and, when you are ready to take on employees, payroll. By using it you will develop the accounting savvy necessary for successfully jumping to computers, should you wish to make the leap.

Purchasing and using a one-write system

If you purchase a one-write system, you will want to consider the options available in your area and select the one that is best for you. Two considerations are most important. Will the system work well for your business and is good support for the system available? If you need help learning how to use the system, will you be able to get it promptly?

COMING UP

Buying a One-Write System

Setting Up a One-Write System

Achieving Consistency with a Chart of Accounts

Accounts Basic and Beyond

Controls

Basic Chart of Accounts

Charts of accounts can become extremely involved. The chart in one accounting book for builders comprises more than 400 different categories of income, expense, assets, equity, and liabilities. A more basic chart of accounts, such as the one shown here, should be adequate so long as you are still running a small-volume operation.

Income
- Preconstruction services—for planning, design, and estimating
- Progress payments—for completed construction work
- Interest—bank payments of interest on balance in account
- Insurance refunds

Overhead expenses
GENERAL EXPENSES
- Rent
  —Office
  —Shop/storage
- Continuing education—publications, classes, and seminars
- Office supplies—paper, tape, pens, desk tools, etc.
- Telephone—telephone service
- ISP fees—Internet service provider
- Utilities
- Postage
- Bank charges—fees for business checking account; other charges
- Insurance
  —Vehicle
  —Theft
  —General liability (base payment)
- Professional services—accountants and lawyers
- Business licenses
- Computers and other business information technology
  —Hardware and software
  —Technical support & training
  —Operation and maintenance
  —Supplies

For me, the answers were a resounding "yes" and "yes." My system was designed in collaboration with a national construction association. My local representative stopped by my office to orient me to the system. In your area, you may find that similar or even superior support from vendors of one-write systems are available from a variety of sources, including other specialty houses, banks, and full-line vendors of office and business supplies. It will be worth your while to do a bit of comparison shopping, not so much to get the cheapest price but to see which system and supplier will provide you with the best fit and support.

Along with buying your one-write system, if you have not already done so, you should upgrade from your shoebox to a filing cabinet. As with any other tool, when you purchase a file cabinet, get a good one. It should be fireproof, have a sturdy lock, and feature full extension drawers that allow you to easily access documents at the back of the cabinet. In the cabinet, set up folders for the same categories of records as for the shoebox system, including income, overhead costs, direct job costs, and petty cash.

With your one-write system and filing cabinet in place, doing the clerical part of your accounting will be simple. For invoicing, use the same procedure as with your shoebox to bill clients and monitor their payments. When you receive a payment, enter it in the check register and in one of the income accounts in the one-write register/spreadsheet. When you write a check for an expense, your one-write system will automatically create both a duplicate and an entry in the check register. With the check completed, you detach it, mail it, staple the duplicate to the bill, and file it. Then you record the amount

- ■ Construction Equip.
  - —Major overhaul or repair of vehicles
  - —Power tools
  - —Nonpower equipment
- ■ Vehicles
  - —Purchase
  - —Operation and maintenance

MARKETING EXPENSES
- ■ Advertising—job signs, business cards
- ■ Promotion—mailings to past clients, open houses
- ■ Entertainment—meals, etc., for prospective clients

ADMINISTRATIVE EXPENSES
- ■ Bookkeeping service

- ■ Office staff
  - —Salary
  - —Insurance
  - —Payroll taxes
  - —Benefits
- ■ Travel—bridge tolls, parking

Direct job expenses
- ■ Material
- ■ Labor
  - —Wages
  - —Insurance
  - —Payroll taxes
  - —Benefits
  - —Payroll service charges
  - —Consumables—small tools and materials rapidly used up by crew on projects
- ■ Subcontractors
  - —Payments to subcontractors
  - —Liability insurance based on payments to subs

- ■ Temporary labor—payments to temporary agencies for part-time labor on jobs
- ■ Construction services— permits, inspections, surveys, recycling, etc.
- ■ Equipment rental
- ■ Design services—architects, engineers, kitchen and bath designers, landscape designers, other designers
- ■ Callbacks

Other
- ■ Transfers
  - —Owner's pay (draw)
  - —Other transfers out
- ■ Petty cash
- ■ Adjustments—corrections of errors
- ■ Miscellaneous

of the check on the spreadsheet portion of your one-write system.

When you have completed a spreadsheet, total all the columns and—here is the built-in proof that prevents entry errors or omissions—check that the total of the checks you have written equals the total of the figures entered in the spreadsheet for expenses. Likewise, proof deposit entries in the register against entries in the income accounts. If there is a discrepancy, you have added wrong or made an entry error that you must find and correct.

Creating a chart of accounts for a one-write system

The spreadsheet in my one-write system covered five pages, two on the front and three on the back of the foldout. Altogether, they provided approximately 50 columns in which to categorize and record deposits and expenses—enough for

a quite detailed general ledger of income and expense accounts for a small-volume building business. When you are just converting from a shoebox to a one-write system, you may wish to use only a few of the columns. With greater experience, however, you will want to take advantage of more columns to gain a more detailed breakdown of your income and expenses. As you increase your use of columns to create more categories, it becomes progressively easier to confuse them, to enter one kind of income or expense in one account one time and in another the next, thereby distorting your accounting picture.

To avoid confusion, create a chart of accounts as shown above that will guide you to making your spreadsheet entries consistently. For efficient use and correlation of the chart and spreadsheet, the names of the accounts listed in the chart should be as precise and clearly dif-

▪ SAMPLE LETTERS AND FORMS   One-Write System

The spreadsheet I use with my one-write system serves to record both income and costs.

Month July, 2002

Income Accounts

	date	to the order of	description gross	discount	check number		bank balance	deposits date	amount	1 Pre-Const. Services	2 Const. Progress Payments	3 Interest
1	7/01	───────────	Payment: Aird Garage		──	1		7/02	4000 00		4000 00	
2	7/07	Truitt & White Lumber	Tape, Chalk dust, etc.		436	2						
3	7/07	Pac Bell	Phone		437	3						
4	7/07	Quik Computer Repair	Recover lost data		438	4						
5	7/07	───────────	Payment: Rose Estimate		──	5		7/02	500 00	500 00		
6						6						
7												

Off-Spreadsheet Overhead Costs

Especially if you are doing a small volume of work and operating out of your home, your overhead is likely to include expenses for which you do not write checks. Therefore, they will not get entered in your spreadsheet even though they may be in your chart of accounts. Such expenses include:

- ▪ *Rent.* If you are using a space in your home its fair market rental value is an expense of operating your company.
- ▪ *Cost of capital.* This the interest you lose by having money in your business operating capital accounts rather than in an account that earns higher interest. For example, if you keep $10,000 in a bank as operating capital and earn 1 percent interest on it rather than 6 percent in a money market fund, you are losing $500 annually in interest. That is your cost of capital.
- ▪ *Your pay.* As I have stressed repeatedly, you must learn to pay yourself for all the work you do of running your company. When your company is small, your pay is, by far, the greatest of your overhead costs.

When you figure the overhead costs of running your company, it is important to include these off-spreadsheet expenses.

ferentiated as possible. For example, don't use "professional services" twice—once for lawyers and accountants under overhead and again for designers under direct job expenses. Instead, use different terms as shown in the sample chart.

Also, as illustrated on pp. 70–71, the names of the accounts from the chart should be used as column headings in your spreadsheet. Then, when you are in doubt as to where to record a deposit or expense, your chart will guide you exactly to the right column. If you want to go a step further, number the accounts and use the numbers as column headings. There is no way to mistake account 401 for 206. For ease of discussion, however, I will hold off adding numbers to a chart of accounts till we get to the more involved chart in our computer accounting chapter.

Overhead accounts

For the basic chart of accounts shown on pp. 70–71, I have grouped accounts into broad areas already familiar to you from reading previous chapters. We have income accounts. We have overhead accounts—which are further divided into general, sales, and administrative accounts. And we have direct job cost

Overhead Cost Accounts						Direct Job Cost Accounts						Other___
4 Office Salaries	5 Telephone	6 Postage	7 Computer	8 Const. Equip.		9 Material	10 Consum-ables	11 Subs	12 Services	13 Callbacks	14 Transfers	
					1							
					2		96 21					
	41 10				3							
			180 00		4							
					5							
					6							
					7							

accounts, followed by a short list of "other" accounts. The accounts for income, which are explained in the shoe-box chapter, are self-explanatory. The overhead (and also direct job and other) expense accounts are much more detailed and require discussion.

Accounting accurately for overhead in sufficient detail is key to building a financially sound company. Here is why. On each of your projects you need to "recapture," that is, charge for, a portion of the cost of running your company. To recapture the cost, you have to know what it is. And to know what it is you have to track it in your accounting records. That logic may seem as obvious to you as it does to me. But you would be amazed at the number of builders who have no idea what their overhead is. If you learn to track your overhead and charge adequately for it, you will be joining an elite group.

Overhead accounts in the chart that need a bit of explanation include:

GENERAL LIABILITY INSURANCE
Some insurance companies charge you a minimum base premium and additional premiums equal to percentages of employee wages and subcontractor

charges. The base fee is a cost of running your company. The additional charges are direct job costs, incurred as a result of building projects with employees and subs.

COMPUTERS Computers and related information technology can become a major overhead cost for even a small-volume construction company. You need

A Petty Cash Accounting Procedure

1. Cash a check for $100, and record the check in the petty cash account.

2. Put the cash in an envelope marked "petty cash," and label it with the check number and amount.

3. To make a cash purchase, remove cash from the envelope and replace it with the receipt.

4. When you run out of cash, seal the envelope and file it.

5. Repeat the process.

To see how much petty cash you have used for a given period, look at the total of the checks in your petty cash account. If you see that you are using too much petty cash, make adjustments in your procedures so that checks are used instead.

to track the cost in at least one separate account, partly to help you determine whether your investment is reasonable for the benefits gained.

POWER TOOLS AND OTHER EQUIP-MENT Given our tendency to go tool crazy, we builders need to track our equipment expenditure in a separate account as a way of keeping a collar and leash on our tool-buying impulses.

BOOKKEEPING SERVICE AND OFFICE STAFF When your business is small, your first administrative expense—other than your own expenditure of labor—is likely to be for a bookkeeping service. If you decide to grow your business to the point that you need permanent office staff, your administrative costs will expand. You will need separate accounts for the salaries of office workers and for each category of labor burden—the taxes, insurance, and benefits that you will pay out along with salaries.

Be aware that when your business is very small, you are especially likely to have overhead expenses that are "off-spreadsheet"—as explained in the sidebar on p. 72. You don't need to doctor your records to pick up these off-spreadsheet costs in your overhead accounts. *But you must make sure to include them when you total your overhead for the sake of recapturing all of it in your charges to your clients.* We will take a more detailed look at how you do that in our coming chapter on marking up for overhead and profit in bids.

Direct job cost accounts

As with overhead costs, certain of the direct costs of building your projects are a little elusive or complex and deserve special attention.

LABOR As with office staff, wages to field employees are "burdened" with tax, insurance, and benefit costs.

LIABILITY INSURANCE While a base portion may be overhead, the portion based on employee wages is labor burden, and the portion based on subcontractor charges is a subcontractor cost. It is

---

Another Way to Slice the Overhead Pie: Fixed, Variable, and Standing-Still Overhead

You can divide overhead into general, sales, and administrative expenses as we have done in our chart of accounts. You can also divide it into "fixed" and "variable" expenses. *Fixed overhead* includes expenses that you incur to keep your business in existence even when you have little or no work under construction. Expenses that are likely to be fixed include rent, telephone, postage, and other office supplies. *Variable* expenses, those which you can likely cut back when work is slow, include computer hardware and software and construction equipment expenses.

Builders differ as to which expenses they define as fixed and which as variable. For example, I categorize crew medical as fixed overhead, because I pay for employees' medical insurance even during periods when I have no work for them. Another builder might not categorize medical benefits as overhead expense at all but see it as a fluctuating direct job cost. Similarly, one builder might see marketing expense as completely variable, while another might feel he must invest in marketing at a steady rate in good times and bad to keep his business strong.

In my operation with my intense emphasis on "turning off leaky faucets" (as one business consultant calls tightening down on unnecessary overhead), I tend to view the majority of expenses as at least somewhat variable and as subject to restraint. I keep an eye on my ultrafixed overhead, what I call *standing-still overhead*. That's the rock-bottom expense of keeping my company in existence should work become scarce for a lengthy period, as I have seen happen in several recessions. I try to keep my business organized so that if a recession comes on rapidly, I can quickly cut back to standing-still overhead. I do not want to be caught in the trap that Thomas Schleifer warns builders of in his outstanding book, *The Contractor's Survival Guide*—namely, being tempted to bid for work at dangerously low prices because you are desperate for cash to pay excessive overhead costs.

important to break out your liability payments into their components. If you lump it all under overhead, you will be overstating your overhead and understating your labor costs. The mistake will play havoc with your numbers when you calculate labor costs and markup for overhead in bidding for projects.

CONSUMABLES During construction, crews rapidly use up saw blades, chalk dust, glue, safety tape, plastic tarps, visqueen, and many other supplies. Some builders lump in expenses for such consumables with other material costs. As a result, they lose sight of the cost of consumables and fail to charge for them in their estimates. When they are estimating framing, they may figure quantities of lumber, plywood, and hardware and get those costs in. But they neglect to include the cost for miscellaneous supplies like tape blades, chalk dust, and saw blades the framers will go through in order to install the lumber and ply. By accounting for consumables separately, you can see what they are costing and then charge for them as a percentage of wages or of material cost. (We'll talk about how much to charge for consumables in the chapter on calculating construction costs. You might be amazed at how much you lose by leaving the cost out of your estimates.)

CALLBACKS It is *critical* to know your costs for getting called back by clients to redo work you, your employees, or subs did not build right the first time. If the expense is significant, you need to find out why—a bad sub? a sloppy carpenter? poor communication on your part?—and make corrections. At stake are your reputation and references. Some builders reportedly spend 5 percent of their revenue on callbacks. Others spend a tenth of a percent. Their reputations and prosperity reflect the spread.

Security Procedures

Cash can wander away more easily than tools left out overnight at a job site. To control cash:

- Deposit all payments immediately. Payment checks from customers do get lost.
- Compare the amount on checks to invoices carefully. You'd be surprised how easy it is to write a check for $2,000 when you owe $200.
- Sign all checks personally, and make sure they are for legitimate vendors even if you let someone else write the checks. Bookkeepers have been known to route checks to themselves, either directly or by creating phony bills.
- Limit writing checks out to "cash" because with such checks it's hard to know where the money went or prove to the IRS they were for real business expenses.
- Use checks in numerical sequence so that you can see that none have wandered away to finance someone's trip to Las Vegas. If you have to void a check, tear off the signature portion, write "void" on the remainder, and file it.
- Reconcile your bank statement promptly to make sure no deposits are missing—banks do lose deposits—and that deductions from your balance are correct.

Accounting for direct job costs in your one-write general ledger as we have been discussing here can give you much insight into your operation. But you should be clear that such accounting—with the material, labor, and subcontractor cost for *all* your projects mingled together—is not what we mean by *job costing*. That involves recording costs for each of your individual projects separately and phase by phase—for demolition, foundation, frame, etc.—as the project is built, then comparing those actual costs to the costs you had estimated. One critical benefit of job costing is that, if done properly, it can produce a record of costs on completed projects you can use for estimating future projects. Job costing is so important a subject we will deal with it in a chapter of its own, right after this one.

Other accounts

As the chart of accounts suggests, a final group of expenses you will need to track in your one-write general ledger can be loosely labeled "Other." It includes, notably:

OWNER'S PAY   This is the money you draw from your business to compensate yourself for the work you do. With my own one-write system I simply recorded my owner's pay as a transfer from my business to my personal accounts. A builder could, instead, record his or her pay partly as an overhead expense of running his company and partly as labor cost for swinging a hammer on his project. Your accountant, adhering to the formal rules of his trade, might insist that your draw be recorded in an "equity" account—which we will discuss later—and correlate correctly with the business form you choose—sole proprietorship or one of the forms of incorporation.

PETTY CASH   With your move to a one-write system you might wish to install more sophisticated petty cash accounting than you used with the shoebox. Rather than just save cash receipts and enter them in your spreadsheet every so often you can use the procedure described in the sidebar on p. 73.

MISCELLANEOUS   This account is important not because you must make certain to use it, but because if your accounting is up to snuff, you will hardly have any use for it. Expenses bunched together under "miscellaneous" are of little use for management purposes. They are a throwback to pile accounting in which expenses are heaped together without discrimination. If you are recording many expenses under "miscellaneous," it's a tip-off that your chart of accounts needs further development.

Controls

One of the benefits of a one-write system is that the proofs and checks built into the register/spreadsheet give you stronger controls than you enjoy with a shoebox system. However, you will need other controls as well—controls that are not so much part of your accounting system as part of the procedures you set up for using it.

You must continue to make sure subs do not overbill you and that you do not over- or under-bill clients. You must put in place procedures to safeguard the cash that flows in and out of your company and to ensure that you alone retain control over that cash.

Make certain never to abdicate control over cash to a bookkeeper—including the bookkeeper friend of the family to whom you would entrust your first born, your life, even your favorite fishing rod. Recently, the highly trusted bookkeeper of a good size construction company, who had been given uncontrolled authority over her company's cash, was arrested after it was discovered that she had directed nearly a million dollars of her company's funds into her personal account over a seven-year period.

Finally, as with the shoebox, you must continue to avoid the deadly cash flow fallacy. If you like, you can continue using the same controls for avoiding it as you did with the shoebox. You can simply update your checkbook balance by adjusting it for unpaid bills and uncollected income to get your real cash picture—and at the same time make sure you do not help yourself to "loans" from one customer to pay for work for another.

You may, however, wish to go beyond such informal adjustments and switch entirely from a cash to an accrual accounting system. Should you wish to convert your one-write system to an accrual system, your supplier should be able to provide you with the requisite payable and receivable journal sheets. Likewise, the supplier should be able to provide you with spreadsheets for taking care of the accounting responsibilities we will take up in our next two chapters—Job Costing and Payroll.

Keeping Job Cost Records

So far, so good. If you have climbed the ladder of number-crunching systems to the rung we are reaching for now, you have come a long way. You have moved your deposit slips and invoices out of a sack and into organized files. You have mastered the spreadsheet and created a general ledger governed by a chart of accounts. Your sources of income, your overhead costs, and your direct job costs are categorized so that you can see in detail how money moves into and out of your company.

Yet, there is a major component of your accounting system still missing. While your general ledger does give you the overall costs of construction—labor, material, subs, and services for all projects *combined*—it does not break out the cost of building *each* project. Nor does it give you your costs for the divisions, phases, and items of work within each project. In other words, your system still does not provide *job costing*.

Recording and analyzing job costs is a critical accounting responsibility. If you have the discipline to take it on, you will be moving into the upper ranks of your chosen profession. Few builders ever get on top of their job costs. Some think it is not worthwhile. Jobs, they rationalize, are going to cost what they are going to cost, and it's impossible to estimate them accurately, so why try? Or they think they are so smart they can estimate costs without the benefit of job cost records. They are like the builder I talked with the other day who told me, "Oh, I've got all kinds

COMING UP

Resistance to Job Costing

The Benefits of Job Costing

Three Layers of
Job Cost Records

Costs in a Can

Creating Your
Labor Cost Records

Levels of Job Cost Records

■ *Projects under construction.* During each job, record costs for labor, material, and subcontractors to see how they are stacking up against estimates.

■ *Completed projects.* At the end of each job, file the record of labor, material, and subcontractor costs versus estimates kept during the job.

■ *Labor productivity.* From completed job cost records or right from time cards, create records of how long it takes you and/or your crew to produce various items of work.

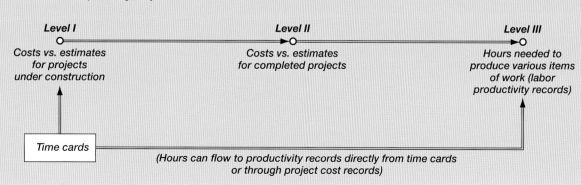

Level I	Level II	Level III
Costs vs. estimates for projects under construction	Costs vs. estimates for completed projects	Hours needed to produce various items of work (labor productivity records)

Time cards

(Hours can flow to productivity records directly from time cards or through project cost records)

This simplified cost record for a small deck still under construction, with the railing and stairs yet to be completed, illustrates the basic principles of tracking costs during a job so that you can compare them to your estimate of costs. If you want to get a look at higher-octane job costing, jump ahead to the illustration on p. 94.

JOB COST RECORD

Job Name: Gonzalez Home   Address: 269 Coral Rd.

Type of Job: Deck   Completion Date:

	Cost 1	% Est.	Cost 2	% Est.	Cost 3	% Est.	Total Cost	Est.	Variance
Setup and Demo Labor	$400	80%	$50	90%	—	—	$450	$500	-$50/10%
Frame Labor	$300	37%	$500	100%	$200	125%	$1000	$800	+$200/25%
Frame Materials	$400	100%	—	—	—	—	$400	$400	$0/0%
Decking Labor	$500	33%	$500	66%	$400	93%	$1400	$1500	-$100/7%
Decking Materials	$682	91%	—	—	—	—	$682	$750	-$68/9%
Railing Labor	$300	20%	$300	20%				$1500	
Railing Materials	$400	66%						$600	
Stair Labor								$800	
Stair Materials	$350	87.5%						$400	
Electrical Sub	$110	25%							

of computer programs for job costing, but I don't need them. The costs are right here in my head." We'll see about that.

Job costing at three levels

Builders who do have the foresight (and humility) to attend to their job costing enjoy several major benefits. They are able to track and control costs during jobs. They are able to see in what areas of work their costs chronically run over, or under, their estimates of costs. They develop the data bank they need to clean up their errors and to calculate their job costs with increasing accuracy as time goes on.

To get such benefits from job costing, you must attend to it at three levels. They are mapped out in the sidebar on p. 77. Below the levels are described in a bit more detail, and the benefits of doing the work required at each level are explained.

MONITORING COSTS ON ONGOING JOBS   As the illustration above suggests, you want to track costs in such a way that you can compare them to your estimates of cost. Monitoring of costs versus estimates is not without problems. The primary problem is that it is difficult to match cost records with work in the field. For example, your records may show you have used 75 percent of your budget, or estimate, for framing. But how can you know from looking around your job site whether framing is 75 percent complete or not? The truth is, you cannot know with exactitude, and best guesses, even when they are made by seasoned builders, tend to be on the optimistic side. Still, if you see a radical mismatch, you will be prompted to take a close look at the work in the field. If you've spent 75 percent of what you had allowed for framing, and framing is obviously less than 50 percent done, you will want to find out why. You may discover your crew lead has failed to tell you he's had to do a lot of reframing due to existing substandard work that he found hidden behind existing surfaces. Of course, that hidden work was not shown on the plans you bid from, so it wasn't covered in your bid. As a result, you are doing it for free. Your job costing has alerted you that it's time to educate your lead about the necessity of obtaining approval for extra charges before doing work not covered by the construction contract. (See p. 191 for more on writing change orders to charge for extra work.)

FILING COST RECORDS FOR COMPLETED PROJECTS   Once projects are complete, and the cost records for them are complete, the records should be filed, preferably by type of job—kitchen remodel, retaining wall, new home, commercial renovation, and so on. The files will enable you to find patterns in and improve upon your performance on costs versus estimates. You may see that you consistently spend more on framing lumber than you have provided for in your estimates. As a result, you decide to track framing costs on your next few jobs not only for framing overall but separately for floor frames, wall frames, and roof frames. That way you will be able to pin down just where your shortfall is occurring and where you need to sharpen your estimates. Similarly, you can see on which types of jobs you tend to earn a reasonable profit and which not. You may see that on kitchens designed by a certain designer, the work needed to make up for oversights in her work costs you so much you don't earn enough to pay your overhead, much less earn a profit. You decide to politely turn away her next request for a bid.

DEVELOPING AND MAINTAINING LABOR PRODUCTIVITY RECORDS   To a builder, records of how many hours of labor his or her crew needed to produce specific items of work are like Grandma's dog-eared recipe cards—nobody else's records (or recipes) will quite do. Labor costs (as opposed to material costs, which are relatively easy to pinpoint, and subcontractor costs, which should be whatever your subs' bids tell you they will be) are the most difficult costs to get right in your bids for new projects. With a good file of labor productivity records from your *own* experience, for your *own* crews, for your way of doing things, you can accurately calculate *your* costs for the new projects you are planning or bidding. Without such records, you will be guesstimating, approximating, operating on a wing and a prayer and a hope—or, just about as bad, using the canned costs that will allow you only to calculate what it would take some *other* builder to do the job.

As you look over the three levels of cost records, it may seem to you that it is not necessary to keep labor productivity records apart from the cost records for completed jobs. After all, don't you have your labor costs right there in those completed job records? That misunderstanding took me a while to work through as well. There are two primary reasons why

A Veteran's View of Canned Costs

Rather than do the work of developing their own record of labor costs, many builders buy "costs in a can" from one of the national services that publish books and CDs of construction cost data. In my experience, these canned costs can be dangerous. The difference between canned costs and what it actually takes to produce tight, durable, attractive work can readily exceed your markup for overhead and profit. A veteran builder once told me he owned every cost guide ever published, that they made "fine bookends," were fun to look at to "see how you are doing in a general sort of way compared to the rest of the nation," and were, otherwise, "not worth a darn." He had it right.

you must keep separate productivity records. First, the job records, as shown in the illustration on p. 78, are typically kept in dollars. Since the value of dollars lessens as time goes on (due to inflation), old dollar costs for completed work won't help you to estimate the cost of new work. Second, even if the completed project cost records show hours also, digging through completed project records for labor costs of particular items of work is just too slow. You need much more accessible costs. Below, we will discuss how to create cost records including an accessible and *incredibly* useful labor productivity record.

Creating your cost records

To monitor project costs against estimates, enter the phases of work in the project and your budget for each of those phases on a job cost sheet. As construction proceeds and your costs come in, enter them one after another on the sheet. Compare the accumulating total to the budget in both dollars and percentage terms.

Make sure, when creating your cost record of a job under construction, that you enter the costs on an accrual (i.e. *payable*), not a cash, basis. If you wait till you have actually paid for the material, labor, or sub's work, rather than entering the costs as soon as they are incurred, your cost entries will run way behind the actual costs of work done. You'll have a wildly optimistic picture of how you are doing on the job. At least that will be the case until the project is completed and all bills paid and entered in the cost records. Then an ugly truth—that you were running way over budget all along—may suddenly surface.

The second level of cost records, that of completed projects, is the easiest to accomplish. At the end of each ongoing job, you simply make sure all your costs are entered and totaled, then file the cost

record. If there is a subtlety here, it is in making sure all the costs *are* actually entered. It is easy to neglect to enter a cost in your job record even if you enter it in your general ledger when you pay it. Some computer accounting systems help safeguard against such errors. If you are using a one-write manual system or a less sophisticated computer program, however, you will need to devise a safeguard of your own, perhaps with help from your sales representative.

The last of the three levels of job cost records, namely the labor productivity records, can be produced in one of two ways—from completed project cost records, if they include hours of labor for different phases of work and not just dollars, or from time cards. In both cases, it is worth reemphasizing, *productivity records are valuable only if expressed in terms of hours as opposed to dollars*. If you are estimating the cost of a new retaining wall, it will do you little good to know that you spent $16,300 on carpentry labor six years ago to form, reinforce, pour, and strip a retaining wall. Six-year-old dollars are of no value for estimating the retaining wall plans now on your desk. It would be immensely helpful, on the other hand, to know that six years ago a crew needed five hours per foot for a retaining wall of size and complexity similar to the one now being estimated.

The first step in creating a useful labor productivity record is to take the *hours* from either your job cost record or from time cards. If you personally produce most of the items of work on your job sites, the "cards" can be sheets in a binder on which you tally the hours you spend on various items. When you move to the point where you have a crew, you can move to a more elaborate card like the one shown on p. 85. The second step is to obtain the quantity of work from the job plans or your estimate. Then it's a matter of simply doing the math to come up with your labor productivity records. For example:

- The time card you have kept for your own labor in building a small deck tells you that you spent 20 patient hours installing 4/4 × 6 mahogany decking with bronze boat nails that resisted bending under hammer blows about as well as a strand of bubble gum.
- Your estimate and plans show 100 sq. ft. of decking.
- Your labor productivity rate is 5 sq. ft. per hour (100/20 = 5).

Narrative labor productivity records

For my own labor productivity records, I prefer narrative records such as the one illustrated below. I find such records, which narrate the circumstances under which work was accomplished and describe the crew that did the work, to be immensely helpful. They serve to root the productivity numbers, which I refer to constantly when doing estimates, in vivid images of carpenters actually at work under real conditions. If I have two productivity rates for decking, it is important to know which is for 2×6 pine installed with a screw gun by a crack journey-level carpenter on a sunny day and which is for mahogany installed

SAMPLE LETTERS AND FORMS   Narrative Labor Cost Record

LABOR COST RECORD

PHASE/ASSEMBLY/ITEM:

Phase:	Concrete
Assembly:	Two-story T-Foundation
Item:	Form stem
Total length:	170 feet
Complexity:	Moderate (Rectangle with three popouts for bays, three blockouts for entries), rebar stubs for slab

PROJECT: Evanston Street Development (Two live-work spaces)

CLIENT & DESIGNER: Janet and Robert Gravenstein (General partners for project)

COMMENTS ON CLIENT: Great! Careful not to distract crew.

DATE OF CONSTRUCTION: May-June 1999

CONDITIONS FOR WORK: Excellent. Level lot. Easy digging. No rain. Warm. Only distraction: Neighbor's dog begged carpenters to play.

CREW LEADER: Fred (highly experienced, well organized)

OTHER CREW INVOLVED: Leslie (Solid journey-level carpenter), Jake and Pete (Advanced-level laborers)

HOURS ON ASSEMBLY/ITEM:

Layout, excavate footing with Bobcat, form two sides of stem for integral pour with footing, install rebar and AB's, pour, strip and clean, backfill:

Fred:	116 hours
Leslie:	126 hours
Jake/Pete:	124 hours/124 hours

Form stem only:

Fred:	44 hours
Leslie:	56 hours
Jake/Pete:	70 hours/70 hours

UNIT COSTS:

Assembly—Two-story T-wall layout to backfill: 490 hours for 170 ft. = approx. 3 hours per ft.; skill level = strong lead, carpenter, and laborers.

Item—Form stem. 1.5 hours per foot. Skill level = same as above.

A Ladder of Labor Productivity Units

It is useful to develop labor cost records for a range of unit sizes, from parts to assemblies to whole projects. There are gray areas between the different-size units. Where one builder might see a "part" another might see a combination of parts complex enough to be called an "assembly." Also, different builders use different terms for the same level on the ladder. For example, some builders use "items" to mean "parts." What is important for your own records is not so much how you label each one, but that you do develop records for the units that will be most helpful to you in your estimating.

■ *Parts.* A single small element of a job. A stick of rebar. A sheet of ¾-in. t&g subfloor. A prehung door.

■ *Assemblies.* A combination of many parts. A door including jambs, door, hardware, casings. A floor frame including joists, rims, blocks, subfloor, glue, screws.

■ *Phases.* Multiple assemblies combined. All floor frames. All wall frames. Finish carpentry.

■ *Divisions.* Several phases grouped together. All framing including floor, wall, and roof.

■ *Projects.* An entire project. A restaurant. A home. A kitchen remodel. A retaining wall.

As I punch up an estimate on my computer, I leaf through my binder of labor records, finding the productivity rates I need to calculate labor costs accurately for the new job.

by an apprentice working in the rain. They will vary hugely. If I have a number only, no narrative, how can I decide which to use?

In the illustrated record, I have come up with two productivity numbers. One is for an entire foundation "assembly" and the other is for an "item" within the assembly. There is, in fact, a whole ladder of productivity units ranging in size from small to very large, as laid out in the sidebar at left. You will find it worthwhile to keep records for the whole range of the unit sizes.

Developing the records is not a huge job, just one that requires persistent effort. At the completion of each project, I typically spend from an hour for a small project up to several hours for a big one (such as a whole-house reconstruction), tallying hours from time cards, taking quantities from estimates, figuring productivity rates, and writing up from a couple to half a dozen or so narrative records. I concentrate on producing new records for items and assemblies for which my existing records are relatively thin. If I'm short on records for two-story pier-and-grade beam foundations, that is an assembly for which I will make a record.

When I have completed my new records, I add them to the three-ring binder where I store productivity records. Carpentry records are arranged in the sequence in which I typically estimate work—foundation, floor frame, wall frame, etc., all the way through to casework and hardware installation. Whole project records go into a separately tabbed section, as do records for sub-trades that are occasionally done by my crew, such as drywall and tile. When estimating, I can simply leaf through the records as I go, easily finding my way to the needed ones.

Having built my narrative labor records for some years, when it comes time to create an estimate, I can usually locate a record that closely matches the work (item, crew, and circumstances) in the new project. If I plan on lead person Leslie's crew installing roof sheathing on a cut-up 5/12 pitch roof during the winter of 2001, I will readily find my way to the record for Fred's crew for sheathing a similarly cut-up 6/12 pitch during February of '96. I figure Leslie's production will about match Fred's, since she was his apprentice at the time. So I use Fred's productivity number—half a person hour per 4×8 sheet including handling, cutting, and nailing—in the new estimate for Leslie's project.

I *urge* you to build a narrative cost record of your own. You will never get a higher return on investment in dollars or peace of mind from any work you do. Capable builders understand construction is too complex to intuitively know the labor cost of all the items and assemblies. They recognize that the rationalization that you can't know what something will cost till it is built is pure bunk. They are willing to make the steady effort necessary to build labor productivity records. As a result, they are able to estimate the costs of even very complex projects within *a few percent or closer of the actual costs*.

Those of us who develop cost records enjoy another advantage. We position ourselves to charge for our preconstruction services as well as our construction work. We have something tangible to offer during preconstruction. We have the records that enable us to accurately project the costs of alternative designs during the planning stage of projects. Such "cost planning," as I call it, is a valuable service. You can learn to get paid for it rather than pump out all your estimating work for free. To reap

the benefits as soon as possible, you should begin creating your own binder of labor productivity records with your first project. And if you are past that point, may I take the liberty of suggesting a good time to start would be tomorrow or this afternoon.

Adding Payroll

At the beginning of your career as a builder, you are likely, as the old industry adage has it, to "wear all the hats." You are salesperson, estimator, office manager, bookkeeper, project manager, carpenter, and laborer. You may stay with your one-person show for a long while. It can be fun. You can make a good living producing first-class work. But as time passes and your body begins to give out or your brain requires a fresh challenge, you may want to enlarge your company and hand off some of the hats—first field production and routine office work, then other functions.

You may find it possible and even desirable, with the trades becoming so complex and even routine office work demanding serious computer skills, to distribute the hats to subcontractors who are highly efficient specialists in their areas. Perhaps you will prefer developing relationships with foundation, framing, and finish subcontractors to building a carpentry crew. Maybe you will elect to contract with an accounting service rather than hire an office manager/bookkeeper.

On the other hand, as you grow, you may prefer to take on employees along with subcontractors. On smaller projects, using subcontractors for the minor amounts of work in each trade may be inefficient. On all projects, you may get better results by dispatching employees to jobs as needed than by trying to get

COMING UP

Becoming an Employer

New Responsibilities

Time Card Choices and Challenges

Making Payroll

Payroll Taxes and Tax Reports

The Benefits of Payroll Services

urge you to build a narrative cost record of your own. You will never get a higher return on investment in dollars or peace of mind from any work you do.

Playing by the Rules

To avoid the work of developing a legitimate payroll system or to avoid paying their share of employment taxes, builders often treat employees as subcontractors. It seems so easy to just write carpenters a check, skip all the withholding and reporting, stick the tax and insurance payments in your pocket, and account for payments to employees as "framing subcontractor" or "cabinet installer." Especially when you are starting out, desperately juggling all those unfamiliar balls of running a construction business, the temptation can be hard to resist. But if you give in to it for a time, you'd be wise to start playing by the rules after a short while. The tax guys are likely to discover your employee-as-subcontractor gambit. When they do, they will eat you right up.

For starters, they can demand all your unpaid back taxes for social security, disability, and unemployment. Next, they will carve into you for interest—compounded—on those taxes. After such appetizers, they're ready for rump steak. If your employees did not report the payments from you on their tax returns, *you* can be required to pay all *their* unpaid income tax—and for dessert you can be asked to serve up interest (compounded) on those taxes. A person determined to run a sound construction company will not allow a liability like that to build up behind him.

A well-run construction company, with long-term employees who share a commitment to good work and respectful relationships, fills the need of its employees (and their employer) for community.

subcontractors to turn up in a timely fashion. Along with control, though it is not often mentioned, comes a social benefit of "employerhood." A well-run construction company with long-term employees who share a commitment to good work and respectful relationships, fills the need of its employees—and their employer—for community.

A major, new responsibility

Like a lot of builders, I first became an employer—eventually of about a dozen people—so casually I have tended to forget what a momentous step it was. I was building a small artist's studio. A young man, who would mature a few years later into a superb carpenter and become my first lead person, walked onto my job site and asked if I needed help. I liked him and thought it would

be nice to have some help, so I hired him. For a time we remained a crew of two, then gradually other people added themselves, or we recruited them. As the crew's skills improved and their appetite for responsibility and job site control grew, they pushed me off the site, and I began to concentrate on hiring new people and winning new jobs to keep everyone employed.

The new responsibilities that come with employerhood are huge. First of all, if you are a good employer and can attract good people, you will develop with them a powerful mutual sense of obligation that comes close to that felt between family members. As part of holding up your end of the bargain, you must provide your employees with steady work so that they can eat, pay their rent or mortgage, and support their kids. Along with these obligations come very specific financial and accounting responsibilities.

You must have the cash to pay your employees at the end of each payroll period. If you fail to do so even a few times, you will engender their disappointment, then their distrust, then their justified anger, and finally legal confrontation—which you will lose big-time. To make sure you have cash on hand when each payday arrives, you need to maintain an adequate supply of operating capital and monitor cash flow carefully. In addition, you must create systems for punctually making payroll week after week. You will need procedures for:

- Having time cards filled out
- Withholding and depositing taxes
- Making reports to the tax authorities
- Logging payroll costs in your general ledger and job cost records.

Once you have these systems and procedures in place, making payroll becomes a routine clerical task. Getting them into place requires forethought and decision making.

Time cards and checks

"There are many ways to skin this cat," a construction industry veteran remarked about the variety of ways successful builders do business, and his observation nowhere holds more true than for time cards. At one end of the spectrum, you find builders using cards produced at a print shop. At the other end are those who have gone high-tech, eliminating paper cards altogether, and have employees enter hours right into a job

site device that shoots the hours to an office computer.

My approach is halfway along the spectrum to fully computerized. I create time cards on my computer, print them out, and distribute them to job sites to be filled out by hand. Over the years, I have developed a computer file of standard time cards—an example of which is illustrated below—for different types of projects. There is one for foundation replacements, another for kitchen remodels, another for small additions, and so on up the ladder. For large projects, I use a series of time cards as my

---

■ SAMPLE LETTERS AND FORMS Time Card

Time cards vary greatly from company to company. My time card provides for:
- **A two- instead of one-week pay period, which halves the expense of making payroll.**
- **Four 9.5-hour workdays each week, because the four-day schedule is a huge benefit to my employees, clients, company, and me.**
- **Breakdown and totaling of employee hours by tasks so I can create the labor productivity records necessary for accurate estimating.**
- **Totaling of hours by insurance categories, since some categories, like plumbing and sheet metal, can carry much lower insurance rates than others, like carpentry.**

TIME CARD

Name James Jones
Beginning date 12/11/01
Job 4321 Southdale Dr.

Task	Task Total	Insurance Total
Site grd.		
Fnd. grd.		
Reinfor.		
Cement		
Fore org.		
Setup		
Demo		
Form	14	
Pour	8	
Strip	7	
Flr Fra	7	
Subflr	4	
Wall fra	10	69.5
Wall she	7	
Roof fra	4	
Roof dec		
Deck fra	3	
Deck rail		
Decking		
Doors		
Windows		
Siding		
Ex trm		
Int trm		
Oth carp		
Clean	4½	
Pickups	1	
Cab		
Plumb	2	2
Sheet met	4½	4½
Elect		
Drywall		
Tile		
Paint		
	76	76

Week 1: TU WED THU FRI — 8 6 / 8 / 7 / 7 / 3 / ½ 1 ½ ½ / 1 / 2 / ½ / 9½ 9½ 9½ 9½
Week 2: TU WED THU FRI — 7 / 4 / 4 6 / 2 2 / ½ ½ ½ ½ / 1 3 / 9½ 9½ 9½ 9½

Comments:

Weekly or biweekly: timecards collected

Hours phoned or faxed to payroll service

Paychecks sent to builder

Federal
Depository

Taxes withheld from paychecks deposited at approved bank

Reports of wages and withholdings sent to builder

Net wages and withholdings entered in general ledger. Gross wages entered in job cost records.

Quarterly summary of wages submitted to federal government

Annual summary submitted to employees and government

crew moves through the stages of the project. I use one card for setup, demo, and the foundation, a second for framing through close-up, and another for finish work. Often, I customize the cards to track labor needed for an unusual element, such as framing a dormer atop an existing roof.

My flexible time cards support all the goals of a payroll system:

PAYMENT OF WAGES, TAX WITHHOLDING, AND TAX REPORTING
With time cards in hand, I can figure my employees take-home pay and the payroll taxes I need to withhold, deposit, and report (or better yet, I can call the hours into my payroll service and have them do the rest of the work).

INPUTTING OF LABOR COSTS INTO JOB COST RECORDS DURING CONSTRUCTION The cards break out hours into the phases of work for which I track costs during construction.

DEVELOPMENT OF LABOR PRODUCTIVITY RECORDS At the completion of each project, I can tally hours spent on items for which I want to create labor productivity records.

CONTROL OF INSURANCE COSTS
Some categories of work, like sheet metal, can carry lower insurance rates than others, like framing. My card separates out the hours of the lower rate from the higher-rate categories.

Whichever way you choose to create time cards, you will almost certainly have to keep after your employees to fill them out accurately. Even in my company, with conscientious employees who understand that accurate time cards contribute to the profits we all share, I find the task neglected. I get to a project site

and discover the crew is two days behind filling out their cards. When they finally get around to the task, they will be able only roughly to recall how their hours were spent. The problem is not only mine; other builders regularly groan about it, too. The only thing I know to do is to entrust time card completion to the project lead and/or keep insisting (whine, moan, groan, beg, plead, snarl) that accurate time cards *do* matter and urging that they be filled out daily.

Taxes, tax reports, and payroll services

With time cards collected at the end of each pay period, employees' checks can be prepared. Those checks are, of course, for *net wages*—namely the amount that is left after hours worked are multiplied by wage and then income, social security, and other employee taxes are withheld. After withholding taxes from our employees' wages, we cannot (though I gather some employers don't quite get this) head over to the mall and spend the takings on a spree through our favorite sporting goods emporium. We are required to deposit the withheld taxes at an approved bank and to follow up with reports to the government detailing employees' earnings and withholdings. The frequency and promptness with which you must make deposits and file reports depends on your total amount of payroll. But basically it can be described in one word—*fast*. Miss the deadline and you get hit with a nasty fine.

All the payroll check-writing, withholding, depositing, and reporting adds up to a lot of work. You can extend your accounting system to take care of it in one of three ways:

ADD ON TO A ONE-WRITE SYSTEM
From your supplier you should be able to get an add-on to the one-write system illustrated on p. 68 that will allow you to

make out payroll checks and record net pay and tax deductions. From the federal and state tax authorities you can obtain annually updated charts that show you how much tax to withhold and forms for the reports you must file.

COMPUTER   Some generic small-business programs and all specialized construction programs I have seen will generate payroll checks, distribute payroll costs to your job cost records and general ledger, and produce the reports required by the tax authorities. Annual upgrades modify your program to conform to changing tax laws.

CONTRACT WITH A PAYROLL SERVICE   By asking around at small businesses in your area you can find a payroll service offered by banks or other corporations that will fill your needs inexpensively and reliably.

Of the three options, handling payroll on their computer may, for many builders, ultimately prove the most efficient. I have, however, liked using payroll services and think they are of special benefit to builders who are not yet computerized and/or who do not employ an office person capable of handling payroll. A good service allows you to take care of payroll very efficiently. I have found that once I have time cards in hand, I can report hours to my payroll service in a quarter hour or so. For a modest charge— considerably less than it would cost me to do the work in-house—the service takes the job from there. It cuts the checks, makes the tax deposits (by transferring money from my bank account), submits the reports required by the tax guys, and sends over a copy of the reports for my office files. All I need do is monitor the service's work for accuracy and distribute the payroll costs to my general ledger and job costing records. As a bonus, if the service makes a mistake, it pays the penalty. It is easy to make mistakes doing payroll, and the penalties are brutal and swift, so it's nice to not be at risk.

A most attractive part of hiring a payroll service is that you increase your personal freedom. With payroll checks, you don't have the flexibility you do with other bills; you can't pay them a little sooner or a little later as you can sub and supplier bills. But with a payroll service, you don't have to schedule your life around payday. You can go out of town for a spontaneous vacation, and when payday comes, all you need do is call your project leads for crew hours, then phone the hours into your service. The service will, as you prefer, deposit wages right to the employees' accounts or have their checks in your mailbox by the time you get home. With 15 or 20 minutes work you have taken care of payroll and are back in the surf.

Leaping to a Computer Program

In previous sections, I have used words like "straightforward" to describe each of the steps we were taking up the ladder of accounting systems. The next step is not so straightforward. Computer programs do hold out the *possibility* of increased accounting efficiency, power, and effectiveness. They *can* pay solid returns for time and money invested. Some builders swear that computerizing their accounting has given them control of their business for the first time. But the programs are by no means "easy to use"—though the people who sell the programs sprinkle such phrases across their ads like powdered sugar on a Swedish pancake. Believe me, when you start chewing on computer accounting software for the first time it will go down more like boot leather (with steel studs) than any pan-

COMING UP

The Challenge of Moving Up to Computer-based Accounting

Reasons for Making the Leap

Getting Yourself Ready to Make the Leap

A Ladder of Computer Accounting Programs

Choosing Your Program

Accounting with a Computer

Construction and construction management are very complicated. There is no reason to expect construction accounting software to be simple.

cake. Judith Miller, a consultant expert in both basic and advanced computer accounting programs, tells it like it is: "Construction and construction management are very complicated. There is no reason to expect construction accounting software to be simple. It is not simple."

Why make the leap

You may have doubts about your ability to make the challenging conversion to computer accounting. You may wonder whether it is really necessary, in order to run a successful construction company in this day and age, to make the leap. In my view the answer is no. You can grow a strong construction company using a one-write system. People have done so for decades. Whether or not the manual system will cost you more to maintain than a computer program over the long run is anybody's guess. The outcome depends on your particular combination of skills and circumstance.

Nevertheless, though, a paper-and-pencil system may be your best choice for a start-up system, there are a number of compelling reasons to convert to computer accounting fairly early in your career. The reasons can be divided roughly into two groups. The first is negative, the second positive.

On the negative side, if you stay with a paper-and-pencil system, you may find

yourself increasingly without support. It may become difficult to get the supplies you need from commercial vendors; the maker of the one-write system that I once used no longer offers the job costing sheets that were once a part of its system for builders. Education in the use of paper-and-pencil systems seems to be drying up. On a recent trip to a store specializing in books for builders, I found virtually nothing about paper-and-pencil accounting while there were several books on computer accounting. If you continue to use a paper-and-pencil system, you will have increasing difficulty finding bookkeepers experienced with or even willing to use it.

On the positive side, while paper-and-pencil systems are fading into obscurity, the names of the most widely used computer accounting programs have become household words. The programs are available from many sources. Training, consulting services, and online courses and forums, though of uneven quality and reliability, are all increasingly available.

Furthermore, computer accounting *can be a really cost-effective investment.* If you already use a computer for other applications, you can add computer accounting for a modest additional out-of-pocket cost. A good-quality, generic, small-business program (specialized construction programs are another question) can be purchased for the price of a good circular saw. You will need to invest in training, but if you are willing to put in the hours, you can self-educate rather than rely on expensive consultants to get yourself up to speed.

For your investment, while there are no guarantees, you can get good returns on the time and money you put into making the conversion, including:

Why Convert to Computer Accounting

■ Support for manual systems is disappearing.
■ Support for computer accounting programs is increasing.
■ The costs of conversion can be minimized.
■ Computers can speed up your accounting chores.
■ Computers can improve access to the numbers needed for understanding your company's financial performance.

BOOKKEEPING EFFICIENCY Computer programs automate the repetitive tasks of accounting—entering income and expenses, filling out and writing checks, totaling up numbers. The programs save you a lot of grueling clerical work.

CONTROLS To varying degrees, depending on their cost and power, computer programs incorporate checks and proofs that help you avoid such classical accounting errors as overpaying subs, underbilling clients, and miscalculating your cash situation.

UNDERSTANDING OF ACCOUNTING When you use a computer accounting program designed by accounting experts, you absorb some of their expertise.

INSIGHT INTO BUSINESS PERFORMANCE With a click of a key, an accounting program produces information—such as percentage of revenue being spent on callbacks—needed for analysis of a company's financial performance. Because digging out such information with a paper-and-pencil system is a relatively laborious process, you may not get around to it. As a result, you will make management decisions based on inadequate information, and those decisions will cost you money.

As we move deeper into the twenty-first century, the reasons for switching to computer accounting will become steadily more compelling. While people who stay with paper-and-pencil systems will be operating in relative isolation, those who use computer-based systems will find many sources of support. Though computer accounting is not cheap, the costs can be managed and constrained. Computer accounting is not an easy way to go, but the work it demands can produce good returns.

Bare-Bones Accounting Literacy Test

To take on construction accounting software, you need to be as comfortable with these terms as you are with "rebar," "joist," and "t&g."
Instructions:
1) Define each of the terms and concepts listed below, and use it in a sentence.
2) Mark an "x" in the box by any term you can confidently define and use.
3) Take test repeatedly until you pass.

Time allowed: Five minutes
Passing score: 100 percent

- ☐ Income
- ☐ Expense
- ☐ Cost
- ☐ Receipt
- ☐ Disbursement
- ☐ Checkbook
- ☐ Check register
- ☐ Balance
- ☐ Reconcile
- ☐ Chart of accounts
- ☐ Cost codes
- ☐ Spreadsheet
- ☐ General ledger
- ☐ Overhead costs
- ☐ Fixed overhead costs
- ☐ Variable overhead costs
- ☐ Gross profit margin
- ☐ Net profit margin
- ☐ Job costing
- ☐ Labor productivity rates
- ☐ Payroll
- ☐ Withholding
- ☐ Net pay
- ☐ Labor burden
- ☐ Consumables
- ☐ Draw
- ☐ Principal and interest
- ☐ Cash flow analysis
- ☐ Cash accounting
- ☐ Accrual accounting
- ☐ Payable
- ☐ Receivable
- ☐ Asset
- ☐ Liability
- ☐ Equity
- ☐ The accounting equation
- ☐ Ratios

here are few business mistakes worse than adopting a computer accounting program before having achieved both accounting and computer literacy.

Getting yourself ready

If you come to the conclusion that computer accounting is for you, then before plunging in, make certain you are ready for it. There are few business mistakes worse than adopting a computer accounting program before having achieved both accounting and computer literacy. Builders often make the leap too soon, become deeply frustrated, and lose control of the financial side of their businesses.

To achieve accounting literacy, become fluent with a paper-and-pencil system before attempting computer accounting. Study the accounting chapters in this book until you understand them thoroughly. Go further if you like. Take accounting classes. Read other books. At the very least, advance your accounting literacy to the point that you can pass my "Bare Bones Accounting Literacy Test" shown on p. 89.

You would benefit from mastering the concepts covered in "Bare Bones" even if you stick with paper-and-pencil accounting. For computer accounting, mastery is essential. The trainers and manuals that support and explain the use of computer accounting programs all constantly draw on the concepts. If you don't understand them, you will quickly lose track of the explanations and get lost in your program. With paper-and-

Charts of Accounts

Charts of accounts for computer accounting, such as these reproduced from *Contractor's Guide to Quick Books Pro* (see Resources on p. 258) use a "code," i.e. a number, as well as a name to label each account. At first glance, this chart may seem overwhelming. Look closely and you will see it breaks out into our now familiar groupings of accounts. First come *asset, liability, and equity* accounts. Next are *income accounts*. Next come *direct job cost* accounts, here called "costs of goods sold." Finally, there are accounts for *overhead* costs, here called "expenses."

Account Number/Name	Type
1110 · Company Checking Account	Bank
1120 · Company Savings Account	Bank
1140 · Petty Cash Account	Bank
1210 · Accounts Receivable	Accounts Receivable
1310 · Employee Advances	Other Current Asset
1320 · Retentions Receivable	Other Current Asset
1330 · Security Deposit	Other Current Asset
1390 · Undeposited Funds	Other Current Asset
1400 · Refundable Workers' Comp Deposit	Other Current Asset
1510 · Automobiles & Trucks	Fixed Asset
1520 · Computer & Office Equipment	Fixed Asset
1530 · Machinery & Equipment	Fixed Asset
1540 · Accumulated Depreciation	Fixed Asset
1590 · Work in Progress	Fixed Asset
2010 · Accounts Payable	Accounts Payable
2050 · MasterCard	Payable Credit Card
2060 · Visa Card	Payable Credit Card

Account Number/Name	Type
2100 · Payroll Liabilities Other Current	Liability
2200 · Customer Deposits Other Current	Liability
2240 · Workers' Comp Payable Other Current	Liability
2410 · Construction Loan Long-Term	Liability
2460 · Truck Loan Long-Term	Liability
3000 · Opening Balance Equity	Equity
3100 · Owners' Capital	Equity
3110 · Investments	Equity
3130 · Draws	Equity
3910 · Retained Earnings	Equity
4110 · Construction Income	Income
4810 · Vendor Refunds	Income
4910 · Workers' Comp Dividend	Income
4999 · Uncategorized Income	Income
5110 · Job-Related Costs	Cost of Goods Sold
5200 · Job Labor Costs	Cost of Goods Sold
5210 · Job Labor (Gross Wages)	Cost of Goods Sold
5220 · Workers' Compensation Costs	Cost of Goods Sold
5230 · Employers' Payroll Taxes	Cost of Goods Sold
5240 · Employee Benefits Costs	Cost of Goods Sold
6220 · Advertising	Expense
6240 · Amortization Expense	Expense
6060 · Bank Service Charges	Expense
6070 · Bid Deposit	Expense

pencil systems you can always see what is going on. You can place all the spreadsheets on your desk and see your entire system at once. You see the numbers appear as you make and total entries. With a computer program, you see only one screen's—i.e. sheet's—worth of information at a time. The action of entering and totaling numbers takes place out of sight, down in the innards of your machine. Therefore, understanding the concepts that govern the action is critical. Otherwise, when the results pop up on your screen, your response will be, "Where in the heck is this coming from?" (It might even be language con-

veying a level of frustration somewhat deeper than that implied by "heck.")

As for achieving computer literacy, you may have done so even before you decided to go into business as a builder. If not, I'd suggest you choose a path to acquiring it that suits your learning style. For some readers, that path may include classes, while others may prefer to plow back and forth through computer programs till they get a feel for their structure and function. If you are uncertain as to how to proceed, you might find the following steps useful:

1. *Purchase a computer* that comes bundled with basic software applications

Account Number/Name	Type
6075 · Bond Expense	Expense
6090 · Business License & Fees	Expense
6100 · Car/Truck Expense	Expense
6101 · Gas & Oil	Expense
6103 · Repairs & Maintenance	Expense
6105 · Registration & License	Expense
6107 · Insurance—Auto	Expense
6130 · Cleaning/Janitorial	Expense
6140 · Contributions	Expense
6150 · Depreciation Expense	Expense
6160 · Dues and Subscriptions	Expense
6180 · Insurance	Expense
6181 · Disability Insurance	Expense
6182 · Liability Insurance	Expense
6185 · Workers' Comp	Expense
6200 · Interest Expense	Expense
6201 · Finance Charge	Expense
6202 · Loan Interest	Expense
6203 · Mortgage	Expense
6230 · Licenses and Permits	Expense
6240 · Miscellaneous	Expense
6500 · Payroll Expenses (office)	Expense
6501 · Payroll (office staff)	Expense

Account Number/Name	Type
6502 · Payroll Tax Expense	Expense
6570 · Professional Fees	Expense
6571 · Accounting	Expense
6572 · Legal Fees	Expense
6610 · Postage and Delivery	Expense
6650 · Rent	Expense
6670 · Repairs	Expense
6671 · Building Repairs	Expense
6672 · Computer Repairs	Expense
6673 · Equipment Repairs	Expense
6800 · Telephone	Expense
6820 · Taxes	Expense
6900 · Travel & Ent.	Expense
6901 · Entertainment	Expense
6902 · Meals	Expense
6903 · Travel	Expense
6920 · Tools and Machinery	Expense
6970 · Utilities	Expense
6999 · Uncategorized Expenses	Expense
7010 · Interest Income	Other Income
7030 · Other Income	Other Income
8010 · Other Expenses	Other Expense
2 · *Purchase Orders	Non-Posting
4 · *Estimates	Non-Posting

A Ladder of Computer Accounting Programs

■ Personal money management

■ Basic generic small business

■ Heavy-duty generic small business

■ Light-duty specialized construction management

■ Heavy-duty specialized construction management

and learn to use them. If necessary, take a course in basic computer use.

2. *Get connected to the Internet.* Cruise Web sites (see Resources on p. 258 for interesting construction-related Web sites). Information on Web sites is presented and accessed as it is in accounting software, and by clicking through Web site screens, you will get a feeling for how to find your way around an accounting program.

3. *Work your way through demonstration versions* of accounting programs, many of which are available free via the Web or on CDs (see Resources on p. 258). From the demonstrations, you will come to understand the "functionality" and organization of a range of programs.

Once you have acquired computer literacy—meaning you can find your way around computer programs with reasonable confidence, not that you are a master of them—you can move on to deciding which accounting program, if any, you want to use in your business. You may settle on a program for which you have already run a demo. Or you may want to take a look at still other programs before deciding which ones to consider seriously.

Choosing your computer accounting program

If you do decide to buckle into your computer and probe deeper into the thicket of accounting programs, you are going to find yourself facing a tangle of possibilities. For our purposes as builders, however, the programs can be sorted into the four levels described in the sidebar on p. 88.

Some builders have adapted personal money management programs to their business accounting needs. The likelihood, however, is that you will be better off going up at least one level and purchasing a program designed for small businesses. While more expensive and more challenging to learn, they also offer more accounting power and will prepare you better for later steps up the ladder. Some makers of generic small-business systems offer a basic version and a heavy-duty version. A great advantage of certain heavy-duty versions is that they perform the vital function of job costing.

A *long step* up from advanced generic small-business systems are several levels of specialized programs designed for construction accounting. Sometimes called "construction management programs," these programs integrate accounting including job costing and estimating into one package. Of particular interest to builders are "lite" versions of the specialized programs, intended for small construction companies, those with half a dozen or so employees. Such programs, while costing a dozen times as much as generic programs and demanding much greater investment of time and money to learn and keep up, are still much less expensive than the full versions. A benefit of moving directly to a lite program from your paper system is that if you choose the right one, you may never have to change programs again, though you may at some point have to upgrade to the full version.

One of the toughest decisions when making the switch to computer accounting is whether to go for a generic, small-business program and stretch it to function as a construction program or to bite the bullet and take on all the costs of a specialized program. Both options have their knowledgeable advocates. Your choice of program should depend on what is available when you decide to make the leap to computer accounting, what programs are best supported where you live, and your own judgment as to what level of program you can use most cost-effectively. Because programs change constantly and because support for them varies so much from locale to locale, I cannot tell you exactly which program will be right for you. I can, however, suggest a procedure for making your choice:

1. From builders in your area, ask for evaluations of the programs they are using. Ask particularly about built-in proofs and checks that will safeguard against input and output errors; clarity of reports that will help you view and analyze your numbers; and availability of reliable support from consultants skilled at construction accounting, not merely accounting in general.

2. Narrow your possibilities down to promising programs for which you will be able to get support, interview the recommended consultants, and check their references, particularly long-term builder clients.

3. As best you can, project the long-term costs of the programs that interest you—not just the purchase price and support costs, but the value of the time you will put into learning the program. If you consider a specialized construction management program, do not underestimate the learning effort.

Disregard any well-meant salesperson's assurances that his program is easy to use. It won't be.

Take time to make your selection. One builder impulsively spent thousands of dollars on a specialized accounting program without really checking out either the program or the company that sells it. Now it sits unused because he can get no training. His story is a common one.

Using a computer accounting program

Though computers can turbo-charge your accounting, a number of the pitfalls inherent in paper-and-pencil accounting remain a danger. You can still fall prey to that old bugaboo, the cash flow fallacy. If you are up to date in your recording of deposits but way behind on paying expenses, you will see a large cash balance in your checking account that suggests a financial picture much rosier than reality.

By switching from cash accounting to accrual accounting (less labor intensive

Turtle Creek Payable Journal

Using a computer payables journal, such as the one from Turtle Creek illustrated here, you get a detailed picture of your outstanding bills, including when payment of them is due and when it is overdue. If it is up to date, the journal helps you monitor your cash flow needs.

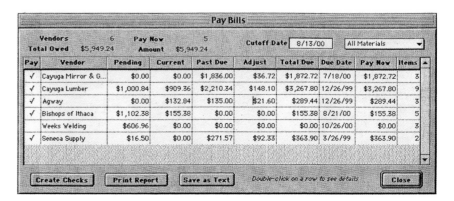

▪ SAMPLE LETTERS AND FORMS   Job Cost Monitoring

American Contractor, a specialized construction accounting program, gives you a clear format for job cost monitoring. Scan the lines for concrete footings from left to right. You will see that in the second group of columns, the budget (i.e. estimate) can be

adjusted for change orders (though in this case it has not been). In the next columns labor costs to date are recorded in both dollars and hours, and the amount spent is compared to the amount estimated in percentage terms.

Job: 10201—Van Deusen Project (Continued)

| CODE | DESCRIPTION | TYPE | CONTRACT & BUDGET AMOUNTS | | | COSTS & BILLINGS | | |
			ORIGINAL	CHANGES	TOTAL	TO DATE	%	REMAINING
03	FOUNDATION	CONTRACT	1,493		1,493	1,493.00	100%	.00
		BILLINGS						
0330	Concrete Footings	MATERIAL	704		704	699.01	99%	4.99
		LABOR HRS	24.4 hr		24.4 hr	16.00 hr	66%	8.40 hr
		LABOR $	537		537	340.97	63%	196.03
06	FRAMING	CONTRACT	7,434		7,434			
		BILLINGS				2,973.60	40%	4,460.40
0610	Frame First Floor	MATERIAL	3,259		3,259	2,354.04	72%	904.96
		LABOR HRS	77.7 hr	2.0 hr	79.7 hr	81.00 hr	102%	−1.30 hr
		LABOR $	2,093	54	2,147	2,030.40	95%	116.60
0660	Frame Roof	LABOR HRS	30.0 hr		30.0 hr	24.00 hr	80%	6.00 hr
		LABOR $	808		808	663.58	82%	144.42
07	THERM/MOIST PROTECT	CONTRACT	1,598		1,598			1,598.00
0720	Insulation	MATERIAL	138		138	.00	0%	138.00
		SUBCON	840		840	840.00	100%	.00
0730	Roofing	LABOR HRS	12.4 hr		12.4 hr	.00 hr	0%	12.40 hr
		LABOR $	334		334	.00 hr	0%	334.00
08	DOORS & WINDOWS	CONTRACT	1,201		1,201			1,201.00
0820	Doors	MATERIAL	789		789	.00 hr	0%	789.00
		LABOR HRS	5.3 hr		5.3 hr	.00 hr	0%	5.30 hr
		LABOR $	142		142	.00 hr	0%	142.00
0850	Windows	LABOR HRS	3.2 hr		3.2 hr	.00 hr	0%	3.20 hr
		LABOR $	86		86	.00 hr	0%	86.00
09	FINISHING	CONTRACT	2,489		2,489			2,489.00
0910	Finish Carpentry	MATERIAL	355		355	274.13	77%	80.87
		LABOR HRS	5.0 hr		5.0 hr	.00 hr	0%	5.00 hr
		LABOR $	135		135	.00 hr	0%	135.00
0925	Drywall	LABOR HRS	9.5 hr		9.5 hr	6.00 hr	63%	3.50 hr
		LABOR $	256		256	154.19	60%	101.81
		SUBCON	400		400	.00 hr	0%	400.00
09᠁	᠁ing	SUBCON	910		910	.00 hr	0%	910.00

with a computer than with paper-and-pencil accounting) and using journals such as the one illustrated on p. 93, you can better defend against the cash flow fallacy. But the defense is not absolute. There is still a tendency for receivables to be recorded promptly, as soon as you get invoices off to clients, and for payables to lag. Subs forget to bill. Invoices for materials get lost in a stack of paper or a notebook at a job site, never make it to the office, and never get entered in payables. To make sure your books are showing your true cash picture, you must still make sure that all your payables and receivables are being entered promptly.

With a computer program, you must still bear down on all three levels of job costing, as described on pp. 78–80. You must resist letting the computer lull you into thinking it will do all the work. It is true that computers can make the job easier. With a little additional input from you beyond what it takes to do your other accounting, computer programs will give you detailed job cost records such as that illustrated on the facing page. The records allow you to monitor costs during a project. At project completion, they can be stored on the computer and later easily retrieved if you want to review your success at estimating a particular phase of work or a particular type of job. You do, however, still need to study, think about, and act on the reports—and that, not the work of entering and totaling numbers, is the harder and more important part of job costing.

Even with computers, you must create the labor productivity records necessary for accurate estimating. While the computer may store bare-bones productivity rates in a database and retrieve them for an estimate, I strongly recommend going further. I still urge you to keep labor productivity records in the narrative form illustrated on p. 81. Such

records, with numbers accompanied by descriptions of work site conditions and of the crew who did the work, will be enormously valuable in helping you create estimates tailored to the specifics of your projects. The computer can power your production of the narrative records. With a word processing application, you'll produce more legible records and produce them more easily than you would scrawling them out by hand.

Going Deeper into Your Numbers

With a well-developed manual or computer accounting system up and running, you can do a good job of recording and sorting your numbers. Your ledgers, journals, and other spreadsheets give you detailed displays of income and expenses—and even of assets, liability, and equity if you have set up a balance sheet. All this nicely tabulated information—while pleasing in its orderliness and handy at tax reporting time—is actually not of much use for managing your company unless you do two things. You have to view your numbers in relationship to each other—in terms of "ratios," as people in the financial business say. If your ratios are substandard, you must consider what moves you can make to improve them.

Ratios, as you may recall, can be expressed as either fractions or percentages. A

COMING UP

Thinking about Your Numbers

Ratios: An Analytical Tool

Key Ratios

Other Measures of Financial Health

Viewing Your Business as a Shareholder

A Ratio

Net Profit Ratio for Alexander Construction in 2002:

Total revenue for 2002:	$312,000
Profit for 2002:	$44,570
Net Profit Ratio:	14.28%

(Math: 44,570/312,000 = 1/ 7 (or 1:7) = 14.28%)

ratio of 1 to 4 can be expressed as ¼ (1:4) or as 25 percent. One to ten can be expressed as ¹⁄₁₀ (1:10) or 10 percent, and so on. We have earlier made use of ratios without calling them that—for example, in discussing the relationship of the costs of

consumables (miscellaneous supplies such as saw blades consumed by a crew) to wages or material costs. Another helpful ratio is that of profit to revenue, as shown in the sidebar on p. 95. If you are a small-volume builder and your profit is just a few percent of revenue, you are not operating a sound business. If it's 14.28 percent as for the Alexander Company, and you are not making the mistake of including your pay in your profit instead of viewing it as overhead, you have reason to celebrate.

With a paper-and-pencil accounting system you can extract ratios from your spreadsheets fairly quickly with a calculator. If you punch in revenue at $80,000 and marketing expense at $800 through the first quarter of the year, your calculator will tell you that you are spending one-hundredth (0.01), or 1 percent of revenue on marketing. One of the benefits of using computer programs for accounting is that some will give you whole sets of ratios with a few clicks of the mouse—and not only in percentage terms but in graphic form, such as a bar or a pie chart. Whether you are using paper or computer, you do need to think about your ratios regularly. One builder wisely advises picking out a few key ratios from the many that can be generated and concentrating on those. It's good advice.

Key ratios

Several key ratios of special value to small-volume builders are:

REVENUE   It can be helpful to compare revenue for a period such as a quarter or a whole year to prior periods of the same duration. If your revenue is increasing too quickly, for example doubling or tripling from year to year, you may risk losing control of your business. If your revenue is falling off and the reason is not simply that the economy is in recession, you will want to find out whether

A Builder's Essential Ratios

One of the best ways to track your company's financial performance is by keeping an eye on certain key ratios. Here, several are pictured as a series of bars representing a company's total revenue and one important component of the revenue. Alongside each bar the ratio—the component over the revenue—is stated as both a fraction and as a percentage.

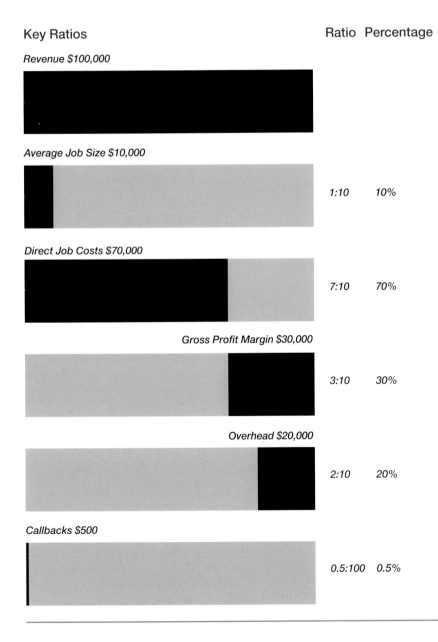

Key Ratios	Ratio	Percentage
Revenue $100,000		
Average Job Size $10,000	1:10	10%
Direct Job Costs $70,000	7:10	70%
Gross Profit Margin $30,000	3:10	30%
Overhead $20,000	2:10	20%
Callbacks $500	0.5:100	0.5%

the decline is a result of mismanagement, such as lack of marketing effort.

AVERAGE JOB SIZE   By comparing average job size for different years, you may discover that you earn more profit doing one size job than another. You can decide to concentrate on the profitable size job, or you can dedicate yourself to learning how to earn a profit on the other sizes as well.

DIRECT JOB COSTS AND GROSS PROFIT MARGIN   As discussed earlier, revenue can be divided into two large components, direct job costs and whatever remains, namely gross profit margin (GPM), which includes both overhead and profit. Knowing GPM is helpful for comparing your company's performance to that of companies doing similar work. The GPM of 30 percent, shown in the illustration on the facing page, would be exceptional for a custom-home builder. For a small-volume remodeling company, that amount would be respectable, though some remodelers boast of GPMs ranging from 40 to 45 percent.

OVERHEAD   Keeping an eye on your overhead ratio is critical, for if overhead is allowed to inflate, less of GPM is left over as profit. With discipline, the owner of a small-volume company should be able to keep overhead, including a good salary for himself, to less than 20 percent.

CALLBACKS   Callbacks are a part of your direct job costs. If callbacks expand, direct job costs expand, and GPM goes down. With good quality control, you should be able to hold callbacks to a tiny percentage of revenue such as the $\frac{5}{10}$ percent shown on the facing page.

If you are keeping an eye on the ratios discussed so far, you will be doing a respectable job of monitoring your business' financial performance. Beyond these basic ratios, however, there are other measures of financial performance worth attending to.

Deeper yet

The first of the additional measures, builder's earnings, illustrated on p. 96 is my concoction, adapted to the world of small-volume construction companies from the ideas of Warren Buffett, the famous investor. You won't hear it discussed in conventional accounting books or classes. But I think it is of value to builders.

To get a look at builder's earnings, divide GPM into four instead of only two components. Two of the four, builder's pay and other overhead, have come up

A Builder's Earnings

Dividing gross profit margin into four parts allows you to see how much you can really take home as owner's pay and profit from your construction operation.

		Gross profit margin		
Direct job costs	Other overhead	Bldrs' pay	Bldrs' profit	Company profit

Builders' earnings

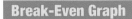
Break-Even Graph

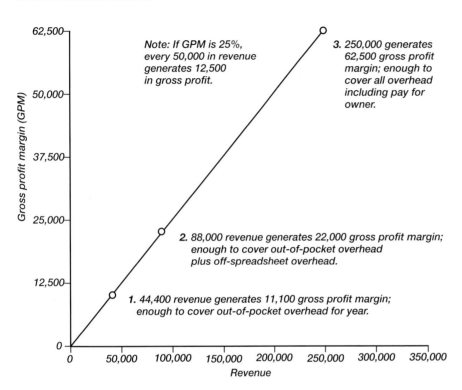

Note: If GPM is 25%, every 50,000 in revenue generates 12,500 in gross profit.

3. 250,000 generates 62,500 gross profit margin; enough to cover all overhead including pay for owner.

2. 88,000 revenue generates 22,000 gross profit margin; enough to cover out-of-pocket overhead plus off-spreadsheet overhead.

1. 44,400 revenue generates 11,100 gross profit margin; enough to cover out-of-pocket overhead for year.

y-axis: Gross profit margin (GPM)
x-axis: Revenue

often before. The division of profit is new. Company profit is the profit that must be left in the company to bolster its operating capital, replace equipment, and otherwise maintain the company. Builder's profit is the portion of profit that the builder is free to either leave in his or her company to support its growth or to pull out of the company for personal use. Builder's profit also can be thought of as "free cash," the cash that can be freed up from a company's ongoing operations without causing injury to the company.

Builder's pay and builder's profit combined make up *builder's earnings*—what you as manager and owner of your company enjoy as financial reward for the hard work and risk of being in the construction business. In a well-run, small-volume company, builder's pay and profit combined might run 15 to 20 percent of revenue. For a builder

doing half a million dollars of work a year, that would be $75,000 to $100,000. I know builders doing a few million who have enjoyed earnings of $500,000 pay and profit combined in good years.

Along with ratios, both conventional and Buffett inspired, another and closely related measure of financial health worth keeping an eye on is your break-even point, or better yet, points as illustrated in the graph at left. A company with tightly managed overhead can hit its break-even points relatively early in the year. Afterward, any earnings are pure profit.

■ *Point 1.* The level at which you earn enough above direct job costs (gross profit) to pay the out-of-pocket overhead costs of running your company for the year. Once there, you will not have to dip into operating capital to pay the costs of vehicle operation, liability insurance, or other overhead.

■ *Point 2.* The level at which gross profit additionally covers overhead costs that may not show up in your general ledger—such as fair market value for the use of space in your home as an office and your cost of capital.

■ *Point 3.* Here you have reached the *real* break-even point, the one at which a company earns enough beyond direct job costs to also pay its owner for all general, marketing, and administrative work. In years when you do not reach that point, you are not only shy of making a profit, you are failing to break even because you are losing the value of your time.

As you advance deeper into your career, another measure of financial performance needing your attention is balance sheet ratios—the relationships between assets, liabilities, and equity (see p. 58 for an introduction to the balance sheet concept). Some accountants may advise you to watch balance sheet ratios right from the start. In my opinion, if your business is debt-free and involves few assets—merely a truck, a collection of carpenter's tools, and inexpensive office equipment—maintaining a balance sheet for your company is hardly worth the effort. Your time will be much better spent concentrating on the operational ratios and other measures discussed earlier in this chapter.

But the picture changes if you begin to accumulate substantial debt or assets for use in your business such as multiple computers, more trucks, heavy construction equipment, and real estate outside your home. In particular, you will want to keep an eye on the ratio of *assets to long-term liabilities,* such as a loan for a truck.

Conventional wisdom has it that a business is okay with an assets to long-term liabilities ratio of 1:1 or better. I propose, however, that as businesses particularly liable to boom and then bust, construction companies should keep long-term liabilities as close to zero as possible. Debt and the interest on it will kill you when business unexpectedly and violently turns down, as it will repeatedly during your career as a builder. Remember the advice of William Shakespeare, "Better a lender than a borrower be." Don't borrow.

A second helpful ratio drawing on the balance sheet is *net profit to assets.* Well-run companies earn 20 cents to 25 cents a year for each dollar they hold in assets. If you have gathered $300,000 worth of office space, shop space, and equipment into your business, you may feel that you have become quite the substantial businessperson. In fact, if you are realizing $60,000 a year profit from working those assets, you are doing well. However, if your profit is only $18,000,

When a builder has acquired substantial assets, such as this shop and office belonging to Silver Hammer Construction, he must make certain that his company does a sufficient volume of work at a sufficient profit margin to justify the investment. In the case of Silver Hammer, the owner has worked hard to do just that.

the $300,000 assets are profoundly underutilized. Your profit to asset ratio is about 6 percent, or about 15 to 20 percent below par.

Financially successful builders are as prudent in their use of assets as they are strict in their management of overhead. They feed their ego not by sitting on a lot of real estate and equipment but by running a healthy business. Just as they are willing to incur overhead only for real gains in productivity, they are willing to spend on assets only if they feel they can earn at least a reasonable return on those assets. They stand back from the daily grind of managing their businesses and view them as an owner—as a shareholder you could say—and study their business' ratios and other measures of financial performance. They want to make certain that this enterprise, in which they have invested so much not only of their money but of themselves, is making good use of its resources and bringing them a reasonable return.

PART TWO

Getting the Right Jobs

4 Entering the Marketplace

Marketing

Connecting with Design Professionals

Evaluating Projects

Competitive Bidding

Design/Build

Cost Planning

5 Estimating and Bidding

Nailing Your Numbers

Gathering Information

Calculating Direct Costs

Figuring Overhead

Figuring Profit

Alternative Methods

6 Construction Contracts

Why and Which One

The Agreement

The Conditions

Two Critical Conditions:
Change Orders and Dispute Resolution

Subcontracts

CHAPTER 4

Entering the Marketplace

Marketing

MARKETING IS the work of letting your potential customers know you are available to help them meet their needs. Simple as that may seem, many of us feel uneasy about marketing. One builder says, "Selling does not seem like honest work." He has good reasons to feel that way. Too often marketing gurus and training programs promote sleazy tactics and encourage treating prospective clients as targets, as adversaries, as objects for manipulation.

Fortunately, because marketing *is* a necessity, a different approach is offered by other experts, notably Salli Raspberry and Michael Phillips in their remarkably good book, *Marketing Without Advertising* (see Resources on p. 258). Raspberry and Phillips teach you to market in a spirit of community service. Rather than manipulate, you listen carefully, attempt to understand your clients' needs, and offer guidance. Rather than charm or seduce, you teach and share your knowledge. Rather than slight of hand, you explain candidly what you can do for clients and what you cannot.

As a starting point, Raspberry and Phillips urge that you create a statement of 25 words or less describing the services your business offers. If you have created a concise statement of purpose (i.e. mission statement) for your company, it should provide a good starting point for your description of services. Whatever your starting point, you need to cover four issues:

- What you do
- Where you do it
- Who you do it for
- How you do it

You'll find it's not easy to boil *what, where, who,* and *how* down to 25 words (on my first attempt, I ended up with approximately enough words for a short novel). But the effort is worth making. When you succeed, you will have achieved focus for your marketing program.

Your natural client network

With your 25 words assembled, you are ready to reach out to people who need the construction services you offer. You can start with the people with whom you already have established a friendly connection, the members of your "club" I

COMING UP

Resistance to Marketing

A First Step into Marketing

Your Natural Client Network

Connecting with Prospective Clients

Your Most Important Marketing

The Three Laws of Marketing

Advertising

Your Client Ring

The farther out you attempt to reach in the rings of possible clients, the more complex, costly, and questionable the marketing you will need to do.

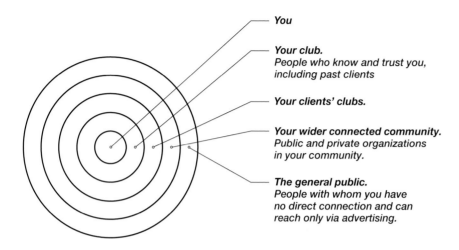

You

Your club.
People who know and trust you, including past clients

Your clients' clubs.

Your wider connected community.
Public and private organizations in your community.

The general public.
People with whom you have no direct connection and can reach only via advertising.

like to call them. One builder, whose company grew to the point it was doing millions of dollars worth of high-end remodeling annually, began by letting women on her softball team know she was available for small home improvement jobs. Another successful builder began by offering repair and improvement services to his church members.

I made my first sale to a motorcycling buddy. I built him a little shop for his classic English bike and woodworking tools.

Sources of Jobs

- Realtors
- Property-management firms
- Other builders
- Building materials suppliers
- Home improvement centers
- Small businesses and large corporations
- Universities, colleges, schools
- Public-housing agencies
- Other government organizations
- Civic and professional organizations
- Classes, both those you take and those you teach

Then, as so often happens, he referred me to members of his "club," people I did not know but who were willing to consider me for their projects on the basis of his recommendation. Happy with my work, they in turn referred me to others in their circles of friends and colleagues.

While enjoying a growing flow of references, I also worked to develop connections with other possible customers in my immediate community beyond already established friendships. During encounters on the neighborhood sidewalks, at parties, in coffee shops, or between games of pick-up basketball, I found opportunities to slip in my 25 words. By such "networking," as it has come to be called, I gathered some good projects—a concrete retaining wall, an office renovation, a second-story addition. In later years, when I would brag that I had never advertised, that my business had been built up entirely by "word of mouth," my wife would gently remind me, "That's right, dear, *your* mouth."

After a short time, I reached out further to organizations in my community with which I had some connection, however slight. I called on realtors, architects, schools, law firms. I asked building inspectors who had spoken favorably of my work to introduce me to the agencies that handled renovation in low-income neighborhoods—and as a result got some large and challenging jobs early in my career. Everywhere, I found projects.

Whether your emphasis is residential work or commercial work, through networking you will be able to connect with individuals and organizations in your own community that need what you offer. A number of the traditional possibilities are listed at left. About several of them I should sound a few words of caution. While there are surely exceptions, realtors and property-management firms are notorious for squeezing contractors to do work cheaply. Home improvement centers, while selling a huge percentage of the remodeling jobs now done in the U.S., want as much of the profit in the job as possible to be attached to the materials and fixtures they provide. That means they don't leave much to be attached to your pay for installation. You may have a hard time preserving enough margin to cover your overhead, much less allow for a profit.

On the other hand, with each job that you do through a home improvement center (or lumberyard), you have a chance to add important "friends" to the inner circle of your client ring. You contract for a bathroom remodel through a home improvement center, do a great job, and the clients recommend you to members of their club. With these new clients you have a better shot at preserving a fair margin.

At the same time, you may be surprised how well you can do with other organizations in your community. One builder has established an excellent business by serving the construction needs of a bank corporation with utter reliability. Another wins a steady stream of projects from a university testing laboratory. A third enjoys a flow of jobs at fair overhead and profit markups from a very large commercial construction firm for whom he handles the smaller projects of their clients. Many builders have acquired good long-term clients in the design professions—a market so important we will deal with it later in a section all its own.

Connecting with prospective clients

If you do go out into your community, talk to people, and tell them about the services you offer, your phone will ring. On the line will be a prospective client wanting to tell you about his project. Now it's show time! You have arrived at a crucial moment, especially if you don't know the person, because, as sales experts

point out, you only get one chance to make a first impression (and, I might add, you only get one chance to form your own first impression of the client).

Builders handle that crucial moment in different ways. Some ask callers a detailed series of questions to determine if they are interested in the project. One hard-nosed guy claims to put callers through a sieve so fine he disqualifies 80 percent as he sorts out the few focused on finding a reliable builder, not just a low price.

Others adopt a less strict approach. Personally, I rarely close the door on a potential client during an initial phone call. There are exceptions. There was the guy who, 45 seconds into our conversation, demanded to know, "What's the absolute lowest price per square foot you have ever built for?" Realizing I had run into a true "bottom feeder" (to use an old industry adage), I suggested we were probably not destined to work together since I sell "value, not price" and let him end the conversation with a disdainful good-bye. In general, though, even if I suspect I will not work with the prospec-

Phone Interview Checklist
■ Clients' mailing address, phone and Fax numbers, E-mail address
■ Project address
■ How client learned about your company
■ Description of project
■ Reasons for wanting to build project
■ Designer
■ Stage of design
■ Progress in applying for permit
■ What client is looking for in a builder
■ Preferred process for choosing builder
■ Openness to process other than competitive bidding
■ Preferred schedule
■ Flexibility in schedule
■ Budget

tive client because their project seems poorly conceived or underfunded, I listen to their ideas and try to offer constructive feedback. I enjoy the teaching, see it as part of the service I offer, and have a more self-interested motivation as well. Quite a few people I have helped have referred me to good jobs, even though I never drove a nail on their project.

I have always instinctively favored a relaxed conversational style for initial phone contacts, and in recent years I have heard sales experts advise that approach. Lean back in your chair or wander around your office as you get acquainted, they urge. If the caller seems receptive, you can offer a bit of your expertise: "Well, you're not alone there, worrying about the cost of structural changes," you might say. "But really, in my experience they're usually pretty straightforward. What you're describing sounds very doable. I will take a careful look at the structural issues when we meet at your place."

Using the conversational style, you will find that almost everything you need to know about the project will come naturally to the surface in the course of 15 to 20 minutes. If it does not, at the end of the call, you can ask a few questions to pick up the balance of what you need to know. If you are interested in going fur-

> S elling is not a performance art.

ther with the prospective client, you likely will suggest a face-to-face meeting.

First meetings with prospective clients

As with initial phone contacts, builders handle initial face-to-face meetings with potential clients in a variety of ways. But there does seem wide agreement among successful builders on certain guidelines. Though they will make exceptions, they generally push for a meeting during regular working hours. If the clients resist, the builder explains that given the cost, duration, and complexity of construction jobs, it really is important that both clients and builder be fresh and at their best for the first discussion of the project. Some builders go further, explaining to clients who continue to resist that evenings and weekends are reserved for their children. Generally, I am told, that does the trick. If it doesn't, unless the clients' circumstances absolutely do not permit a working hours meeting, a refusal probably signals that they are grinders of the type you best avoid anyhow.

For the initial meeting, successful builders generally dress like professionals, which for some means canvas work pants, for others a conservative sport coat and low-key tie, but for all means neat and clean. They show up on time. They'll tell you that they have won jobs by being punctual while every competitor was late.

Once inside the clients' home or office, builders who are good at marketing devote themselves to *listening*. They understand that selling is not a performance art. The meeting is not about you. It is about the clients' project. You listen to their nuts-and-bolts descriptions of their plans. You listen for their underlying dreams and hopes. Understanding that they may be self-conscious—after all, you are an old hand at this and they are beginners—you encourage them along with "active

Guidelines for Meeting Clients

- Encourage meeting during regular working hours.
- Require that all decision-makers (both spouses, all partners, etc.) be at the first meeting.
- Dress in comfortably professional fashion.
- Arrive on time.
- Listen! Listen! Listen!
- Use your portfolio sparingly.
- Never give off-the-top estimates.
- Always get the clients' budget.

listening"—nods, smiles, recognition of good points, occasional questions to help them sharpen their focus. "So am I getting it right?" you ask. "What you envision is..."

One capable builder I know feels so strongly about keeping his own agenda in the background and "bonding with the clients over their project" that he brings only a notepad and pencil to the first meeting. Other builders carry a thin portfolio of past work and hold their presentation to 5 or 10 minutes. While I respect these approaches, I prefer to bring an extensive portfolio, as described at right, but I use it flexibly. Some clients skim though it quickly, and that's fine. Others become absorbed, and the portfolio serves to bring us together in further conversation about their project.

The money thing

Savvy builders adhere to two other guidelines for initial client meetings: They never give an off-the-top estimate. They make certain to get the clients' budget. They know that if you give an estimate that is too low, you are stuck with it. Hit the number dead-on, and if the clients are not ready for it, you'll be shown the door. Guess high, and you may kill the project or your own participation in it. On top of that, as we will discuss further in later chapters, estimating is something you want to get paid for. You don't want to just give one away.

If the clients do ask for an estimate, you can explain that an accurate estimate takes careful work and inaccurate ones do damage, or that without plans and specifications you don't really know what to estimate. If the clients press for "a ballpark figure," you might like to joke, as I do, "a ballpark's a big place. You want a bunt or a line drive to left center?" Clients get the point. A ballpark estimate will not be close enough to their likely costs to be of much value.

My Portfolio, and Yours

I visit clients with a briefcase containing four binders of job photos and documents. Three are conventional. They contain before-and-after photos of past jobs, letters of appreciation from clients, and articles about my company's work. These portfolios build the new clients' confidence that I have the experience necessary to build their project. Specific photos usually catch the clients' attention and stimulate conversation.

The fourth of my binders I call my "management portfolio." It intersperses photos illustrating construction from foundation through finish with the forms and documents I use in managing projects (a subject we will take up in our closing chapter). The management binder makes visible to clients the behind-the-scenes effort my company makes to ensure that projects are organized tightly as well as crafted tightly. The portfolio makes an impact on clients. They worry about whether their project will be managed well. They have heard the horror stories about disorganized contractors.

Even when you are just starting out you can create effective portfolios. Collect photos of work you have done as a tradesman. Gather letters of recommendation from past bosses or from clients for whom you have done side jobs. Mix into your portfolio the management forms you will learn to use for controlling your projects. With imaginative use of just a few photos, letters, and forms, you can create a starter portfolio that will demonstrate your competence, stimulate conversation, and help build a connection between you and potential clients.

Alternately, you may want to turn the request for an estimate around and ask the clients what they think, what they have in mind as a budget for the project. One way or the other, you need to ask for the clients' budget. Many builders fail to do so. That was vividly illustrated at a marketing seminar I attended a few years back. The speaker asked how many of the 60 or so attendees inquired about budget during initial phone conversations with prospective clients, or failing that, during first meetings. Only one person other than me raised his hand. I was startled. The speaker was not. She knew to expect the response, and she went right to work straightening out her audience. You need to know the budget. If you don't, you can put in huge amounts of time estimating and bidding projects that can be built only for a price so low the builder will lose money on it.

To get their budget, I ask clients, "May I raise the subject of cost?" If they hesitate, I explain I can't put in the great amount of time it takes to produce a good estimate if I am not assured they have a realistic idea of costs. Fair-minded clients respond. I have rarely had clients refuse to give me their budget (and the same holds true for other builders who make certain to ask their clients what they think they can reasonably spend on their projects).

When I hear the budget I try to tell the client where it stands in relation to reality. Sometimes I have to say, "I just don't know. I won't know until I do some detailed estimating." *If you are just starting out in business, just coming to terms with construction costs and unable to gauge budgets quickly, such a response will keep you out of trouble while at the same time winning clients' confidence in your integrity.* To most budgets, I am able to say, "That's not going to get you everything on your wish list, but it should be enough for what I, at least, would consider a nice project. To really know, however, we need to develop a preliminary design and estimate." Occasionally I have to say, "If that is your limit, I advise you to not undertake this project. You will end up

with a lowball contractor who may lead you into terrible trouble." People appreciate that feedback also.

One remodeler tries never to close the door on clients whose budget is inadequate. If he has to tell them that their budget is low for the project they originally called about, he'll ask if they have other work they have been considering or will even suggest possibilities. Sometimes he meets clients to talk about a kitchen remodel and ends up with a contract to renovate a bathroom.

Just how you proceed after your initial meeting with prospective clients will depend on the type of work you do. If you are a specialty contractor doing standardized work such as roofing, siding, window replacement, or plug-in bathroom remodels, you may be able to go back to your office and get off a proposal immediately. If you are doing custom work, leave the clients a brief statement describing your company and a list of references. A week or so later call to inquire whether they are interested in working with you and affirm your interest if you want to build their project. If you do not or suddenly have gotten too busy to take care of them, let the clients know right away. Remember, they are now part of your network, people with whom you have shared ideas about a project near and dear to them. Honor the relationship; it is valuable.

The most important marketing you do

With careful listening at initial meetings and attentive follow-up, you will win projects. Building those projects is the most important marketing you do. Build well, and you will be referred on by satisfied clients to their personal friends and other members of their club. Those referrals inspire trust and open doors like no other connection can. As an old marketing axiom has it, you tell a potential

The Three Laws of Marketing for Builders

1. Build and they will come!

2. Build and they will forget you!

3. Do not let them forget you!

client you'll do a good job and that's a sales pitch. One of their friends tells them the same thing, and it's a fact.

Building well includes tight construction and good management, putting up structures that are plumb and level, waterproof, skillfully trimmed out, and completed on schedule. It also includes courtesy toward clients. A few years ago, a survey revealed that 70 percent of the time when people did not go back to a contractor after doing one project with him or her it was because of discourtesy. Builder's courtesy includes patience and respect along with everyday politeness. It means listening carefully to client questions, no matter how naive or edgy, and giving thoughtful and honest answers. It means keeping clients fully informed of what is going on with their project.

Builder's courtesy includes keeping a job site neat. Clients and their neighbors justifiably resent cowboy contractors turning job sites into trash heaps for months on end. Keep your debris in bins. Sweep up. Stack your material neatly. With debris and litter-strewn sites the norm, your orderly site will distinguish you as a class act. I've had calls from prospective clients who took the looked-after appearance of one of our sites to be a sign that we did the actual construction work with care, too. They were right.

Build well in all ways and the references will come. For clients, references are a way of saying thanks to you for a job well done. They are a way of helping their friends; it's not easy to find good builders. Giving you an enthusiastic reference is even a way of bragging a little: "Hey," the clients are saying, "I got my job done right!"

Marketing axioms

"Build and they will come," though surely the first principle of construction marketing, is only the first of three vital

A List of Reminders

There are innumerable ways to make sure your clients do not forget you. The ways I like best involve service, education, or something useful. My least favorite way is the Christmas Eve delivery of a bottle of Scotch. I got such a bottle of Scotch once—it was delivered by the only subcontractor I ever had to take to court, and I don't like hard liquor. Maybe that incident prejudiced me against a grand old tradition. But I do think service is more effective marketing than booze. It is not as readily forgotten once the bright blush of the holiday season has passed.

Ways to Make Sure Clients Don't Forget You:

- Call or write to ask about a project during the warranty period.
- Check in on the project after the warranty period has expired.
- Provide minor free maintenance after the warranty period.
- Send a friendly letter accompanied by a building maintenance checklist for the coming season or year.
- Provide a list of tips on how to make a home healthier, safer, and more energy efficient.
- Send a postcard with a picture of a recent project of yours and some helpful information.
- Send a Thanksgiving card listing subcontractors whom you recommend for service work.

builder's laws of marketing. My own lesson on the other two came as I stepped out of my truck in a parking lot. A woman passing by called out, "David?" I recognized her as a wonderful client I'd worked for years earlier. In a brief conversation I learned she had assumed I was no longer in the building business and wished she'd known I was. She had just finished an extensive remodeling of her home with a terribly disorganized contractor who had needed 18 months to do the job—a very nice half-year project for one of my crews.

With that encounter, I began to grasp the other laws of marketing. No matter how good a job you do for clients, their appreciative memory of you will dim. *They will forget you.* You can't afford to let that happen. *Don't let them forget you.*

When builder Robert Malone completed his first design/build restaurant project, he sent out a card to past clients and professional associates to let them know he was available for more such work in the future and recommended they give the restaurant a try. The card meshed nicely with another of Malone's marketing efforts— an annual letter featuring a comprehensive list of his favorite places to eat.

Of the many ways of keeping your relationship with past customers alive, most powerful is active servicing of their projects. If they don't call you, contact them in a month, then in a few months, and again a year after completing their project. Practically plead for an opportunity to make any needed adjustments, for often your best customers will not want to bother you with "piddling little things."

You may find those calls hard to make. We all cringe at the thought of going back to old projects; we have so much to do on our current ones. Actually trying to gener-ate callbacks really goes against the grain. But taking care of problems at a past project will like nothing else reignite the customers' enthusiasm and their desire to refer you to their friends. One builder advises: "Treat warranty work like an emergency. Get it done within 24 hours." Yes! It's both the right thing to do and an invaluable opportunity to market with service instead of hype. As Larry Hayden, owner of the 75-year-old Federal Building Company and one of my mentors, taught me years ago, "You're much better off spending your time with an existing client than you are going out and looking for 10 new ones. They're your best salespeople."

As the years pass, however, servicing of projects is not enough to keep you in touch with past clients. You can't reasonably keep going back to their projects forever. They are likely to lose track of you. Believe it or not, they will even forget your name and lose your phone number. You must, as I learned in that parking lot encounter, have a program to keep alive your connection to past customers—and also all the other members of your inner client rings. There are many ways to do so, and I have suggested a few in the sidebar on p. 107. You can learn about many more from the marvelous tape *Low Cost, High Impact Marketing* by builder/marketer extraordinaire Devon Hartman (see Resources on p. 258).

Other marketing

Beyond adhering to the three laws in order to sustain a referral-based business, some builders choose to do other marketing—namely, advertising. Personally, I question its value. I think advertising is not only of little value to general building contractors, but it is likely to be counterproductive. It can readily cost you more than you receive.

While I cannot advocate for advertising, I can tell you about the surprisingly

Other Marketing

- Business cards
- Brochures
- Mailings
- Job site signs
- Truck signs
- Yellow Pages
- Web sites
- Listings with referral services

divergent points of view builders have about even the most taken for granted forms of advertising. Take business cards to begin with. One builder claims to distribute about 25,000 a year (now, that's advertising)! He sticks a cluster on every grocery store billboard he passes, leaves a couple with every tip at a restaurant, hands them out in the grocery line. He probably drops a few into the basket when the minister sends it down the aisles at church services. He seems to think his time and money is well spent. But on the other side, there's the canny old-timer, among the most prominent builders in the U.S. during his time. Here's what he says about business cards: "Forget 'em. Leave 'em in the drawer. You meet someone, have a nice little chat, and give them your card. You know what happens. You never hear from them again. Tell 'em, 'I don't have my card with me, but if I could get your phone number and address, I'd love to send you something.' Their address goes into your contact file. Then every year they get a nice card from you. One day they will call you about a project."

Similarly, many builders invest heavily to have beautiful brochures designed and printed. But one builder points out that brochures become obsolete rapidly as the economy changes. You print them up during a boom period when you are seeking large projects. Then the economy dives. Now it's the service side of your business you need to remind clients of. While you drum up small jobs, the old brochures become stale.

Likewise, with job site signs and truck signs, builders invest in them reflexively. But when I surveyed builders about the results some years ago, their justifications were vague. "They keep our name out there." None reported actually getting work from the signs. No surprise, I thought. Americans are blitzed

Web Referral Services: A Skeptical View

Web referral services are in the business of making money by charging contractors for recommendations to potential clients. The services advertise themselves to the general public as a source of prequalified contractors. Owners who respond are asked to E-mail descriptions of their projects for referrals to contractors willing to give bids. The owners do not pay for the referrals. Instead, the contractors pay for being referred.

The problem with subscribing to these services as a builder is that although the services boast about their process for qualifying contractors, it doesn't take much to qualify. Basically, any contractor who has managed to remain in business a few years and who can provide minimal references will make it through. As a result, when you seek referrals via a Web service, many of the guys you will be invited to bid against are likely to be marginal operators.

For the privilege of bidding against them you will pay the service not only a subscriber fee. You pay a percentage of the contract price of each job you win. While that percentage may look like only a very small portion of the contract price, it will translate into a *very high percentage of the potential profit.* Thus, the Web referral services push builders' major dilemma—the presumption by the public that it's your job to provide estimates without charge, even though estimating is highly skilled work—to a new level. Now you not only provide free estimates—you pay through the nose for the opportunity!

with a couple of thousand ads a day. What chance did a builder have to be heard amidst the general din by affixing his company name to a small sign and sticking it out by the lumber pile? More recently, however, I have met a few builders who report getting good projects or even a steady stream of inquiries from their signs.

Why the change? It may be that my first survey reflects results during a slow period while the later reports come from a boom time when clients were having difficulty finding builders and were more willing to call someone whose name they had picked off a sign. Or it may be that the difference results from the quality of the

COMING UP

Benefits of Working with
Design Professionals

Hazards

Evaluating Designers

Building Successfully
with Designers

Realistic Expectations

signage used by the people I was talking to. I *have* come to suspect that results do vary according to the quality and visibility of the signage. Almost certainly, if you use signage—job site, truck, or other—you need to do it right. Too often I see signs done in a delicate rose and lavender scroll, readable from no more than 17 inches away and tilting crazily out of debris-littered mud at a project site. Great marketing, huh? Signage needs to be attractive but it also must be clear, with large and visible lettering. It should be placed in a way and against a background that suggests competence. Why put a sign on that rusting 19-year-old pickup that looks like it just went through an encounter with the Terminator?

Beyond business cards, brochures, job signs, and truck signs, advertising gets even dicier. For years contractors have tried Yellow Page ads. Though some specialty contractors, like my painter, report good results, builders generally tell me they get endless "tire kickers" seeking free information. After the Yellow Pages, we come to the world of newspaper and radio ads and Web referral services. But aside from my editorial in the sidebar on p. 109, I will leave them alone and end this chapter by advising that if you do invest in any advertising, track the results very carefully. Set up a chart. On it record every call you get from prospective clients. Record the way in which they learned about you—referral from a past customer, job site sign, Yellow Page ad, etc. Keep track of which connections lead to good jobs and which result in your simply wasting lots of time on the phone and in meetings with clients who are not candidates for working with your company. From such tracking you'll see which marketing actually brings in good business. And you will find out which merely wastes your time and enlarges your overhead more than your profit margin.

Connecting with Design Professionals

One source of work deserves a section all to itself, and that is the community of "design professionals" (a term I use somewhat loosely to include the whole spectrum of designers from architects and engineers to kitchen designers, interior designers, and space planners). Builders often are able to develop relationships with design professionals that bring them one job after another over the course of many years. Those jobs can be financially rewarding. It is true that there is a built-in tension between a builder's profit margin and the designer's desire to have all the details and features he includes in his designs actually built. Many builders complain about design professionals squeezing their profit margin too tightly. But at the same time, though it is rarely noted, there is a significant financial benefit from having a design firm pump a steady stream of projects into your pipeline. They are minimizing your overhead. They are saving you the marketing effort that you would otherwise have to make to bring in those projects.

At its best, a good working relationship with a professional designer offers great rewards beyond the financial ones. You join forces with the designer at the conception of the project. As the designer develops plans, you provide cost estimates and input about construction methods and materials to help create as high quality a project as the owners' budget will allow. The designer seizes upon your ideas or politely explains why he or she would rather go a different direction, and thereby increases your understanding of the design. The result is a design you feel invested in and that has a good probability of being built by you.

If you do build the project, the chances are good that when it is done

Working with professional designers, you get involved in challenging and interesting projects. This stairwell, built by Gerstel's crew and designed by architect Mike Thomas and engineer Tek Pei, rises four stories from the basement to a rooftop skylight, houses the owner's extensive library, and also acts as a main structural element, anchoring the home against earthquakes.

Building this small but complex studio, which was designed by architect John McLean and engineer Tek Pei, for a steep, downhill lot tested the craft and management skills of Gerstel's company and delighted the photographer, who now works in its sunshine-filled rooms.

you will be able to stand back and admire your work, and that you will have something substantial to show to future clients. Projects that involve a design professional are typically of superior quality. Charles Miller, a senior editor at *Fine Homebuilding* magazine, states the case crisply: "Knowing how to build is important only after you know what to build. Buildings designed by builders are often awful, just terrible. They squander materials."

Good designers bring special skills to the table. Architect John McLean writes that sunlight is among his most powerful design tools. Sunlight, he explains, can "define, dramatize, animate, and color the buildings and the rooms that it brightens. When handled with artistic intent and skill, it can give us much pleasure" and add "value to the buildings and the interior spaces that capture [it] in abundance and in striking ways." How many builders, intent on the linear processes of construction and business management, have learned to think like that? Not me.

Hazards

While there are rewards to be had from working with design professionals, it is also true that there is much tension between the designer and builder camps. The uneasiness designers feel about builders comes about, among other causes, as a result of builders ignoring the details in their plans and undermining the designers' relationship with owners. Their fear was neatly captured by the architect who suggested the first edition of this book be marketed to design schools with the subtitle "Know Thy Enemy." For their part, builders speak with frustration about an arrogant and cavalier attitude toward builders and a sloppiness around construction cost issues among designers. They complain as well of serious inadequacies in the plans designers' produce.

The puzzling, off-putting condescension that permeates the design profession's stance (though by no means the stance of individual designers) toward the people who actually build their visions is a subject fit for a separate book. Here I will confine myself to offering a couple of characteristic examples. A few years ago, *The Not So Big House*, written by architect Sarah Susanka, was published to promote to homeowners the idea of building beautifully crafted smaller homes rather than the crummy mini-mansions being slapped up all over the country. The book admirably accomplishes its mission, using wonderful photos and clear, concise prose. The singular problem with it is that not a line is spent explaining how homeowners might find and work with good builders. It is as if designers are the sole actors in the drama of producing well-crafted homes. Within the pages of the book, builders are consigned to invisibility.

Such dismissiveness is a feature not merely of design publications (where it is virtually universal). It comes up in the day-to-day encounters of builders with designers, as in the experience of a builder who rebuilt a Frank Lloyd Wright Usonian house that had been destroyed by fire. At completion of the project, when a local journalist showed interest in writing about it, the project's designer pushed for the article to focus entirely on *his* contribution. The builder listened in amusement for a while to the designer's

pitch and finally said to him, "So, you think the contractor's role is to just do the grunt work?" The designer answered unhesitatingly, "Yes."

While the condescension among design professionals is merely off-putting, or at worst insulting, other difficulties builders have with designers are of a practical nature. Builders complain of serious shortfalls in the plans produced by many design professionals—including architects and engineers, and even more so designers, such as those specializing in kitchens and baths, who must fulfill only relatively modest requirements to obtain their certifications. The plans are too vague to support efficient production of accurate estimates. Their details, as drawn, are nonbuildable. Dimensioning is contradictory. Structural elements conflict with mechanical and plumbing requirements. Waterproofing details seem deliberately designed to produce leaks. Window schedules are full of errors. Other items are left out altogether.

Most troubling of the difficulties in working with designers is the all too common disconnect between a design firm's plans and its clients' financial reality. Designers regularly sketch away without obtaining knowledgeable input on the costs of the construction they are dreaming up. As a result, the designers produce an expensive set of plans for a project far beyond the owner's budget. The owners then search frantically for someone who will commit to constructing this vision that has cost them thousands of dollars. Builder after builder is sucked into working up a bid for the job. And builder after builder, not to mention their many dozens of subs and suppliers, consumes countless hours pricing work they have no chance of ever doing— unless they make a very bad mistake and price it so low they will take a financial beating during construction.

> t is as if designers are the sole actors in the drama of producing well-crafted homes. Within the pages of the book, builders are consigned to invisibility.

Finding, qualifying, and succeeding with design professionals

Minimizing the hazards of working with design professionals and building successful relationships require systematic effort:

- Locate design firms whose work appeals to you and which you feel you are qualified to build.
- To the extent you reasonably can, evaluate them before marketing your services to them.
- Market your services with a focus on their needs, not your own.
- Take great care to respect the designers' concerns during the construction of their projects. Try to appreciate the difficulties they face and support them even while standing firm for your own interests.

You can locate designers in a number of ways. Go to meetings of their associations. Ask other builders to recommend designers they like working with. Note the names of firms posted at projects whose designs you like, though only if the construction work is of good quality. (You do not want to compete for the work of designers who are content to bring in cheap contractors who do a shoddy job.) Before attempting to contact the designers, learn what you can about them from fellow builders.

Especially if you are just starting out, make a particular effort to gauge designers' experience in the kind of work at which you are competent. You want to find designers whose experience and interests align with your own. They will have the expertise to produce the good plans you will need to work efficiently. They will understand the protocol of designer and builder relationships for the type of work you do. Protocol varies greatly from area to area of construction.

Qualifying Designers

Learn what you can about a design firm before embarking on a working relationship. Important questions to ask of your fellow builders about design firms include:

- What kinds of projects are they experienced and competent at designing?
- What proportion of their projects get built; what proportion "go in the drawer"?
- Are they successful at designing to budget?
- Do they value good craftsmanship and management and accept their cost?
- Do they tend to sacrifice building quality (or the builder) to get their designs constructed?
- How complete, clear, and competent are their drawings?
- Will you be able to rely on them for prompt answers to your questions during construction?
- If they will be involved in approving change orders, are they fair?
- At a project's conclusion, do they make up a reasonable punch list promptly?
- If you build well for them, will they be interested in involving you in future projects on a basis other than competitive bidding?
- If you refer them work, can they be counted on to not feed it to other builders?

Commercial work tends to be hardball. Residential work tends to include more give and take. Thus, if certain designers you are considering might be interested in you for the occasional remodel they do for a friend, but their main line is commercial interiors for Sneaker Rebellion, Dungarees Forever, and Tank Tops 'R Us, that should raise red flags. Their remodel plans are likely to be sketchy and to include inappropriate details. If you decide to work with them, expect to have a lot of difficulty both estimating from and building from their plans.

When qualifying designers, bear down hard on the subject of change orders. You want designers who are fair about them, who make it clear to owners that items not included in their plans

f a design firm has
strengths and is a good
source of projects, you can
find ways to work around
its deficiencies.

will inevitably turn up during construction and that owners, not builders, are responsible for their costs. Such extras can be embarrassing to designers, and some do attempt to slough off the cost onto builders.

Finally, but by no means of least importance, try to find designers who welcome working with builders on a "cost planning" or "negotiated" basis, such as described in the section beginning on p. 133, as opposed to solely a competitive bid basis. Such designers are like gold to builders. They are the ones you really want to build a relationship with.

Once you have a reasonably good take on a design firm and feel it might be worthwhile to establish a relationship, arrange a meeting. Write a letter, send in your resume, call, or do all three. Offer to meet the designers in their offices. They will probably expect that, and it is a good chance for you to continue evaluating them. As you look around the office do you see photos of completed projects, or do you see largely presentation drawings? If it's the latter, beware. With some firms, a high percentage of projects that are designed are never constructed. If you get involved with such a firm, you can burn hours estimating projects that will not be built.

Be prepared when you go to the meeting to present your portfolio. The designers will want to see what you've built and determine whether you are qualified to build their projects. But at least as important, just as when you visit potential clients, be prepared to listen attentively. The designers do not want to see you glance over the plans for a project and declare "Oh yeah, I built 10 of these." Again, Charles Miller of *Fine Homebuilding* explains: "[Designers] live in fear that builders will take some shortcut that will sabotage the effect of their details." They want reassurance that you understand and will respect the uniqueness of their work.

Building with design professionals

Once work on a project has started, it is primarily by taking great care to respect their plans that you will build enduring and mutually beneficial relations with designers. "So much of our work is based on trust that we are working in the owner's best interest," explains one architect. "Nothing can blow that trust like the contractor saying, 'See the way the architect drew this? We could save you a lot of money and do it better.' " If you have a question about the plans, route it through the designer. It is the right and respectful thing to do, and you'll build future business.

In return for your support you can expect the designers in turn to abide by certain fundamental ground rules:

DESIGNERS MUST NEVER GIVE AWAY YOUR PROJECTS If a design firm hooked you up with one of their clients, they would be rightfully outraged if you suggested another designer to the owner. Likewise, if you bring a designer into a job, the designer must take care to not undermine your relationship with the clients.

BUILDERS DO NOT PAY FOR OMISSIONS IN THE DRAWINGS Construction projects include thousands of items of work. Not every single one will be anticipated during design. Normally, the owners should pay for those items. The fact that owners are finding out about them during construction does not relieve them of responsibility of paying for the work they receive. Designers sometimes are responsible for oversights, and to protect against the risk they have available errors and omissions insurance, though it is often prohibitively expensive for small firms. Builders should not be asked to pay for unanticipated items unless the need to build them was clearly implied by details that were brought out in the drawings and specifications.

BUILDERS DO NOT PAY FOR OUT-RIGHT ERRORS BY THE ARCHITECT THAT RESULT IN WASTED MATERIALS
An architect I know once specified a load of custom windows. When they arrived at the job site, it was discovered they could not be made to work with the design. He willingly, if sadly, paid for them and took them home to his basement.

While you do want your designers to abide by the rules, you should cut them a bit of slack. Design of good buildings—graceful and functional, comfortable yet efficient, uplifting of the spirit while up to code—is difficult to achieve, and plans for those buildings must provide an immense amount of information. So you may want to appreciate that if a design firm's plan sometimes seem insufficiently detailed, it's not necessarily because the designers are negligent. Rather, it may be because they can't charge enough to include the level of detail they would like to put in. As it is, design firms frequently invest many unbilled hours on their projects simply out of a desire to get them right, and to enable the builders to get them right.

If a design firm has strengths and is a good source of projects, you can find ways to work around its deficiencies. A young builder told me how he had established a successful working relationship with an architect that several of his more senior competitors found frustratingly difficult. "Sure, she's volatile. Her details are sketchy, and she gets pissed off if you bother her about them during a project. But she's talented. She's fun. She sends us good jobs. So we just count on doing a bit of design completion for her and allow for the projected cost in our estimates."

Evaluating Projects

In the process of marketing your services, networking with potential clients, and connecting to design professionals, you will have already begun the process of evaluating potential projects. With clients, you have learned their budget, listened to their hopes and wishes. You have a preliminary sense of whether they are being realistic and probably a good first take on the kind of working relationship you might have with them. With designers you have gone even further, finding out what you can about their competence, responsiveness, and attitude toward builders.

The process of evaluating projects, however, should be extended beyond those initial takes. To continue evaluating a project as you get deeper into it, you should concern yourself with several broad issues: the owner's attitude toward builders, funding for the project, the quality of the design services, and the project's fit with your own and your company's capabilities.

Eventually you may be able to evaluate projects intuitively. Early in your career, if you have repeatedly gotten yourself into bad projects or if you feel uncertain about a project, you should evaluate them using the kinds of checklists and forms that we will discuss in this chapter. You want to learn to recognize and turn away from bad projects as promptly as possible. Estimating and planning projects that you have little chance of building or that you should not be building adds enormously to your overhead burden. Winning the wrong one is worse. I will spare you the "blood on the tracks" stories, but I have seen a single job go bad and wipe out the benefits a builder had accrued from many successful ones. I have even seen a bad job destroy a company.

COMING UP

Grinders

Co-contracting with Owners

The Clients You Want

Evaluating a Project's Fit

Glamour Projects and Glamour Volume

Benefits of Small Projects

Portrait of a Grinder

It was the late 1980s. George and Sally Smith called their architect friend, Jerome Nice, and asked him to design a home for the lot they had purchased. To avoid paying the cost of a full set of plans, the Smiths struck a deal with Nice. He would reduce his fee to a minimum. They would accept minimally detailed plans and work with a builder selected by Nice whom he could count on to not take advantage of the plans and cut corners during construction.

Immediately upon receiving the plans, the Smiths ditched Nice's builder and solicited bids from half a dozen others. When their bids came in clustered around $200,000, the Smiths shopped further, finally finding a tract builder who agreed to build their custom home for $130,000.

Once construction was under way, the Smiths capitalized on the plans' sketchiness to pounce on the builder for free upgrades. Those rough Mexican pavers in the foyer, they insisted, constituted a "tripping hazard." They had to be torn out and replaced with a more refined and costly product. The standard brass-plated hinges on the doors did not properly complement other decor. They had to be replaced with polished steel hinges. The exterior paint did not exactly match the sample chip. The charges for the paint job should be voided. So George and Sally went, grinding down the builder till undoubtedly they got their house for less than his material and labor costs.

Grinders

If you stay in the building business long, you'll likely hear an industry expert voice a caution such as, "One out of five customers will do everything they can to prevent you from making a profit on his project." I am less pessimistic. Sure, people often have a pizza budget and a yen for lobster and steak, but they don't expect you to pick up the balance of their tab. Here and there, however, you do run into what one builder aptly calls a "grinder," someone who is going to try to manipulate a surf and turf dinner out of you for the price of fish sticks and a soft drink. Sometimes, they will tip their hand at your first meeting, like the guy who asked me for the absolute lowest square-foot price I had ever built for. But

in other cases they will hold their fire till late in negotiations, like the man who called me the day he was to sign our contract and asked if I could cut my price by 7 percent—which amounted to most of my markup for profit.

Grinders, though relatively few in number, do seem to be fairly evenly distributed across the spectrum of humanity—including the community of design professionals. Sometimes builders do not understand that early in their careers. When they get that first feeler from a well-established design firm, they think their careers have suddenly taken off, and they jump to meet the designer's demands for cutbacks in their charges. Do not make that mistake. While there are many fair-minded designers, there are others who make a career out of exploiting builders. One I know says that since his clients normally would not be able to afford the construction of his beloved details, he finds them contractors too naive to charge market prices. Another regularly reports that a contractor has barely survived one of his projects and declared, "I'd never do it for that price again." A third admits, he would "never get a commission" if he actually told clients what they should reasonably expect to pay to get their projects built.

Realism

Instead of grinding, what you want from owners and designers is realism tempered by a sense of fairness. Rather than pressing for fire sale prices, they respond thoughtfully when you explain, "Good construction is expensive; this may run more than you have in mind." They appreciate the value of your time. If they plan to put their project "out to bid," they are willing to limit themselves to the traditional three bids. They understand it is not fair to ask that you do the work of costing out their job if you are to have even less than a one in three chance of winning it. If they have not come to that realization on their own, they get it when you explain that estimating their job will take 10, or 20, or 40 hours of skilled work. "Oh my," they respond. "I had no idea!"

The clients you want grasp the reality that good construction must necessarily be preceded by design and planning. They do not expect you to deliver those services to them for free as part of an estimate that is also free. As they look to the construction itself, they do not attempt to reduce their own costs by slicing away at your fair margin for overhead and profit unless they transfer to themselves commensurate responsibility and risk. True, at the outset they may assume you will be delighted to work with brother Tom from Duluth who remodeled his own house all by himself! With naive excitement they tell you of their plans to fly Tom in for a week to run water supply lines and DWV, thereby saving themselves much of the cost of plumbing their project. Similarly, they'll take for granted that you will welcome their providing the kitchen cabinets so they don't have to pay your markup on them.

But when you explain the impact of their proposal from your point of view, they will get it. They will understand that by having Tom install the plumbing or by supplying cabinets and fixtures they put you in the position of working with an amateur in place of a member of your team of professional subs and suppliers. They will see that even as you take on the responsibility of supervising their amateur effort and cut your remuneration for the job, the span of time you will need to commit to it and your liabilities will not change at all, or will even increase. When you explain that is not a reality you can work with and offer guidelines under which you can fairly involve them in the project as a co-contractor they will accept them.

Respect

You want to work with an owner who, along with demonstrating a sense of financial reality joined with a sense of fairness, shows respect not only for the craft skills but also the management your company brings to a project. Even if you could feel okay walking away from a second-rate product, you simply cannot—in this century of total quality management enforced by the threat of litigation—go along with owners who claim they will accept mediocre work in exchange for cut-rate prices. Down that path await angry messages in your voice-mail box, costly callbacks, soaring insurance rates, and lawsuits.

Even owners who are looking for someone to do a skilled job of putting together their project do not necessarily realize how much behind-the-scenes management it takes to deliver good craftsmanship at the job site. You can tell them by their question, "Now, do you work on the job yourself?" By that they mean, "Do you drive nails? Do you saw lumber?" They do not want to pay you for anything else. They do not comprehend the need

Owners as Co-contractors

From time to time you will meet owners who qualify as good clients but who genuinely cannot afford to have you do all the work, or who want to play a hands-on role in the construction of their own shelter. For working with such "co-contractors," I have established a simple guideline. *The project must be organized so that there is a clear boundary between my work and the owners' work.* Owners can elect to do work at the front end of the job—typically deconstruction or excavation—but their work must be completed before the agreed upon start date for my crew. If it is not, my crew completes it for a fixed price or on a time and material basis, as I deem most fair. Similarly, the owners may take on tasks at any point during the finish sequence of their project, or even earlier. But from whatever point they do step in, they must take the project all the way through to completion.

for and cost of project management, much less the overhead costs of keeping a company up and running smoothly so that it's available to do their project in the first place and stand behind it for the long run. They think "profit" means wages for the carpentry, plumbing, etc., you personally do at the job site.

Sometimes you can turn on the light for such owners. The founder of a contractor referral service told me he had luck getting owners to appreciate the management function of good builders by inquiring, "Well, Mr. Jones, if you act as your own contractor you could potentially save the builder's fee for overhead and profit. How much of your time do you think you will use to do that? What is that time worth? How many mistakes do you think you can make before their cost has exceeded your potential savings?"

Maybe you will also have luck with such questions. But I have found that owners who do not appreciate management generally need to discover its value for themselves (sometimes over and over before the truth sinks in)! They need to experience the proverbial "contractor from hell" who is incessantly running short of materials, spreading too thin over too many projects and not turning up for days on end, leaving a dangerous tangle of nail-embedded lumber and trash spread over their property. Then their sense of reality shifts. They realize there is more to building a project than fitting pieces of material together. I sometimes tell potential clients, "I am rarely hired by owners who are building for the first time. I get hired the second time around, when they've learned what it takes to do a project right."

Funding

Before taking on a project, you need to make sure that you have an owner not only willing but able to pay you. Builders sometimes take an owner's declaration of a reasonable budget as a sign that funding is in place for a project. After all, if someone says they are going to invest thousands of dollars in a job, they must have it. Not necessarily. If the project is public work, quite likely. If a bank loan to cover the projected costs is in place, yes. But in other cases, maybe not. The Association of General Contractors warns, "Many contractors have gone broke because they didn't ask where the money was coming from to fund private jobs."

That builders do not, as a matter of course, check out clients for financial reliability is fairly incredible. We regularly make huge, short-term loans to our customers in the form of materials installed at their projects. You'd think it would be part of our standard business practices to make the small investment necessary to learn whether our expectation of being paid was grounded on anything more than blind faith. But it is not standard business practice. It is rare. As a result, even small-volume builders regularly report being ripped off for $5,000, $20,000, $50,000 at a pop, then facing the choice of letting their money go or taking on the distraction, cost, and anxiety of a lawsuit. If you want to make sure of getting paid, take two steps early in your relationship with an owner and the third when negotiating your construction agreement:

- Check the owner's credit.
- Check courthouse records for any history of civil litigation by or against the owner.
- Require that funds for construction be placed in an escrow account before work begins.

Credit and courthouse checks are an inexpensive way to assure you of a client's credit worthiness before getting deeply involved in the preconstruction phase of a project. Credit checks cost a

■ SAMPLE LETTERS AND FORMS   Project Evaluation Form

PROJECT EVALUATION FORM

Project: Smith Addition, Emeryville   Date: 1/16/2002

/----Trouble----/So-So/----O.K.----/
1   2   3   4   5   6   7   8   9   10

Category	Score	Comment
Client	9	Direct, fair, respectful
Designer	6	Responsive, plans sketchy
Funding	7.5	Budget a little tight
Schedule	9	We have opening
Type/Size	9	Up our alley
Crew Lead	7.5	Enrique – good, still learning our systems
Crew	7.5	Pete, Anna
Subcontractors	7.5	Project too far out for plumber; others o.k
Suppliers	6.5	Too far for Sugar City Concrete
Commute	6	Long; snarly traffic
Other Projects	6	Opposite direction from other main job

Overall/Conclusion — Avg. score 6.86 – Let's take it; work is slow and the clients will be good future references.

few dollars, court record checks not much more. One builder told me he'd been uneasy about a client from the first meeting, gone ahead and built her project anyhow, and was refused payment of his last bill for $20,000. Then he decided to stop off at the courthouse. With a little research, he discovered he was only one in a line of contractors she had bilked for big bucks.

Before actually beginning construction, you can take a fourth step to assure yourself of getting paid. *Require that funds for the project go into a joint control account at your bank from which neither you nor the client can make a withdrawal without the other's consent.* When a payment is due, you present a voucher to the owners. They sign off, thereby authorizing you to withdraw your money, and then you sign off to authorize transfer of the funds from the joint control account to your operating account. The owners can, of course, refuse to sign, but simply knowing the money's there in an account at your bank is a great reassurance and an advantage in the event of a legal dispute. (See Contracts on p. 185 for detail on the use of such accounts.)

Fit, glamour projects, and small ones

Though the owner and the funding pass muster, as you get more deeply involved with a project you may sense it may not be a good fit for you. If you are finding it difficult to estimate the direct costs of building the project, it is a tip-off that you may be operating outside your range of competence. Evaluating the project on paper as illustrated above can help you make a

Glamour Volume

Equally as dangerous as the glamour project is taking on more work than you should so that you, too, can puff your chest at the meeting of your builder's group and say, "Yeah, we've got a million plus already booked for this year." After warning others about glamour projects in the first edition of this book, I fell for glamour volume myself, taking on a number of large and complex jobs simultaneously and pushing my annual volume to double its previous levels. Because of outstanding work by my company's project leads, carpenters, and subcontractors we pulled through. My systems for construction, communication, and control, however, were all strained to the limit. I was barely able to keep up with change orders and job costing. Marketing fell by the wayside. And I took a loss of a sort I had not been aware existed. The pressure was so great, I was often on a short fuse and, as a result, damaged good relationships. I did get to puff my chest at builder's meetings, but the ego trip turned out not to be worth nearly the price of the ticket.

rational decision whether or not to move ahead with it. Using such a form (which you can easily create on your computer or by hand), you can grade a project one facet at a time, then average the grades to obtain an overall ranking as somewhere between big trouble and top notch.

As you can see, the hypothetical project scored in the illustration, qualified only weakly in several areas. It was out of the contractor's normal area of operation. A key sub and supplier would not be able to service it, and new, untested people would have to be found. The designer, while having a reputation for responsiveness to requests for information (RIFs), would have to be sent a lot of them because her plans were sketchy. The crew that would be doing the job was the company's newest. They were still getting dialed into the company systems. They would need extra management support and that would be doubly burdensome given the distance of the project from the other large job the company would be doing at the same time.

On the other hand, the crew was skilled. It was reliable. And in other respects, the job scored solidly to very high. Given that work was slow, that she needed projects, and the likelihood of the clients becoming good references for future projects, the contractor took on the project.

While use of an evaluation form will help you guide yourself to prudent decisions about many projects, it won't always save you from the siren song of the glamour job. Excited by its size, challenged by its complexity, thrilled by its beauty, awed by the prestige of its designer, seduced by the wealth or prominence of its owners, blinded by the profits it seems to promise, you can downplay the trauma it will cause you and score it higher than is realistic. "Often," one builder realized after spending a year working at minimum wage because of underestimating the difficulty of a project, "I have been so eager to do a job that I would do less (evaluating) of it than I should have. I have learned to be realistic, to not become so enamored of a project that I kid myself about what it will cost me to do it."

The glamour of a project, its potential to move you up a level or two in the construction world, can be a good justification for taking it, but not in isolation from more fundamental reasons. You still need to have a good shot at making a reasonable income doing quality work that will enhance your reputation and build future references. When you allow yourself to be seduced by a glamour job beyond your competence, you can take a double or triple hit. You suffer anxiety all through the project and lose money on it. You also lose the income and the satisfaction of the projects you could have been successfully doing instead. And you lose the references from those projects. Instead, you do damage to your reputation, for as you visibly stumble and struggle with the glamour project your client grows increasingly frustrated and angry. And angry clients, an old saying has it, will tell 10 times as many people about you as happy ones. You would have been much better off foregoing the big glamour job and taking on several smaller jobs. Thereby, instead of setting yourself back, you would have successfully sowed seeds from which future projects would sprout—including, no doubt, some real glamour jobs when you are ready for them.

Competitive Bidding

If you are building a network of clients, connecting with design professionals, and learning to systematically evaluate potential projects, you are well on your way to contracting for jobs successfully. But there is still considerable work to do. Over the years, builders have used three ways to cover the final mile to winning projects. They are competitive bidding, design/build, and a third way that goes under various names including "negotiated bidding" and "cost planning."

COMPETITIVE BIDDING   Builders who do competitive bidding submit a price—i.e., a "bid"—for the work shown on a set of plans in hopes of winning a contract for construction of the work. Contractors who build their businesses around competitive bidding know that their customers are typically focused on price, that quality is a secondary consideration (whether or not the owners admit it). To win a job, they realize, they will usually have to be the low bidder.

DESIGN/BUILD   Builders who operate design/build firms offer their customers one-stop shopping. They provide a complete package of services from design and estimating through construction. Design/builders realize that while price and quality are always a consideration for their customers, time is at a premium. They do not want to have to coordinate separate design and construction services; they want to walk into a design/build store and order their new kitchen or office and be done with it.

COST PLANNING   For the third way, builders use a variety of names. "Negotiated bidding" is favored by many. Others speak of offering "preconstruction services." In my work, I use the term "cost planning," and I have noticed that the term has caught on around the country. Builders who offer cost planning

COMING UP

Three Ways of Winning Jobs

The Appeal of
Competitive Bidding

Hazards

Making the Best of It

Beyond Competitive Bidding

Project Tree

Young Home

↑

Jabbar Second-Story Addition

↑

Levinson Kitchen

↑

Johnson Foundation

↑

Hui Deck

Every small project you do will seed a whole new branch of your client network. From time to time, I trace the origin of the large projects my company has built. I find myself going back to a small improvement, renovation, or repair job done years earlier.

Three Ways of Acquiring Work

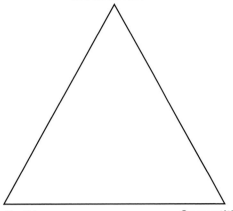

Cost planning
Builder teams with owner and designer through preconstruction and construction.

Design/build
Builder provides owners with one-stop shopping for complete services from design through construction.

Competitive bidding
Builder bids for construction contract against other builders by submitting as low a price as possible.

work in a team relationship with an owner and an independent designer from the conceptual stage of a project forward. Their job is to provide estimating and construction ideas to keep the developing project within budget and, just as importantly, to help optimize the quality of the project the owners will be able to build for the dollars they have available. Builders who provide cost planning typically tie preconstruction services to the actual construction of the project. They are offering cost plan/build just as design/builders offer linked design and construction services.

Like many other builders, while I see promise in both the design/build and cost planning approaches to acquiring construction jobs, I have misgivings about competitive bidding, in part because com-

The Competitive Bid

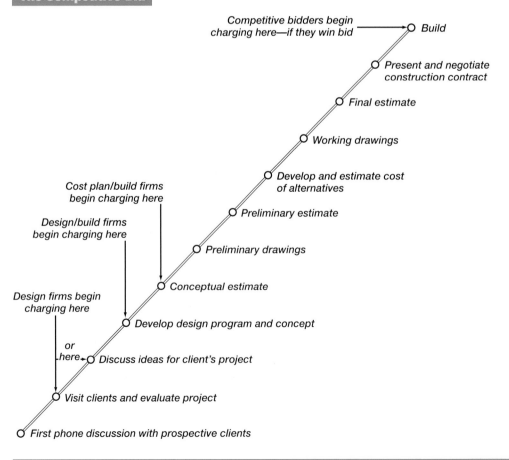

Competitive bidders begin charging here—if they win bid → **Build**

Present and negotiate construction contract

Final estimate

Working drawings

Develop and estimate cost of alternatives

Cost plan/build firms begin charging here

Preliminary estimate

Design/build firms begin charging here

Preliminary drawings

Conceptual estimate

Design firms begin charging here

Develop design program and concept

or here→ **Discuss ideas for client's project**

Visit clients and evaluate project

First phone discussion with prospective clients

pensation for builders kicks in so late, as illustrated in the graph on the facing page. Since builders don't get paid directly for competitive bids, they must recover the costs of bidding in their markups for overhead. Thereby, the people who hire them end up paying for the bids generated for the people who do not.

Toward the end of this chapter I will go further into the shortcomings of competitive bidding. But for here it must be granted that competitive bidding has a hold on many of the owners and designers with whom builders work. As builders we must, at the very least, understand its appeal and be prepared to make the best of it when circumstances require.

Competitive bidding's appeal to owners and designers

You've seen the standard newspaper feature, "How to get your construction project done without going crazy." It opens with a "contractor from hell" story, promises to lay out a strategy for success, and then proceeds to recite the mantra: Get three bids. View the bidders as if you were contending with an infestation of poisonous vipers. Check references for the lowest bidder, hire him, and during construction watch every move he makes.

These articles program the public to believe that the adversarial approach, pitting bidders against one another and the owner against the winner, is the one most likely to protect an owner from being ripped off by a contractor. Even when they don't buy fully into the adversarial approach, owners are drawn to competitive bidding as a form of price shopping. For many, price shopping is a must when it comes to big-ticket items, and construction projects are the biggest ticket items of all.

Moreover, from time to time, owners do get a real bargain by bid shopping. They get a low price from a good builder who needs their project to keep a crew busy or to pay his overhead during a slow time. The possibility for such a score enhances the appeal of competitive bidding to designers as well. Designers see it as an opportunity to get their client the best deal possible. They may even feel a legal obligation, a "fiduciary duty," as one designer puts it, to use competitive bidding as a means of protecting their clients' financial interests.

At times design firms reach for competitive bidding as not only the cheapest but the *only* way to get the their design built. Often, a design firm will discover late in the game that the experienced, reliable, and skilled contractors they prefer working with won't build their design for the dollars the owners can make available. That's when temptation sets in. "You want to believe the project can be done for the amount of money you have," explained one architect in a regretful tone. "You go out on the limb for the cheaper contractor." The limb you go out on is competitive bidding. At the end of it, you just might find that low price that matches the owner's budget. Frequently, the limb snaps off; owner and designer end up struggling through months of construction with a builder who is in way over his head. But then again, sometimes it does not.

Why builders do competitive bidding

For some, perhaps most builders, competitive bidding simply comes with their territory. It's their only avenue into projects. They do a type of commercial or public work for which it is not often possible to win contracts by any other means. Some builders who might be able to go down another road actually

> These articles program the public to believe that the adversarial approach, pitting bidders against one another and the owner against the winner, is the one most likely to protect an owner from being ripped off by a contractor.

> f you do no competitive
> bidding, you can lose your
> edge. You lose touch with
> marketplace realities
> and grow lazy at
> controlling costs.

prefer competitive bidding for the relatively arm's-length nature of the process. Owners ask you for a bid. You give it. It's low. You win. You feel no obligation to warn of problems in the design or hold the hand of an anxious client. You just build to the plans and specs. That's it. As one contractor says, "You get the job, get it done, get your money, get out. I like it that way."

A few builders seize upon competitive bidding as a fast track to high volumes of work. They pay wages as low as they can get away with, squeeze their subcontractors and suppliers, rush work to completion, build to the loosest standard that will pass inspection. Thereby they position themselves to bid work as tightly as possible, bid a lot of it, and win often. Using such a "lowballer" strategy, one builder—notorious for the shabbiness of his work but envied for the ubiquity of his job site signs—went from a few hundred thousand to tens of millions of dollars in volume during the 1980s. During the next decade, he went bankrupt, but maybe he feels he had a heck of a ride while it lasted.

For almost all builders, including those who prefer to acquire jobs via design/build or cost planning, competitive bidding is a necessity at times. It's a way to keep a crew busy rather than lay off and lose key employees during a slow economy or to simply fill a hole in the schedule during better times. One builder, who had $35 million in work under contract during the boom of the late 1990s (almost all of it acquired on a cost planning basis), a few years earlier had to crank out several dozen free bids before finally landing a project to keep his key people working.

Even for builders who have the option of avoiding competitive bidding altogether, it may be wise to not move away from it entirely. Deva Rajan, a West Coast builder with vast experience points out that if you do no competitive bidding, you can lose your edge. You lose touch with marketplace realities and grow lazy at controlling costs. You loosen the reins on your subcontractors and allow their prices to creep up, slacken your requirements for productivity by your crews, and let your overhead inflate. Then, if you must suddenly enter the competitive marketplace, you can't compete. You have grown lazy and sluggish, and cannot run with the wolves.

Finally, competitive bidding can be a way of breaking into a new market. A builder who started out plugging in stock bathroom and kitchen remodels for Sears Roebuck and Co. moved on to contracting for many of the largest and most challenging projects in his city. At first, he had to bid against other contractors for those coveted jobs. But by providing exceptionally reliable construction services, he reached the point where his was often the only company many owners and design firms would consider.

Success at competitive bidding

Though there is opportunity within competitive bidding, it places serious burdens on its practitioners. One is the time that it takes to do all the estimating and other work necessary to put together a bid—skilled work that designers and owners typically expect you to do without pay. For small-volume builders the burdens can be quite destructive. I think, for example, of a young builder on the East Coast with whom I had a brief on-line chat. He was in his home office, still hacking away at an estimate as his clock neared midnight. Such late-night stands are too often the experience of builders who have not yet worked their way beyond competitive bidding. When they should be with their family or resting for the next day's work, they are instead holed up with plans and a computer, calculating costs for a job they *might* get—or that they will get only by pricing the project so low they are almost certain to lose money on it.

Given the burdens of competitive bidding, if and when you must produce free bids, you will likely want to pick and choose between the opportunities rather than cranking out an estimate for every set of plans you can lay your hands on. You will need a set of guidelines—such as those as suggested in the sidebar below—to determine which projects to bid. To begin with, as described in the last chapter, you'll want to evaluate the project, its owner, and the designer. Going further, determine as best you can not only the number of bidders, but the quality of the bidders and your position in the pack. Why? Because too many builders do not understand their overhead burden or lack an adequate estimating system. As a result, they bid projects for less than their costs, and that is especially true when they are "hungry" and liable to infuse their estimate with wishful thinking. There's not much point getting into a race with those guys when you can win only by submitting a bid that guarantees you'll lose money on the job.

Another frequent hazard you need to steer around is the owner who already favors one bidder and is using your bid merely as a control. He wants your number only to make sure his guy's number is not too high or as a tool for levering his guy down. How do you determine if someone is trying to use you? Ask questions of the designer and owner. Often, though not always, you'll get telltale answers. Ask, "How many

other professionals are you requesting to price your project, Mr. Jones? Have you worked with one of them before? Did he do a good job for you? If our bid is reasonably competitive with respect to price, is there any reason why we would not be selected to build the job?" From the answers, you will get a sense whether the owner really is interested in working with you or merely looking to get some free information.

Finally, you can ask about the ground rules for the bid. One designer argues persuasively that the *only* fair way to run a competitive bid is to request three builders of closely equal quality to submit bids with the understanding that the low bid will win. In Europe, similar ground rules are used but with the twist that the middle bid wins—a good practice because it encourages competition while not forcing contractors to cut corners on subcontractor selection and other costs in order to produce the low bid. By looking for bids for which such rules are in force and by adhering to the other guidelines, you can improve the chances that the investment of time you make in competitive bidding will bring returns.

From time to time, however, for a project you intensely want, you can choose instead to break all the rules, so to speak. Act as if you are not even in a

Bidding to Win

■ Evaluate the project.
■ Find out the number of bidders.
■ Evaluate other bidders.
■ Learn your position in the pack.
■ Don't win a job on which you are sure to lose money.
■ Do not bid for owners interested in using you only to gain leverage over other builders.
■ Learn the ground rules for each bid.
■ Act as if you have already won.

> "**B**idding for free is a self-esteem issue," she said. "You are unwilling to say you should be paid for your services."

competitive bid or as if you have already won. Submit your bid but then service the owners as if they are already your clients. Give them a complete project schedule. Give them a detailed cost breakdown, and ask if any line items seem high. If so, get together with them, offer lower-cost alternatives, explain the trade-offs, and offer to pursue any avenues they think promising. Ask each of your subcontractors to knock a small amount off their bids, throw in a bit of your markup for overhead and profit, and offer the total to the owners as a goodwill discount. Invite the owners to tour some of your best projects. Show them how you'll build important details of their project. In other words, demonstrate your interest in the project and your commitment to build it not only for as tight a price as you reasonably can, but to a high level of quality as well.

The limits of competitive bidding

While there are ways to optimize what opportunity there is within competitive bidding, they unfortunately amount to merely making the best of a bad situation. The double bind of competitive bidding is just too severe. On the one hand, you spend endless hours bidding on projects you will never get because you will be too high. On the other, you bid low enough to get them, and the corners you must cut to build within your estimate come back to haunt you for years afterward.

William Mitchell, a contractor who went bankrupt and then wrote a how-not-to book, warns, "For builders who have to survive on low bids, construction contracting is a real jungle with few survivors." A builder who *has* survived for many years, while acquiring a broad range of projects from bare-bones commercial to estate-level residential by

both competitive bid and other means, was asked whether competitive bidding is a viable business proposition over the long term. Though a normally garrulous guy, he answered that question in one word: "No."

For builders, along with the financial hazards, there is an additional downside to competitive bidding—a psychological burden. The public's assumption that builders have a virtual duty to provide free cost estimates to anyone who contemplates doing a construction project can be deeply frustrating. Explain the burden estimating places on you and your company, and you'll often hear, "But I thought contractors were supposed to give free estimates," or "Oh, well, that just gets rolled into your overhead." Memorably, I got just that response from an architect who, in a subsequent conversation, explained to me why he charged for even his get-acquainted meeting with new clients. "My ideas and time are valuable," he declared. "I don't like to give them away for nothing."

All this adds up to a situation that some builders regard as genuinely demeaning. In a powerful essay in *Fine Homebuilding* in the 1980s, Sam Clark, a New England builder, noted: "The fact that highly skilled work (estimating) is provided gratis says a lot about how people in general and builders themselves value a builder's time." Iris Harrell, a remodeler who operates on the opposite side of the country, speaking at a construction conference in Silicone Valley a decade and a half later, echoed Clark's view. "Bidding for free is a self-esteem issue," she said. "You are unwilling to say you should be paid for your services." I agree with Sam and Iris, and for that reason in the next two chapters I will discuss other ways that builders have developed to acquire work.

Design/Build

When I contemplate the dominance of competitive bidding in the construction world and the slapdash quality of the work it so often produces, I often ask myself, How did we ever get to this situation? How did we evolve to a system where the people expert at constructing buildings are left out of the loop until the plans and specifications for a project are completely drawn up, and even then asked for no input other than to name a price for building it?

For years, builders have recognized the defects of competitive bidding and have sought to develop other means of acquiring work. They have had three requirements for any alternative. First, it must appeal to clients as well as builders. There's no point in developing a service for which there would be no market. Second, it must enable builders to acquire projects on the basis of the quality of their work and the reliability of their performance, not merely lowest price. Third, it must release them from exploitation as a source of free estimating and other preconstruction service by owners and designers. It must dignify and reward the contributions they make during the preconstruction phase of the project.

The first of the two alternatives builders have developed is known as design/build, which offers clients one-stop shopping for the entire package of services they need to get their projects built. Design/build seems to be gaining increasing market share and is practiced by construction companies ranging from those that do kitchen and bath remodels to large firms that build major commercial projects. Design/build incorporates five major elements:

- *Planning* to meet zoning and other government requirements, as well as those of owners and their neighbors

- *Design* (including engineering) to help the owners define their project
- *Specifying* of construction materials and methods
- *Estimating and budget control* (including guiding the owner to sources of financing)
- *Construction*, actually building the project

Design/builders provide all five of the services. They get paid for them all. And they surely earn their pay.

Challenges and hazards

Design/build is a complex process. Along with the usual construction, communication, and control systems, you need whole other systems to govern the design side of your operation and mesh it with the construction side. In fact, articulating all the requirements for successful design/build operations is beyond the scope of this book. I will give you a broad overview of the subject, highlight the principal challenges and hazards, and suggest a path into design/build for those readers who find it appealing. But if you want to pursue design/build, you should research the subject further.

Design/build work carries with it three challenges beyond those faced by builders who offer construction services only, or even those who practice cost planning as a way of winning construction projects. First, design/build firms are prone to acquiring heavy overhead burdens. Second, their projects impose complex management requirements. Third, design/build companies are exposed to substantial additional legal liabilities.

Many design/builders seem to feel that to appeal to the well-heeled clients they depend on, they must invest heavily in image. They tend to maintain fancy digs featuring showrooms, design studios, and conference rooms where they

COMING UP

Why Design/Build

Challenges and Hazards

A Path into Design/Build

Marketing Design/Build

Prudent Practices

Limits

Phases of a Design/Build Project

One design/build firm reports using *nearly five dozen* different documents to track and control their process from the initial design agreement with a prospective client to project completion. Design/build is not for the contractor who thrives on "no-brainers."

- Evaluate project.
- Sign design agreement.
- Collect retainer for design services.
- Schedule design services.
- Block out tentative place in schedule for construction.
- Establish feasibility of project.
- Verify zoning.
- Create conceptual design.
- Verify that concept is within budget.
- Assist owner to secure funding.
- Develop design and budget.
- Create preliminary design.
- Create preliminary estimates.
- Design alternatives.
- Estimate cost of alternatives.
- Produce final design drawings, specifications, and final estimate.
- Sign construction contract.
- Collect construction deposit.
- Schedule construction.
- Schedule design support for construction.
- Complete preconstruction work.
- Produce working drawings.
- Obtain permits.
- Build project.
- Coordinate designers with construction crew and subs.
- Design for change orders.
- Manage and control all construction.

construction costs. During slow times, when they have few jobs, it can squeeze out all their profit or even force them to operate at a loss as the only alternative to closing their doors entirely.

When they do sell a project, design/build firms embark on a process much more complex than that of a company that does design or construction only. Design/build is not just a matter of sticking design on the front end of the construction process. Design must be ceaselessly coordinated with other preconstruction services and then with construction from the inception of each project to its completion. To make matters yet more difficult, the two functions—design, then build—often refuse to dovetail. One design/builder says his greatest challenge is to "get the other shoe to fall," to obtain a construction contract once design is completed. He regularly finds himself finishing a design for a project, planning for a crew to build it, then having the owner balk at signing the construction agreement so that he must suddenly scramble to keep his crew busy. Another design/builder says he needs to keep two projects in the design "pipeline" for every opening in his construction schedule so that his crews are not left unemployed. But the result is that when more than one out of two customers do want to build, he faces the ticklish, tense task of informing some of them they are facing a long wait.

Sometimes clients grow frustrated waiting for construction of their project to begin—or while they are waiting they bolt to another contractor. That is a prospect a design/builder contemplates with horror. What happens if the contractor turns out to be an incompetent who blames his errors on the design/build company's plans? Or suppose the building fails and the owner attributes the failure to the design. What will be the outcome for the design/build company? It may be dragged

can host potential clients and sell them on their services. They spend heavily on marketing, including expensive advertising, mailings, and handouts. Their trucks, their job site signs, even their Web sites are first rate and in pristine condition. During relatively good times, all that overhead consumes a large proportion of their margin above direct

into a lawsuit, one which it may very well have to face without support from its insurance company. Design/build firms (at least at the level of small-volume operations), while carrying contractor's general liability, rarely have access to the "errors and omissions" (E&O) coverage available for design-only firms. Even when a design/build firm can locate an insurer willing to provide an E&O policy to a general contractor, it's likely to find the policy unaffordable. The rates run from high to truly staggering—25 percent of revenue in one case I heard of recently.

A path into design/build

For all the hazards, design/build still holds great appeal (and, as we shall see in a few pages, there are ways of contending with its hazards). There is an enormous amount of satisfaction to be had from working with clients to sharpen their ideas for a project, designing it, and then building it. If you become proficient at design/build, you can make a good living at it. Design/build, unlike competitive bidding on a lowest-price-wins basis, is a viable long-term business proposition.

Even if you do not want to go 100 percent design/build, it is a useful arrow to have in your quiver. Design/build is a way to service past clients or connect to new clients on projects for which bringing in an independent design firm seems overkill. At the beginning of your career it can, therefore, be a good way of acquiring small projects such as a laundry room, a deck, or a fence. Even these jobs need thoughtful and careful design so that costly labor and material are not poured into a badly conceived project.

If you want do to move into design/build you can, as the illustration on p. 130 suggests, follow a quite natural path. Once you have educated yourself about the process and created a design/build proposal, you can begin by taking

on small projects. If you are an experienced builder who is interested in and pays attention to design, you may be able to do a quite respectable job of designing the projects yourself. Alternately, you can find professional designers who will willingly work for you on a subcontract basis. There are design firms happy to work directly for builders. Many architects and other designers employed by large firms, home improvement centers, and government agencies are eager to do small projects (and large ones) on the side. One of my best projects ever was building a large home/music studio designed by an architect who seemed to enjoy our project much more than his day job planning hotel resorts.

As you push further into design/build, you will continue to have a range of options for handling design, from doing it all personally, to hiring it out, to combining in-house with outside services. One design/builder began by personally producing designs for small remodel projects. He now employs four architects full time. Another uses a flexible approach, designing some projects himself while on others subcontracting

Even small projects need design. To give the owners of this backyard bridge the rustic look they wanted as well as a durable structure, Gerstel designed the span to use two 8″ × 21″ × 12′ beams milled from a fallen redwood tree.

Research design/build	Develop basic design/build systems	Create a design/build contract	Practice presentation of design/build service	Recruit designers and engineers to work on your projects	(Option: study design and obtain certification as a designer)	Sell design/build services for small projects	Hone design/build management systems	Take on larger design/build projects

to an outside design firm. There are many ways to skin the design cat. All of them can work so long as the design services are of professional quality and well integrated with construction operations.

Marketing design/build

If design/build did not benefit owners as well as builders, there would be few customers for the service. But design/build does offer benefits to owners. Understanding and being able to explain them is key to marketing design/build services successfully.

The benefits of design/build arise in good part out of its advantages over competitive bidding in half a dozen areas, including:

DESIGN COSTS   Design/build firms typically charge about half as much as do pure design firms preparing plans for competitive bids. When designing for competitive bids, design firms often feel compelled to create exceedingly detailed plans and specifications for two reasons: First, they try to solve the proverbial "apples to apples" conundrum; that is, they are trying to assure that all bidders are covering exactly the same scope and quality of work in their bid, selling the same apples, so to speak. Second, they are trying to protect themselves from lawsuits for "omissions and errors" should the owner award the job to an incompetent bidder who might blame his mistake on alleged inadequacies in the plans. Design/

build firms, facing no such pressures, can make do with simpler plans and therefore charge less for design services.

FINANCIAL FEASIBILITY   In the design/build process, design and estimating proceed in lock step, with the result that the final design can be built for the owner's budget. For competitive bidding, however, design typically proceeds with little or no builder input on costs until the plans are complete. As a result, the owners' investment in highly detailed and costly design sometimes leads to a grotesquely ironic result. The plans go out for bid. All bids come back far above the owners' budget. Having forked out all that money for a process that was supposed to bring them the lowest price, they end up with nothing but prices they can't afford to pay.

QUALITY OF CONSTRUCTION
Because design/build companies are acquiring jobs not on the basis of lowest price but of value, they are motivated not to cut corners but to produce good work. In competitive bidding as one architect warns, owners must "beware [of] the low price" even as they seek it. Bids are low, he explains, because lower-cost material substitutions have been made, not enough time has been allowed to properly build elements of the project, and price, not quality, is emphasized in choosing subs. To his caution I would add that because no builder is involved during design and

The benefits of design/build arise in good part out of its advantages over competitive bidding in half a dozen areas.

because designers often do not understand construction methods, their plans can call for unnecessarily complicated and/or inferior construction details.

CHANGE ORDER ARTISTRY Well-delivered design/build services alert owners to the costs they are likely to face during construction for work beyond that shown in the plans. Competitive bidding, on the other hand, often leads to the owner getting nailed during construction for numerous extra charges by a builder intent on making up for the too low price he had to submit to win the job in the first place.

QUALITY OF RELATIONSHIPS Often, competitive bidding results in a tension between the design firm and the builder. The designers fear the builder will place blame for problems on their plans or take liberties with details to cut costs. The builder is furious with the designer for inadequacies in the plans, which add to the financial pressure he is already feeling. As a result, the owners find themselves in the middle of a nasty adversarial relationship. With design/build, since design and construction is provided by the same entity, the potential for the owners to get caught in the cross fire virtually disappears.

The design/build process certainly does not always work perfectly. Design/builders do occasionally produce over-budget designs (sometimes because of unexpectedly high engineering requirements). They do falter and bring in marginal subs. Communication between designers and builders within the design/build company breaks down and details are drawn or built improperly. But the design/build process diminishes the problems, and if it is well presented, owners will often come to see design/build as a good way to go.

Change Order Artistry

Architects and designers rarely are able to produce a set of plans complete in all details. When incomplete plans go out for competitive bids, knowledgeable builders quickly spot the gaps, and they respond in a variety of ways. In the estimators' offices at some large companies competing in the hardball world of commercial construction, every oversight and omission in the plans is marked, and a calculation is done to figure how much profit can be made on change orders for the omissions. If a bountiful harvest of extra charges seems likely, a bid for the project which is actually *below* estimated costs for work shown on the plans may be submitted on the assumption that the loss will be amply made up for by the change order profits.

In the world of residential contracting, many builders balk at practicing such "change order artistry," as it is called in the industry. They feel a moral obligation to include the costs of omissions in their bids and to alert the designer and owner that the gaps exist. They do not feel right about setting up their clients, many of them naive about the realities of construction and its costs, for a change order ambush.

The result of such conscientiousness, builders often discover, is that they bushwhack themselves. Because their bids include work not shown in the plans, they end up too high to win the job. And so, caught between cutting their own throats and cutting the clients', they retreat to a more neutral position. One builder says, "I no longer educate owners for free. I write down all the questions about the holes in the plans, but I submit them *after* I have started construction." Others try to protect themselves while still providing a bit of cover for owners by bidding only what is on the plans and in the specs but also giving the clients a muted warning that it is typical for additional costs to crop up during construction.

It's difficult, this change order artistry issue. I know of no really good solutions. It is part and parcel of competitive bidding. It is one reason we need better ways for owners, designers, and builders to get together for projects.

Prudent protections

Though you may see design/build as offering benefits both to yourself and your clients, you might still hesitate to go down the design/build road. You may be intimidated by the additional management burden and by the potentially greater overhead. You may hesitate to expose yourself to the additional risks. However,

Virtual Showrooms

Design/build firms often burden themselves with heavy overhead, especially fancy real estate for a showroom and impressive offices. When work is slow, the cost of that real estate can be crushing. It's possible, however, to offer design/build services yet maintain a lean operation. One of the most intriguing ideas I have seen for keeping overhead down is to create what builder Scott Shelley calls a "virtual showroom." Shelley maintains a list of Web sites for the manufacturers of finish fixtures and materials he likes to use in his projects. When he signs a design agreement with a client, he sends them an E-mail with links to the Web sites. By clicking on the links, clients are able to cruise through the myriad "rooms" of his "showroom" and select products for their projects.

> "Everyone at this table, if they're honest with themselves, would admit they've been in a situation where without the (designer) on the other side of the table, they might have been able to get away with something."

if you have what it takes to organize a successful construction company, you likely have what it takes to integrate design/build successfully into your operation. You will find, also, that both the overhead and risk associated with design/build can be restrained and minimized.

By subcontracting design services, you can avoid the heavy fixed overhead for design facilities (including office space, computers, and specialized software) burdening design/build firms that try to provide all design in-house. Likewise, you will find that the heavy marketing overhead that high-profile design/build firms choose to assume is not necessary. Many design/builders work from quite compact spaces, foregoing the trophy offices and the fancy advertising. After all, if you are selling design/build, the clients are not going to be buying your office space or elegant brochure. They are going to be buying a building for their own use, and it is a reputation for delivering well-designed projects on time and on budget with good quality control that will win you their business.

While the liabilities of design/build are substantial, those who have gone down the road before you have worked out sound strategies you can adopt to minimize your exposure. They include:

- *To ensure your designs are of professional quality*, use designers competent to handle the type of project you are taking on. For some projects, that may be you. For others it may be certified kitchen and bath designers. For yet others, you may need an experienced architect. Always, for a project including significant structural work, hire a licensed engineer—preferably one who carries his own insurance. Lastly, bear down on waterproofing details, the greatest source of lawsuits in the construction business.
- *For protection against incompetent contractors building from your designs*, state in your design agreement that the plans are the property not of the client but of your company and are for use only on projects that it builds. Stamp all design drawings "Not For Construction Purposes," and create working drawings only after the construction contract is signed. Retain custody of all working drawings till construction is complete.
- *To protect yourself against lawsuits for failures due to design*, work only with skilled and reliable tradespeople and with first-rate, licensed, and insured subcontractors. Militantly manage, check, and recheck the design and construction of waterproofing (roofs, flashings, membranes, drainage) and structural work. One design/builder employs an expert roofer who handles all waterproofing on his company's projects. Your operation may not be large enough to keep a waterproofing specialist on the payroll. In that case, you and your lead people must become experts.

Limits to design/build

For all its strengths and the opportunities that do exist to practice design/build successfully, it does have limits. Something is lost in design/build—namely, independent persons playing the roles of designer and builder and the check and balance they provide for each other. One builder, speaking on a panel with other contractors, stated the case with admirable honesty, "Everyone at this table, if they're honest with themselves, would admit they've been in a situation where without the (designer) on the other side of the table, they might have been able to get away with something."

With no independent firm lobbying for first-class design, design/build operations rarely, in my opinion, produce excellent design. The design possibilities are likely to be suffocated by the builder's need, or decision, to maintain a certain level of gross profit margin. Good design ideas often are not let out of the office. Why? Because if the client sees and falls for them but doesn't have the budget to build them—at least not at the design/build firm's rates—the firm may face a choice between sacrificing profit or losing the client to a less expensive builder. Recently, a major remodeling magazine pictured the results of its annual competition. For the most part, the winning projects featured designs that ran from predictable to downright clumsy. There was only one really outstanding design, and it won best of show. Tellingly, it was the only one of the winning designs that was produced by an independent architect working with an independent builder. The others were the products of design/build companies.

I do know design/builders who overcome the temptation to sacrifice design for higher profit. You may be able to do so in your own design/build practice. But another option is to go to a program that retains independent entities for design and construction, yet also overcomes many of the problems inherent in competitive bidding. We will next look at that program and how builders acquire work by using it.

Cost Planning

In response to the defects of competitive bidding and because design/build, too, has its problems, builders have developed yet another way of acquiring jobs. They work in a team relationship with the owners and an independent designer hired by the owners from early in the preconstruction phase of a project through to its completion. The owners' role is to make their wishes, preferences, and budget clear. The designer focuses primarily on function and aesthetic considerations. The builder provides information about construction costs and methods to help optimize the quality of the project and keep it within budget.

The third way goes by various names. Some builders call it "negotiated bidding." Builders who use that term seem to be those who favor a loose, intuitive approach to their work. They engage in a give-and-take with the owner and designer to develop as good a project as possible while at the same time safeguarding their own needs to build reliable structures at reasonable profit margins. Other builders, favoring a more systematic approach, speak of offering "preconstruction services." To describe my own preconstruction services, I use the term "cost planning." While it's not exactly a poetic phrase, I like it because it describes concisely a valuable role builders can play during preconstruction— namely, to help plan a project so that it can be built to an optimal quality level for an acceptable cost.

COMING UP

A Third Method of Acquiring Work

Cost Planning Defined

A Range of Cost Planning Services

A Sample Contract

Guidelines and Safeguards

Marketing Cost Planning

Charging for It

An Idea Whose Time Has Come

SAMPLE LETTERS AND FORMS   Cost Planning Services

Each builder who develops a cost planning program puts his unique spin on it. The services you include in your cost planning agreements will be determined by your skills, values, and tolerance for risk and responsibility.

A COST PLANNING CHECKLIST

EVALUATING
- ☐ Qualify and recommend designers and engineers.
- ☐ Inspect site/structure for existing conditions that will impact design and construction costs.
- ☐ Forecast areas and magnitude of likely change orders.
- ☐ Flag other necessary construction that can be most cost-effectively done at same time as primary project

ESTIMATING
- ☐ Develop conceptual estimates based on conceptual drawings.
- ☐ Create preliminary estimates based on preliminary design drawings.
- ☐ Punch up what-if estimates based on optional features and alternative designs, specifications, or subcontractors.
- ☐ Make final estimates based on final working drawings.

SPECIFYING
- ☐ Write statements of the assumptions and specifications underlying estimates.
- ☐ Provide design development (i.e. design completion) of plans produced by others but needing construction details.

CONSULTING
- ☐ Propose ideas for construction methods that will lower cost of realizing design.
- ☐ Suggest technologies for decreasing long-term costs for operation and maintenance.
- ☐ Propose recapturing of existing on-site resources for new project.
- ☐ Present ideas for maximizing environmental benefits.
- ☐ Present alternative contracts for construction.

Cost planning fulfills the three requirements builders have for alternatives to competitive bidding. First, the cost planning approach is *a way to acquire work on the basis of quality of service, not merely lowest price*. Second, it *releases you from exploitation as a source of free estimates*, for builders who do cost planning charge for the service. Third, *cost planning is marketable* because it offers benefits both to clients and designers. Cost planning protects clients against the risks of investing heavily in design only to find out they cannot afford to build the project. It protects against the excessively detailed and costly design as well as the inferior construction that so often results from competitive bidding. At the same time, it restores the check and balance between builder and designer that clients lose when they go with a design/build firm.

Designers benefit from cost planning because, as one architect puts it, they are not "particularly aware (of the) cost implications of many common construction practices and procedures." As a result, designers often labor long and hard over their details only to discover their clients cannot afford to build the project and are angry at having been charged thousands of dollars for a pile of drawings that will never be used for construction. Over the course of his career, a designer can, as one architect admits is the case for himself, end up with "a vault full of plans for unbuilt projects." Cost planning guards against that.

Cost planning services

The range of services you can provide if you elect to offer cost planning is suggested above. Your evaluation of designers and engineers is valuable to owners because often, as a result of not appreciating the vast difference in skills and interests among designers, they make costly mistakes when selecting a designer for their project. One homeowner hired a very

SAMPLE LETTERS AND FORMS   Cost Planning Agreement

For small projects, a bare-bones agreement such as this may do. For larger projects, additional clauses regarding services, charges, and limits of liability may be advisable. *To assure that it is in conformity with the laws of your state, have any agreement you develop reviewed by an attorney knowledgeable about construction law.*

THE CONSTRUCTION COMPANY
License #897654 · Phone: 000-342-5679

Cost/Planning Agreement

Date:

Project:

The Company, working in cooperation with the owner and the owners' designer,_____, will provide the following services in order to prepare the above named project for construction by The Company beginning (tentatively) _____.

- Inspect for preexisting conditions that will affect design and cost and present findings to owner and designer.
- Suggest to the designer and owner construction technologies and methods to maximize environmental benefits of the project.
- Create and present to the owner a detailed estimate accompanied by detailed assumptions based on preliminary plans drawn by the designer.
- Suggest alternative construction methods to help maintain alignment of design with the owner's budget.
- Create what-if estimates based on alternative versions of and optional features for the project.
- Create a final estimate together with necessary assumptions based on final working drawings for the project.
- Present to the owners a fixed-price contract for construction of the project.

Charges: The Company will provide the cost planning services described above for $60.00 per hour charged against a retainer of $2,400.00 to be deposited with a signed copy of this contract. If the owners contract with The Company for the project, one half of the cost planning charges will be credited against the costs of construction.

Dispute Resolution: Should any dispute arise between The Company and the owners during cost planning, they will attempt to settle the dispute through nonbinding mediation provided by _____ mediation services. If they do not succeed in settling the dispute through nonbinding mediation, they will settle their dispute in small-claims court. In no case is The Company to be held liable for damages in excess of The Company's cost planning fees up to the time of the dispute.

Signatures:

Builder: _____   Owners: _____

---

good architect who, however, happens to be a devout modernist and ended up with a crisp stucco box stuck on the back of her half-timbered English Tudor-style home. The owners of a food-processing plant hired an architect who was passionate about fine residential work and ended up paying for the design of much intricate detailing irrelevant to the plant reconfiguration the owners wanted to accomplish. On the other hand, homeowners working with a builder on a cost planning basis were guided to a kitchen designer who produced plans for a new kitchen that

Story of a Cost Planning Failure

A few years ago, I was asked to remodel a small kitchen for clients with a very tight budget. I agreed to take the job on a cost planning basis, then immediately headed off in the wrong direction by inviting in a designer accustomed to working with well-to-do clients but not with folks of limited means.

The designer produced sketches that included, among other costly ideas, an expansion of the project from the kitchen into adjacent spaces of the house. Rather than doing the hard-nosed conceptual estimating that would have made clear this ambitious design was much too expensive, I fell in love with the design and joined the owners and designer in hoping that it could somehow be built for the dollars available. When I finally did produce an estimate after completion of the preliminary design, it was 75 percent over what the owners could afford. They were devastated and justifiably upset with me for having failed to provide the very controls that I had claimed cost planning offered.

My experience brings into sharp relief a basic rule of cost planning. *Never fall in love with a job to the point you are blinded to cost realities.* If a design is running over budget, give the owners the facts, including that if they want to build the design, they will need to look for a cheaper contractor—which is exactly what the owners did in this case. Fortunately, they are happy with his work, part of which they paid for with my cost planning fee, for I did dare bill them for all the hours I had put in.

included the functionality they desired while blending nicely with their traditional home.

Once a designer has been selected, you can provide additional valuable service to both owner and designer by scoping out existing conditions at the project site, particularly if the project is a remodel. By locating pipes, ducts, electrical home runs, and bearing walls; by checking on the quality and strength of existing foundations and frames; by noting where new work may unnecessarily lead to disruption of existing finishes; you can guide the design away from prohibitively costly choices and in the direction of affordable ones. You can become quite systematic about existing

condition surveys. One builder who provides them as part of his cost planning service has developed a checklist of existing conditions for every phase of work, from excavation through painting.

With existing-condition surveys you will be able to spot areas where change orders are likely to crop up during construction. In a crawl space, you'll note dry rot extending into walls above. You'll see evidence that existing plumbing is near the end of its life and will likely give out as the result of vibration from the new work. By forecasting areas of potential change orders, you can help owners project the actual final cost, as opposed to merely the initial contract price, and adequately budget for it.

After designer selection and existing condition surveys come the work that is at the heart of cost planning—namely cost estimating at four levels: conceptual (also called "feasibility"), preliminary, alternatives, and final. Conceptual estimating is worthwhile if there is doubt whether the owners can afford the project they have in mind. For example, the owner may be considering two options for remodeling his kitchen. One involves gutting the existing kitchen space and building a new kitchen into it. The other involves extending the new kitchen into an existing laundry room, opening it to the living room and backyard, and expanding it by adding a large bay window. Working from schematic floor plans and using your job cost records from past projects, you cost out the project by area. With figures in hand you are able to show the owners that while the smaller version should be doable, the larger project is clearly beyond their budget. They would be wasting their money if they had it designed.

Conceptual estimates, by nature, are rough, intended only to determine whether a project is potentially feasible or clearly not. To get cost figures that will come close to actual construction costs, design and estimating need to move up a notch to the preliminary level. Here, you need the designer to provide you with exterior elevations and selected interior elevations, in addition to floor plans. If the project involves significant structural elements, you also will need input from the engineer. Will the foundation be a simple T-footing and stem wall, or is there a chance that the engineer will require deep piers and a grade beam? Is he going to allow the roof to be framed with manufactured trusses, or will it need to incorporate welded steel ridges and hips? Using the designer's preliminary drawings and the engineer's input, you create a detailed, line-by-line estimate of every labor, material, and subcontractor cost that you can anticipate. The result is a cost estimate that will give the owners a close idea of what it will really take to build their project, though their design investment is thus far minimal.

With preliminary estimating done, in order to help the owners and designers trim costs or determine optimal approaches to construction, you can provide them with cost estimates of alternative construction methods and materials. If you are using a computer estimating system, you can efficiently create what-if scenarios for the whole project. How much will it cost with asphalt shingle roofing, aluminum windows, and drywall? How much will it cost if upgraded to include a standing seam roof, wood windows, and veneer plaster?

If your preliminary and alternative estimates are thorough, production of the final estimate will be quite easy. Using your preliminary estimate as a base, you will be able to quickly adjust line item costs to reflect the designer's final drawings, then present your price for construction to the owners. If the price is within budget and your delivery of cost planning services has won the owner's trust, you should be on your way

to signing a contract for construction. Of the many projects for which I have provided cost planning, there are only four I have not built. In one case, the couple decided to get divorced rather than build. For two others the owners decided to hire a cheaper contractor. The fourth I royally screwed up (as described on p. 136).

Guidelines and safeguards

From years of practicing cost planning and watching other builders practice it as well, I have developed guidelines to help ensure the success of the process. They include:

STAY WITHIN YOUR LIMITS OF COMPETENCE Resist the temptation to use cost planning as a way of getting an inside track on a job if it is too big or complex for you to estimate accurately on the basis of past experience. At the start of your career when you have not yet developed your cost records (see p. 78), strictly limit the size projects for which you offer cost planning.

MAINTAIN A MARGIN OF SAFETY IN YOUR COST ESTIMATES Tend toward conservatism, not optimism, about costs at the conceptual and preliminary level of estimating. Thereby, you will provide a margin to cover the costs that may unexpectedly show themselves when the designer completes the final drawings.

SELECT DESIGNERS OBJECTIVELY When you recommend a designer, do so with an eye on the owner's budget and tastes, not your own preferences.

INFORM THE OWNERS OF THE LIMITS OF CHANGE ORDER FORECASTING Make clear, and in writing, that change orders involve the unknown, namely hidden conditions or upgrades elected in the middle of a job. Emphasize that it is impossible to determine in advance the exact costs of dealing with them. Declare that the best you can do is to forecast areas where they might occur and to report the magnitude of change order costs experienced on similar projects with similar conditions. Underscore the fact that past experience is no guarantee of future results.

CONTROL DESIGNERS DURING CONCEPTUAL AND PRELIMINARY ESTIMATING Encourage the designer to give you what you need for estimating, but no more. Holding back designers can be difficult. They love to draw! But if the designers go further than necessary and the project turns out not to be feasible, the owner will have wasted money on a design that won't be built, one of the missteps cost planning is intended to prevent.

BE CANDID WITH OWNERS If the costs to build a design are exceeding the

owners' budget, tell them their choices. Cut back the design. Increase funding for the project. Look for a cheaper builder.

RESIST CUTTING COSTS BY BRINGING IN CHEAP SUBS Refuse to use second-rate subs for those trades that do the heavy lifting—carpentry, plumbing, electrical, mechanical, and waterproofing, including roofing. The liabilities for builder and owner outweigh any potential savings. Emphasize that even for less critical work, cheaper subs require more management, the cost of which negates some of the immediate dollar savings they might provide, and that the lower quality of their work will negate the rest of it in the long run.

GET INPUT FROM ENGINEERS EARLY ON Structural requirements for buildings grow increasingly demanding and can easily put a project out of a client's financial reach.

NEVER PROMISE TOO MUCH Make clear to owners that conceptual estimates are rough and that even preliminary estimates, while often close to final costs, can be 10 to 15 percent off.

At all levels of estimating, you should write up the assumptions underlying costs. State your assumption that joists will be TJIs, not solid lumber; that walls and ceilings will be veneer plaster and not drywall; that trim will be paint-grade poplar, not stained clear pine or fir. To clarify assumptions for a project, you will need to talk with the designers and engineers, time for which you and they must be paid. But those conversations save the owners the expense of the designers and engineers drawing up every detail before the costs of the project are clear.

Though your cost planning agreement will be with owners, the service also entails obligations to designers. The most

Overhead, Truth, and Profit

Some builders, feeling owners and designers will not accept their markup for overhead and profit, choose to hide part of the markup, even going so far as to create two versions of their bids—one for the clients and one for use in their offices. In the version created for use in their offices, they will show estimated costs for each item of work and their markups for overhead and profit for the project as they have actually figured them. In the version they give the owners, they will attach a portion of overhead and profit to each item of work so that they can show a smaller amount at the lines for markup.

Such hiding of markup—or what builders who practice it and accountants who condone it like more elegantly to term "dual allocation of overhead"—may be justifiable in competitive bidding. The owner has invited you into a poker game, and you can play your cards as close to your chest as you like.

In cost planning (and design/build) the situation is different. You are being trusted and paid to provide accurate cost information. You violate that trust if you shape your numbers in such a way that direct costs are misrepresented and the overhead and profit you are charging is deliberately hidden. One builder I know calls the practice "lying." Another calls it "double dipping." To me, it smacks of consumer fraud.

important is *running all ideas that impact a design by the designer* before presenting them to the owner. By doing so you avoid preempting the designer's role and preserve the trust that allows cost planning to go forward as a team effort.

Of the other special obligations of cost planning, there's one I feel so strongly about that I have sounded off about it in a special editorial on the facing page. Some builders sincerely disagree with the position I take. A contractor from the East Coast says it's un-American, that it is his right to charge for profit any way he likes. One further ethical obligation of cost planning is, however, beyond dispute. When your clients hire you for cost planning, coupled with an understanding that you will build their project, they have put all their eggs in one basket. You are holding it. You cannot dump it and run. If another, more attractive project suddenly crops up, you cannot discard your cost planning clients to make room for the new project. One builder did just that. He bowed out so late in the process that his client could not find another good builder before winter rains made construction impossible. His name is now dirt with the client, the designers, and their circles of friends.

Marketing

Cost planning is an alternative to competitive bidding. It is not, however, a way out of competing for work. In a sense, you must compete harder because you are going after a larger role in the project. Builders who are eager to get beyond competitive bidding often ask me how to acquire jobs on a cost planning basis. My answer boils down to a few paragraphs: To begin with, you must build a company that provides top-notch product. Potential clients for cost planning are not looking for the lowest price. They want something harder to deliver.

They want high-quality work, delivered on schedule and for charges that represent good value.

Once you can deliver all that and have references to back up your claim that you can, position yourself to market cost planning by doing two things: Create a clear cost planning agreement with alternative clauses to serve the needs of different projects, and develop a clear, concise presentation of those services (see Resources on p. 258).

For my own presentation, I first ask clients, many of whom have initially contacted me hoping that I will do a free bid for their project, whether they would like to hear about alternatives to competitive bidding. Virtually all say "Yes." People are incredibly confused about how the construction industry works and welcome any offer to shed light. With those who show no or little interest, I don't force the issue; I don't try to convert people who are sold on competitive bidding. Instead, I thank them for inviting me to bid their project, thereby leaving the door open to my actually giving them a bid. After all, I did participate in a competitive bid back in 1974, and I might want to again during this next quarter century.

I begin my presentation by describing in a few sentences the three ways in which builders acquire work and the pros and cons of each. I am careful to not slam design/build or even competitive bidding excessively—though I do emphasize the tendency of competitive bidding to produce inferior-quality work and the drawbacks of not involving the people who will actually build the project until it is completely designed.

When I get to cost planning I *take care to not oversell it*. I simply go over a few of the basic services, including the three levels of estimating and describe a few of the basic benefits, including protection against paying for a design too expensive to build. Recently, I have begun emphasizing my ability to contribute to "environmentally considerate" construction—space that is not destructive to its occupants' health, as so much conventional construction is, and that is built so as to minimize damage to the larger environment.

That's it. As I mentioned earlier, I cannot offer much in the way of razzle-dazzle marketing technique. I approach selling as a listening, sharing, and teaching. For me, the approach works. A good proportion of the clients who approach me for a free bid end up hiring me on a cost planning basis. If it is clearly presented, clients see cost planning's benefits. It is their surest shot at getting the most for their money.

Charging for cost planning and reaping the rewards

If you do adopt cost planning, you may find your greatest challenge will be charging for your preconstruction services. You may find it a challenge not because clients are unwilling to pay but because you are concerned that if you ask for pay, you will lose opportunities to bid work.

Such concern is valid; there's a hazard here. As you become known as someone who resists doing preconstruction work as an unpaid volunteer, people in your client network, especially some designers, may stop calling you to bid jobs. That has happened to me.

You may or may not think the risk is worth taking. However, consider this. Charging for preconstruction may filter out people who want as much from you for as little as possible. But it will also filter *in* the people who recognize the benefits of having their builder involved in planning their project and who are sufficiently fair-minded to realize they must pay for the valuable service they will receive.

Builders' charges for cost planning divide into three levels—beginner, intermediate, and advanced. At the beginning level are builders who offer cost planning as a loss leader. They give away the time it takes to do cost planning in the hopes that it will lead to a contract for the construction of the job. Some experienced builders get stuck at that level. One says that out of ten jobs he cost plans each year, he builds seven, two do not get built, one "goes away." He says he is happy with his score. But I wonder whether, when he reaches retirement, he will still feel content as he looks back over his career and realizes that he has given away hundreds of thousands of dollars' worth of skilled work that his devoted clients would have been willing to pay for.

Moving up to the intermediate level, we find builders who offer cost planning partly as a loss leader, partly as a service for pay. They charge for their cost planning but apply half of the charge to construction costs if they contract to build the project. For projects they don't build, they keep the entire fee.

Finally, there are those builders who have moved all the way up to charging a professional fee for their preconstruction

A Range of Cost Planning Charges

BEGINNING
- No charge; service provided as loss leader
- Fixed fee credited against construction cost if you build the project

INTERMEDIATE
- Fixed fee with one-half credited against construction cost if you build
- Hourly rate billed against a retainer with a portion credited against construction cost

ADVANCED
- Fixed fee or hourly rate billed against a retainer with no credit against construction cost
- Additional forfeitable deposit to reserve place in schedule

work, either in a series of fixed installments for a defined amount of work or at an hourly rate. Some go a last mile and ask for a deposit to hold a place in their construction schedule for the project. If the owner cancels the project or goes to competitive bidding, they keep the deposit to compensate themselves for "lost opportunity," the projects they passed up to keep the schedule slot open.

Charging for cost planning at a professional level is entirely fair. *Cost planning is highly skilled work, and it is right that men and women who do it well get paid for it.* Cost planning often makes a huge contribution to a project. In one case the builder showed a designer how to save thousands of dollars by cantilevering a new structure from existing foundations rather than creating a new one. In another, the builder turned up an $80,000 savings for an owner by locating a nonprofit firm to handle deconstruction of the existing structure and donate the recovered materials to charities. During a typical cost planning effort, my company suggested virtually every finish specification, from gutter profile and material to interior and exterior plaster, finish flooring, shower doors, cabinet and countertop material and details, window manufacturer, interior trim materials and detailing, and paint luster. With every suggestion we saved the owner construction costs or long-term operating costs and enhanced the design. The savings exceeded my charges for the cost planning.

If you learn to acquire work via cost planning and learn to charge for it at a professional level, you can turn what was once a severe overhead burden—namely the estimating you did for free—into a profit center for your company. You will reap other rewards. Because you come to know each project so well from costing it out repeatedly, you are much less likely than in competitive bidding to overlook

Letter from a Reader

Since writing about cost planning (then called "price planning") in the first edition of this book, I have regularly heard from readers who have tried it out. Many find it a good method of acquiring work.

April 17, 1993

Dear Dave,

After reading your book and hearing you speak, I was inspired to try your ideas. I've now done [cost] planning on five projects and gotten the following results:

$1,500,000 contract for new house
$950,000 contract for new house
$500,000 contract for new house

One other job was abandoned. On another project, they hired someone else. But at least I got paid to bid it . . .

Sincerely,
Paul R. Conrado
President, The Conrado Company

costs. Your more accurate estimates translate into better earnings and a great deal less financial anxiety during jobs.

Perhaps best of all, cost planning usually turns out to be "cost plan/build." You construct most of the projects you estimate. They mean more to you, for you have made a greater investment than in projects for which you merely squeeze out a low price in a competitive bid. As a final bonus, you position yourself to work with the many excellent designers who would not be available as subcontractors on design/build projects but who do want to get beyond competitive bidding. With these designers you can work together through preconstruction as colleagues to deliver the best possible product to the owners. Your relationship, as one designer puts it, is transformed "from power theater to mutual learning."

CHAPTER 5

Estimating and Bidding

COMING UP

An Overview

Basic Estimating

Estimating Checklists

Catching the Slippery Items

Professional Estimating

Computerizing Your
Estimates and Bids

Nailing Your Numbers

WHEN I SET OUT to write this section, I considered calling it "Calculating Costs and Charges," not "Estimating and Bidding." I decided against the change. With "estimating" and "bidding" so embedded in builder-speak, new terms would have only caused confusion. But I wanted to make a point: Estimating is not the rough, vague process that the term, and its rogue cousin, "guesstimating" can imply. Capable builders do not roughly estimate/ guesstimate the costs of building projects they submit to clients. They *calculate* the costs. They *figure* the charges. They nail down those numbers and get them right!

You will hear all kinds of rationalizations for sloppy estimating and bidding. "A construction job is like a lawsuit," some contractors will tell you. "You don't really know how much it's going to cost until it's done." If asked about their estimating procedures, they'll respond, "Oh, I just kinda eyeball the thing. I know pretty much what it will take to build it." Or they claim that throwing in a big "fudge factor" is the real key to successful estimating. I was astonished to hear a builder, who often speaks at construction conferences and holds himself out as an authority, tell an audience that he typically piles 17 percent worth of fudge into each estimate.

In actuality, "fudge" is analogous to an "other" column in an accounting general ledger. If you have much in the "other" column, you are doing a sloppy job of accounting. You don't really know where your expenses lie. Similarly for fudge, smear it all over an estimate and you've obscured your view of where a project's cost will come from.

Fudging is not necessary. Construction is not like a lawsuit. Costs can be accurately projected in advance. By developing systematic procedures, capable builders are able to turn out estimates and bids that come within a few percentage points of the work shown in the plans and specifications.

An overview of estimating and bidding

Estimating and bidding are not the same thing. Estimating involves calculating the direct costs of building a project. Bidding involves figuring markups for overhead and for profit and then adding the markups to direct costs to get a bid price. In other words, bidding includes estimating, but estimating does not include bidding.

Estimating and bidding require a different mind-set. Estimating should be based on hard numbers—on quotes from subs and suppliers and on cost records from past jobs. To as great an extent as practicable, intuition and judgment should be kept out of the process of cost estimating. Bidding, on the other hand, inevitably involves judgment calls about the amount of company overhead costs you need to recover on the job and what amount of profit to shoot for.

At some larger construction firms, you will see an actual wall between the processes of estimating and bidding. In one room sit the estimators figuring the direct costs of doing a job, relying on their cost records, gathering quotes from suppliers and subs, consulting with a project manager for those few items for which they have no records and need to construct a cost. On the other side of the wall sits the owner. When he receives an estimator's cost calculations, he adds overhead based on his analysis of the company's general, sales, and administrative costs. Then he adds profit based on his reading of the project, the economy, and the company's needs. Smaller-volume builders who personally do the calculating of direct costs and figuring of overhead and profit need to maintain a mental wall between the processes.

To estimate and bid a job successfully, use a four-step process that separates calculation of direct costs from figuring overhead and figuring profit:

1. GATHER INFORMATION   Set up a binder for the job, inspect the job site, and walk your subs through it. Study the plans and figure the quantities of each

---

Key Concepts

- *Direct job cost*—The costs for labor, materials, and subcontractors on a job.
- *Overhead*—A company's general, sales, and administrative costs.
- *Profit*—Revenue a company takes in over and above what it pays out for direct job costs and overhead costs.
- *Labor burden*—The costs of labor that come on top of wages.
- *Labor productivity records*—Records of the hours your crews have worked to produce different items or assemblies.
- *Spreadsheet*—A sheet of paper, or a computer screen, divided into rows and columns on which numbers can be spread and totaled.

---

item of work to be done by your crews. Get quotes from the subs. Get material prices from suppliers.

2. CALCULATE DIRECT COSTS   Figure material costs. Use your labor productivity records to determine costs for all work to be done by your crew. Enter and total all material, labor, and sub costs on your estimating sheets.

3. FIGURE OVERHEAD   Determine how much overhead to charge to the job. Overhead is usually figured as a percentage markup of total direct costs. The percentage can vary widely from job to job. Typically, it is higher for the smaller jobs. I have used percentage markups varying from 5 to 15 percent in a single year and know other builders whose percentages have varied from 3 to 30 percent.

4. FIGURE PROFIT   Based on your assessment of the project, figure out how much profit to charge. Judgment will play a large role. What do you feel is fair? What will the market allow? How high do you need to go to make it worth your while to work again with that pouty, scolding client with those two dreadful, screeching terriers and the spitting cat?

Smaller-volume builders who personally do both the calculating of direct costs and figuring of overhead and profit need to maintain a mental wall between the processes.

With these four steps complete, you can figure your bid—or what is often called *selling price*—the amount you will charge the owners for the job. A bid is determined by adding together estimated direct costs, markup for overhead, and markup for profit together. In other words: *Estimated Direct Costs + Markup for Overhead + Markup for Profit = Bid (Selling Price)*

In the following chapters we will discuss in greater detail each of the steps that lead up to the determination of the selling price. But first, in the balance of this chapter, we will look at a series of tools and procedures for estimating and bidding that run the gamut from the most basic to heavy-duty computer programs.

Handwritten Estimate

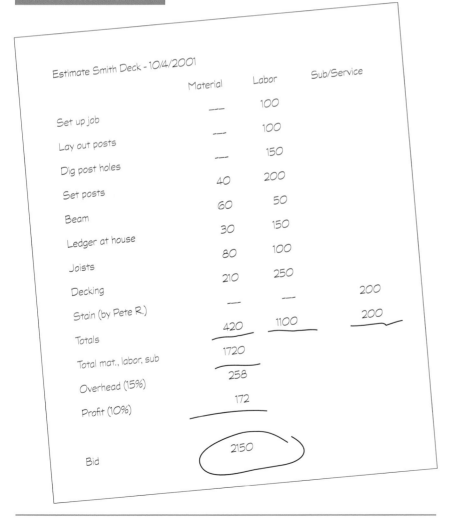

Basic estimating and bidding

At the start of your career as a builder, you may have, as I did, instinctively used a homemade procedure that results in estimates and bids looking something like the one for a small deck illustrated below. To create such an estimate—which requires nothing more than paper, a pencil, and an adding machine (preferably one with a paper tape, so that you can double-check, i.e. proof, your math)—you would simply:

1. Write the items in the job from beginning to end down the left-hand side of the sheet.
2. Set up columns across the top for labor, materials, and subs.
3. Figure and enter costs for each item in the columns.
4. Total the cost columns.
5. Figure an amount for overhead.
6. Figure an amount for profit.
7. Total the cost, overhead, and profit to get your bid price.

Such a system comes naturally to experienced tradespeople, because unlike accounting, which is a world unto itself, estimating is closely related to the work that goes on at a construction site. Just as construction is accomplished one step at a time, beginning with the foundation and moving by logical stages to finish, estimating is a matter of figuring costs for items to be constructed one step at a time and more or less in the same order as they are built.

Checklists and forms

As you gain experience with estimating and bidding, you realize that by writing out the steps for each job, you're wasting time. Many of the steps are identical from job to job. You are also prone to miss items because you have no system for reminding yourself of all the steps involved. To solve both problems, create a checklist that doubles as an estimating form, such as the one illustrated on the right.

Using the checklist form involves the same procedures as the handwritten estimate. You enter numbers, and then total them up with an adding machine. But it also represents a big step up in sophistication. It includes two extra columns. In the column for "quantities/units" the amount of work of each item is entered as a number of units—hours, pieces, linear feet, square feet, or cubic yards. The quantities/units column is a compressed version of what is known as a *take-off sheet*—one on which all quantities of work in a job are re-corded after having been "taken off" the plans.

The checklist form also includes separate columns for subcontractors and services. Many estimators make do with a single column tagged "subcontractors." For my estimates, I like to distinguish between the subcontractors, such as plumbers and electricians who install material on a project, and those who provide support services, such as special inspections, sani-cans, hauling, rental equipment, and so on.

Note, also, that on the checklist form I have taken the jump from estimating by items to estimating by assemblies for part of the work. Joists, blocking, rims, and subfloor are estimated not as separate items but as an assembly on a square-foot basis. So is the roof frame and deck.

Although a checklist form can be written out by hand and copied, it is best to create it on a computer. A computer checklist form can be quickly customized for individual jobs. It can be easily expanded. When you think of or learn about new items, you simply type them in, then they are there in the checklist form when you print it out for your next estimate.

My own checklist/form eventually grew to about 15 pages. You can extend your checklist by using the sources described on p. 146. As your checklist grows in length, for control and clarity divide it into phases of work such as the

---

■ SAMPLE LETTERS AND FORMS
Word Processed Estimating Checklist Form

Once you have a word processed checklist/form on your computer, you can create a customized version for each estimate, fill it out by hand, and total and proof the numbers with an adding machine

Project: Alfano porch rebuild

Date: 4/21/02

Phase/Item	Quantity	Units	Labor	Material	Subcontractors	Services/Other
Project manage	10	hr.	500			
Set up	10 ¼	hr.	125	50		
Clean up	10 ¼	hr.	125			
Recycle	21	hr.	100			
Pickups	21	hr.	100			
Rough demo	7	hr.	350			
Precise demo	3	hr.	150			100 (haul)
Excavation	2	cubic yd.	160			
Foundation	3	cubic yd.	1200	600	(pump truck)	300
Framing						
Walls	16	lin. ft.	800	120		
Joists	} 80	⌀	200	100		
Blocks						
Rims						
Subfloor						
Posts	2	pc.	150	100		
Railing	16	lin. ft.	400	400		
Rafters	} 110	⌀	450	150		
Blocks						
Roof deck						
Siding	100	⌀	250	220		
Corner trim	4	pc.	100	60		
Stairs	2	step	200	200		
Roofing	110	⌀	50	---	700	
Stucco	300	⌀	100	----	1600	
SUBTOTALS			5510	2000	2300	400
TOTAL DIRECT COSTS				10,210		
OVERHEAD } PROFIT		to be determined				

Sources of Items for an Estimating Checklist

■ *Your experience as a tradesperson.* From having worked in the trades, you will be able to create a good starter list of items.

■ *Your experience as a building contractor.* As you build projects, you will become aware of items not covered in your estimating checklist. Make a note of items as soon as you spot them. Drop your notes in your in-box and add the items to your checklist the next time you do your office work.

■ *Lists in this book.* Include in your own checklist the slippery items and general conditions items provided here.

■ *Other published lists.* See Resources on p. 258 for sources of books that will provide you with comprehensive lists of items for the type of work you specialize in. The books aren't cheap—except when compared with the cost of missing a few items in your next estimates and building them for free.

■ *Lists incorporated into construction-estimating software.*

CSI Masterformat divisions shown on p. 149, or develop your own set of divisions to fit your business. Take special care to get in the subtle, slippery items that don't jump out at you on a set of plans. Those items are a big part of doing any job. You want your checklist to remind you of them.

General conditions

One entire division of slippery items that tend to elude builders is known as *general conditions*—the conditions that create costs across a major part or even the whole span of a project. In the handwritten estimate on p. 144, only one general condition is covered—job setup, which has to be done every day of the project. There are almost certainly other general costs required in the deck project (perhaps you can think of others). Even the checklist form on p. 145 only has five.

A really thorough estimating checklist will cover many more general conditions. The list on the facing page, while not inclusive, has served me well over the years. Of

the general conditions mentioned there, a few deserve special attention.

PERMITS You need to provide not only for the cost of the permits, but for the labor of obtaining them. Some building departments now enable you to apply for and receive permits efficiently via the Internet. At others, you must still spend hours slogging through one line after another.

CLEANUP It's a significant cost on any well-run job. Job sites must be kept organized and swept up for the sake of safety, to maintain crew morale, and as a gesture of respect for the clients and the neighborhood.

RECYCLING As dump fees rise steadily, recycling becomes a way to save money or even generate cash. But it is also often a cost.

SAFETY It takes time, but it is a lot less costly than accidents and is required by law.

DAILY SETUP AND ROLL-UP Both require from a quarter hour to half an hour, depending on the size of the project. Over the course of a three-month job, those fractions of hours add up to somewhere between 30 and 60 person hours. At current labor rates, even for apprentices, that is enough to buy a laptop computer.

PROJECT MANAGEMENT On many jobs it is by far the largest general condition cost. It includes your supervision time if you take the role of project manager in your company. Also, and often overlooked, it includes any management work by a lead carpenter. Even if you or someone else is providing project management, the lead will spend time studying plans and specs, ordering materials, and communicating with clients, subcontractors, and suppliers. In my company, where leads handle most project management with some backup from me, I have found that depending on a project's size, they will spend from 15 to 50 percent of their time on management.

General conditions typically comprise 8 to 10 percent—*more than the profit margins builders typically enjoy*—of the direct costs of building a project. Yet many builders, even quite experienced ones, hardly cover them in their estimates. No wonder general contractors so often operate on a nonprofit basis!

Other slippery items

Beyond general conditions, in every division and phase of rough and finish work there are slippery items that can elude you when you are calculating the costs of building a project. A few of the most treacherous ones are listed in the sidebar on p. 148. During the rough phase, though the gross demolition or dismantling for a project may be fairly obvious, after it is done there may remain items of what I call "precise deconstruction." They can be trickier to spot. Examples include removal of thousands of nails still sticking in the studs after plaster and lath have been torn away; carefully cutting away part of an old piece of trim and leaving the remainder to join to a new piece; or notching old framing to make room for an electrical box.

For start-up builders, the most dangerous of the slippery rough work is often excavation. It is *so* easy to underestimate. After all, what is there to digging a hole in the ground and hauling away some dirt? The answer is a great deal when the "dirt" is clay, rock, or similar material that must be chiseled out with a power shovel, sticks to tools like glue so that the tools must be scraped clean and lubricated repeatedly, or expands by 50 percent and more between the time you dig it out and load it into a truck to be hauled away. I initially thought of excavation as incidental to concrete

At the site of this old Masonic temple, being rebuilt into four apartments by builder Seth Melchert, there are half a dozen general conditions visible, and that's after the job has been shut down for the day.

▪ SAMPLE LETTERS AND FORMS General Conditions

General conditions include phases or items of work that occur throughout a project. Here, I have included a selection from my estimating checklist.

PERMITS AND INSPECTIONS
- ☐ Plan check
- ☐ Building permit
- ☐ Inspection fees
- ☐ Street-use deposit
- ☐ Parking permits
- ☐ Bonds

SITE SERVICES AND MAINTENANCE
- ☐ Office
- ☐ Storage
- ☐ Sanitation
- ☐ Phone
- ☐ Power pole
- ☐ Temporary power
- ☐ Temporary water hookup
- ☐ Water
- ☐ Security
- ☐ Weather protection
- ☐ Scaffolding
- ☐ Daily cleanup
- ☐ Final cleanup
- ☐ Recycling
- ☐ Waste

SAFETY
- ☐ Safety meetings
- ☐ Safety rails
- ☐ Hole covers
- ☐ Ditch covers
- ☐ Special equipment

PREPARATION AND CLOSEOUT
- ☐ Initial setup
- ☐ Final rollup
- ☐ Daily setup
- ☐ Daily rollup
- ☐ Yard protection
- ☐ Building protection, interior
- ☐ Building protection, exterior
- ☐ Vehicle, plant, other protection

PROJECT MANAGEMENT
- ☐ Project manager
- ☐ Lead person

SAMPLE LETTERS AND FORMS
A Checklist of Slippery Items in Rough and Finish Work

ROUGH WORK
- ☐ Precise deconstruction
- ☐ Excavation
- ☐ Shoring
- ☐ Furring
- ☐ Flashing

ROUGH AND FINISH WORK
- ☐ Layout
- ☐ Carpentry support for subcontractors
- ☐ Pickup and delivery
- ☐ Material handling
- ☐ Access
- ☐ Tie-ins to existing work
- ☐ Overtime to meet a tight schedule
- ☐ Extreme weather
- ☐ Intrusive owner
- ☐ Overbearing or sloppy designer

COMPLETION
- ☐ Corrections
- ☐ Adjustments
- ☐ Breakage
- ☐ Touch-up
- ☐ Returns
- ☐ Callbacks
- ☐ Customer instruction

SPECIALTY TRADES
- ☐ Overlaps between trades

Areas of a project where the work of many trades comes together—such as this food-prep and cooking area for the Nutritiously Gourmet Cooking School where the work of eight different specialties meet—involve many slippery costs for supervision and for miscellaneous items that fall between the trades.

work. With experience, I have become so leery of it that I now provide for it half a dozen or more times under different phases of work including site work, foundations, and sewers and plumbing. I have met builders who have gone broke on a job due to underestimated excavation costs. If you cannot accurately estimate excavation, subcontract it to an expert.

Flashing is equally critical and tricky. Often it is not shown on plans. But you must spot it and allow for the labor and material costs of installing it. If you do not, once the project is under way, you may face a choice of doing the work without pay or ending up in a lawsuit for failing to do it. Remember, leaks are *the* prime cause of construction litigation.

Other slippery items crop up in both rough and finish phases. Are you allowing for the time to lay out as well as nail together and install the items in your projects? For the pickup and delivery of material and for handling and storing it once it reaches your project site? Have you allowed for tie-ins of old to new work? I have often found that blending an old to new floor frame or tying new trim into the existing can take as long as all the associated new framing or trim itself.

Some conditions can add cost to every item in a job. A project that is difficult to access or too tight on space for workers to move around easily can soak up an extra 20 percent in labor. An excessively intrusive or inattentive owner or designer can exact a similar toll. So can severe weather.

At the end of all phases of work and all projects, there will be completion work to do. No project is ever perfect. Adjustments, corrections, touch ups, and callbacks are a normal part of getting a job up to standard. In my estimates, I include a lengthy list of completion items in the rough and finish divisions and allow a couple of percent of the cost of all other labor in the division for completion.

A final group of slippery items occurs in the areas of overlap between the trades. Who is going to set blocks for the plumbing supply lines, your crew or the plumbers? Who notches framing for electrical boxes? Who provides scaffolding for gutter installation and exterior painting? In our next chapter, we will look at a great tool, developed by one of the best subcontractors I know, for eliminating confusion about overlap items.

Professional estimating

Estimating, clearly, is highly skilled work—so skilled that it has evolved into a well-paid profession in its own right. Professional estimators use a supersize checklist known as Construction Standards Industry Masterformat. CSI Masterformat, to a large degree, parallels construction sequence. Each of the 16 divisions shown below is subdivided into progressively smaller categories (not shown) with all of them carrying a number code. For example, under division six for wood and plastics, you can work down through progressive subdivisions to Formica plastic laminates in solid colors, which carries the code 06241.101.

Some builders find CSI's Masterformat a pain and prefer to stick with their own sequence of items for estimating. It feels more natural. It corresponds to their experience of how projects are put together. They don't like trying to estimate according to someone else's prescription. Such objections to Masterformat are reasonable, and it is not likely to be of much use to a new builder at the start of his or her career. Down the road, however, you may enjoy benefits from adopting Masterformat.

Masterformat is very much part of the construction industry language. Although there are other formats in use in specific industry sectors, such as residential remodeling, they really amount to Masterformat with some of its divi-

sions broken into smaller ones and somewhat rearranged. Important catalogs of and guides to materials, including guides to environmentally considerate (i.e. "green") building materials, are organized according to Masterformat. Design firms organize their specifications according to Masterformat. If you plan to grow your company to the point where you will hire estimators, the likelihood is they will be accustomed to thinking in "Masterformatese," or some variation of it. They will have a lot less trouble getting up to speed in your company if it is using Masterformat rather than a format you have invented and they have never seen before.

Computerized estimating and bidding

Once you become comfortable with estimating on a word-processed checklist/form, consider moving to computerized estimating. The leap is much less difficult than the transition from manual to computerized accounting, and there are good reasons for making it as early in your career as possible, including:

▪ *Speed.* Even a very basic estimating program will save you a lot of time

CSI Masterformat Divisions
Masterformat includes these 16 primary divisions. Each is progressively subdivided until you get down to the level of specific items.

- General
- Site work
- Concrete
- Masonry
- Metals
- Woods and plastic
- Thermal and moisture protection
- Doors and windows
- Finishes
- Specialties
- Equipment
- Furnishings
- Special construction
- Conveying systems
- Mechanical
- Electrical

A Ladder of Computer Estimating Options

■ Generic electronic spreadsheet (basic use)
■ Generic electronic spreadsheet (advanced use)
■ Specialized construction-estimating software
■ Integrated construction-estimating software
■ Model-based estimating software

totaling numbers and checking your math. More advanced programs will even take over much of the work of entering numbers!

■ *Clarity of presentation.* The crisp look of a computer-printed estimate and bid inspires confidence in clients.

■ *Low cost.* If you already own a computer, it likely came with a generic electronic spreadsheet that you can build into a powerful estimating tool. Specialized estimating programs can be purchased for a few hundred dollars.

When you make the move to estimating by computer you can choose from a number of software options as listed above. To save money (though not necessarily time), you can start with the generic spreadsheet included with your computer. Initially, you will set it up much like a word-processed checklist. Create a list of items of work down the left-hand column. Across the top, set up other columns for labor, material, subs, and services. When you create an estimate you will enter all the quantities of work and the costs. The computer can take it from there, totaling and summarizing your costs in any way you program it to, thereby saving you a lot of tedious labor with your adding machine and, possibly, costly errors in arithmetic.

From such a basic level your generic spreadsheet can be developed into an advanced estimating and bidding tool. You can set it up to automatically enter

markups for overhead and profit or even go further and have it handle the multiplication involved in entering costs once you have entered quantities. You enter 100 ft. of 2×4 wall, for example, and the machine automatically fills in dollar amounts for labor and materials. One design/build remodeler I know built so much power into his generic spreadsheet that he could enter a dozen quantities for a highly complex remodel job, such as a custom kitchen incorporating an addition, and his estimating program would then crank out a complete estimate and bid.

Unfortunately, there is another side to the remodeler's story. It took him two years' worth of evenings and weekends to build his wondrous spreadsheet. If you are not that much of a computer geek, you may wish instead to buy a program specially designed for construction cost estimating and bidding. By checking in with the usual suspects—builder friends, Web sites, and the builder journals and bookstores listed in Resources on p. 258— you will be able to turn up promising products. Check out the demos and determine which program is for you. But be prepared for one downside. Programs designed by others will force you to estimate in ways that are different from your natural approach.

Among the specialized programs are a number that are integrated into accounting software packages. They offer a benefit but also have one drawback. The program may automatically set up a job cost record once you have created an estimate. But the estimating program may not suit your needs as well as a stand-alone program. In other words, efficiency gained from integration might be outweighed by effectiveness lost in estimating.

None of the estimating programs packaged with accounting programs I have seen approach the power of "model-based estimating programs." Essentially, these

▪ SAMPLE LETTERS AND FORMS   **Electronic Spreadsheet**

A computer estimating program can total all the labor, material, and subcontractor figures for each division of work in a project, then forward the totals to a summary sheet, such as the one shown here from American Contractor.

ABC Construction Co.   **BID SHEET SUMMARY**   Page 1
                                          Summary by Division   3/31/99

CLIENT: Van Deusen, Jay   JOB: Van Deusen Project   BID: 102.01.01   LAB BURD: 60.0%   OVERHEAD: 15.00% L
                                                          12/15/98   SALES TAX: 8.00%   5.00% M
                                                                                                     10.00% S
                                                                                                      5.00% E
                                                                                                      5.00% O

CODE	DIVISION	COMPL	LAB-HRS	LABOR (+Burd)	MATERIAL	SUBCON (+Tax)	EQUIP	OTHER	TOT COST	PROF%	BID
01	GENERAL REQUIREMI	Y	.0	0	758	758	0	1387	2,145		2,520
02	SITE WORK	Y	44.0	847	0	1,984	258	0	3,089		3,771
03	FOUNDATION	Y	24.4	537	704	0	0	0	1,241		1,493
06	FRAMING	Y	24.4	537	704	0	0	0	1,241		1,493
07	THERM/MOIST PROTE	Y	12.4	334	138	840	0	0	1,312		1,598
08	DOORS & WINDOWS	Y	8.5	228	789	0	0	0	1,017		1,201
09	FINISHING	Y	14.5	391	355	1,310	0	0	2,056		2.489
10	SPECIALTIES	Y	7.0	189	734	0	0	0	923		1,087
12	FURNISHINGS	Y	0.0	0	0	790	0	0	790		956
15	MECHANICAL	Y	0.0	0	0	2,500	0	0	2,500		3,025
16	ELECTRICAL	Y	0.0	0	0	2,670	0	0	2,670		3,231
	BID SHEET TOTALS:	Y	218.5	5,427	5,979	10,852	258	1,387	23,903		

                                                                    OVERHEAD: 9.5%   2,282
                                                                    PROFIT: 10.0%   2,620 =========
                                                                    ORIGINAL BID   28,805

CHANGE ORDERS

# CHANGE ORDER	COMPL	LAB-HRS	LABOR (+Burd)	MATERIAL	SUBCON (+Tax)	EQUIP	OTHER	TOT COST	BID
1 WET BAR	Y	2.00	54	0	345	0	0	399	486
TOTAL CHANGES	Y	2.00	54	0	345	0	0	399	486
		220.5	5,481	5,979	11,197	258	1,387	24,302	

                                                                    OVERHEAD: 9.6%   2,325
                                                                    PROFIT: 10.0%   2,664 =========
                                                                    ORIGINAL BID   29,291

programs work like the one developed by the design/build remodeler I described previously. You simply key in a few basic quantities, such as square feet of floor space, number of windows, length and height of walls, and so on. The program returns a complete, detailed estimate and bid. Such programs are costly, but the investment may come back to you many times over in hours saved, never mind tedium avoided, in performing cost calculations we will discuss in the next chapter. If you have been laboring over hand-written estimates, watching a model-based program perform feels like the next best thing to being present for the Second Coming. You feel like you have been saved from eternal estimating damnation.

COMING UP

Setting Up a Project Binder

Preparing the Plans

Calculating Quantities of Work

Inspecting the Site
with Subcontractors

Taking Sub Quotes

Establishing Labor Costs

Gathering Information

To calculate costs for a project, you need information from many sources—plans, specifications, the site, subcontractors, and suppliers. All that information must be gathered efficiently, then organized so that it can be readily accessed when the time comes to sit down and calculate costs. To gather it, you need systematic procedures. To organize it, you need a good information management system.

Fortunately, a really good information management system is widely available, and it's cheap. I remember when another builder, who started out in business about the time I did, discovered this system and told me about it. His tone expressed profound appreciation, mingled with amusement that he had not thought of it before. "Three-ring binders with tabbed dividers, David," he said. "You've got to start using them. They're *great*." He's right. Three-ring binders are wonderful for keeping track of all the procedures and managing all the information necessary to estimate, bid, and then run a construction project. I now set one up for every single project I get involved with. Someday, I may trade my binders for a laptop computer. But I doubt it. I will use a computer to generate and update documents. But I will keep on using the binder to store and access them. It can't be beat for low cost, accessibility, portability, and reliability.

Setting up a project binder

For each of my own projects, I set up a binder with approximately a dozen divisions, including:

GENERAL PROJECT INFORMATION
A page or two for the project address and the phone numbers, E-mail addresses, etc., of major participants in the job.

TO-DO LISTS A master list covers the entire process of estimating and bidding, and coordinates with subordinate to-do lists for plan preparation and site inspection.

QUESTIONS Here I keep separate pages for questions for the owner, the designer, each supplier and each sub, the building department, and the project lead. During estimating and bidding, and later during construction, when I think of a question I write it down immediately.

TAKE-OFF SHEETS Here are recorded the quantities of work that are, to use a construction industry term "taken off" of—i.e. figured from—the plans.

THE ESTIMATE AND BID All cost calculations are done on spreadsheets. When cost calculations are complete, a cover sheet showing the costs summarized by phase of work, the markups for overhead and for profit, and the bid price is added.

THE ASSUMPTIONS This is a really critical section. As I calculate costs, I typically have to make assumptions about materials and construction technique. Concrete is to be high-volume fly-flash, mix #pq3479; drywall to be level 5 smooth, except textured in garage, and so on. I write down all assumptions as I make them, run them by the owner and designer, and include them in the contract as necessary. If you go into construction with assumptions different from the owners and designers, you've got problems. Catch and clear your assumptions during estimating.

BUILDING NOTES Occasionally during estimating, I enjoy a brainstorm about how to build a project. I write down my idea. When construction starts, if it still seems useful, I bring it up for discussion with the project lead.

PROJECT PLANS AND SPECIFICA-TIONS FROM THE DESIGNER   Most builders roll up their plans. I like all my documentation to be in one place, so I fold up my estimating set and clip it into the back of the binder, dividing it into sections if necessary.

CONTRACTS AND CHANGE ORDERS
Preconstruction contracts, construction contracts, and change orders are placed in the binder in the order in which they are signed.

SUBCONTRACTOR BIDS AND CON-TRACTS   They are stored in the order in which the subs will first work on the job during construction.

At a glance, setting up so many divisions may seem like overkill. *It is not.* Once you have gone through the process a few times, setting up each new binder takes minutes. Those minutes save many hours of searching for information during estimating and bidding and during construction. I once heard a construction business consultant say that in the well-organized company you can find any piece of information you need within 15 minutes. With well-organized three-ring binders, you can find the information you need to estimate and run projects in seconds.

Preparing the plans and figuring quantities

With a binder set up, you are ready to study the plans and prepare them for cost calculations. For my projects, I study plans systematically, first scanning them loosely and taking in the overall scope of work, then carefully reading each page. During the second pass, I highlight several kinds of items with different-color pens to make sure I do not miss them during the cost calculations.

■ SAMPLE LETTERS AND FORMS
Estimate/Bid To-Do List

1. Set up project binder with sections for:
   - ☐ Cost plan agreement
   - ☐ Questions for: owner, designer, subs, suppliers, building department, others
   - ☐ Estimate and bid
   - ☐ Assumptions
   - ☐ Building notes
   - ☐ Project plans and specifications
   - ☐ Construction contract and change orders

2. Study plans and specifications (see checklist)

3. Order sets for subcontractors and suppliers

4. Take off material and labor quantities (see checklist)

5. Set up site visit with owner and schedule subs (check off when quotes received)
   - ☐ Excavator
   - ☐ Deconstruction, salvage and recycle
   - ☐ Mechanical & sheet metal
   - ☐ Plumbing
   - ☐ Electrical
   - ☐ Insulation
   - ☐ Drywall
   - ☐ Roofing
   - ☐ _____
   - ☐ _____
   - ☐ _____

6. Visit site (see checklist)
   - ☐ Give each sub plans and walk through project
   - ☐ Inspect site
   - ☐ Submit requests for quotes to suppliers and fabricators
   - ☐ _____
   - ☐ _____
   - ☐ _____
   - ☐ _____

7. Calculate all costs for crew labor and materials

8. Enter quotes from subs and suppliers

9. Figure overhead

10. Figure profit

11. Create summary sheet with bid

12. Present bid

With plan study and highlighting complete, the next step is to take off (to figure) the quantities of labor and material in the project. You will greatly increase efficiency if you complete your take-offs before starting to calculate costs. In other words, efficiency in estimating is

SAMPLE LETTERS AND FORMS
Plan Study and Preparation Checklist

1. Review plans overall.

2. Read each page top to bottom; note all questions.

3. Correlate plans; note questions:
   - ☐ Relate site plan to foundation plan.
   - ☐ Relate floor plans to roof plan.
   - ☐ Relate floor and roof plans to elevations.
   - ☐ Relate structural plans to floor and roof plans and elevations.
   - ☐ Relate mechanical, plumbing, and electrical plans to structural plans and to one another.

4. Call designer and engineer about any conflicts between requirements in plans.

5. Highlight plans
   - ☐ Unusual sub work—red
   - ☐ Unusual crew work—green
   - ☐ Structural hardware—yellow
   - ☐ Beams—orange
   - ☐ Other unusual conditions and high cost items—purple

The Stud Conundrum: Where Have all the 2×4s gone

Allowing a stud per foot is a great rule of thumb for estimating, but as you have probably discovered, no matter how many studs you order, you will not have enough—you will be three pieces short. If you order one stud for every *inch* instead of every foot, you will still be three short. I can't explain why. I have talked to many builders about the problem. None seem to know where the darn studs get to.

Stud evaporation is one of the greatest of all construction mysteries, right up there with how the Egyptians built the pyramids without beer and pizza available for TGIF parties. The best stab at solving the stud conundrum came from the old-timer who told me that when he died, prior to checking in with St. Peter, he was going to take a side trip to the fifth dimension. He had it on good authority, he said, that he'd find his 2×4s there, along with decades' worth of missing truck keys, socks, and nail pullers. I asked him to keep me posted on the results of his explorations. Any word I get back I will pass on to you at my Web site.

achieved in the same way it is achieved in framing. *You consolidate your operations.* You don't want to be going back and forth between take-offs and cost calculating any more than you want to go back and forth between laying out centers on your top plates and running your joists across the top of them.

Often, for a given item or assembly, the same take-offs will serve for both materials and labor costs. If the crew is going to install prehung doors, you need only one number to tell you how many doors to order and for how many to calculate labor cost. Sometimes, however, you'll need take-offs for labor beyond what you will need for material. For interior baseboard material costs, you'll need only the species, grade, pieces, and dimensions—for example, Clear VG Fir, 10 pcs. @ $1 \times 4 \times 10'$. For labor, however, you'll also need the number of corners. A complex living room with bays and built-ins featuring 10 inside scribes and 10 outside miters may require the same amount of baseboard material as a rectangular bedroom with four inside corners and four butt joints at doorways. But installing base in the two rooms will take very different amounts of labor.

Take-offs can be done in a variety of different units:

- ▪ *Number of pieces.* Particularly useful for finish items such as casings and baseboard.
- ▪ *Linear feet.* Often you'll need the linear footage of pieces, say 1×4—6/10' and 8/12' for a total of 156'.
- ▪ *Square feet.* For sheet material such as subfloor and wall sheathing.
- ▪ *Board feet.* An alternative to pieces and linear feet for framing lumber. Board feet are figured with the following formula:
  Nominal Thickness (inches) × Nominal Width (inches) × Length (feet) / 12 = Board Feet

Examples:

1" × 1" × 1' = 1 board foot

2" × 6" × 1'= 1 board foot

2" × 12" × 1' = 2 board feet

2" × 4" × 8' = 5.33 board feet

300 2 × 6s each 10 ft. long contain 3,000 board feet

There can be a benefit and a loss to taking off material quantities in board footage. Using the board footage formula, you can sometimes figure your quantities more rapidly. On the other hand, if you use board footage for costs, when it comes to building the job, you will have to do take-offs again to create a "lumber list," that is, a list of pieces to actually order from your supplier.

Several time-honored rules of thumb will help you figure quantities both quickly and accurately:

- *Volumes of excavation.* Soil expands when you dig it up. In my area, I allow 50 percent to be on the safe side.
- *Volumes of concrete.* You need to allow for spillage and a little extra so you are not sending the truck back for a last quarter yard. For small projects, 5 percent extra can be tight; 10 percent is normally safe.
- *Joists and rafters.* At 16 in. on center, allow three for every 4 ft., another for the end of each run, plus additional pieces for rims and blocks. Figure the rim and block stock at the same length as the joists or rafters, and count on selecting the best sticks for the joists or rafters while using the culls for rims and blocks.
- *Studs.* At 16 in. o.c., allow one per foot of wall. Figure gable ends as if each stud were the length of the tallest. Then you should have enough materials for corners, window doublers, and partitions.

SAMPLE LETTERS AND FORMS   Take-off Form

As with other forms, you can create a generic take-off form with your word processor, then modify it to fit particular jobs. For complex jobs, take-off sheets could run twice the length or more of the partially completed form shown here.

Project: Alfano porch rebuild

Date: 4/21/02

Phase/Item/Assembly	Unit	Quantity	Comment/Cost
Site Prep.			
Grading	cubic yd.	3 (expanded)	hand-dig
Concrete			
Excavation	cubic yd.	3 (expanded)	hand-dig
Footings	cubic yd.	3	$246
Grade beams			
Stem walls	cubic yd.	1	Form w/ joists/ $82 per yd.
Rebar	pcs.	10 @ 5/8×20	$3.00 each
Floor Frame			
Joists	pcs./lin. ft.	16 @ 2×10×8	$1.60 ft.
Rims, blocks			
Subflooring	sheets	4 @ 5/8×4×8	T+G/$24 sheet
Wall Frame			
Exterior walls	pcs.	3 @ 2×4×20	#1/$.50 ft.
Interior walls		45 @ 2×4×10	
Headers	pcs.	3 @ 4×10×10	#2/$4.90 ft.
Sheathing	sheets	8 @ 1/2×4×10	CDX/$32 sheet
Roof Frame			
Ridge			
Rafters			
Exposed tails			
Blocks			
Structural Hardware		to be determined	
Hold-downs			
Straps			
MBs, nuts, washers			
Other			
Doors & Windows			
Doors		See supplier quote	
Windows			
Exterior Finish			
Siding			
Trim		To be determined	
Interior Finish			
Other	By owner		

SAMPLE LETTERS AND FORMS Site Visit Checklist

BRING!!!

☐ Ladders

☐ Tape measures

☐ Flashlights

☐ Overalls

☐ Rain gear

☐ Project binder

☐ Laptop

☐ Lunch bucket (with lunch)

☐ Stop off for subcontractor doughnuts (jelly, chocolate covered, glazed)

SUBS

☐ Introduce to owner

☐ Each sub: give plans and orient to job; point out unusual features; clarify which sub handles which items of work where trades overlap

☐ Walk-through

NEIGHBORHOOD

☐ Access

☐ Parking

☐ Adjacent properties (protection needs)

SITE

☐ Access

☐ Power availability

☐ Sanitary facilities availability

☐ Phone availability

☐ Water availability

☐ Area for material drops

☐ Area for recyclables and waste

☐ Excavation concerns

☐ Protection (plants, structures, vehicles, other)

☐ Utility tie-ins—water, waste, power, communications cables

☐ Distractions (pets! children! hovering neighbors!)

EXISTING BUILDINGS

☐ Access and movement—space for crew and subs?

☐ Deconstruction concerns

☐ Hazards

☐ Plumb and level conditions

☐ Areas to set up temporary facilities for owner

☐ Interior protection requirements

☐ Structural tie-ins, old to new

☐ Finish tie-ins, old to new

☐ Deteriorated existing rough or finish work (photo; note in assumptions)

Site visit and subcontractor quotes

Rather than just sending them plans, meet with subcontractors at the project site. Invariably, they will spot issues and cost items you overlook. For competitive bids, you and your subs will likely be herded through the site in an hour or two along with the teams from other companies. For my own projects, which are almost all done on a cost planning or design/build basis, I like to set aside at least a half day for subs to visit the site and study it myself. I phone each of the subs and write down their estimated time of arrival (ETA), trying to space them out so they do not end up in a long line.

When the subs arrive, I have a set of plans and specs for each of them. I require providing plans and specs under "Owner's Responsibilities" in my cost planning agreements. Working up quotes, I explain to my clients, is time-consuming work for subcontractors. They can be much more efficient with a set of plans they can take back to their offices. Providing each sub with a set creates good will for the long working relationship that lies ahead and reduces the chance the subs will overlook an aspect of their work and need to make up for the miss with change order artistry during construction. I do not remember an owner ever balking at providing sets. I often hear subs exclaim "Wonderful!" when I tell them they will have their own plans and specifications. Apparently it's a courtesy they are not often paid.

At the site, I give each subcontractor his plans and walk him through the project, pointing out any special features or difficulties associated with the work in his trade. Sometimes noting a problem for subs may result in higher quotes. Left to themselves, they might have missed

■ SAMPLE LETTERS AND FORMS   Lunt-Marymor Checklist

The final step in gathering information is to get quotes from your subcontractors. Asking them to submit a checklist, such as this one from The Lunt Marymor Plumbing and Heating Company, eliminates estimating oversights in areas of work where the

responsibilities of the different trades overlap. It also eliminates arguments during the job as to who is responsible for what items of work.

BUDGET ESTIMATE

Mobilizations: The base bid assumes one mobilization only per rough and finish phases, unless otherwise specified above. Extra mobilizations will accrue an extra staging charge of $89.00 per man. All work is assumed to occur during normal business hours.

Owner-Provided Materials: Fixtures and materials provided by others must be delivered to the point of installation complete with dimensioned rough-in sheets, in a timely and defect-free condition to avoid extra charges for downtime, repairs, and/or reinstallations.

Payment Terms: Our bid proposal is based on payment-in-full on progress completion, no retention allowed. Our quote is good for 30 calendar days from the date of this bid proposal. We reserve the right to review the Primary Contract.

Our time and materials rates are as follows:

Journeyman Plumber $____/hour

Apprentice Plumber $____/hour

Materials *Modern* Wholesale Trade List Price

Exclusions

	Included	N.I.C.		Included	N.I.C.
Utility coordination and fees	_____	_____	Install roof jacks	_____	_____
Water meter coordination and fees	_____	_____	Install tub/shower protection	_____	_____
Sewer, sewer permit, and fees	_____	_____	Install mortar base	_____	_____
Plumbing permit and fees	_____	_____	Install appliances	_____	_____
Water pressure reducing valve	_____	_____	Cut and/or drill countertops	_____	_____
Electrical wiring	_____	_____	Provide and install nail plates	_____	_____
Trench and backfill	_____	_____	Patch and paint finish surfaces	_____	_____
Concrete demo, cut, haul, core	_____	_____	Install blocking	_____	_____
Import backfill materials	_____	_____	Install fire stopping	_____	_____
Insulate hot water lines	_____	_____	Provide and install scaffolding	_____	_____
Install foundation and site drainage	_____	_____	Offsite debris removal	_____	_____
Sheet metal	_____	_____	Clean-up of fixtures	_____	_____

1270 45th St., Emeryville, CA 94608 • TEL (510) 985-2889 • FAX (510) 985-2692 • BidProposal.bid.wpd License #764839

the problem and the extra work it requires. But you don't want to let your subs walk into a trap. In the long run, your support will be compensated. Once a sub told me I was known among my subcontractors as "tough but fair." The toughness protects my company and clients. The fairness seems to go a long way with the subs. Never has one of my subs declined to work with me or walked away from his or her responsibilities on a job. On the contrary, they've returned fair play with stunning reliability.

While the subs are exploring the site, I look it over myself, if I have not already done so, working through my site visit checklist. I write on the plans or in my binder any conditions that will affect costs, assumptions, or charges for overhead and profit. If parking is going to be a problem, I write a note on the site plan. If a site for new construction borders property with vulnerable plantings, I note the need for protecting them. If I have questions for anyone involved with the project, I write those down, too.

Finally, I take special care to note the conditions for tie-ins between existing and new work. Tie-ins—of a new floor to a warped old one, of a new wall to a stucco-covered existing one—consume huge amounts of labor.

As I look over the site, I frequently pause to exchange information with my subcontractors and occasionally ask the owner to discuss questions with us. I prefer subcontractors to visit the site when the owners are there. If your subcontractors are knowledgeable, candid, and friendly they will strengthen your bid for the project. The owners see they are the kind of people who they want working on their property. Their trust in your team—and the chances that they will take the step to contracting with you for construction—go up.

COMING UP

The Key

Subcontractor Costs

Material Costs

Allowances

Labor Costs

Checking Your Cost Estimate

Calculating Direct Costs

Calculating direct costs for a project within a few percent requires no fancy tricks or razzle-dazzle technology. Along with fluency at basic arithmetic, you need only a determination to be thorough. As the first person who taught me about estimating explained, the worst mistake you can make is to leave the cost of an item out of your estimate; that's likely to hurt you more than getting a cost wrong. If you have systematic procedures and checklists in place, you have what you need to be thorough in calculating all your direct costs.

Subcontractor costs and material costs

For my estimates, I begin by calculating and entering costs for subcontractors and materials. That's the easy part of estimating. It goes fast, and it warms you up for the harder work to come.

For subcontractor costs, transfer the number from the subcontractor's quotes (i.e. bids) to your estimating sheet. For a trusted sub doing a very small amount of work, you might make use of a phone quote that you have written down and read back for confirmation. But for any larger amount of work, a written quote with an included/not included checklist such as the one on p. 153 is essential. I strongly advise against guesstimating the costs of sub trade work at which you are not expert. You will make errors exceeding your entire markup for overhead and profit on the project. Enter sub quotes carefully. It is distressingly easy to enter $3,400 worth of plumbing as $340.

The sub's bid is not the total cost of sub trade work. As noted in our slippery-items checklist on p. 148, there's also the cost of support work by your crew (or yourself if you are the crew). For plumbers, you must cut and block framing, for electricians set blocks and open walls, for all subs coordinate layout and lend a hand every so often, and, of course, provide doughnuts—jelly, chocolate-covered, *and* plain, weekly, at least. For the material you can usually just toss in a "plug figure." To calculate labor costs, draw on your labor cost records or construct a cost as best you can. When you have completed entering a sub trade cost, you'll have a line in your estimate that looks like this:

	Quantity	Labor	Material	Sub-contractor	Service/Other
Plumbing	------	$80	$30	$270	------

To complete sub costs, make certain that any related general condition costs are entered. If a job involves scaffolding for the plasterer and painter, be sure that cost is included in your general conditions division if the subs are not providing it.

For material costs, it is important to get written quotes from your supplier for any other than very small quantities. Those quotes must be recent and should include a "good until" date. Do not use a quote from a project you estimated half a year ago. Construction material costs race up and down, and you need fresh numbers to calculate the costs accurately for your estimates.

When calculating material costs, make certain that sales tax is included as well as a percentage for miscellaneous and waste. Your crew will need a little extra material for furring and blocking. They will make occasional mis-cuts and have to throw away a stick.

With material calculations, allow for the supplier's charges for delivering material and—very important—your costs for receiving it, checking the load to make sure it is right, and handling it from initial storage to bringing it to the point of installation. *These delivery, storage, and handling costs add up over the course of a job.*

Allowances

For some subcontractor and material costs, you will not be able to come up with an exact cost for your estimate. In the case of sub costs, the work may involve so many unknown conditions that it will have to be done on a time and material basis. In the case of materials, the costs sometimes can't be known at the time of estimating. During periods of steep inflation in the overall economy or when construction is booming and bottlenecks and shortages are developing, costs can fluctuate wildly, doubling or tripling in the course of a few months, then plunging back down. Even during stable times, there are materials or fixtures such as tile, appliances, or electrical fixtures in nearly every project that are not selected till after the contract for construction is signed.

In all these cases, you can use allowances in place of fixed costs. The allowances go in your estimate. They also go in

---

▪ SAMPLE LETTERS AND FORMS
Subcontractor and Material Cost Checklist

SUBCONTRACTOR COSTS
- ☐ Enter subcontractor costs from written quote.
- ☐ Use phone quotes only for very small quantities of work.
- ☐ Check entry for accuracy.
- ☐ Enter cost of material needed to support sub work.
- ☐ Enter cost of labor needed to support sub work.
- ☐ Check that related general condition costs are entered.

MATERIAL COSTS
- ☐ Use only recent quotes.
- ☐ Count number of items in plans.
- ☐ Add a percentage for waste where appropriate.
- ☐ Multiply items by cost per item and enter in estimate.
- ☐ Make sure tax included.
- ☐ Make sure delivery and handling covered.
- ☐ Check entry for accuracy of quote used and for math.

---

your contract with the explanation that the allowances will be adjusted for actual costs during construction. If you allow $4 per sq. ft. for 100 sq. ft. of tile and the owners later choose $10 per sq. ft. tile, you adjust the allowance of $400 to $1,000. (With a large allowance adjustment, both for the owner's information and to protect yourself, you should submit a change order prior to buying the material.)

Exercise restraint in using allowances. Too often, they are used to make up for failure to think through a design sufficiently in advance or to avoid the work of accurately calculating costs. Such short cutting comes back to haunt you. Design and estimating get shoved into the middle of construction, opening the possibility for tension between builder and owner and for delays in construction. Owners get angry when they are pushed to make important design decisions in a hurry in the middle of a job. They become contentious when they see actual costs outstripping allowances. If the owner is unable to make the design decisions or contests the costs, then construction can grind to a halt with serious consequences all around.

> Too often, allowances are used to make up for failure to think through a design sufficiently in advance or to avoid the work of accurately calculating costs.

Constructing a Labor Productivity Rate

A builder was calculating costs for a second-story addition with a steep gable end roof. He had no productivity records for rafter framing. To construct a productivity rate, he took the following steps:

1. *Made the assumption* that he would be able to frame the side walls and ridge so that they were level and parallel and that he would, therefore, be able to gang-cut the rafters and not have to fit each one individually.

2. *Found his nearest existing productivity record*, two person hours to lay out, cut, set and nail off 11 ceiling joists.

3. *Figured the time needed to install each joist* to be 11 minutes (2 hours = 120 minutes. 120 divided by 11 joists = 10.9 minutes per joist. Rounded off, that gives a productivity rate of 11 minutes per joist).

4. *Adjusted the rate for the joists to get a rate for the rafters.* 11 minutes + 2 minutes extra for layout + 2 minutes to cut bird's mouth + 3 minutes to lay out, cut, and sand exposed tail + 2 minutes extra install time = 20 minutes per rafter.

5. *Calculated a new productivity rate* of 3 rafters per hour to lay out, cut, and install (60 minutes/20 minutes = 3).

The builder wisely decided to use a labor productivity rate of two rafters per hour instead of three, figuring that since he did not have a rate based on actual experience, he wanted to give himself a margin of safety.

Calculating labor costs

While material cost can be pinned down closely, labor costs are a more elusive target. You cannot know in advance exactly how productive your crew will be on a given task. The productivity of even a reliable employee can vary from job to job. If a terrific carpenter's marriage goes through a bad patch, he may be so distracted and upset his productivity may drop by 50 percent temporarily. You can't do much to adjust your estimates for such unpredictable *future* events, but what you can do to foster accurate estimates of labor costs is to use a four-step process, using knowledge from *past* efforts:

1. For each item of work *pull the quantity* from your take-off sheets.

2. *Determine the productivity rate* for the item, either from your productivity records or by constructing a rate.

3. *Determine hourly labor costs* (wage plus labor burden) you will incur on the project.

4. Multiply quantity of items x productivity rate × burdened wage to get the cost of labor for the item, as in this example: ½ hour per sheet of subfloor × $45 per hour × 50 sheets = $2,250.

Step one of the process is self explanatory. For step two, determining the productivity rate for an item, the best choice is to draw on the kinds of narrative labor productivity records I have described in "Keeping Job Cost Records" on p. 78. If you are starting out or have not yet begun the work of creating them, your productivity records may be thin. In that case, you can construct a productivity rate.

On occasion, you may want to take a hands-on approach to constructing a rate. I was once asked by an owner to use threaded bronze boat nails to install 2×6s on a large deck. I'd never heard of such nails and figured I'd better find out what it was like to use them, so I picked up a bag from my supplier. What I discovered was that the nails hold like a pit bull once in, but drive about as well as wax candles. You don't drive them. You tap each one gently into a predrilled hole. After bending a dozen, I tapped another dozen into predrilled holes and saw the bronze boat nail requirement was going to at least triple the usual amount of labor needed to install decking. I never would have guessed the difference to be half that great, so my test saved me from underestimating the labor costs of the job by thousands of dollars. Not bad pay for a quarter hour's work. Usually, constructing a productivity rate takes even less effort, as illustrated on the facing page.

Labor burden

For the third step in calculating labor costs for a project, determining hourly costs for employees who will work on the project, the critical thing is to include not only wages but also labor burden. If you are paying a carpenter $30 an hour and burden is 50 percent, then your burdened cost for that carpenter is $45 an hour ($30 × 150% = $45). This is the figure you must use in calculating labor costs of items he will build. Not incidentally, unless you feel like giving away the value of your labor, if you are doing hands-on work yourself, figure the charges at what it would cost—namely, wages plus labor burden—to put another person of equal skill on the job. If a good lead carpenter is earning $35 an hour in wages, it's going to cost you at least $52 an hour to put one to work on a project. If you are working as lead carpenter, you should aim to charge your time at $52 an hour—and that's before overhead and profit markups.

In the chart of accounts for a one-write system (pp. 70–71), I have listed labor burden items. You may be able to project your burdened labor costs for a new project right from your accounting records, but it's probably not the way to go. Figuring from your accounting records is likely to be clumsy. Moreover, burden costs fluctuate constantly, and the latest fluctuations may not show up in your accounts. Social security taxes go up; unemployment taxes go up and down; workers' compensation and liability insurance rates explode upward, then sink. Therefore, you don't want to project what labor burden will be from what it has been during past projects as shown in your accounting records. You are better off figuring what it is likely to

be (by checking your most recent insurance and tax rates) when construction gets under way.

In calculating burden include all the costs listed in the sidebar below that apply to your company. If you are new to all this, you may be taken aback at how high your burden is. But the fact is, 50 percent of wages for labor burden is a tight figure for any company if consumables are included at a prudent 10 percent. For a company incurring the majority of the basic and additional labor burden components listed in the sidebar, the burden can easily reach

Components of Labor Burden

Labor burden is made up of the costs beyond wages of having employees. The basic costs are those any company with a legitimate payroll will have. Additional costs are those that established companies providing good employee benefits may have. Alternative costs are those that fall into a gray area. They could be considered either labor burden, general company overhead, or in the case of profit-sharing, a part of profit.

Basic
- Employer's share of social security tax
- Employer's share of Medicare/Medicaid taxes
- Unemployment insurance
- Disability insurance
- Workers' compensation insurance
- Liability insurance (portion based on employee wages)
- Consumables, a.k.a. crew supplies (small tools and supplies used up on projects)
- Employee education

Additional
- Health insurance
- Dental insurance
- Vision insurance
- Retirement plan
- Vacation pay
- Vehicles
- Union charges

Alternative
- Hiring and firing
- Payroll processing
- Profit-sharing

Checking Your Estimate

- Let it sit a few days.
- Confirm assumptions with designer and client.
- Scan plans for any overlooked items.
- Scan estimating checklist for any overlooked items.
- Check quotes from suppliers against entries in spreadsheet.
- Check quotes from subcontractors against entries in spreadsheet.
- Check accuracy of labor rates.
- Check math.
- Reanalyze high-cost phases, assemblies, and items.
- Evaluate overall labor costs.

Unless you feel like giving away the value of your labor, if you are doing hands-on work yourself, figure the charges at what it would cost—namely, wages plus labor burden—to put another person of equal skill on the job.

65 percent. For companies that are unionized and/or provide top field employees with a vehicle, labor burden rises past 100 percent.

Checking your cost calculations

When a cost estimate is complete, it should be checked over from beginning to end. Ideally, the check is done by another estimator. If you run a compact operation like I do, however, you probably do not have anyone else to do the check. Instead, set aside your estimate for a few days, then go back and recheck it, taking the steps included in the sidebar above.

Although the steps may appear a bit intimidating at a glance, it actually takes little time to go through them. Scanning the plans, checking quotes from subcontractors and suppliers, and making certain the productivity rates and hourly charges used to calculate labor costs are right is mechanical work. If you are using a computer program, you probably don't even need to check the math. The program should get it right.

The next couple of steps require gearing down into a more thoughtful mode, but the payoff is great. Reanalyzing high-cost phases, assem-

blies, and items does a lot to ensure your estimate stays within a tight margin of error. If you have created a $50,000 estimate for a job and made a 50 percent error on a $100 item—estimated it at $50 instead of $100—that translates into a 0.1% error at the bottom line (50,000/50 = 0.1%).

However, if you make merely a 10 percent mistake on a $7,500 item, your mistake translates into a 1.5% error on the bottom line ($7,500 × 10% = $750; 50,000/750 = 1.5%). And 1.5% could be a fifth of your potential profit on the job. Moreover, on many jobs, a number of big costs dominate the overall cost of the project. So if you reanalyze the big items and get their costs right, you have taken a huge step to making certain your whole estimate is within a tight margin of error.

The biggest cost of all in a project, and also the toughest to calculate, as we have already stressed, is likely to be the labor of your crew. For that reason, running a check on labor, not only line by line but for the project overall, is really important. To do so, follow these steps:

1. *Total all the labor hours in a project.* For example, for a moderate-size remodel, the labor in your estimate totals up to 967 hours.
2. *Convert those hours into weeks of crew work.* The 967 hours boils down to just over eight 40-hour weeks for a crew of three [967/(40 × 3) = 8.1]. During the job, the actual crew size will vary: A carpenter and apprentice will be on the job beginning to end, but the number of laborers will vary from three early on to none at the end. Still, three will be about the average crew size.
3. *Compare to similar projects.* Your records show that two similar projects employing similar crews

took seven weeks and nine weeks, respectively. You are assured that your estimate of eight plus weeks of crew labor for the new project is reasonably close.

Even if your labor cost estimate ends up being off 10 percent, if that eight plus week job takes close to nine, your overall cost estimate may be very close. Here is why. Your subcontractor costs, based as they are largely on sub bids, should be right on. Material estimates, if you have been thorough, and not missed anything, should likewise be very close, based as they are on supplier quotes or allowances. While it is not always true, labor often represents only one-third or so of total direct costs. Therefore, even if the labor estimate is off 10 percent, your overall estimate will be off only a few percent ($\frac{1}{3} \times 10\% = 3.3\%$). Thus it is that with methodical work you can quite regularly create cost estimates that come within a very few percent of actual cost.

As I said at the beginning of this section, there's no fancy footwork required. With systems and thoroughness, you eliminate guesstimating. You get rid of fudge factoring. You sweep aside all the excuses for sloppy estimating. You create professional estimates.

If you are working on a cost plan/build or design/build basis, your estimates will genuinely be worth the professional fee you charge for them. Whether you are cost planning or bidding competitively, with accurate cost estimating you will also create a solid base from which to take the next steps in estimating and bidding, namely adding charges for overhead and profit. Both are figured on the basis of the direct costs. They can be figured accurately only to the extent the direct cost basis is accurate.

Figuring Overhead

One successful design/builder recalls that when he was starting his business, he was so in love with building he would have "*paid* people to work on their homes." After a time it dawned on him he actually was, in effect, paying his clients. He was footing the bill for his clients' projects three different ways: By charging less than market rates for his hands-on work on their projects; by failing to recover any of his overhead costs from them; and by foregoing the profit that he deserved in exchange for taking on the financial risks associated with building their bathrooms, kitchens, and additions. Like a lot of us early in our careers (and a lot of others all through their careers), he was subsidizing his clients' shopping spree.

To succeed financially as a builder you need to move beyond the point of

COMING UP

Why You Must Charge for Overhead and Profit

Resistance to Charging

Identifying Your Overhead Costs

The Uniform Percentage Method

The Capacity-Based Method

A Moving Target

Figuring Overhead

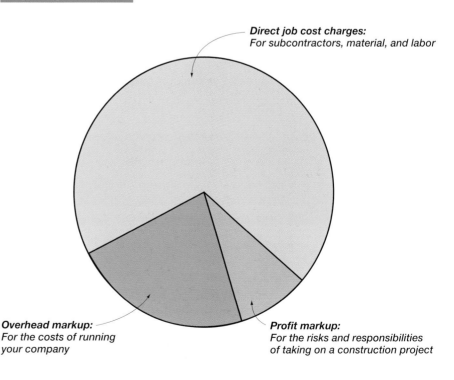

Direct job cost charges:
For subcontractors, material, and labor

Overhead markup:
For the costs of running your company

Profit markup:
For the risks and responsibilities of taking on a construction project

footing the bill for your clients' projects. You need to charge them at three levels:

■ *Direct job costs.* As stressed previously, your calculations of labor, material, and subcontractor costs must be thorough so that you recover them all from clients during construction.

■ *Overhead (indirect costs).* A portion of your company's overhead costs must be recovered on each job.

■ *Profit.* You must charge a profit in order to build a cash reserve against unexpected costs, to support your company through hard times, to fund growth, and as compensation for taking on the risks of the construction business.

A Story of Three Builders

Three builders put up identical small additions. Each of them worked 125 hours at project management and carpentry. After paying for labor, materials, and subcontractors, each had $5,000 remaining, but they viewed their $5,000 very differently.

The least experienced divided his $5,000 by 125 hours, came up with $40 an hour and concluded he had made a "good profit" on the job.

The midlevel builder looked at the $40 an hour and concluded "at least I broke even." He figured that, though he had made no profit, at least he had $40 an hour to show for his work on the project.

The veteran builder looked at the $5,000 and concluded, "I lost my butt on this one." He realized that he had lost money three ways:

■ The $40 an hour was $20 less than he would have had to pay (in wages and labor burden) to a good lead to work in his place on the job. Therefore, he had lost about $20 of the value of his labor for every hour he had worked.

■ He had incurred $1,000 in overhead, none of which he had recovered.

■ He had no profit to show for the job. He had taken on all the risks and responsibilities of building the addition without any compensating profit at all.

Though only the veteran builder realized it, all three builders had lost money three ways. They had lost part of the value of their labor, their overhead costs, and a fair profit.

We have discussed the attitudes and lack of procedures that lead to builders undercharging for direct costs. Failure to charge for overhead and profit occurs for two reasons: confusion and fear. The confusion, as the story of three builders below illustrates, comes from not understanding the difference between wages, overhead including salary for managing the company, and profit. Their fear is that they will not be able to get jobs if they charge what those jobs are actually costing them in overhead, risk, and responsibility. One remodeler in my area recalls the first time that a consultant told him that on his projects about 30 percent of his total charges to the owner should be for overhead and profit. "I thought she was crazy," he says. "I thought if I charged that much, I'd never get another job." Eventually, he came to see her figure as quite conservative.

To overcome confusion and fear, and learn to charge fairly for overhead and profit, you must first identify the costs and risks beyond direct job costs that your company incurs. Then you must convince yourself of this truth: Many thousands of successful construction companies do charge for overhead and profit to compensate themselves for those costs and risks. Those companies win projects and stay in business. You can do the same. You can come to grips with and charge adequately for overhead and profit. Maybe you can't do it in one fell swoop. If you are now barely getting a wage out of your projects, it may take you a couple of years—or even longer if you have to bridge a recession. But a step at a time you can get there.

Identifying overhead costs

Identifying overhead requires, first of all, tracking it in your accounting records as described on pp. 72–74. From your accounts you can pick up your disbursements for both fixed and variable overhead. But like direct costs, overhead includes slippery items—in particular, three costs that won't necessarily show up in your accounting records because you don't write a check for them. They include:

- *Rent* for space used by your company but not paid for out of your company accounts, such as a room for an office or shop space in your home.
- *Cost of capital*, the money you are losing by having your operating (i.e. working) capital tied up in a bank account that is earning ½ percent instead of substantially more in a money market account or index fund.
- *Your salary,* for running your company.

To determine your overhead accurately, you must figure and add in these slippery items. Determining rent and cost of capital is pretty easy—ask around and you will quickly learn what is a fair market rent for the space used by your company and what you could earn on the cash tied up in your operating account.

Identifying your salary for running your company (not to be confused with your pay for hands-on work, which is a direct cost of construction) is trickier. At the outset of your career as a builder, you may not be very good at company management and, to be blunt, not worthy of much pay for your work. To draw a bead on an appropriate starting salary, ask yourself this question: "How much would I be willing to pay someone with my business and management skills to run a construction company?" A realistic answer might be the same as mine when I was starting out: "Not very much." In more discouraged moments you might even be tempted to grumble, "I'd pay them to stay away."

One way to set your starting salary is to estimate the number of hours per week you spend at general, administrative, and mar-

Identifying Overhead

To determine charges for overhead during an upcoming year, first estimate total overhead cost for that year. Start with the previous year's overhead and adjust up or down for any changes you can foresee. If you are just beginning your career and do not have a previous year's figures, then estimate as best you can. Include amounts for:

- All *fixed overhead* items from your chart of accounts
- All *variable overhead* items from your chart of accounts
- *Market value rent* for space used by but not paid for by your company
- *Cost of capital*
- Your *salary* for running your company
- *Other costs* that do not show up in your chart of accounts

keting tasks (including estimating and everything else that goes into running your outfit and getting jobs). Multiply the total hours times your cost for a beginning carpenter's apprentice—for example, 20 hours per week × $11. The result, $220 per week, becomes your starting salary as chief executive of Your Construction Company. That's pretty low pay for a CEO. But like your carpentry apprentice, you are just learning your job. Because your salary is low, you won't have to add much to your bids to cover it. That's helpful at the outset of your career, when your bids will likely need to be tight for you to get work. On the other hand, you will be establishing the habit of charging a salary for yourself in your overhead markup, an important step.

In time your CEO skills will sharpen. You will deserve raises. If you are establishing a company with a reputation for integrity and reliability, you will be able to provide for those raises in your bids and still get work.

How fast and how much can you increase your salary? That will depend on how rapidly you develop your skills and your company and on the strength of the economy. (During stiff recessions, even experienced builders find they have to cut their salaries to the bone to survive in business.) Probably, you will be able to increase your salary in stages, first to a level on par with your cost for a carpenter, then a project lead. As you become really capable, you can aim for compensation at the level of other seasoned builders. One group of such men and women, predominantly residential remodelers, are members of an organization called Business Networks (BN), which publishes the financial performance of its members. In 1996, a year when the economy was strong but not booming, BN reported that its members were able to take salaries averaging roughly 10 percent of the direct costs of building their projects.

Figuring charges for overhead

Once you have identified your overhead costs for the year, you are ready for the task of figuring the amount to *recover* (to charge for) on each of your projects. You can choose from among several methods, including:

■ *The uniform percentage method* by which direct costs on all projects are marked up by the same percentage.

■ *The capacity-based markup method,* which leads to higher percentage markups for smaller jobs.

■ *Alternative methods,* including especially the gross profit margin method, in which overhead markups are lumped together with profit markups.

The uniform percentage-based method involves the following steps (illustrated below):

■ *Total your direct job costs* for the past year and anticipate for the new year.

■ *Total your overhead costs* for the past year and anticipate for the new year.

■ *Divide new overhead by new direct job costs* to figure the percentage markup of direct costs needed to recover overhead for the new year.

■ *Mark up direct costs on each of your jobs by the percentage* to get the amount of overhead you will charge on the job.

In the example, direct costs on each project would need to be marked up by 13.5 percent to recover the overhead. If the builder did ten jobs averaging $26,000 and marked up each of them by 13.5 percent he would take in $35,100 in overhead, or $100 more than his goal.

The uniform percentage method has the great appeal of simplicity. It is adequate for a construction company that does projects of fairly uniform size and type. A uniform percentage markup can work for a builder specializing in moderate-size residential additions or small retail store interiors and never straying far beyond his or her niche. However, you can run into trouble using a uniform percentage if you move away from a narrow range to a much wider range of projects—or if you experience large variations in your total volume of work.

To understand the potential problems, think of your company as a shop with "X" amount of capacity and with all

An Example of Figuring a Uniform Percentage Overhead Markup

Previous year's direct costs—$150,000

Previous year's overhead—$17,000

(Includes low salary for builder and all other fixed and variable overhead)

Anticipated new year's direct costs—$260,000

Anticipated new overhead—$35,000

(Includes sizable raise for builder but only nominal increases in other overhead)

Calculation of percentage—35,000/260,000 = 0.1346

Uniform percentage markup on direct costs: 13.5%

of your overhead costs going to support that capacity. If you are at the early stages of your career and are working as your own project lead as well as general manager of your company, your capacity may be one job at a time. Later, you may employ three leads, each of whom runs a job so that you have a capacity of three jobs. For practical purposes—and here is the key point—you can generally figure that each lead uses the same amount of your overhead support, regardless of the size of job he or she is running.

As the top sidebar at right suggests, those jobs can vary greatly in terms of the direct costs of building them, yet take roughly the same length of time with the result the small one will soak up as much of your capacity—and as much overhead—as the larger one. When that is the case, if you are using uniform percentage markups, the small job is recovering less than the overhead needed to support it. If you have a year packed with such jobs and you are marking up with a percentage derived from a prior year of larger jobs, you may end up falling far short of recovering your overhead, as the figures in the bottom sidebar illustrate.

Capacity-based markup

Because of the limits of the uniform percentage method, companies doing projects of varying size and experiencing large variations in volume year to year need another method of marking up for overhead. I call this method "capacity-based markup." It works like this:

- ■ Figure capacity.
- ■ Figure overhead for the year.
- ■ Figure amount of overhead you need to recover weekly per job.
- ■ Figure the number of weeks a job will take.

Danger of Using Uniform Percentage Markup on Different-size Projects

Experienced builders know that they must use much higher percentage markups to recover overhead costs on small jobs than on large ones. If you use the same markup, on small jobs you fail to recover sufficient overhead as shown here.

Costs	Repair job	Remodel project
Materials	$4,012	$21,962
Labor	$15,119	$37,312
Subcontractors	$1,023	$29,617
Services/Other	$0	$4,109
Total Costs	*$20,154*	*$93,000*
20% Markup	$4,030	$18,600
Time for job	6.5 weeks	8.5 weeks
Recovery of overhead per week	$620	$2,188

Danger of Using Percentage Markup Figured on Basis of Previous High-Volume Year for a Lower-Volume Year

Your overhead costs do not necessarily change when you move from doing large projects to small ones. You can move from doing a few large projects in one year to many smaller ones with half the total revenue the next year, but have virtually the same costs for vehicles, insurance, office systems and supplies, your own work for running your company, and other overhead costs. If you use the overhead markup percentage that recovered those overhead costs during the higher-volume year for the subsequent, smaller-volume year, you will end up way short of your needed charges for overhead.

	Year 2004	Year 2005
Direct job costs on projects	$800,000	$400,000
Overhead including your salary for running your company	$100,000	$100,000
Overhead markup needed to recover overhead	12.5%	25%
Overhead recovered using 12.5% markup on job costs	$100,000	$50,000
Percentage of overhead recovered with 12.5% markup	100%	50%

■ Multiply your weekly overhead figure by the number of weeks to get the amount of overhead you need to charge on the job.

Here is an example of using capacity-based markup right at the beginning of your career when you are doing a range of projects from small repairs to moderate-sized remodel projects. First, you figure your capacity. It's one job at a time. Then figure your overhead. It's $39,000 a year, or roughly $750 a week, half for your beginning CEO salary.

Now comes the challenging part, adding that $750 in overhead to the direct costs of each and every job for every week you spend on it, no matter how small the job. If you are doing a tricky repair job that takes $2,000 a week worth of labor and $500 in materials, you are looking at direct costs of $2,500. If you add $750, that's the equivalent of a 30 percent markup (2,500 × 30% = 750), and that is just for overhead. You have not even gotten to profit. You may say "no way." But the fact is 30 percent overhead markup on small jobs is moderate. The numbers don't lie. If you don't charge that amount, you are standing in the boots of those builders described earlier who were, in effect, footing part of the bill for their customers' projects out of fear of not getting any work. The fear may be justified at times; you may have no choice but to buy jobs and the chance to earn a wage for your hands-on work by throwing in your overhead and profit. Do it if you must, but don't kid yourself about the business reality.

Using capacity-based markup, when you move to a small remodel from the repair job, you will find yourself confronting less troubling numbers. If you build an addition with costs for labor, materials, and subcontractors running $7,000 a week, then your $750 markup for overhead is a more palatable 10 per-

cent. As we shall see in a few pages, that will leave you room to add a decent profit markup and still keep your total markups within market range.

You can continue using capacity-based markup as you develop your company, delegate project control largely to your lead people, and begin working full time at marketing and general management. You grow to the point that you have two leads and basically do two projects at a time. Your overhead is now $2,000 a week with three-quarters of it for your salary. To recover that overhead and pay your salary, you simply charge $1,000 a week on each project run by each of your leads. As before, you will have high percentage markups on small jobs and low percentage on large ones—which is the industry norm. If work is tight and you cannot get jobs at the full markup, you may have to cut it and take less in salary, again normal. You may even need to go back to doing hands-on work to get through the difficult period before you can resume growing your company. You will not be the first builder to go through that experience either!

In short, capacity-based markup is a flexible system that allows you to recover overhead—or consciously sacrifice it when conditions demand—on a wide range of jobs and over a wide range of capacities. It will continue to work even if you reach the point of doing several jobs at a time, and your overhead includes salary for full-time office people in addition to yourself. You will continue to figure your total overhead per week and parcel it out to your jobs in order to recover it.

Of course, capacity markup has its limits. It becomes more difficult to use if your number of jobs fluctuates rapidly or if your leads have widely different capabilities, but all overhead markup systems have limits. Marking up for overhead is one of the most difficult tasks

---

The numbers don't lie. If you don't charge that amount, you are standing in the boots of those builders described earlier who were, in effect, footing part of the bill for their customers' projects out of fear of not getting any work.

business owners face. As one consultant says, "Overhead is a moving target," and you will need a variety of nets to capture it in your career as a builder.

Figuring Profit

Of the three levels of charges—direct costs, overhead, and profit—it is the last one that causes builders the most puzzlement. Some builders, like the first two guys in the sidebar on p. 162, are confused about the difference between wages for working directly on a project, salary for running the company, and profit. Others hesitate to charge a profit just as they hesitate to charge overhead for fear of pricing themselves out of their market.

Still others, however, hesitate to charge a profit not from confusion or fear but because profit does not seem quite legitimate to them. A Maine-based builder entering his fifth year in business expressed the hesitation clearly. "Do I deserve to make a profit?" he wondered. "I'm comfortable getting a wage for my labor and a markup for my investment in tools and office equipment. But is it right to take profit in addition to that?"

"*Yes!*" I told him emphatically, though I admire the sense of fair play behind his hesitation. As the business cycles roll by, I see with increasing clarity that in order to be fair to themselves even as they are fair to clients, builders must charge a profit. Profit is compensation for risks and responsibilities, beyond merely paying your bills for direct and indirect costs, that you assume with every project you build.

Risks (and just rewards) of the construction business

Among the risks of being in the construction business are those suggested at right. The risks are real. They do come home to

roost. The builder who first introduced me to the concepts of overhead and profit marked up her costs by 10 to 30 percent. But she counted on only 1.5 percent remaining in her accounts. The rest of it went back out to cover costs resulting from the high-risk, structural repair work her company performed.

Her's is an extreme case. The risks arising from the type of work you do are not likely to be so high, but they will be plentiful. You may develop the most thorough estimating procedures, but now and again a project's costs will greatly exceed what was anticipated because of some bolt from the blue. Extreme weather or an injury to a key person will cut productivity by one-third or even bring the project to a halt. While it sits, overhead costs beyond what was provided for in the bid will mount up. With every project come change orders, and no matter how completely you prepare your client for them and tool your systems to catch and charge for them, you'll do some for free. Occasionally, clients who experience great stress during a project will become very difficult. They will distract your crew or fight your

COMING UP

Why You Must Charge a Profit

Resistance to
Charging a Profit

Construction Business Risks

The Uniform
Percentage Method

The Market-Based Method

Builder Business Risks

- Estimating errors
- Project delays and disruption due to:
  —Extreme weather
  —Man-made and natural disasters
  —Loss of key employees
  —Subcontractor failure
- Equipment failure and loss
- Uncharged or unchargeable change orders
- Callbacks and warranty work
- Difficult and labor-consuming clients
- Litigation
- Management errors
- Recession

While it is not possible to erect a shield against business risk, you can put in place a pretty tightly woven grate.

requests for payment. They may even file a lawsuit—which will consume a great deal of your resources, win or lose. Likewise, you will have bad times when you are distracted and make poor judgment calls, which lead to costly errors.

No matter how good you are, how excellent your skills, you will experience the costs arising from the risks of being in the construction business. To think otherwise would be the height of arrogance. Though I run what a number of people have called a "bulletproof" operation, I have experienced most of these costs at some point in my career, and many more than once. Jobs have been shut down for weeks because of torrential rain. One job slowed to a snail's pace and took extra months to build, eating up proportionate extra overhead, because the lead carpenter dislocated his shoulder. I have had clients throw tantrums, threaten me, and ply my crews with cookies (big, thick, chocolate chip cookies!) and soft drinks to get extras done for free. I have goofed up estimates and made bad judgment calls.

In short, my company is *not* bulletproof. No construction company can be. The costs arising out of risk are inevitable. It is also true, however, that while risks cannot be eliminated, they can be held in check by good management. Build a supportive environment for workers, one in which they are treated with respect and fairly compensated, and you will minimize employees and subs leaving you in the lurch. Communicate clearly and fully with clients, build reliable and attractive structures, and you'll hold down callbacks and disputes. Run a lean, debt-free operation, and you will ride out recessions without hemorrhaging cash.

In short, while it is not possible to erect a shield against business risk, you can put in place a pretty tightly woven grate. With hard work and a little luck, you will build a grate that will hold back most of the potential assaults on your business's well being. You'll enjoy the rewards of successful risk management. Not all profit will need to be paid back out to cover losses. Some of it, in many years a good deal of it, can be retained for growing and strengthening your business. You will be able to create a profit-sharing program for your employees, thereby intensifying their loyalty. You will have the cash to invest in new equipment or facilities that give your company new capacities. You'll even be able to put some of the profit in your personal bank account as a return on your investment in a business enterprise, your construction company.

Figuring charges for profit

Once you have accepted the rightness of charging for profit, you face the question, "How do I do it?" The answer is not quite as easy to come by as it is for overhead. With overhead, the previous year's costs give you a good starting point for figuring a current year's overhead markup. The costs arising out of the risk of being in business—and therefore the amount of profit markup needed to cover them—are not so decipherable. The costs may be hard to pull from your accounts. How do you extrapolate the losses from a patch of bad weather or of dealing with a temperamental client? Moreover, the costs that go against profit vary enormously year to year. For several years, they may be insignificant. Then in a single year you get hit with brutal weather, the failure of a computer and a truck transmission, the loss of a key employee, and uninsured theft of a dozen costly tools.

For all the difficulty, just as with overhead, you can charge for profit in different ways:

- *Uniform percentage.* Markup by the same percentage on every project.

■ *Mark up to market.* Charge what the market allows. More in good times, almost nothing in bad times.

■ *Alternative methods,* such as attaching all markup to labor costs, marketing to meet markup goals, and GPM method.

To use the uniform percentage method, begin by selecting a percentage that is prevalent in your segment of the construction industry, then adjust it to suit your own situation. Percentages vary enormously across the industry. At the low end is the approximately 2 percent markup for profit charged by companies that do large-scale commercial construction. (I mention this in case you are thinking that building skyscrapers might offer a cushier ride than your line of work and were planning to bolt to the high-rise business.) Next up the scale is the 4 to 9 percent of direct costs charged by builders of medium-size, commercial projects. Ten percent is a figure often insisted upon by insurance companies and design firms seeking contractors for residential work. Fourteen percent of direct costs is the markup for profit promoted by the Business Networks, an organization that sponsors mutual support groups for remodeling contractors. Less than 5 percent, however, is the average profit markup actually realized by the members of Business Networks in 1996.

The last two figures are particularly instructive. They suggest that Business Networks members were unable to preserve their profit markups against erosion by all those costs arising from the risks of the construction business. Their experience is a good reminder of the "grate, not shield," nature of managing the risks, because the members of Business Networks are a dedicated bunch. If they aim for 14 percent profit markups and end up with less than

5 percent, you can bet most other contractors in their line of work do even worse.

If you do elect to use a uniform percentage profit markup, bear in mind that you will get different amounts of markup depending on how you apply the percentage. For the sake of consistency, I have spoken of markups on direct cost. In practice, many builders mark up direct costs *plus* overhead for profit. For each $100 in direct costs, they do *not* figure $100 costs × 10% profit = $10. Rather they figure $100 costs + $10 overhead = $110. And $110 × 10% profit = $11 profit. At that rate, on a job with $40,000 in direct costs, marking up direct costs plus overhead works out to $400 extra profit.

Market-based markup

For my own bids, rather than a uniform percentage method, I use what I call *market-based markup* to figure profit charges on projects. Like capacity-based markup for overhead, market-based markup for profit is more demanding than the formulaic use of uniform percentages. It is not a cookie-cutter approach. It may not be suitable for the start-up phase of

> ike capacity-based markup for overhead, market-based markup for profit is more demanding than the formulaic use of uniform percentages. It is not a cookie-cutter approach.

An Example of Market-based Profit Markup

If you are a very efficient builder with tightly managed overhead, you can enjoy wide profit margins, yet offer your clients total overhead and profit markups better than those of your more lax peers. (Bingo!)

■ Direct costs = $100,000
■ Overhead charges for 12 weeks at $1,000 a week = $12,000
■ Overhead markup percentage = 12% (12,000/100,000)
■ Combined overhead plus profit markup used by comparable builders = 32%
■ 32% minus 12% overhead markup = 20% profit markup
■ 20% reduced to 16% results in a total overhead and profit markup of 28% (12% + 16% = 28%), quite competitive relative to your peer's 32%
■ 100,000 × 16% = $16,000 profit markup

COMING UP

Attaching Markup to Labor

Marketing to Markup

The Gross Profit
Margin Method

Standing by Your Bids

your career, when you need to keep things as simple as possible. Later, however, you may find it valuable, particularly if you are handling a wide range of projects that call for differing levels of markup. Market-based profit markup comprises the following steps:

■ Calculate the direct costs of a project.
■ Figure your overhead charges for the project by whatever method you prefer.
■ Determine the percentage markup on direct costs your overhead markup represents.
■ Determine the combined overhead and profit markup percentage used by comparable builders for comparable projects in your area.
■ Subtract your overhead markup from the going combined rate.
■ Adjust the remainder for use as your profit markup.
■ Mark up your direct costs for profit.

While this process may seem complex, it is very much what seasoned builders do instinctively, without having to think about the steps when they are figuring profit. They calculate direct costs, figure the overhead they must add, and then with an eye on market conditions, add profit as they feel they can. In good times, when their competitors are busy and marking up by high percentages, they can be generous with profit markup. In bad times, they have to rein it in, sometimes to near zero.

Of course, to use market-based markup, you need to know what percentage of overhead and profit other builders in your market are including in their bids. You will get that information (it's a matter of constant discussion) by participating in a builders' association and reading trade journals. As stressed in earlier chapters, those are things you ought to be doing anyhow if you are serious about succeeding as a builder.

Alternative Methods

By now you may feel you've seen enough methods of marking up for overhead and profit to last a lifetime. However, overhead is a moving target. Profit is yet more elusive. Builders do keep inventing ways to corral the beasts. Three more ways, each a variation on others we have already looked at, are worth knowing about. They are:

■ *Attaching all markup to labor costs*, a variation on capacity-based markup.
■ *Marketing to meet markup goals (or marketing to markup for short)*, which amounts to marking up to market turned 180 degrees.
■ *The gross profit margin method*, a variation on uniform percentage markups, but with overhead and profit figured and included in the bid price in one whiz-bang mathematical manipulation.

Attaching all markup to labor costs

This method is simple; you may find it particularly helpful during the early stages of your career. To use it, take the following steps:

1. Figure the total required overhead and profit dollars for the year.
2. Figure the total number of hours of labor your crew and/or yourself will work directly on your projects.
3. Divide the total of overhead and profit dollars by the total hours.
4. Add the result to hourly labor rates (i.e., wages plus burden).

For example, a builder who does all his own construction with one helper figures his overhead to be $24,000 a year and aims to keep a profit of $18,000, for a total of $42,000 overhead plus profit (24,000 + 18,000 = 42,000).

He puts in about 30 hours a week on job sites and the remainder of his time running his company. The helper puts in 40 hours a week. They both work about 44 weeks a year (going fishing is a high priority in this outfit). So the total number of hours they work on the jobs is 3,080 ($44 \times 70 = 3,080$).

Dividing $42,000 by 3,080 hours, the builder comes up with $13.64. ($42,000/3,080 = 13.64$). He rounds the $13.64 to $14. He knows he won't be able to hang on to all of his profit markup, that some of it will go back out the door for callbacks due to bad weather, and so on. To give himself a margin of safety, he kicks the $14 up to $18. That's the amount he adds to his labor charges.

His helper costs him, in wages and burden, $36 an hour, so he charges the helper's time at $54 an hour ($36 + 18 = 54$). He values his own labor at $50 an hour. With the 18 added, that figure goes to $68 ($50 + 18 = 70$).

This method can work for larger companies as well. The builder I know who has refined it to the highest level operates a design/build remodeling company with about half a dozen field employees. He attaches all overhead and profit to labor, none to subcontractors or materials, and reports great side benefits from the method. His clients like it. They like the fact that they can upgrade a material, go from plastic laminate to Corian countertops, for example, without incurring any extra markup on the material. And they like the fact that since there is no markup at stake, the builder lets them pay for the materials directly, using their credit cards, so they get to earn frequent-flyer miles.

Like all markup methods, attaching overhead and profit to labor has limits. It works well so long as your projects are of relatively consistent size and involve consistent proportions of labor. But it could break down if you took on an unusually large project that involved relatively little labor by employees and was built mostly by subcontractors. Even though you were taking on larger responsibilities and risk, you would end up with less overhead and profit than you would on a job that was much smaller but was built largely by your crew. To handle the larger and subcontractor-heavy project, you'd need to alter your system, perhaps by attaching markup to labor as always, but also adding percentages for overhead and profit to subcontractor work.

Marketing to markup

This method is not so simple and is likely to be of value more to a well-established builder than to a start-up guy. Marketing to markup means selling jobs at a predetermined markup, refusing to sell if you cannot get that markup, and marketing until you've made enough sales to meet overhead and profit goals. To use the method:

1. Determine the combined percentage of overhead and profit markup desired for the year.
2. Determine the dollars of overhead and profit desired for the year.
3. Determine the dollar volume of sales necessary to bring in the desired overhead and profit dollars at the desired markup.
4. Keep selling until you have reached the necessary dollar volume.

One remodeler who swears by this method insists on approximately 40 percent combined markup for overhead and profit—a high but by no means unheard of level for remodelers operating as design/builders. For a given year, he might set his goals for overhead and profit at $120,000. To meet the goal, he would have to sell $420,000 worth of work, incorporating $300,000 in direct costs and $120,000 in markups ($300,000 \times 40\% = 120,000$, and $300,000 + 120,000 = 420,000$).

The benefits of the marketing to markup approach are that it sets strict, businesslike goals for sales and forces its users to market vigorously.

The benefits of the marketing to markup approach are that it sets strict, businesslike goals for sales and forces its users to market vigorously until they have enough work at desirable markups to enjoy a financially successful year. One primary drawback of the method is that, to achieve his sales goal, a builder may have to invest much more in marketing (an overhead expense) than he intended. As a result, even though he gets his 40 percent combined markup, more of it may have to go for overhead than he had envisioned, leaving an anemic profit percentage.

A second drawback is that taking jobs on the basis of whether or not they will carry a given percentage of markup can be self-defeating. For example, a successful remodeler has been able to earn combined markups in the 40 percent range for quite a few years. He becomes wedded to his markups and resists selling jobs for lower markups. Then opportunities for jobs available in his market area change and much larger projects, including new homes and whole house makeovers, come his way. To be reasonably competitive for those jobs, he would have to cut his markups to half their usual level. He hesitates to do so. He has come to believe that accepting lower markups would be unbusinesslike. Yet something tickling the back of his brain

tells him he might be making a mistake. He goes to a long-time mentor for advice.

His mentor simply shows him the numbers. In eight months, one of the remodeler's senior lead carpenters can handle four smaller remodels or the makeover of a large house. The four small remodels involve $200,000 in direct costs. At a combined markup of 40 percent, they bring in $80,000 for overhead and profit. The large house project involves $800,000 in direct costs. At a 20 percent markup that's $160,000 for overhead and profit.

After staring at his mentor's numbers for a few seconds, the remodeler gets the picture. The whole house makeover ties up essentially the same amount of his capacity, namely one of his crack lead carpenters and a crew, as the small remodels. But it brings in twice the money for overhead and profit. His dedication to his historical markups had almost cost him the best business opportunity he had ever had.

Gross profit margin method

A third alternative method for figuring overhead and profit charges is known as the *gross profit margin* method and has become popular in recent years. It is fairly sophisticated and is probably most suitable for established builders. Gross profit is that part of gross income, i.e. total income, that does not go for direct costs—materials, subs, labor. In other words, gross profit actually includes both overhead and profit. Builders who use the GPM method aim to figure a dollar amount for gross profit that will correspond to a predetermined percentage of the selling price of the project. That's a mouthful, isn't it? A look at the steps involved in this method will help clarify matters:

1. Set desired gross profit margin in terms of a percentage.
2. Calculate the direct costs of construction.

The Gross Profit Margin Formula

The formula: $\text{Project Selling Price} = \dfrac{\text{Project Direct Costs}}{1 - \text{GPM}}$

Example: $\text{Selling price} = \dfrac{\$70,000}{1 - 0.30} = \dfrac{\$70,000}{0.70} = \$100,000$

You may wonder where this weird GPM formula comes from. It is derived algebraically from the commonsense formula, selling price × (100% − GPM%) = project direct costs.

3. Calculate the selling price for the project by means of the gross profit margin formula (shown on the facing page).
4. Check your calculation.

Here is an example: A builder sets 30 percent as his gross profit margin goal. He calculates the direct costs of a project to be $70,000. Using the formula, he comes up with a selling price of $100,000 (100% – 30% = 70%; or $70,000/0.70 = $100,00).

To check his calculation, he subtracts his direct costs from his selling price and gets $30,000 gross profit (100,000 – 70,000 = 30,000). Then he divides the $30,000 by $100,000. Sure enough, the $30,000 corresponds to a gross profit margin of 30%. (30,000/100,000 = 30/100 = 30%).

If you use the GPM method, you must take care to not confuse it with markup methods. If you do, you can make real hash out of your bids. As the sidebar at right suggests, the same percentage used with one method will give you very different dollar results than when used with the other.

The GPM method has the appeal of simplicity. Plug your direct costs into your formula, and bingo, you've got your bid for the project. You have to do only one calculation, not two as is required with the percentage-markup methods.

Therein, however, also lies the shortcoming of the GPM method. Overhead and profit are very different creatures. By determining charges for these two very different entities with one computation, the GPM method can blur the distinctions between overhead and profit, and fuzz understanding of financial performance.

This is no theoretical speculation on my part. I hear builders who are part of the GPM crowd speak admiringly of one another, "He gets great gross profit margins," or say of a particular job of their own, "The GPM was fine." In doing so, they brush aside the fact that it's not margins you take to the bank—it's your salary

Warning: Same Percentage, Very Different Dollars

Please note carefully, so you don't end up costing yourself a bundle, the same percentage gives very different results when used to figure markup than when used in the gross profit margin formula:

30% GPM means *$30,000* for overhead and profit in a *$100,000* selling price ($70,000 direct costs + $30,000 GPM = $100,000 selling price).

Given the same direct costs, 30% markup for overhead and profit combined produces only *$21,000* for overhead and profit and only a $91,000 selling price ($70,000 direct costs × 30% markup = $21,000; $70,000 + $21,000 = $91,000).

To avoid errors, avoid using GPM part of the time and markups at other times. Choose one method, and stick with it.

and a share of your company's profits. Valuing a company or rating a particular project for its gross profit margins is a bit like valuing sales volume for its own sake—and the crash of the dot.com industry has exposed the sheer idiocy of that approach.

It is neither revenue nor GPM that determines the value of a company or the financial success of a project. It is *retained earnings resulting from attentive management of overhead and risk*. A company or a project could have a great gross profit margin, but if it is made up of all overhead and no profit, it is a financial bust. If you elect to use the gross profit margin method of adding overhead and profit to direct costs, you need also to backtrack on each project, as well as for the company as a whole, and keep a close eye on the overhead and profit components separately. And frankly, if you are going to do that (notwithstanding the current fashionability of the gross profit margin method in at least some parts of the construction industry), you may as well do so from the get-go, figuring overhead and profit in two distinct steps using the markup method of your choice.

Adjusting your bid (and sticking with it)

Regardless of which method of figuring overhead and profit you use, you'll find that your charges will have to flex with the times. Some builders would disagree. They will do virtually anything to maintain their markups or margins when times are slow. Their unwillingness to work without adequate compensation is admirable. But emulating their strategy can be shortsighted. In particular, you may face a choice between taking on projects at sharply reduced markups or letting go seasoned and loyal employees. Sticking with your people may be not only the ethical thing to do but the best business strategy. When business turns up, the expense of having built a few projects with tight markups may look like a wise investment. You will be ready to capitalize on expanding opportunity without the huge cost of integrating new people into your operation.

If you decide it's necessary to trim your markups to get through slow times, you can:

■ Make doubly sure overhead is trimmed as far as practicable.

■ Trim profit, and expect the same of your subs. You do not have to protect their markups at the expense of your own.

■ Cut your pay or take part of it from the cash reserves you have built up during better times.

Just how far you go in trimming overhead and profit to keep your people employed is a judgment call. Personally, I am willing to sacrifice profit and even my salary for running the company, so long as I can earn enough above direct costs to cover my out-of-pocket overhead costs. But the sacrifices are acceptable for a limited time. The risks of construction are just too great to work without pay and profit for an extended period.

When business picks up, lose no time in pushing profit markups back to competitive levels. Restore your salary. Or raise it. You deserve the raise for leading your company through an economic slump. You'll notice that a lot of the other builders in your community will not have managed that feat. There are typically a lot less builders in business after a recession than before.

Whether you are marking up austerely in bad times or generously in good times, stand by your markups once you have submitted a bid. If you are using the procedures discussed in preceding chapters, your charges for overhead and profit are rational and fair-minded. They are your appropriate compensations for the real costs and burdens of bringing construction services to your clients. You do not want to absorb those costs on your clients' behalf. In the long run, you really cannot afford to be giving your overhead and profit to your clients as gifts in exchange for the privilege of working on their property.

Stand by Your Bid

An old-timer taught me years back, once a bid is in don't back down from it out of fear of not getting the job. I remembered his advice not long ago. A client, whose project I had been cost planning for over a year, called me up after I had given him a contract for construction. Would I knock $5,000 off of my proposed contract price? he asked me. No, I explained. That would amount to most of my potential profit in the job. I could not build without profit. I would have responsibilities for his project for years after building it—and that was just the beginning of the risk I would be assuming. I also could not trim the $5,000 from the direct costs or the overhead costs I had included in my estimate and bid. I was sure to incur those costs over the course of the project. "Sorry," I concluded. "I just can't come up with $5,000 unless I cut the quality of material and craftsmanship, and I think neither of us is willing to do that." "Hmmm," said the client. "Let me talk to my wife. We'll get back to you." They did the next morning, with a signed contract.

CHAPTER 6

Construction Contracts

Why and Which One

A CLIENT ONCE told me that what she most liked about working with my company was that there were "no surprises." Her expectations of what we would build for her, how long it would take to build, and how much we would charge were all met. Meeting clients' expectations, and as a result improving the likelihood that yours will be satisfied as well, requires they be understood and aligned in the first place. The clients are given to understand, for example, that almost inevitably during the course of a project, extra costs will crop up. You, on the other hand, understand that it is your responsibility to keep the client up to date on those costs as they arise and not hit them with the extras after they have piled up for weeks or months.

Along with thorough preconstruction planning, the best tool you have for aligning your expectations and the owners' is a good construction contract. Many builders resist developing a thorough contract. They feel overwhelmed enough without *that* headache, or they take pride in working on a handshake, on

being taken at their word rather than having to rely on lawyers and legalisms to define their relationship with clients.

Even experienced contractors who build large projects resist. "My clients don't want to deal with all that paperwork," they say. My reply to them is this: You are letting your clients take control of your business and of the building process. You need to stay in control, because you are the expert, not them. It is up to you to make certain that your own and your clients' expectations are fully matched up before construction begins. Agreeing on a detailed contract is an indispensable step in that process.

Often I hear builders wish for a simpler, briefer contract. I tried to come up with one for this book that I could recommend in good conscience. I was not able to do so. Every single clause mentioned in the Table of Contents to my own contract is essential, even for relatively small projects such as a bathroom renovation or deck. It is well worth your time to create a thorough contract. It is well worth your clients' time—regardless of the size of their project—to spend an hour reading it and getting straight on

COMING UP

Setting Expectations

The Structure of Construction Contracts

The Contents of a Thorough Construction Contract

Sources of Contracts

Lump Sum Contracts

Time and Materials Contracts

SAMPLE LETTERS AND FORMS
The Contents of a Construction Contract

DAVID GERSTEL / GENERAL BUILDING CONTRACTOR
License #325650   Kensington, California 94707   Phone: (510) 524-1039

CONTENTS OF CONTRACT BETWEEN OWNERS AND BUILDER

THE AGREEMENT
Project Description . . . . p. 1
Change Orders . . . . p. 1
Billing and Payment. . . . . p. 1
Substantial Commencement Date . . . . p. 1
Substantial Completion Date . . . . p. 1
Signatures . . . . p. 1

THE CONDITIONS
Owners Obligations
Proof of Ownership . . . . p. 1
Provide Utilities . . . . p. 1
Maintain Access for Builder . . . . .p. 1
Children and Pets on Work Site . . . . p. 1
Safety Precautions . . . . p. 2
Punch list. . . . . p. 2
Make Decisions & Discharge Other Obligations in Timely Fashion . . . . p. 2
Builder's Obligations
Selection of Subcontractors and Suppliers . . . . p. 3
Diligence, Supervision and Work Force. . . . . p. 3
Delays Beyond Builder Control . . . . p. 3
Charges for Preparation of Change Orders . . . . p. 3
Charges and Credits for Work Stipulated by Change Order . . . . p. 3
Responsibility for Damage. . . . . p. 4
Failures of Existing Work. . . . . p. 4
Matching Existing Finishes or Samples. . . . . p. 4
Installation of Material Provided by Owner . . . . p. 4
Quality of Work . . . . p. 4
Mutual and Reciprocal Obligations
Owner's Insurance. . . . . p. 5
Builder's Insurance . . . . p. 5
Termination by Owner . . . . p. 5
Termination by Builder. . . . . p. 5
Indemnification . . . . p. 6
Warranties and Callbacks. . . . . p. 6
Dispute Resolution. . . . . p. 6

THE PLANS

THE SPECIFICATIONS

THE ADDENDA
Notification of Owner's Rights of Rescission
Payment Schedule
Change Order Form with Explanation of Change Orders
Notification of Builder's Lien Rights and of Owner's Rights

the ground rules before embarking with you on the costly process of construction. Gary Ransone, a construction lawyer and author of *The Contractor's Legal Kit* (see Resources on p. 258) says that nine out of ten disputes he gets involved with could have been avoided if the contractor had a thorough construction contract and stuck with it.

The structure and contents of a construction contract

Construction contracts typically involve five sections. In some off-the-shelf contracts, the sections are run together. But in better contracts, those that really do the job of matching up your and the clients' expectations, the sections are distinct from one another, so much so that in construction legalese they are referred to as separate "documents." The documents included in a good construction contract are:

- ▪ *The Agreement*. A cover document setting the broad goals of the job: what is to be built, on what schedule, and for how much.
- ▪ *The Conditions*. A collection of clauses setting out the ground rules under which the goals established in the Agreement will be accomplished.
- ▪ *The Plans*. Drawings with dimensions and notes that describe just what is to be built.
- ▪ *The Specifications*. Added written detail about what is to be built.
- ▪ *The Addenda*. A variety of documents that spell out legal rights, such as your lien rights, and expand on information in The Agreement and Conditions.

Even if you are just starting out with your business, from your years in the field as a tradesperson you understand two of the documents, namely the plans and the specifications. In the following sections of this chapter, after discussing sources of contracts, I will go on to the structure, purposes, and key clauses of the other contract documents—The Agreement, Conditions, and Addenda.

Sources of contracts

If you have accepted the importance of having a good contract, you may still be wondering how to come up with one other than by hiring a lawyer to write it up from scratch at a cost roughly equivalent to that of a new pickup. There are two good, low-cost sources of construction contracts. First is *The Contractor's Legal Kit*. Second is the American Institute of Architects. Particularly useful among the AIA contracts for start-up builders is the AIA small projects contract consisting of document A105, the Agreement, and A205, the General Conditions. (See Resources on p. 258 for information on obtaining both *The Contractor's Legal Kit* and the AIA documents.)

The *Legal Kit* and AIA documents provide much of what you need in a contract for projects ranging from small remodels up to sizable new structures. The more you learn about contracts, however, the more you will see opportunities to improve these starter documents. In the case of the AIA contract, as the sidebar at right indicates, some modification is imperative.

As an alternative to beginning with someone else's contract, then bending it into a shape that suits your business, you can create your own using the following procedure:

1. Study the following chapters to strengthen your understanding of the purpose and structure of contracts.
2. Gather several contracts, including those mentioned above and a selection of those available through your local builder's group and other construction industry associations.
3. Read the contracts. Cut them up into their various clauses, group the clauses by type, arrange the clauses in a logical order, and use them as a guide in writing your own Agreement and Conditions.

Regardless of how you develop your contract, periodic review by an attorney knowledgeable about construction law in your state is essential. I tell you this

AIA Small Project Contract: User Beware!

The American Institute of Architects (AIA) is the trade association of architects. It is no surprise, then, that the contract documents the AIA produces look after the interests of architects first, the interests of owners to whom architects have legal obligations second, and the interests of general building contractors last, by a mile. That is as much the case for the new AIA small project contract (A105 and A205) as for earlier AIA contract documents. If you use the contract, consider modifying it in at least the following areas:

- *Dispute resolution.* No provision is made for alternate means of dispute resolution, meaning that a dispute between owner and builder can go right into full-blown litigation—a disaster.
- *Change orders.* They are hardly mentioned in the contract, leaving naive owners open to some horrible surprises during construction.
- *Owner's right to perform work on the project.* It's wide open, allowing an owner to step right into the middle of a job, take over various sub trades, wreck your schedule, and endanger your crew.
- *Builder's responsibility for failure of existing work.* It is excessive. You are required to "remedy" even the "damage" you cause "only in part."
- *Architect's power.* The architect is positioned as the impartial arbiter over the construction process in which he or she has a vital interest, a "startling professional conceit," as one lawyer nicely puts it. Especially troubling, the architect is granted authority over your change orders for extra work, even though those orders could arise from deficiencies in the architect's work.

I t is up to you to make certain that your own and your clients' expectations are fully matched up before construction begins. Agreeing on a detailed contract is an indispensable step in that process.

R egardless of how you develop your contract, periodic review by an attorney knowledgeable about construction law in your state is essential.

not merely to cover my backside. It's real advice. Contracts are communication tools, but they also involve technical legal requirements, varying from state to state and ever fluctuating in response to judicial decisions and legislation. You do not want your contract to be invalidated in case of a dispute because its clauses contain some sort of internal contradiction or fail to conform to the latest demands of the law.

That's just what happened to a friend of mine. He took a client to court over a cut-and-dry claim for $15,000 worth of change orders. His claim was rejected. Why? Because his contract did not yet conform to a recent requirement for a notification—in just the right-size letters and using the exactly prescribed wording—regarding certain of the clients' legal rights. Have your contract reviewed by a construction attorney.

Two kinds of construction contracts

Construction contracts can be divided into two basic types, distinguished by the way they provide for builders to charge for their work. *Lump Sum* contracts set a fixed price and provide that the builder bill against that price in installments as work progresses. *Time and Materials* (T&M) contracts provide that the builder collect reimbursement from the client for labor, material, and subcontractor costs plus a fee for overhead and profit.

A case can be made for both types of contracts, but lump sum agreements do have clear advantages. First, they place responsibility for determining project costs in the builder's hands, rather than letting them fall where they may with the customer picking up the tab. That is as it should be. You are the professional. Owners are often naive about costs. You should be responsible for projecting and

controlling costs. Second, lump sum agreements more closely set expectations about price, thereby reducing the possibility for disagreements and disputes. Third, they minimize your paperwork and chances of undercharging. You simply set the contract price based upon your estimate and bid and collect a series of agreed upon payments during the job. You don't have to repeatedly gather labor, material, and sub costs into a bill, each time running the risk you will leave something out, as is the case with time and materials contracts.

T&M contracts are more complex. With their relative vagueness about price, T&M contracts open the door to tension arising around money matters. When the clients see the project lead stop to study the plans or talk with you, they fret, wondering whether they are paying for the lead to loaf or chat. You and your lead, in turn, know you are being watched and are distracted from your work by feelings of resentment.

With a T&M contract, if mistakes are made during construction, the clients may fight having to pay for them, leaving you frustrated at their unwillingness to appreciate that no project is perfect, that occasional corrections are a normal part of building. When you submit bills, the clients may resist your charges, arguing, for example, that as a builder you should own scaffolding and provide for it as part of your overhead fee rather than rent the scaffolding and charge for it as a direct job cost. For all the efforts that have been made to create T&M agreements that build in resolutions to such potential conflicts, it remains a challenge to keep tension over money out of T&M work.

Despite the drawbacks of T&M contracts, all builders need to understand them. Often T&M contracts are necessary for projects of the following types:

FAST-TRACK JOBS   The plans are adequate to get a permit, but not far enough along for complete estimating. The client wants to get going, so you agree to a T&M arrangement.

RENOVATION AND REMODELING OF DILAPIDATED STRUCTURES

The project involves an existing structure with so many problems that change orders for hidden conditions may exceed the cost of work that is visible. A fixed-price agreement would be meaningless.

CHALLENGING PROJECTS COMING EARLY IN A BUILDER'S CAREER

T&M contracts can be a way of contracting for a project you are not ready to handle on a fixed-price basis. You have not yet built up a record of costs and are not confident of your ability to estimate a project that is a good deal larger and more complex than anything you have previously built. Nevertheless, you know you can do a good job and want to do it. The owner wants you as their builder. You propose to the owners that you will charge labor (including your own), material, and subs at cost, a markup for overhead including only a modest salary for yourself, and a markup for profit that is hardly more than symbolic of your recognition that every builder *must* earn one.

From such an arrangement, benefits can flow to both you and the owner. You have a chance to demonstrate an ability to build a challenging project. You have an opportunity to develop extensive cost records for future use. The owners, while flying blind on costs, know that almost all of what they spend will be for the actual construction with little going for your overhead and profit.

If such circumstances tempt you to propose T&M contracts, do so with some caution. What you are really doing is using T&M to take on a project you are not yet fully qualified to contract for. Deep in the project, you may find yourself in terrible conflict with the owners about cost, especially if you have given them some off-the-cuff reassurance that their budget seems reasonable.

If you elect to use T&M contracts, take care also not to let them spoil you and retard your development as a builder. Since they allow you to charge as you go, T&M can lull you into skimping on the work of building up cost records and learning to estimate with professional accuracy. In the long run you'll lose out. You will find yourself unqualified to take on those projects that require accurate estimating. You may find yourself without the data and skills needed to survive in hard times when T&M work is hard to come by and competitive bidding rules the day.

Three Sheets Worth of Resentment

At the very beginning of my career, I contracted on a T&M basis with a wealthy couple to build a trellis in their backyard and replace about 1,000 sq. ft. of crumbling plaster in their dining room with drywall finished smooth. The project proceeded without a hitch, and at its end, when I had a few sticks of lumber and three sheets of drywall remaining, I gave myself a pat on the back for an accurate take-off.

But when the wife saw the three sheets, her face tightened with anger, and she complained about the "terrible excess" of material I had ordered. Conceivably, she would have responded in the same way had the job been done under a lump sum contract. But it's not likely.

Under lump sum contracts, if you waste an hour or a sheet of drywall, the clients see the cost as falling on you, not on them. With time and material contracts (T&M), on the other hand, the clients are likely to perceive you as wasting their dollars instead of your own. They are afraid they are going to have to pay for that misspent hour or "excess" drywall. They can become quite anxious about the costs, even angry and suspicious, and their distrust can distract you from your work and drain the pleasure out of a project.

Builders assume that T&M agreements greatly reduce their risks. In my view, the assumption is wrong.

A ladder of time and material contracts

Over the years, the construction industry has invented a variety of T&M contracts in an attempt to come up with one that fairly divides financial risk and reward between builder and owner. The contracts can be arranged in a series, with each seen as a further step toward the creation of an equitable arrangement.

COST PLUS FEE AS A PERCENTAGE

The builder charges the owner direct costs for labor, material, and subcontractors plus a percentage of those costs as a fee for overhead and profit. For example, if your fee is set at 22 percent, for each $1,000 in direct costs you also bill for $220 in overhead and profit. The weakness of the cost plus a percentage contract is that it gives the builder no financial incentive to control costs. In fact, it does the reverse. The more the project costs, the more the builder receives as fee.

COST PLUS FIXED FEE

The builder charges the owner for labor, material, and subcontractors as those direct costs are incurred, but the fee for overhead and profit is fixed at a set dollar amount. Now, the builder does not benefit from costs piling up. His fee won't rise with them. But there's also little incentive for him to control the costs since he'll get his fee no matter how high the costs go.

COST PLUS A FIXED FEE WITH A GUARANTEED MAXIMUM

As in the previous arrangement, direct costs are charged as incurred and the fee is fixed. The added twist is that costs are charged only up to a maximum amount, typically the estimated costs plus a percentage of those costs. For example, if you are building a dental office and had estimated the costs for work shown on the plans and specs at $100,000, your guaranteed maxi-

mum might be 15 percent higher, or $115,000. If costs exceed the guaranteed maximum, say the project uses $121,000 in labor, material, and sub work, the excess $6,000 comes out of your fee. While the guaranteed maximum contract gives builders an incentive to control costs on the owner's behalf, it has the drawback that all reward for the builder's effort accrues to the owner.

COST PLUS FEE WITH GUARANTEED MAXIMUM AND A SPLIT DIFFERENCE

In the dental office example used above, if you bring the project in for $107,000 the "difference"—meaning the $8,000 below the guaranteed maximum—will be split between you and the owner. You collect an additional $4,000. If you go over the maximum, however, you eat the excess. Now there's an incentive for controlling costs, including a reward if you do.

A builder I admire for his high ethical standards has added one more wrinkle to time and material contracts. Reflecting the fact that the builder has a responsibility to estimate correctly, his contract splits any difference below guaranteed maximum cost not 50/50 but 40/60 in favor of the owner.

Time and materials contracts and risk

The more evolved T&M contracts have considerable appeal. One architect makes a case that in cost plan/build arrangements (i.e., negotiated as opposed to competitively bid work), the fixed fee with guaranteed maximum contract is a necessity. He contends that it's the only way to provide owners with assurance that the builder's charges are fair.

Builders, however, need to avoid embracing an inflated sense of the benefits of T&M contracts. Commonly, builders assume that T&M agreements greatly reduce their risks. In my view, the assumption is wrong. If you refer to "Figuring Profit" on p. 167, you will see that of the many kinds of risk builders experience, only one is impacted at all by changing from a lump sum to a T&M agreement. That is "estimating error" risk. You might suppose that with T&M you avoid the risk, that since you do not contract to build for a fixed price, the clients and not yourself are at risk for any costs that exceed expectations. In fact, the likelihood is high you will produce some sort of cost projections for your T&M jobs. Once you have, you will find yourself laboring under pressure to build for the estimate, even if there is no guaranteed maximum, as the story of Max, at right, illustrates. Moreover, as you move through the series of T&M contracts described previously, you'll find that estimating risk is moved away from the owner's side of the table and over to the builder's.

The risks of construction work, including estimating risks, remain substantially in place under T&M agreements. At the same time, however, the buffer against such risk—namely your profit markup, is often constrained. This is because, ironically, operating under the false assumption that T&M agreements greatly limit risk, builders often constrain their markups. In other words, if you are not careful, by using T&M agreements, you can give away the house—continue to carry the risks of building but surrender too much of your potential compensation for doing so.

The Agreement

If a contract is like an umbrella (a device to shelter both you and your client from misunderstanding and wasteful conflict), then the Agreement is the fabric of the umbrella, and other sections (the plans, specifications, and conditions) are the ribs that hold it place. In other words,

T&M Contracts and Risk

Builders often think that T&M agreements shield them from the risk of underestimating the costs of a project—that if an estimate is low, the owner foots the bill for the difference.

Such was the case with Max, who had taken on a residential remodel project on the basis of a verbal time and materials agreement coupled with an assurance to the owner that his budget of $40,000 should be adequate. When Max submitted a bill for $20,000, bringing his total charges past $60,000, the owner balked at making payment. Max insisted on it. Their dispute went to arbitration.

At their hearing, after much argument and counter-argument about agreed upon scope of work, change orders, and quality of workmanship, Max was awarded $10,000. Most of that went to his attorney. His T&M agreement had not protected him from estimating risk at all. When costs ran over his original projection, he had to eat them, just as if he'd signed a lump sum agreement.

the Agreement broadly covers issues that span the whole project—what work is to be done, for how much money, and over what time period. The other sections provide supporting details. Agreements typically begin by designating the "parties," namely, your company and the owner, then go on to describe work, schedule, and arrangements for payment.

Describing the work

Within the one or two pages of the typical Agreement, there's room for only a few words describing the project—for example, "remodel of Mandarano residence." But the Agreement will also reach out and pull in, or "incorporate," other documents that describe the project in detail. For the Mandarano job the Agreement will go on and say "in accordance with the plans, pages 1–9, and specifications, pages 1–8, by Dixie Morrison, dated July 25, 2002."

It is important that the plans and specifications be *named by date*. Otherwise, it can happen that you prepare a bid based on one set of plans. A couple

COMING UP

Describing the Work

A Change Order Form

Substantial Commencement and Substantial Completion

Collection Procedures

Percentage of Completion Billing

The Retention Issue

Legal Requirements

SAMPLE LETTERS AND FORMS
Builder's Assumptions

You can build a master list of assumptions in a computer file. For each new job, edit the list to include the relevant ones.

Note to Owner: The charges for construction specified in the Agreement are based on the following Assumptions. Departure from the Assumptions during construction will require a change order and may entail additional charges.

OWNER'S RESPONSIBILITIES
- ☐ Select roofing shingle—by July 10
- ☐ Choose floor tiles—by August 21
- ☐ Determine paint colors—by September 26

ITEMS NOT INCLUDED IN THE CONTRACT PRICE
- ☐ Awning (to be installed by owner after substantial completion by builder)
- ☐ Final cleaning (builder will leave site broom clean; other cleaning by owner)

CONSTRUCTION MATERIALS AND METHODS
- ☐ Foundation to be high-volume fly ash concrete
- ☐ All framing to be certified sustainably harvested lumber
- ☐ Existing subfloor nailed tight, not replaced
- ☐ Drywall finished to level 5 smooth except skip trowel in closets
- ☐ All paints to be low VOC

of days later, the designer gives the owner a revised set with new details added. You and the owner sign a contract incorporating your bid price. Two months later you begin building and soon find yourself in disagreement with the owner as to which details, those in the first or those in the second set of plans, are covered by the contract and which require change orders.

The Agreement can extend the description beyond that provided by the plans and specifications by bringing in two other documents. The first is what I call "builder's assumptions"—alternately titled "additional specifications" or "amendments to specifications."

As the sample above illustrates, assumptions are divided into three main categories. *Owner's Responsibilities* helps owners fulfill their contractual obligation to make decisions in a timely fashion. *Not Included* items are spelled out so the owner can see clearly what costs they will incur other than those covered by the contract price for construction. The *Construction Materials and Methods* section clears up any ambiguity that might exist in the plans and specs. It eliminates surprises for the owners and establishes with them a clear agreement as to just how, of what materials, and to what level of finish all the items in the project are to be built.

Along with assumptions, an Agreement should incorporate a change-order form, as shown on p. 186. It will provide the invaluable service of educating clients about the change order process while obtaining their consent to it. Such a form goes a long way to achieving the primary purpose of contracts, matching up of expectations.

As a final measure of project description, the Agreement should put the incorporated documents into a hierarchy, stating their order of precedence. In case of conflict, builder's assumptions and conditions are given precedence over specifications, specs over the plans, and the change orders over everything. A statement of precedence ensures that if the assumptions state plastic laminate countertops and the specifications call for granite, plastic laminate it will be until a change order is created to go back to granite or switch to some other material.

Defining the schedule

On the advice of an attorney, some years ago I eliminated the phrase "final completion" from my contract vocabulary. Nothing in life, never mind construction, is ever *finally* complete, the lawyer pointed out, so you do not want to stipulate in your contract you will wait for final payment until a project reaches that never-never land. More recently, I have gone the lawyer one better. I no longer use even the word "complete" in the schedule section of my Agreement. Instead, I use the following phrases and definitions to describe the beginning and end of a project:

- *Substantial commencement*, the moment when my crew or subs begin construction of a project. If the crew stores some materials and equipment on the site, that does not signify commencement of the project. Only the construction work itself does.
- *Substantial completion*, the moment the owners can begin using the project for its intended purposes, though a few punch list items might still need to be done. A kitchen is at substantial completion though a couple of pieces of backordered accent tile or a few light fixtures remain to be installed.

The definition of substantial completion is coupled with a punch list requirement. When substantial completion is reached, the owner must promptly make out a *single* list of all items they deem in need of attention. When those items are attended to, the job is at an end for contractual purposes and for payment purposes. The owner cannot then make out another punch list—and another and another and another for a whole year, all the while withholding payment, as happened on one nightmare project that ensnared a friend of mine. Of course, if an owner has additional requests after the punch list has been executed and *payment is made*, a smart builder will take care of them promptly so long as they are reasonable. For one thing, it's great marketing.

Provisions for payment

Agreements state the price for the project, and along with the price they describe the terms under which the builder will request and receive payment. In all cases, Agreements should provide

that the owners give you a down payment when they sign the contract. Before you begin construction, you will experience overhead costs, including the time you or your staff or crew spend communicating with the owners, scheduling subs, and otherwise gearing up. The down payment will offset those costs.

Beyond the down payment, the type of Agreement, lump sum or time and materials, will determine the payment terms for the project. If your Agreement is for a fixed price, payment can be provided for in one of two basic ways. You can divide the price into a series of fixed

SAMPLE LETTERS AND FORMS
Percentage of Completion Payment Form

Using a percentage of completion form, you request payment for work completed since the last billing.

PAYMENT REQUEST

Borrower __Drayman, Louis__ Disbursement no. __3__ Date __3/14/02__
Location __432 Boynton/Berkeley__
Project __Bed & Bath Addition/Remodel__

No.	Item	Estimated Cost	Previously Disbursed	This Request	Total	Balance
1	Demolition	6,012	3,900	2,112	6,012	0
2	Foundation	9,014	0	9,014	9,014	0
3	Frame	7,206	1,000	2,600	3,600	3,606
4	Furnace	2,986	0	0	0	2,986
5	Sheet Metal	2,400	0	0	0	2,400
6	Plumbing	4,672	600	1,171	1,771	2,901
7	Electrical	1,186	0	0	0	1,186
8	Roofing	1,600	0	0	0	1,600
9	Doors & Windows	2,413	0	0	0	2,413
10	Stucco	3,331	0	0	0	3,331
11	Drywall	1,450	0	0	0	1,450
12	Cabinets	2,010	0	0	0	2,010
13	Finish Carpentry	3,011	0	0	0	3,011
14	Tile	3,697	0	0	0	3,697
15	Supervision	3,000	600	300	900	2,100
16	Overhead & Profit	11,311	1,000	1,000	2,000	9,311

payments. For small jobs you might need only half a dozen payments—$1,000 after setup, $2,000 after rough work, on through to $500 after substantial completion. For larger jobs, you will need to schedule more payments. Alternately, with lump-sum agreements and especially for larger jobs, you can bill by the percentage of completion method, illustrated on p. 185.

SAMPLE LETTERS AND FORMS   Change Order Form

You can keep several change order forms in your computer. One should be blank so that copies can be printed out for projects. Others, for use in contracts, can include variations of the explanation shown on this one.

DAVID GERSTEL / GENERAL BUILDING CONTRACTOR
License #325650   Kensington, California 94707   Phone: (510) 524-1039

CHANGE ORDER

OWNERS: _____

PROJECT: _____

DATE: _____   NUMBER: _____

We hereby agree to make the following changes in the work:

Dear owners: When it is necessary to make a change in the work during your project, the change will be written up on this form. After signing, it becomes incorporated into the contract and subject to the contract Conditions. Change orders can be required for reasons including but not limited to:

Subsurface Conditions: Conditions below existing grade requiring extra efforts to accomplish excavation or drilling. Example: Boulders

Hidden Conditions: Substandard and/or deteriorated mechanical, plumbing, electrical, or structural work beneath or behind existing finish surfaces. Examples: Dry rot or rusted plumbing lines.

Changes desired by the owners. Example: Upgrade bathroom tub.

Change orders are a normal part of any construction job. If you have any questions at all about the change order process please ask. Please signify your acceptance of the change order process provided for in our contract by initialing here_____/_____.

Cost of this change: _____ Cost of changes to date: _____

Original contract price: _____ Contract price plus changes: _____

Change in construction schedule from this change: _____

Change in construction schedule from all changes: _____

Change order preparation charges: This Change: _____   All Changes: _____

Builder's signatures: _____

Owners' signatures: _____

If your Agreement is for time and materials, you will simply bill for your direct job costs and a proportionate amount for your markups on a regular basis. T&M agreements do, however, require one additional feature not necessary with fixed price contracts. Either right in the agreement or with an incorporated addendum, you must make clear to the owners just what costs are passed through to them and which are subsumed within your markups for overhead and profit.

For both lump sum and T&M agreements, your should stipulate frequent billings—weekly or at most biweekly. Clients should be expected to pay immediately, in three days or less. Frequent billing and speedy payment should be provided for work done by change order as well as the work covered in the contract. As an old builder's proverb has it, we're in the construction business, not the loan business. If clients are hanging on to money due for work completed, you are giving them an interest-free loan. Don't do it. Using invoicing methods such as those discussed in chapter 3 or a computerized billing system, invoice and collect promptly when work is done.

You want to avoid scripting a scenario like this one: Your Agreement calls for monthly billing, with the owners allowed ten days to pay. Near the end of the project, they fail to pay within the ten days, offering various excuses and apologies. Two weeks further along, because they still have not paid, you pull off the job, leaving behind nearly two months of unpaid production. A few more weeks pass. You drive by the project and see a carpenter putting the finishing touches on it. Then you get a letter from the owner informing you that they owe nothing more and that any further contact with them, including attempts to collect, will have to go through their lawyer. They wish you luck, implying that with *their* lawyer you are going to need it. I have repeatedly seen builders in just such a predicament. Often, they walk away from tens of thousands of dollars, figuring it would cost them even more than that in legal fees and personal grief to recover their money.

A last measure to ensure that you get paid for the work you produce is use of a joint-control account and payment voucher such as that illustrated at right. By putting the builder in a position to deny the owner access to the project funds should they unfairly try to withhold payment, the joint-control account and voucher agreement go a long way toward reversing the most burdensome of payment terms, those having to do with retention.

Payment retentions

You will see payment retentions called for in AIA contracts and in the construction loan documents of certain banks. Here's how retention works. You do $10,000 worth of work. The owner pays you $9,000 and retains $1,000 until the project is complete. Retentions can get ugly, as in the example narrated on p. 188.

Reliable builders, feeling retention is a control appropriate only to builders who can't be counted on to finish their jobs, rage against the practice. Builders respond to requirements for retention in a variety of ways. Arranged from painfully burdensome to tolerable the responses include:

■ Accept a retention of 10 percent—the highest level of retention I have seen—as the price they must pay for getting a project.
■ Accept the 10 percent retention, but with the provision that it goes into

The two-party direct-payment voucher may be the best protection a builder can have against getting bilked by a client. Federal Building Company, a design/build firm that uses the voucher shown here, has clients deposit the funds for their project in an account at Federal's bank. At the completion of each stage of the project, Federal asks the client to sign a voucher, then presents it to the bank to have funds transferred from the project to the company's account.

DIRECT PAYMENT VOUCHER
NUMBER ONE
DATE:
(INSERT DATE)

PAY TO: FEDERAL BUILDING COMPANY:
$22,000.00

FOR:
START FRAMING

which has been incorporated in the work of improvement located at:

THE UNDERSIGNED WARRANTS AND REPRESENTS TO (name of bank) AS AN INDUCEMENT TO PAY THE VOUCHERS:

That the foregoing sum is in full payment to date for labor and/or material above described and represents the fair market price therefore, and that Federal Building Company hereby releases all liens and claims for labor and/or materials provided to date and agrees to hold harmless the client(s) against all claims for labor and/or materials provided to date.

Client: (One signature required):

_____
(CLIENTS' NAMES)
Contractor: Federal Building Company

_____
Contractor's signature

A Case of Retention

A builder contracts to build a $120,000 office addition to a small manufacturing plant and signs an agreement stipulating 10 percent retention by the owner from each of the payments—$12,000 in total. Three months later, the project is substantially complete and the punch list is done, excepting $890 worth of custom light fixtures specified in a late change order and months away from being delivered. Since the contract permits the owners to keep the retention until "final completion," they elect to hold onto the $12,000. While the builder waits for the fixtures to arrive, the owners collect interest on the $12,000. The builder, on the other hand, *pays* interest for funds he has had to borrow to meet operating expenses on his next jobs—and, of course, to order the light fixtures which, being custom items, had to be paid for in advance.

an escrow account with interest accruing to the builder.

- Require the retention be reduced to 5 percent (or less) and go into an escrow account with interest accruing to the builder.
- Require that retention be reduced to 5 percent or less, applied only through the rough stages of the work, and put in an escrow account with interest going to the builder.
- Require that the retention be limited in one of the ways described previously and be released when substantial completion is reached.
- Refuse to allow retention on the premise that the builder has a sterling record for reliability or that retention amounts to his financing the owner's project for free.
- Allow only a single retention—one from the substantial completion payment of 200 percent of the value of the punch list until it is done.

Builders who specialize in certain kinds of government or commercial work may have no choice but to live with heavy retentions. They will be forced

down their throats by the owners, the banks, and the AIA contracts. On my projects, I do not accept retentions other than the punch list retention, which I voluntarily offer. It never amounts to much; my company strives to do punch list free work. It reassures my clients. They can see I am making it financially worth my while to come back and take care of those last, niggling details.

As a result of my retention policy, coupled with my insistence on frequent and prompt payment, none of my clients has ever been in a position to deny me large amounts due. A client did try once to hedge on a substantial completion payment amounting to about 2 percent of the contract price. I told him that as soon as I hung up the phone, I'd be on my way to file a lien and begin foreclosure proceedings against his nice, new home—but would do him the favor of stopping by for payment before heading to the courthouse. When I got to his place, the check was ready for me. I believe it is critical for builders to learn to be polite but firm about receiving prompt payment for work completed.

Dotting the "i's" and crossing the "t's"

Along with describing the parties, work, payment, and schedule, your Agreement needs to dot the various legal "i's" and cross the "t's" as prescribed by the construction industry laws of your state. You want to make sure that your contract is not setting up practices that contravene state or federal law—or, for that matter, fair-minded business practices.

Just as you want the payment section of your Agreement to protect you from exploitation, you want it to be fair to the owners. In the interest of fairness, and so as to not violate consumer protection laws, avoid creating a payment schedule that provides you with payment in advance of your doing the work. Some construction industry consultants focused on the residential remodeling business suggest collecting a 50 percent payment before work even starts. Such "front-end loading" is an ethically questionable practice, and in some states it can get you into legal hot water.

Make sure that your Agreement incorporates any legally required notices to owners. Among those to watch out for are those pertaining to:

- *Right of rescission*, the right of owners to change their minds and to cancel a contract after signing it.
- *Arbitration*. If you include binding arbitration in the dispute resolution section (to be discussed in the next chapter) of your contract, you may be required to notify owners that by agreeing to it, they limit their other legal options.
- *Lien rights*. To preserve your lien rights—your right to file a claim against the owners' property if they fail to pay you—you may be required to incorporate notice in your contract.
- *Bonds*. You may be required to inform the owners that they do have the option of asking you to obtain bonding for their project.

Requirements for legal notifications in construction contracts vary from state to state. You will want to make sure that you know and fulfill the requirements in your state, as they may differ from those I have described here. (To learn about them, contact the department of your state government that licenses contractors, and talk with your lawyer.) With an Agreement that does meet notification and other legal requirements as well as covers scope of work, schedule, and payment, you are ready to add the next section of your contract, the Conditions.

The Conditions

In some contracts the Conditions are called "General Conditions." In others they are named "Stipulations." One builder I know refers to them as "fanny armor." As far as he is concerned, they have one purpose only, to cover his backside.

Well-written Conditions can do more than provide cover for the builder. Or maybe I should say they can do it in the best way. By helping to align the owners' expectations with yours, they prevent disagreement during the project over issues about which you had made one assumption while the owners were making another. Well-written Conditions are not all that "general"—they are quite specific, and they cover about every circumstance, contingency, emergency, and ambiguity that can arise during a project.

In developing your Conditions, you should strive to be fair and balanced, seeking to protect the owners' interest as well as your own. It's not an easy thing to do, especially if your starting point is one of the widely published existing contracts. Often, their Conditions are quite adversarial in tone and content. Depending on whose lawyers wrote them, they will tend to protect one party—owners, builders, or designers—at the undue expense of another.

One-sided contract Conditions pose several problems. First, they can offend owners—and upsetting your clients by offering them an unfair, unbalanced contract is certainly no way to start off a project. What usually happens is the clients get their lawyer to review the contract. He suggests revisions that shift the balance too far in their direction. In return, you go to your lawyer, and finally, after expensive back-and-forth negotiations, you arrive at a balance, with both parties a little sore and suspicious of one another. Alternately, the

COMING UP

The Purpose of the Conditions

Fair and Balanced Conditions

Owners' Obligations

Builders' Obligations

Reciprocal Obligations

Using Your Conditions as an Addendum to Other Contracts

owners agree to what they consider unfair Conditions, and then in a dispute you find your claim invalidated because the Conditions are outrageously weighted in your direction. Remember, we live in a society in which it is now "seller beware," at least as much as "buyer beware." Consumers enjoy a great deal of protection. If you slip an unfair contract down a clients' throat, you may end up eating it.

Rather than running the risk of upsetting your clients, getting into a duel with their attorney even before starting the project, or of losing out in the event of a dispute, why not just write fair Conditions to start with? Remember, your contract Conditions are the last document clients will see before signing you up for their project. A fair and balanced set of Conditions can be a sales clincher.

Owners' obligations

To help my clients access and understand my Conditions, I have broken them down into three sections, Owners' Obligations, Builder's Obligations, and Mutual and Reciprocal Obligations as shown in the Contract Table of Contents on p. 178 of "Agreements." I begin my Conditions with two pages of owners' obligations. Noteworthy among them are:

PROVIDING PROOF OF OWNERSHIP

It seems almost laughable to require proof, but apparently it does happen that builders have completed work only to find out the clients did not own the property. Imagine tearing out a kitchen for a remodel the day before the owner returns from a trip abroad to tell you the tenant who contracted with you had no legal right to do so. That would be a head scratcher, would it not?

MAINTAINING ACCESS FOR BUILDER

Access is the handmaiden of efficiency. If your client unexpectedly jams the space around your job with vehicles, furniture, equipment, or other contractors doing other work, you will have little chance of building to your estimate.

KEEPING CHILDREN AND PETS OFF THE WORK SITE

Years ago, one of my first mentors told me the story of the pooch who kept grabbing her crew's tools and dropping them into the backyard swimming pool, amusing the crew no end but killing their productivity. Partly for the sake of a little comic relief, I adopted her pets and kids clause for my own Conditions. Later, when I learned of a child ripping her hand open on a finish carpenter's table saw, I realized there was a deadly serious reason for a clause requiring clients to keep their pets and children out of work areas. Both can cause accidents and both can be hurt.

PUNCH LIST

Clients are obligated to make a single punch list—one only—at substantial completion.

A final owners' obligation applies all across the contract. It is "Make Decisions and Discharge Other Obligations in a Timely Fashion." Or as the lawyers say, "Time is of the essence." Owners have to take care of business promptly so you can move ahead. I've been lucky. I have never had clients who got stuck on a decision, or at least if they were, I could get them unstuck by giving them an organized summary of their options. But if my experience does not illustrate the importance of a time is of the essence clause, the story of a builder I met at a conference does. She signed up clients for an eight-month project. Three years later she was still working on it, having moved on and off the job many times as the clients agonized over their choices. If she'd had a time is of the essence clause in her contract and the moxie to enforce it, she could have collected for work

> A fair and balanced set of Conditions can be a sales clincher.

done, terminated the contract, and moved on. Or she could have shaped up her clients with charges for the real losses their indecision was inflicting on her.

Builder's obligations

The Builder's Obligations section of the Conditions spells out the builder's responsibility, and the limits of that responsibility, for managing the project effectively.

SELECTION OF SUBCONTRACTORS AND SUPPLIERS It should be the builder's responsibility, and the builder's alone. Before signing a contract, you might agree to a plumber suggested by the owners. But during the project, the owners cannot decide to substitute their plumber for yours. If they select the wrong outfit they can endanger your crew, play havoc with the schedule, and impair the quality of the work.

DILIGENCE, SUPERVISION, AND WORK FORCE The builder is required to move the project along diligently toward its substantial completion date by deploying crew and subcontractors in timely fashion and supervising them effectively. The builder cannot conduct himself like a contractor working around the corner from my home as I write these pages. He has taken on a second-story addition he lacks the manpower to handle, with the result that half a year into it, deconstruction is not quite finished and framing is just getting under way.

DELAYS BEYOND BUILDER CONTROL My list of delays, given at right, is so long it might seem to violate my commitment to using a fair and balanced contract. I do give myself a lot of outs. But when push comes to shove, I think they are in the owners' interest as well as my own. In particular, the items relating to loss of

key personnel or subs seem mutually beneficial. If a key carpenter or sub were lost through injury or other reason during a boom period, when it is very difficult to find top people, I want time to do so. Should the clients want to rush, I want to be empowered by my Conditions to hold them off, saying, "No, we need to let the work slow until we can find the people capable of doing it to the level of quality we were both anticipating when we signed our contract."

RESPONSIBILITY FOR DAMAGE AND FOR FAILURES OF EXISTING WORK A builder is responsible for damage caused by the negligence of his or her crew or subs. That responsibility does not, however, extend to collapse of existing work so frail that the normal impacts

Causes of Delay beyond Builder's Control

■ The failure of the owner to make payments when due or to make timely decisions

■ Difficulty obtaining required building permits or other government approvals necessary for the project

■ Acts of God, including earthquakes, floods, and storms

■ Social or political events, including religious and other holidays, strikes, riots or other civil commotion, and acts of war or terrorism

■ Inability on the builder's part, for reasons he could not have reasonably foreseen and provided against, to obtain material through his usual channels and suppliers

■ Failures in performance by subcontractors that the builder could not have reasonably foreseen and provided against

■ Loss of key employees or subcontractors due to injury or other reason the builder could not have reasonably foreseen and provided against

■ Difficulty due to economic or other conditions in hiring replacements for lost personnel adequately skilled to perform to the builder's standards

■ Changes in the work arising for any reason, including hidden conditions and requests by the owner

of nearby construction cause it to fail. If a crew is gutting a room, and cracks appear in the 70-year-old plaster on the other side of the wall, the builder is not responsible for fixing it (though, in practice, you might do it for cost or even a bit less as a good-will gesture).

MATCHING EXISTING FINISHES OR SAMPLES   The Conditions should require a skilled and conscientious effort to achieve a reasonable match. But they should stay clear of words like "exact" or "nearest possible," which open the door to unreasonable demands.

MATERIALS PROVIDED BY OWNER
So that you can provide seamless responsibility for all work, urge your client to let you provide all materials. For the cases when they insist on providing materials, usually fixtures of some sort, your Conditions should make clear that you are not responsible for defects in or failures of that material and that the owners are responsible for extra labor costs arising from problems with the material, including delay in delivery to the job site. A big problem with owners providing materials is that by taking the place of your usual supplier, they put you in the position of working with an amateur instead of a pro. Often, they fail to get the right material to the job site at the right time. When that happens, they should foot the bill for delays or other additional costs.

Finally, any fair set of Conditions will oblige the builder to *produce work of good quality*—both reliable and attractive. They do not attempt to slip over on clients the so-called "quality" standards published by certain industry associations that are intended to give builders a defense against clients who resist mediocre performance. At the same time, Conditions should not swing dangerously in the

> Balance your obligations with a requirement that if there are failures, you will be given a reasonable length of time to correct them before the owner calls in someone else.

other direction. Phrases such as "the highest standard of workmanship," used in the quality clause of some contracts, open the door like "final completion" and "exact match" to endless demands by the occasional grinder of a client.

Reciprocal obligations

The final section of the Conditions states obligations that I think of as reciprocal, applying both to clients and builder. They include:

PROOF OF INSURANCE   The builder is required to provide the clients with certificates of workers' compensation and liability insurance. Clients must submit evidence they have insurance that will insure work against destruction once it is in place. If a storm destroys a frame you have just completed, the owners need insurance to pay for removing and replacing the destroyed work.

TERMINATION RIGHTS   The builder has the right to stop work if the owners fail to live up to their obligations—especially to pay and to make decisions in timely fashion. Likewise, the owner can terminate the builder for failure to build in accordance with the contract documents or failure to pay subs, employees, and suppliers.

WARRANTIES   Your state likely will have laws stating the extent of your liability for failures in your work. You can balance your obligations with a requirement that if there are failures, you'll be given a reasonable length of time to correct them before the owner calls in someone else.

INDEMNIFICATION AND HOLD HARM-LESS CLAUSES   Here we get into a legally technical issue, one with which you will probably need help from your lawyer. Very roughly speaking, these clauses protect you and/or your clients and/or designers from losses, damages, or lawsuits caused by the other.

Once you have completed your Conditions, you can, as with other documents, store them in your computer, printing out copies as needed. For some projects, such as those designed by certain architects who insist on AIA contracts, you may not be able to use your own contract. But even then you can excerpt from your Conditions as you feel necessary to override, supplement, and balance the required contract—though probably with review by an attorney so that you do not create any technical conflicts. Two sets of clauses, in particular, should be added to the Conditions of any contract that lacks them—namely, those governing change orders and alternate dispute resolution.

Two Critical Conditions: Change Orders and Dispute Resolution

In the previous edition of this book, I began the chapter on change order Conditions by describing them as a "yawning stairwell" leading right down to financial disaster. Since writing the first edition, I have heard so many more change order horror stories, I have come to think of my stairwell analogy as wildly upbeat compared with the realities. The change order minefield might be more accurately characterized as a builder's hell, littered with the carcasses of charred and smoldering companies.

If there is a single item in contracting that competes with change orders for sheer damage done, it would be this: The failure of builders to put in their contracts an economical and nonadversarial procedure for settling disagreements with

clients. As a result, they too often end up in full blown lawsuits with their capital accounts hemorrhaging dollars for legal fees. Every set of contract Conditions should, therefore, cover change order charges and provide a procedure that limits the damage done by disputes rather than amplifying it. In the words of the sociologist Gordon Fellman, contracts should provide for "mutualistic" rather than "adversarial" means of settling differences.

Change orders

Change order failure can not only devastate a company in a single blow as illustrated by Laura Loyd's story on the top of p. 194. It can steadily bleed away a company's profitability. If you are catching the big ones but failing to write up and collect for a stream of small extras on your jobs, you may not sense that you are taking much of a hit. But small extras can easily add up to 3 to 4 percent of the value of the job. A little rot repair here, a bit of an upgrade in finish there, and you are very quickly at $1,400 worth of extra labor and materials, or 4 percent on a $35,000 job. That 3 or 4 percent probably translates into a third, a half, or even more of your profit on the job. By hesitating or neglecting to charge for small change orders, you are well down the road to converting your company into a nonprofit operation.

To successfully charge for change orders during construction, you need two things in your contract: The first is a change order form and explanation such as that on p. 186 of "Agreements," which lays out the causes of change orders and the way in which they will be handled. The second is a set of clauses in your Conditions stipulating your charges for change orders—both for writing them up and for executing them.

COMING UP

The Gateway to Hell

An Upside to Change Orders

Charging for Change Order Preparation

Charging for Change Order Work

Two Sticky Wickets: Deletions and Material Upgrades

An American Disaster: Adversarial Civil Litigation

Alternate Ways to Resolve Disputes

A Change Order Story

Whether out of naiveté, unease about asking clients for more money, or resistance to paperwork, even seasoned builders like Laura Loyd experience huge losses because of failure to write change orders for extra work. Looking back on her experience, Loyd could see that she had started down the slippery slope well before the project started.

Hungry for a challenging job, she gave a low bid for a large remodel to a couple who "wanted everything now, but as cheap as they could get it." As the project progressed, the couple asked for many extras including a new master bath. Loyd built the extras, without ever getting a signed change order. "I did not imagine they could contest charges for work not shown in the architectural drawings," she said.

The clients did contest the charges. They refused to pay Loyd's final bill for $60,000. Loyd took them to binding arbitration, but the arbitrator awarded her only half of what the client owed, and most of that was paid to her lawyers.

Charging for the Preparation of Change Orders

In my contract Conditions, I provide for a set number of hours of change order preparation without additional charge. Beyond those hours, preparation is charged at a professional rate for all work including:

- Discussion with owner or designer
- Design
- Cost planning including inspection of existing conditions and development of alternative approaches to doing the work
- Consultant's fees
- Discussion with and obtaining quotes from subs and suppliers
- Estimating of crew labor and of material costs
- Writing of change order

I also specify that my charge for preparing change orders is due three days after invoicing whether or not the clients elect to do the work described in the change orders.

With a good change order procedure and charge clauses, you might even get so far as to turn change orders into a positive experience for your company and your clients. There is a potential upside to change orders. They represent work you do not have to competitively bid for. When change orders crop up during a project, the work is yours. Change orders also represent an opportunity to serve your client well. I do not want to overstate the point. Charges for extras are painful for clients even if they have put aside sufficient contingency funds. But it is also true that if you educate clients to the inevitability and possible sources of change orders before work begins, then prepare and charge for them as you said you would, you will have gone a long way toward meeting client expectations. Finally, change orders are a way of accommodating the good surprises, the great ideas that crop up during construction that no one saw during design and planning.

You can legitimately charge for change orders at two levels: preparation of the change orders and doing the work described in the change orders. Preparation of change orders usually involves little work. On some projects, however, planning for and writing up extras becomes a substantial job in and of itself because there are so many of them.

My worst case was the complete reconstruction/remodel of a large, century-old, and severely deteriorated four-story home. The job was done on a fast-track basis from schematic plans, and involved such constant design revision and correction of so many hidden Conditions during construction that my crew and I encountered extra work almost daily. All told, the change orders I had to write came to more than 100 single-spaced pages. I invested hundreds of hours in planning, designing, and estimating the extra work they specified.

Despite the labor involved in change order preparation, some builders elect to not charge for the work. One such builder says he regards change orders as a "profit center" and does not want to discourage extras by charging directly for preparing the change orders. Instead, he categorizes change order preparation as overhead and charges for it in his markup.

I choose a middle path. In my contract, I include one hour per week of change order preparation for each week the project is estimated to run. On most projects, that's enough to cover all change order preparation. But when a project uses more than the allotted hour per week, I charge for the work rather than absorb the additional labor into general company overhead. As a result, my clients with only a few change orders on their projects do not subsidize the clients with many. My schoolteacher client with the low-budget kitchen remodel that generates few extras is not being burdened with the overhead costs of change order preparation at the real estate magnate's mansion, where work is added every time the owner strolls through the site.

Charging for change order work

Charging for the work called for in change orders is, as the sidebar at right suggests, normally straightforward. You charge a fixed price or do the work on a T&M basis. But two types of change orders—deletions and material upgrades—pose a bit of a sticky wicket.

With small deletions, a reasonable solution is to credit back only direct costs but not markup for overheard and profit. Small deletions require labor for various adjustments in material use, project management, and in office work. Retaining your markups compensates you for the work of making adjustments.

With large deletions, however, the picture gets fuzzier. You are building a master bedroom and bath addition. The client suffers a financial reversal and must delete all work for the project beyond framing and exterior close up.

Would it be fair or even legal to credit back only direct costs on such a large deletion, retaining thousands in markup? Probably not. Large deletions need to be handled on a case-by-case basis. But it is reasonable that you retain enough to compensate yourself for overhead costs and lost opportunity costs—namely, opportunities for jobs you may have passed up to hold a place in your schedule for the work that has now been deleted.

Material changes likewise raise questions. Your client upgrades during the job from plastic laminate to cast concrete countertops. Should you increase your markup? Some construction professionals say no. I say yes to the overhead markup, because you incur costs in canceling one subcontract and negotiating a new price, schedule, and contract with a new sub. I say yes to the profit markup as well because your risk is increased—you are now responsible for a much more expensive item. A case in point is an experience I

Charging for Extras and Deletions

My contract Conditions let clients know the basis on which I charge for work not included in the contract price. While I sometimes revise my clause to fit individual projects, the default clause provides for charges, payment, and schedule as follows:

1. I will give the clients a fixed price for each change order, *or* if the fixed price is not acceptable to the clients, I will perform the work on a T&M basis.

2. Payment for change orders is due at their substantial completion. For large change orders, my charge may be broken down into several payments.

3. I have sole responsibility for determining the impact of change orders on schedule.

4. For small deletions, costs only, not markups, are credited back. For large deletions, I retain enough markup to compensate myself for overhead, risk, and lost opportunity costs.

> "
> **L**itigation is the
> quickest way to turn
> a large sum of money
> into a small sum of
> money. As a simple
> matter of self-preser-
> vation, every con-
> struction contract
> should contain a
> mediation/arbitration
> clause."

am having even as I write this chapter. Ten years ago, I built a new home for an arty sort of client who requested a concrete countertop sealed only with wax and saw the resulting discolorations as a charming patina. The new owner of the home sees the patina not as art but as a hodgepodge of wine, juice, and peanut butter stains. I am inclined to agree with him, so I am helping him research ways of renovating the countertop without charge. I would not be experiencing that cost if the countertops were plastic laminate.

Alternate dispute resolution (ADR)

The "alternate" in ADR refers to ways of settling disputes other than heading into civil litigation. You need to provide for alternates in your Conditions because the courthouse is exactly where you do not want to go with a construction dispute. Take it from U.S. Supreme Court Justice Warren Burger. Our adversarial civil justice system, he says, is "Too costly, too painful, too destructive, too inefficient for a truly civilized society. . . To continue its use for the resolution of conflicting claims is a mistake that simply must be corrected." My attorney, Bryant Byrnes, brings the point home for builders. "Litigation is the quickest way to turn a large sum of money into a small sum of money. As a simple matter of self-preservation, every construction contract should contain a mediation/arbitration clause."

The ADR clause in my contract Conditions calls for a couple of other steps along with the mediation and arbitration Bryant recommends. The result is a process so long that it should give me and my clients, no matter how badly at loggerheads we might be, time to settle down and work out an equitable solution before we plunge into the nightmare of a lawsuit. My ADR clause calls for, in order:

A CANDID CHAT OVER A CUP OF COFFEE IN MY OFFICE The couple of times I have had misunderstandings with clients, I solved the problem by inviting them over to my office where I could hospitably serve them a cup of hot Mocha Java, hear their point of view, and ask that mine be heard. We listened to one another. We each accepted a bit of a hit, then moved ahead.

NONBINDING MEDIATION Here, a third party—a paid professional skilled at helping people settle disputes, is brought in. Mediators use various strategies to get disputants to begin talking and to consider one another's point of view. They encourage, and sometimes push, the disputants to arrive at a solution both can live with. Because mediation is "nonbinding," either party can walk out at any time. But good mediators can keep the conversation going, especially by playing their ace in the hole, reminding you that if you do quit, you are likely to find yourself climbing the ladder of dispute resolution options, which get increasingly expensive the higher you go. What I especially like about mediation is that you have a chance to not only settle up on money issues, but also to restore mutual trust and respect with your clients.

SMALL-CLAIMS COURT It's cheap, at least in dollar terms. It costs you only the time of preparing your case and going before a judge. You do not have to pay a fee to a mediator or arbitrator. Small claims may be a good alternative for disputes involving smaller dollar amounts if mediation doesn't work. The downside to small claims is that you are in a lose-lose situation. If you lose, you are out your money and time, and if you win, you will likely leave the client with a bitterness that, in the long run, may result in damage to your reputation exceeding the value of any settlement you achieve.

ARBITRATION   Originally, arbitration was developed as an economical alternative to courtroom litigation. Unfortunately, arbitration has come to involve so many of the trappings of court—a judge, lawyers, discovery procedures, cross examination—that it has become nearly as costly as going to court—and equally as adversarial. Still, it may have an edge on full-blown litigation. Arbitration is typically binding. You get in, make your case, win or lose or split the difference, and you are done.

With change order and ADR clauses added, you have rounded out a strong prime contract. It clearly describes the work to be done, schedule, payment, and the balance of builder's and owners' obligations. It protects you and your clients from the most common source of conflict and loss during construction—i.e. change orders—and provides a cost-effective way of dealing with any conflict. Even with a strong prime contract, there is, however, another (and mercifully) last mile to go with contracts. That's creating one for use with your subs.

Subcontracts

If you have in place a really thorough, clear, and balanced prime contract for owners (and actually know what it says and why), you are miles ahead of most builders. When working with subs, you may elect to leave the contract to them. That is what I did for years. I worked repeatedly with the same subcontractors, knew them to be highly reliable, and thought their contracts fair though for the most part sketchy. All things considered, I felt comfortable using their docu-

ment. Later in my career, however, I came to appreciate that a fully professional builder does have a thorough subcontract as well as prime contract. He or she may not use it in every situation, but there are projects when it will be best to pull it out rather than rely on the subs' contracts. Such projects include those for which:

- There are pressing legal or insurance reasons for the subcontract to coordinate closely with the prime contract around such issues as retention, rights of the clients to require overtime work, indemnification, and hold harmless clauses.
- You are working with a subcontractor for the first time.
- You are working with a sub you know well, but who is taking responsibility for a high percentage and/or a high dollar volume of the work.

If you want to be a real stickler, you could move to using your subcontract with every sub on every project (some insurance companies now require you to).

Subcontract issues

If you do create a subcontract, it will need to address issues very similar to those in your prime contract, though with a few additional considerations. Among issues covered in the sidebar on p. 198, a few need explanation:

The subcontract should require a sub to demonstrate that he is a qualified operator who has the necessary protections for you and your clients. He needs to warrant that he is properly licensed and an independent contractor. If he works largely for you, he is not an independent subcontractor but rather your employee. If he has employees of his own, he should provide certificates demonstrating that he carries current workers' compensation insurance. If not,

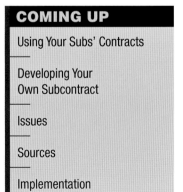

COMING UP

Using Your Subs' Contracts

Developing Your
Own Subcontract

Issues

Sources

Implementation

▪ **SAMPLE LETTERS AND FORMS**
Subcontract Issues Checklist

LEGAL QUALIFICATIONS
- ☐ Independent
- ☐ Licensed
- ☐ Insured

THE WORK
- ☐ Permits
- ☐ Scope of work
- ☐ Quality of work
- ☐ Acceptance and protection of work by other trades
- ☐ Schedule
- ☐ Supervision
- ☐ Sufficient forces
- ☐ Job site behavior
- ☐ Safety

COMMUNICATION
- ☐ Communication with owners
- ☐ Change orders

MONEY MATTERS
- ☐ Payment
- ☐ Overtime
- ☐ Retention
- ☐ Warranty work and back charges

LEGAL FINE POINTS
- ☐ Mutual rights of termination
- ☐ Time of essence
- ☐ Assignment
- ☐ Dispute resolution
- ☐ Addenda

he should provide a letter stating that he has no employees and will work alone on your projects. (Otherwise, you may be hit with a bill by your own workers' compensation insurer.) Lastly, he should provide a certificate of liability insurance, and it should name you and your clients as "additional insureds."

When it comes to the work the sub will perform on a project, the contract should require that he obtains his own permits unless otherwise stipulated (as would be the case in jurisdictions that provide all-in-one permits). Very important, *the contract should spell out that a sub is responsible for all work associated with his trade*. For areas where the responsibilities of trades overlap, the contract should require the sub to be responsible for any work not specifically excluded.

A thorough subcontract will require that each sub accept the work of any preceding trade before building on it, and that the sub protect the work of other trades. Thus, a painter must accept the drywall and protect the finish flooring. When it comes to schedule, the contract will provide for reciprocal obligations. You give the subs repeated and ample advance notice of when they are needed. You make sure the job is ready for them when they show up. They, in turn, are required to show up at the appointed time, with sufficient workers—including a qualified lead person assigned to your project from start to finish—to get the work done efficiently.

During construction, subcontractors should be required to abide by the same standards of job site behavior as your crew, showing respect and consideration for the clients and their property, and all other persons working on the site. They should be required, as well, to abide by all legally required and prudent standards

of safety to protect not only themselves but others on the job as well.

The subcontract should specify that subcontractors must *not* communicate directly with the owner about any issues relating to the construction or management of the project. They must go through you. Subcontractors communicating directly with the owner can create havoc. They will inadvertently lead owners to expect something at odds with the expectations you have sought to establish. They will agree to do work for the owner directly rather than through you, thereby undermining your opportunities to earn overhead and profit, even as you absorb the responsibility of coordinating with them. They might agree to extra work without your knowing about it. The subcontract should make clear that *any*—even the smallest—changes in the work are to be routed through you. The subcontractor is to provide you with a change order so that you can, in turn, create a change order for the owner.

Paying subs immediately after they complete a phase of work, even if you have not yet collected, is a great way to build sub loyalty. To prevent strain on your working capital, however, your subcontract should give you the option of paying subs only after you have collected for their work from the owners. The subcontract should also provide that if you must allow the client to retain part of your charges until substantial completion, you can hold back a proportionate retention from the sub's payment. Be aware, however, that as the sidebar on the facing page describes the retention can be even harder on a sub than on you.

In parallel with the prime contract, the subcontract can require that subs take care of any defects or failures promptly upon being notified, and that if they do not, you can have someone else handle the work and back charge for your costs, overhead, and profit. If that seems harsh, bear in mind that in the time it takes you to handle the sub's work, you could have been doing profitable work of your own.

Your subcontract should require that the subs actually perform the work themselves. They cannot assign the contract to another company. Otherwise, you may find yourself in a situation such as the one I nearly stepped into—almost contracting with one of my favorite plumbers, only to learn that he was so heavily booked he might hand off the work to his brother-in-law, an independent licensed sub in his own right, but not half the craftsman. Finally, like your prime contract, your subcontract should provide for mutual rights of termination, stress that time is of the essence, include balanced indemnification clauses, incorporate legally required addenda, and—by all means—set up alternate means of dispute resolution.

Sources and implementation of subcontracts

To create a subcontract, you can use procedures similar to those suggested for a prime contract. Start with a standard contract and build from there, or create your own contract from several sources. In either case, having a lawyer expert in construction law review your document is a must. Make especially certain it aligns with your prime contract. When it comes to implementing the subcontract, you can go a couple of different routes:

- Use the subcontract selectively, providing it only to the subs who are handling high-dollar amounts of work on a project, are new to you, or to satisfy legal requirements of a project.
- Boil the subcontract down to as tight a format as possible while still hitting all the key issues, and send it

Subcontractors and Payment Retention

Retention can be even harder on subs than on general contractors.

Take the case of a foundation sub who completes his work at the beginning of an eight-month project such as the construction of a new home. Because 10 percent of of the general contractor's pay is held back until the end of the job, the general contractor elects to hold 10 percent of the sub's.

So, while all the other trades from the framers through the painter complete their work, the foundation guy must wait for his money. But even when the painter has touched up the last piece of trim, the foundation sub may not get paid if the contract allows the owner to hang onto the retention until "final completion." In that event, the foundation sub finds himself waiting again while two back-ordered faucets and four cabinet knobs make their way along some manufacturer's assembly line.

Absurd, is it not? The absurdity underscores why we should not tolerate draconian retention practices.

to every sub whose bid you are taking for a project, thereby getting double duty from the subcontract as notification of bid acceptance.
- Create a highly detailed master set of subcontract Conditions, ask each sub to sign it, then for individual projects, simply send out a one- or two-page agreement that incorporates the master Conditions.

With your prime contract and subcontracts in place, you are ready to move on to the best part of being a builder—putting up reliable and attractive structures that will serve your community for many years. To do a top-notch job, you will need systems as thorough and as intelligently selected as the systems you use for accounting, estimating, bidding, and marketing. In Part III, we will turn our attention to those project management systems.

PART THREE

Getting the Jobs Done Right

7 Labor, Materials, and Subcontractors

Hiring and Firing

Crew

Project Leads and Delegation

Pay

Subcontractors and Suppliers

8 Project Management

Safety First

Job Setup

Running Projects

Working with Clients

Labor, Materials, and Subcontractors

Hiring and Firing

WHEN I WAS getting my start in construction in the 1960s, builders commonly organized their carpenters into two separate crews. One handled rough work, from foundations through framing. The other handled the more prestigious finish work. As the carpenters did their work, a few specialty contractors—plumbing and mechanical, electrical, roofing, drywall, and painting—came and went.

That form of organization, the "two-crew model" I have come to call it, worked well in its day. Construction was far less complicated. There were far fewer sub trades. Codes were much simpler. Only a small fraction of today's materials, premanufactured fixtures, and tools were in use. For all those reasons, management of construction jobs was far easier. Few if any builders use the two-crew model today. With its built-in discontinuity between rough and finish responsibilities, it fits poorly with

today's more complex process. In its place, builders have developed a whole series of other models for organizing field labor.

Small-volume models

Of all the models, the Independent Artisan model is the simplest. It's a natural starting point at which to begin a career as a builder. Many contractors return to it after trying their hand at organizing a bigger operation and finding themselves overwhelmed by the complexities. They discover they are happier and make more money mostly working alone or with a helper and an occasional sub. Builders who operate as independent artisans and establish reputations for reliability can enjoy tremendous benefits—great demand for their work, good income, fabulous freedom to work as they like and when they like. The problem is that as your body gives out during middle age. Work is transformed from a source of satisfaction into physical torture. Unless you have

COMING UP

A Choice of Models

Hiring Right

What Employees Want

What You Want

Hiring Procedures

Terminating Employees with Respect

built up investments, your economic security is threatened. The only thing you know how to do you can't do anymore. I have seen a lot of builders caught in that trap. They are scared.

To extend their careers or for other reasons, some builders develop their independent artisan operations into a practice—analogous to that of small law office. They get really good at management but elect not to build a company of any size. Instead, they will employ only a single carpenter, maybe a laborer/apprentice, a team of tested and true subcontractors, and a part-time office manager/bookkeeper. Their own work consists of marketing, estimating and bidding, project management, and a share in the lighter, on-site work.

Builders who elect to take on volumes of work beyond what a practice can handle often instinctively choose the "lead person model"—also called the "lead carpenter model." The leads take responsibility for job site production. The builders are freed up to concentrate on growing their volume of work.

Lead person operations fall into two subcategories—lead and pool, and lead and crew. Builders who use lead and pool feel it is most efficient to have their leads working alone as much as possible, drawing help from a pool of carpenters and laborers when they must have help.

Other builders (including myself) prefer to team each lead permanently with a helper or two. We feel the stable relationship offers several benefits. It maximizes efficiency since lead and helpers have the opportunity to coalesce into a team. It supports quality by allowing workers to take more ownership of a project since it is theirs from start to finish. And it pleases owners who like seeing the same people on their projects every day.

Larger-volume models

Builders ambitious to grow larger companies often move to the "production manager model"—or "project manager model." Rather than leads handling project administration, a production manager takes over supervision of construction from the point the owner, or even a separate sales staff, have negotiated a contract for a project. Builders often move from the lead person to the project manager model prematurely and, as a result, pile up extra overhead and lose efficiency. Good production managers are costly. A production manager represents a layer of bureaucracy between the builder and the on-site construction work. One well-established builder inserted a production manager between himself and his leads, then quickly reversed directions when he saw it was more efficient to have his leads running projects and reporting directly to him.

When a company moves to the production manager model and also employs a salesperson, it often runs into the problem of the sales and production guys ending up at loggerheads with each other. The production manager complains that the salesperson, hot to increase volumes and prove his worth or earn higher commissions, has promised the customers too much for too little and that he, the

---

Builders often move from the lead person to the project manager model prematurely, and as a result, pile up extra overhead and lose efficiency.

Models of Construction Company Organization

- ■ Two-Crew
- ■ Independent Artisan
- ■ The Practice
- ■ Lead Person
- ■ Production Manager
- ■ In-house Contractor
- ■ Developer

production manager, can't possibly get the jobs done in the time and for the money the salesperson has stipulated in the contract. The salesperson accuses the production manager of inefficiency and says he couldn't possibly sell jobs at the prices and schedules the production manager wants.

To solve the problem, one innovative builder created what I call the "in-house contractor" model. He promoted his project managers so that they were functioning like independent contractors, excepting they were on his payroll. Each of them was responsible for selling projects, then building them. With both sales and production in their own hands, his in-house contractors had to create a realistic estimate and build to it, just like a small-volume contractor who calculates costs for a project and then supervises its production. If they sold the project at too low a price or couldn't get work because they built too inefficiently to be competitive, they had no one to blame but themselves.

Other builders who employ production managers move to the "developer model." Rather than the production manager supervising crews, almost all work is subcontracted (as is the case for developers). The production manager's job becomes coordination of the subs. Commercial builders have long favored the developer model. Recently, it has come into use by more custom-home and remodeling contractors. One remodeler runs his operation with three in-house people. He sells projects. A production manager builds them with a team of subcontractors and occasional temporary carpentry or labor help. An office manager handles the bookkeeping and other paperwork.

A disadvantage of the developer model is that you do lose the tight control over production quality as well as the

Legal Concerns

Hiring and firing are both subject to much legal regulation at the federal, state, and even local level. For example, when you hire, you are prohibited by law from asking questions that trespass on an applicant's civil rights; you cannot ask about race, religion, or physical disabilities. When terminating an employee, you can get into a real legal jam if you do so too abruptly, without advance warning and due process.

To make sure your hiring and firing practices are within the law, get summaries of the regulations from the appropriate labor relations boards. Study them. Get help from an attorney if need be. Pay particular attention to requirements for maintaining written documentation of your agreements with and any problems with employees. If an employee is becoming a problem, write up his or her violations of company policies and your attempts to deal with the problem. In the event you must move to termination and the employee disputes it, you will thank your lucky stars for your paper trail.

feeling of community that comes with employing a crew of carpenters. On the other hand, a number of the management burdens, such as meeting payroll and making sure you have enough work to always keep your crews employed, are largely removed. With a very compact operation, you can handle quite large volumes of work. The remodeler with the three-person outfit enjoys revenues of around $1 million a year.

The importance of hiring right

Your own choice of organization will depend on your preferences and opportunities. You may choose one of the models described previously, another that is a blend of two or three, or switch models as your opportunities vary. During a boom period, you might try the lead person model, but then as work slows you find yourself forced back temporarily to something more like a practice. Your choice of models will depend, also, on the people who come your way when and if you set out to hire help. You may find carpenters who can take on the responsibility of project leadership. If not, you may need to hire a production manager to supervise your jobs.

Hiring may be the single greatest step you ever will take in determining the quality of your life as a builder and of your construction operation. When you hire, you determine, quite literally, the company you keep. Your employees are the people with whom you will spend the most waking hours—more than you will with your family or other friends. In fact, when you build a company, it may take on overtones, if not quite of family, then at least of tribe. In strong companies, owner and employees gather at weddings and holiday parties; close out workweeks over a shared pizza; and attend construction conventions together. They are keenly aware of one another's emotional ups and downs and support each other through crises.

Your employees determine the character of the company you will run. As you hand off production responsibility to field employees, you are handing off control over the quality of the work produced. You are handing over responsibility for your company's relationship with your clients. You are putting your reputation, and therefore your economic prospects, in the hands of your workers. You must hire the right people.

What employees want

To hire right, which means to not only initially hire good people but to then keep them hired, you need first and foremost an understanding of what workers want in a job—and what good construction workers can get, if not from you, then elsewhere. You might think there's no mystery in the matter, but as the sidebar on the facing page indicates, builders don't necessarily get it.

Contrary to the assumptions of many employers, workers are looking for a lot more than a paycheck. Study after study shows that they are also looking for a relationship that delivers other rewards. They can be summed up in five words:

Respect. Responsibility. Predictability. Fairness. Control.

For you to attract and hold good workers, all five must be embedded in the daily workings of your operation. They must flow from the statement of purpose and code of values you set for your company, from the policies you establish, from the way you conduct yourself. You can't just write the five words into an ad and expect that will make for successful hiring. You would fool only a few of your hires for a very short period of time.

I personally had to wage a battle with myself around responsibility and control. Even after I had trained my leads, it took me two more years to teach myself to leave a work site when there was nothing more for me to do there. I'd hang around and sweep, straighten lumber piles, and pull nails out of scrap lumber—anything rather than entrust jobs to my very capable employees.

Another builder found his greatest struggle was learning to let his employees know how much he respected their work. He was not even aware of his failing until he hired a management coach who showed him the importance of conveying respect and appreciation. A third builder hired a personal trainer to teach him how to "let go"—and just in time. His key crew members were getting ready to quit due to frustration with his domineering style. His coach taught him how to surrender responsibility and control to his employees. They stayed on. The builder was able to turn his attention to marketing and doubled his company's volume and profitability.

What you're looking for

Whenever you set out to hire someone you will be looking for particular trade skills. There are a few general attributes to keep an eye out for as well. To begin with, you need people with reasonable interpersonal abilities. The building process grows ever more complicated. It requires the passing back and forth of an enormous amount of information. The people you hire and team together need to be adept at taking and giving that information in a receptive and respectful way.

You need to hire productive people. Construction workers seem to come in three speeds—Slow, Medium, and Fast. Slow can't learn to be fast, and Fast can't learn to slow down. Slow is not affordable, especially when Slow takes the form of putting down the tools and gabbing at every opportunity, thus infecting the whole job with slowness. Fast can be okay, so long as speed is not achieved at the expense of consistency. Fast seems to work out best for production work. The fast guys can be great so long as they are in familiar territory. When they hit a problem, they often lack the patience to work it through before reaching for their hammer. Their work gets tangled up, sometimes so badly it needs to be done over or it generates callbacks. For custom work, the best people are the steady, methodical, medium-speed people who move at a rate that allows them to spot and solve a problem and who get their work done right on the first try.

As a general rule, skilled workers are a better deal than beginners. Often, start-up builders hire from the bottom of the skill ladder. They are making the mistake of focusing on labor rate rather than labor cost, of thinking that by hiring low-wage people they will be able to build more cheaply. That's usually not the case. In other words, the person who costs you $26 an hour in wages and labor burden is

not a better deal if he takes three times as long to do the job than the person costing $42 an hour.

That is not to say you should not hire relatively unskilled people now and then. After all, someone gave you and I our start. We have to bring along the next generation. Apprentices can be productive members of your team, especially on projects with a lot of simple, repetitive work for them to do. You should, however, maintain a realistic sense of the productivity costs for lower-skilled versus higher-skilled people.

If you are just starting out as a builder, and are not much past journey-level status yourself, you may resist hiring skilled people in part because you feel self-conscious supervising them. That's understandable, but it's a tendency you want to resist. Actually, you might be better off making your first field hire not a beginner but a seasoned carpenter who could accelerate your education in production technique and in project organization.

A hiring procedure

To hire right, you first need an effective flyer. It's a must. Even as his competitors were desperately looking for help in the

---

What Workers Want

Although it might appear obvious what workers want from a job, it seems those of us who run construction companies don't necessarily get it. A survey of construction workers and of construction company managers revealed that the managers often have a really skewed picture of what matters to workers. On a scale of 1 to 10, with 1 being the highest, here are the survey results on selected key issues.

- *Appreciation:* Workers gave it a 1. Managers gave it a 5.
- *Employers sensitive to workers' problems:* Workers 3, managers 9.
- *Feeling "in on things":* Workers scored it a 2, managers 10.
- *Pay :* Workers scored it only 5, while managers scored it 1.

The True Cost of an Apprentice

	Apprentice	Lead Carpenter
Wage	$10.00	$30.00
Workers' Comp Insurance	$ 5.00	$ 3.00
Other Labor Burden	$ 4.00	$ 9.00
Supervision by Lead	$ 6.00	$ 0.00
Error Correction	$ 1.00	$ 0.00
Total Cost Per Hour	$26.00	$42.00
Total Cost for a Typical Task	$78.00	$42.00

The figures are approximate, but give a realistic picture of the difference in cost as opposed to hourly wage for apprentices and leads because:

■ Workers' comp costs for apprentices are higher for two reasons: Rates tend to be much higher than for journey-level people. Apprentices are much more often injured, and their injuries result in upward adjustments in workers' comp rates for all of a company's employees.

■ Other labor burden is higher on a percentage basis for apprentices because you need to provide them with more tools and other support.

■ For every hour an apprentice works, he or she will need about 10 minutes, or $6 worth, of supervision by the lead.

■ Apprentices spend a good amount of time correcting their errors. Good leads rarely make errors.

With all the costs added up, the hourly cost of an apprentice turns out to be only about 40 percent less than that of a lead person. Meanwhile, except for the most basic tasks, an apprentice's production is likely to be a third as much per hour, if that. While the lead will get that pickup framing done in an hour at a cost of $42, the apprentice might need three hours and cost you $78, close to twice as much for lower-quality work.

super-heated economy of the late 1990s, one builder was having no trouble. He had created an imaginative flyer that effectively played to workers' needs for responsibility and respect along with offering good pay. He had a line of people out the door hoping to be interviewed for jobs in his company. Meanwhile, another builder was struggling to attract promis-

ing applicants. His flyer was humdrum—it sounded like one of those typical newspaper help-wanted ads. You know the type. They give the impression their writers are shopping for flea market merchandise, not motivated human beings. "Wanted: Carp., p/u truck, tools, reliable, clean driver rec., fax res., no phone, comp. wages."

Effective ways to reach out with a flyer include:

■ *Passing it around your own company.* If you already have good employees, they will know other capable tradespeople, and they will, in turn, know still others. Give copies of your flyer to your workers and encourage them to hunt for a good coworker.

■ *Distributing to fellow builders.*

■ *Stapling it to the bulletin board* at your lumberyard and other suppliers.

■ *Posting at schools*—technical colleges and architecture departments.

■ *Placing a boiled-down version in the media.* This one is iffy. Some builders report good results from advertising in newspaper and/or on-line classifieds. Others complain of being overwhelmed with applications from unqualified people.

Luck can make a big contribution to your employee search. You can simply happen into the right person for your company. Capitalize on your luck. Even when all your positions are filled, write down the names and phone numbers of any good prospects you hear about or meet. File their names so that you can call them when you need someone. I have hired some good people whom I first met watching a ballgame or bumped into around the neighborhood. When casting about for upper-level help, don't forget the people already on your payroll. Maybe someone is ready to move up. One builder grew frustrated trying to hire new project leads. He stopped looking, and instead started a program to develop people already in his company.

Selecting your new employee

A traditional process for selecting from among the applicants who respond to your flyer is outlined at the top of p. 208. Tweak it to suit your own inclinations. Many builders request resumes or ask prospective employees to fill out an application. In my company, while I welcome resumes, I do not ask for them. I don't think you can rely on them. Often, they are not even written by the applicant. I would just as well start off talking with the person, typically on the phone, and take notes on a form/ checklist as we go. As in interviews with clients, I concentrate on listening and asking occasional questions to focus the conversation or encourage the applicant. "That's great," I might interject. "I would like to hear more about what you enjoy most about construction and where you want to go in your construction career."

In the course of such a natural exchange, the information called for on an employment application inevitably crops up. The conversational exchange gives a much better feel for the applicant than is acquired by firing questions and taking short answers. Equally as important as prompting interviewees to respond to your interest is requesting them to raise *their* concerns. It's a first gesture of respect toward a person you may work with for many years. Their concerns tell you much about them. Is their focus on quality standards, safety, and the length of time employees have stayed with you as well as on pay? Or is it simply on wages? One set of concerns suggests a person interested in making a commitment to a well-run company, the other an individual merely hunting for a job to pay the bills.

Hiring Strength

A business savant once pointed out that entrepreneurs who have the need to hire people smaller than themselves are always "surrounded by midgets." On the other hand, those who are able to hire people who surpass themselves in important respects end up at the helm of a strong company.

My experience bears that out. All my long-term employees have been much my superior in important technical skills and in various aspects of human relations. The result: They have taught me a great deal about many things—from forming concrete walls, to management techniques, to relating to skittish clients and nervous designers (not to mention ice hockey and river rafting). They have managed and built our projects in a way that has won our clients' appreciation, admiration, and loyalty. All in all, they have taken our company to a level I never would have approached had I hired only people who never overshadowed me.

SAMPLE LETTERS AND FORMS   A Sample Flyer

ARE YOU READY TO MOVE UP?
Come to a Company Where You Can Make
a Real Difference and Be Rewarded for It

David Gerstel/Builder is seeking a top lead carpenter. Your challenges will include:
- Responsibility for construction of your projects to a high quality standard
- Supervision of crew and subs
- Ordering of material
- Maintenance of professional safety and behavior standards at your projects.
- Shared responsibility with the builder for evaluating crew and subcontractors.
- Working with the builder to develop environmentally considerate (i.e., "green" and healthy) building practices
- Project scheduling and change order production (optional)

The individual who fills our lead carpenter position will be a responsible and productive person who will be fairly rewarded for his or her efforts. Compensation will include:
- A legitimate paycheck with all mandated benefits
- A wage at the top of the market scale for your skill and experience level
- Merit raises
- Health benefits after successful completion of a trial period
- Profit sharing
- Tool and travel allowances
- Four day work week (on most projects we work Tuesday though Friday for 9.5 hours a day; we find this schedule more efficient and a better way of life)

PLEASE CONTACT US IN THE MOST CONVENIENT WAY • RESUMES WELCOME
Phone: 510.524.1039 Fax: 510.524.1039 Email: davidugerstel@AOL.com

A Traditional Hiring Procedure

■ Advertise position
■ Take resume and/or written application
■ Phone and/or office interview
■ Check references
■ Job site interview
■ Skills test
■ Policy acceptance
■ Trial period

SAMPLE LETTERS AND FORMS
Employment Application Checklist

BASICS
☐ Date
☐ Name, address, phone, E-mail
☐ Social security number
☐ Person to call in emergency

EXPERIENCE
☐ Education
☐ Three previous employers
☐ Dates of employment and wage level
☐ Job site experience: Rough carpentry/Finish carpentry/Sub trades
☐ Demonstration of knowledge and skills

AMBITIONS
☐ Reasons for applying
☐ Occupational goals
☐ Expected wages and benefits
☐ Vacation needs
☐ Willingness to work overtime
☐ Other interests
☐ Strengths
☐ Weaknesses
☐ Self-assessment

If an applicant seems promising in a phone interview, set up an appointment to talk further, preferably at a job site. In the meanwhile, check references. Talk not to one, but several past employers. An applicant can fool you in an interview, but he won't have fooled all his past employers if he's a dud. When calling former employers, ask first for confirmation of the information the applicant has given you (if he's misled you, the show is over), then inquire in a general way about the applicant's reliability, productivity, and communication skills. Then *listen*. You will be amazed by what you will get. References that start out perfunctorily positive end up decidedly cautionary. Listen for what is not being said as well as what is being said. You may detect evasiveness, for many employers are concerned that they may open themselves to a lawsuit if they make critical remarks about a past employee. If you sense hesitation or hedging it's time to pop the four-seasons, super-strength question: "*Would you hire him (or her) again?*" If the answer is something along the lines of, "Well," then silence, then a bright, "Oh, we're not hiring right now," you can take the response as a veiled warning. If you hear, "You bet! I hated to lose her when she moved to your part of the country," chances are good you've got a strong prospect.

A job site interview

Often your best applicants for a job will already be working. Usually, therefore, the crucial job site interview takes place after hours. For my own interviews, when the applicant pulls up, I try to check out his or her vehicle. I know a lot of good tradespeople don't mind a mess. But I do. So do my clients. If the applicant's pickup bed contains a compost pile of smashed soda cans, sawdust, broken shims, rotting 2×4 blocks, and crumpled coffee cups, the likelihood is we are not a good match.

During the job site interview, the main goal is to assess the applicant's skill levels. Ask questions appropriate to the level you are hiring for. With apprentices make sure they are familiar with building materials so that when the lead asks them to hustle up a 2×4×8 he doesn't get instead two 4×8 blocks. I remember being especially impressed with one apprentice who crisply named off every item in our extensive on-site hardware storage system. Clearly, she had been paying attention to what went on around her at her previous jobs. I hired her. She rapidly matured into a crack journey-level carpenter.

With journey-level people, ask that they show and tell you about their procedures for major tasks such as running joists and hanging doors. With leads, solicit knowledge of plan reading, take-off, and layout technique. With all applicants, work in a request for a self-assessment of strengths and weaknesses. Some people either can't or won't look at their defects, and that can be a real problem when you need to ask for change, as you inevitably must with all employees. To encourage a candid response, relate one or two of your own struggles.

When I decide to hire someone, I usually feel a great rush of excitement and hope. I have worked hard at interviewing.

When I find a promising person and they accept my job offer, I feel like a kid who has just turned up the prize Easter egg. But I have also learned that sometimes my excitement is misplaced. So as a last step in the hiring process, I ask the new person to read our company policy and sign a letter accepting its provisions. Among them is one stipulating a three-month trial period for new employees. I stress to the new employees that getting through the interview with me is just a first step. To win a permanent job they must succeed with their lead and fellow crew members.

Firing

A builder I greatly respect leaves it to his longer-term employees to vote new people in or out after their three-month trial period is over. While I like this democratic process, I prefer to keep the decision in my own hands, though with input from employees. After all, I had the pleasant decision of offering the person a job; I should shoulder the unpleasantness of letting him go if need be.

Letting someone go can be a painful task, even when the person is a new employee still in his trial period, and the process is relatively simple. You have a brief, evaluative conference with the employee and ask for change. If you do not get it, you terminate employment quickly and cleanly, offering a polite handshake, the final paycheck, and best wishes.

More difficult is firing a longer-term employee, a person you've counted on who's gone south and cannot pull out of his nose dive. Suddenly, he or she is turning up late to work several days a week, working sluggishly, not correcting mistakes. Now you need a more deliberate process, what human resource specialists call "progressive discipline."

A progressive-discipline process along the lines of the one outlined in the sidebar on p. 210 accomplishes several important things along with removing a bad employee from your company. With respectful inclusion of the crew lead in the termination process, you'll maintain his or her authority at the job site. By explaining to the crew—with a phrase such as "he just was not working up to our standards"—why you fired the individual you have made clear that their jobs are not in jeopardy and that your appreciation for them is intact. Equally important, you have treated the fired worker with consideration and respect and done everything reasonable to allay bitterness on his or her part. You do not want to send a worker away feeling resentful and humiliated. It's not right, and a bitter employee can spread his bile through your network of clients, subs, and builders.

On Testing and Interviewing

Some construction consultants advocate the use of written tests for evaluating workers, and if you have to narrow down a large group of applicants, they may be a good screening device. Construction workers, however, communicate as much or more by gesture, drawing, and speech as by writing. For those reasons, job site interviews in which prospective employees can show, as well as tell, you what they know are more effective. Guidelines for interviewing include:

■ Never ask trick questions. (Why begin a relationship on a deceitful note?)
■ Avoid yes/no questions; they put people on the spot and elicit only trivial knowledge.
■ Pose broad, open-ended questions.
■ Wait for answers.

Broad, open-ended questions give interviewees a chance to show the depth of their knowledge. What do you think of the way the job site is set up and the materials stored; do you have any ideas how to do it better? How would you frame a partition wall here? How would you lay out the cabinets and plumbing for the kitchen shown in these plans? Such questions require thought by the person answering. Tell interviewees to take time and wait for their answers. (That's not easy. The silence gets uncomfortable.)

Steps in a Progressive Discipline Process

1. *Discuss the situation with the lead,* and give the lead a chance to intervene before you step in.

2. *Invite the employee to meet with you.* Explain the problem as you perceive it, and ask the employee for his perspective. Obtain an agreement from the employee to change.

3. *Follow up with a letter* outlining the agreement and indicating that continuing employment is contingent upon the employee following through.

4. *Monitor the employee's behavior,* expressing appreciation if he or she makes the necessary changes; otherwise move on to the next step.

5. *If the employee does not shape up,* invite him to an exit interview. Explain to the employee why your are terminating him. Ask him if he has any questions, and answer them in as friendly and candid a way as you can manage.

6. *After the termination is complete* and the employee has left the job site, explain to your crew why you fired the individual and express your continuing appreciation for their work.

7. *Call the employment department* and report the termination to ward off a phony unemployment claim that will increase your insurance rates.

COMING UP

Sizing Crews

Meeting the Needs of Your Crew

The Costs of Turnover

Training

Crew

If you are just beginning your career as a builder, you may still feel contented with doing all the work on each project, from estimating to fitting the final door knob. But in all likelihood, the time will come when you will want to get help. You will want to hand off, or delegate, some of your responsibilities. The first big delegation builders make is usually of field production, of the hands-on work. Some jump right to the production manager model (see p. 202 for this and other models of organizing labor), concentrating on marketing, sales, and general administration, while designating an employee to handle the actual construction of projects. But typically builders move away from production in steps, hiring laborers and carpenters until they have built up a crew, leading the crew themselves, then gradually handing off leadership to their most able employee.

Crew size

If you do gravitate to the crew and lead approach, you will need to decide what size crews to work with. Different builders hold different opinions about optimal size. Some favor two-person crews with either two journey-level people or one journey-level person and a helper teamed together. The two-person crew was in favor during my years as an apprentice carpenter. Each journeyman had an apprentice helper who worked "behind" him, absorbing the trade as he filled in details and did chores for the journeyman. I spent thousands of hours cutting and nailing to my journeyman's layout. When a journeyman was well organized and adept at keeping an apprentice moving steadily behind him, the two-person team was efficient. In the right situation it still can be.

In recent years, the one-person crew has come into vogue. Its advocates argue that a builder reaches maximum efficiency by entrusting a single lead carpenter not only with production but also with administration of a job, having him work alone as much as possible and providing him with carpentry or subcontractor help on a stringent, as-needed basis. While I appreciate both the two-person and one-person models, I think builders need to be flexible in establishing crew size. We need to keep in mind two key points. What is most efficient on one job will not be on another. Immediate efficiency does not necessarily equate to long-term effectiveness or even profitability for a company.

Thus, a one-person crew might be just right for a bathroom remodel or small kitchen project, but not effective for building an addition. Moreover, while a one-person crew might give optimal labor productivity on a given project, that productivity may turn out to entail hidden costs. Here's how. The one-person is likely a key company lead. Working alone, the lead takes significantly longer to bring a project to completion. Therefore, because your capacity is limited by your number of leads, by having leads work alone, you reduce the number of projects you can do in a year. With fewer projects on which to recover your overhead, you may need to use higher overhead markups on those projects you do build, thereby squeezing your room for profit. Also, you have fewer projects on which to earn a profit.

You can try to restore speed by having the lead draw intermittent help from a laborer/carpenter pool. But it's questionable whether such a shifting work force will be as productive as a stable crew whose members work with one another day in and day out. I doubt it. Carpentry teams are like sports teams. They take time to coalesce, to get their movements in sync, and to attain top efficiency.

Clearly, sizing crews according to formulas has limited value. You have to make judgment calls and determine what makes sense for your operation. My approach has been to work with two-person teams. For very small projects, such as a bathroom remodel, I occasionally ask a lead to work alone, shifting his sidekick to another site temporarily. For larger projects, such as a new home or reconstruction of a large building, I have either subcontracted part of the

work normally done by my crew or temporarily beefed up the core crew.

I draw on two sources for temporary help. My first choice is other builders who are slow momentarily and who welcome my providing their carpenters with interim employment. My second choice is a temporary construction labor agency where I have cultivated contacts who make sure I am sent reliable people. Construction labor agencies now operate in many parts of the country. You'll find it worthwhile to locate a good one where you work.

In general, it is best to limit crews to three people or less and from that point jump to as large a crew as practicable—five, six, and even more. With one or two other workers on site to supervise, a lead can still effectively do hands-on work. Past two, leads are so involved in supervision of their workers they may as well drop the tool belt in favor of directing as many people as can effectively be fitted on the site.

The Two-Person Crew: a Bit of History

The two-person system reached its pinnacle with the advent of production framing in California during the 1960s and '70s. Carpenters framing on a piecework basis, and motivated by it to pump out work as rapidly as possible, winnowed every unnecessary move out of the framing process. A team of two seasoned production framers could nail up, stand, plumb, and line the walls of a three-bedroom, two-bath house *in a single day.*

I once worked alongside a couple of brothers who ran the floor joists on a piecework basis for the four-story apartment buildings we were framing. The brothers put material in place so rapidly they each earned, in year 2000 inflation-adjusted dollars, around a quarter of a million dollars annually.

To see the two-person system demonstrated, take a look at *The Very Efficient Carpenter* book and video by Larry Haun (see Resources on p. 258). It is a breathtaking study in time and motion efficiency.

Meeting the needs of your crew

Working with crews involves more than balancing immediate efficiency with overall production. It requires taking account of the needs of your crew. In the previous chapter we discussed those needs in the context of hiring and summarized them in five words: Respect. Responsibility. Predictability. Fairness. Control. Here we will look at ways those needs can be met on a day-to day-basis. Then we will look at the costs of failing to do so.

I once had a chance to watch a company owner, who has a real gift for tending to employees' need for respect, as he moved around one of his sites and paused repeatedly to express appreciation to a worker. Particularly striking was how specific he was with his praise. He'd point to one or another detail the worker had executed, telling him exactly what he admired about it. It was clear he was not just glad-handing, that he was really paying attention to his employees' efforts. Specific praise has more impact than generalized pats on the back. Your words more convincingly convey respect when you look right at a carpenter, point to his work, and say, "That scarf joint looks razor sharp," rather than tossing, "Work looks real good" over your shoulder as you pass by.

One important worker need—fair treatment as manifested in fair pay—is so large a subject we'll give it a section of its own (p. 221). Another, giving over control and responsibility, especially for the hands-on work, is for many of us the toughest of employees' needs to meet, and yet in some ways it is the simplest. You simply have to stop trying to dictate process and switch to monitoring results. Let people do things in their own way, so long as the outcomes are respectable.

By contrast, meeting the need for predictability is quite complex, as the sidebar on the facing page outlines. I first began to understand the issue during my years as a journeyman carpenter employed by companies that ambushed workers with sudden layoffs. Carpenters were let go with no warning or explanation, discarded like suddenly obsolete pieces of machinery. Of course, when that happened, the laid-off workers felt humiliated and abused. But the companies paid a price. Those who remained behind were well aware they could easily be in the next round of layoffs and were regarded as disposable. They responded by using the company as they were used, stealing time and material at every opportunity, "hiding" from supervisors in dark corners of the project, and regularly heading home with pilfered materials.

> **S**top trying to dictate process and switch to monitoring results. Let people do things in their own way so long as the outcomes are respectable.

Being a Predictable Builder

Meet your workers' need for predictability.

■ *Provide steady employment.* One builder boasts that for three decades, through boom years and times when profit lay thin on the ground, his employees have never gone without work. Top carpenters vie for jobs in his company.

■ *Maintain a well-organized job site.* A builder lost both of his lead carpenters just as he was about to begin the biggest project of his career. Their need for a reliable flow of material, carpentry help, subcontractor service, and information was not being met. They jumped ship to builders who could provide it.

■ *Maintain a consistent and respectful tone.* When things are going well, it's easy. When they are not, it's tough. A builder's bad moods can be interpreted by employees as criticism and can undermine their morale. When I feel the stress rising to the point that I am liable to tear the head off the next person who crosses my line of fire, I request my employees to not take my grouchiness personally. I am just hitting a bad patch. It's me that's the problem, not them, I explain. That seems to help.

■ *Never suspend agreements abruptly.* Whether agreements are written, spoken, or even unspoken, present your crew with proposals for change, not edicts.

Since starting my company, I have always tried to provide my employees with information about their employment picture for the coming weeks and months. I keep them updated about new jobs we are signing up. When we are facing a possible slow period, I work with them to line up side jobs to fill in the gap. I have been warned that such practice would lead to workers jumping ship and leaving me short-handed rather than risk unemployment. On the contrary, my crews have returned my efforts with gratifying reliability and loyalty.

The costs of turnover

Making sure your workers' needs are met is not an option—it is a priority and one you must stick with day in and day out. Fail to do so and you pay a high price—turnover. One of the most creative builders I have ever known told me that when he started his own company, he tried to create "a bunch of clones, extra sets of my own hands." But then he began to see that he was "taking the enjoyment out of the work for the employees and killing their incentive." Finally, when his top guy walked off a job, he realized he had no choice but to give his employees the control they craved.

Another builder was more easily able to hand off control of production. He was ready and eager to concentrate on marketing and sales. To replace himself as production manager, however, he hired a man who had much technical know-how but was incapable of showing respect and appreciation. On the contrary, the man took satisfaction from demeaning his carpenters for gaps in their knowledge or errors in their work. As a result, the owner constantly had to recruit and hire new carpenters as one after another of them quit to get away from the production manager.

Meeting Your People's Needs—a Nonstop Job

I once heard a builder declare that she worried her subs felt underappreciated. Her solution: treat them to a "sub appreciation night," specifically, a turkey dinner. That, I thought to myself, is a turkey of an idea. Not that it was a bad idea, only that it was woefully insufficient.

You can't take your workers' (or subs') appreciation needs off the table with an annual event. Human confidence and trust is fragile and needs steady replenishment, as I was emphatically reminded by a lead who had worked with me for nearly a decade and is one of the more self-sufficient people I have known.

One day at his project as we finished up our usual exchange of information, he said he had a last question. He wanted to know whether he should be making plans to look for another job. I was so surprised I barely managed to ask why he would even think of such a thing. It turned out he thought I was getting ready to fire him because I had not expressed respect or appreciation for his work for near a month, and I usually did so almost every time I was at his job site!

Turnover is so endemic in the construction industry that we tend to take it as a given and to overlook the costs. The costs are high. Advertising for help, taking applications, interviewing, and hiring for a position take hours of work. Putting a new person on payroll and monitoring him through the trial period consumes additional labor. Training new people, finding the gaps in their knowledge and eliminating those gaps, is often a hit-and-miss proposition. By the time you know what new employees don't know, they have already made costly mistakes, sometimes mistakes that go unnoticed and generate failures, callbacks, and loss of client trust. Integrating even highly skilled, new employees with your existing crew and their way of doing things takes time and effort. All the turnover costs add up to real money.

In short, attending to your crews' needs, sometimes even to the detriment

The Costs of Turnover

- ◼ Advertising for replacements
- ◼ Interviewing applicants
- ◼ Hiring
- ◼ Payroll setup
- ◼ Monitoring new hires during trial period
- ◼ Production errors
- ◼ Callbacks and failures from errors
- ◼ Redundant training
- ◼ Integration of new employees with existing crew
- ◼ Increased accident rates

Training: A Triangle of Opportunities

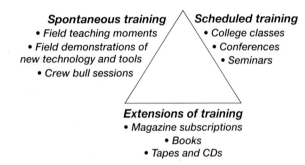

Spontaneous training
- *Field teaching moments*
- *Field demonstrations of new technology and tools*
- *Crew bull sessions*

Scheduled training
- *College classes*
- *Conferences*
- *Seminars*

Extensions of training
- *Magazine subscriptions*
- *Books*
- *Tapes and CDs*

Because construction technology is evolving so rapidly, nonstop training and retraining is a must for all of us in the industry. Offer your employees the kind of training that will work best for them. People learn in different ways. Some will make use of books, others of seminars. Still others will respond best to spontaneous learning opportunities in the field.

of immediate efficiency, is not simply a feel good issue. Because it prevents turnover, because workers stay with and put out for companies who provide them with respect, control, and fair treatment, meeting your crews' needs keeps your costs down. The resultant savings show up in more competitive estimates and on your bottom line. Meeting the needs of your workers makes you money and in addition, though it takes effort, it allows you to relax a bit. You know that they are likely to be there when you need them.

Training

These days technology changes so rapidly that training is a necessity. Not only must apprentices be taught the trade, but veterans must adapt and sharpen their skills constantly. Builders can offer two types of training—spontaneous and scheduled. Both have value. Spontaneous training capitalizes on what professional educators call "teaching moments," timely opportunities to deliver information to a person so that he or she is able to make use of it immediately and, therefore, to retain it. An apprentice is learning how to frame: You see him pulling one nail at a time from his pouch. You step over, show him how to hold a stack of 16d sinkers in his palm and then to roll one onto his fingertips while driving another.

With spontaneous training, and for that matter all other training, checking first for prior knowledge and asking for feedback is crucial. Neglect those steps, and your training will be far less effective. You see a recently hired journey-level carpenter beginning to flash the windows for a new home. You explain to her that moistureproofing is like an emergency medical procedure. If it is not right the patient expires. You ask her to explain her procedure and the thinking behind it. If you spot any blanks in her knowledge, you fill them in by demonstrating your flashing procedure on the next window (and/or correcting the first). Then you watch her flash the third to make sure she's got the idea.

Training that capitalizes on spontaneous teaching moments can be very cost-effective. You teach people just what they need to know for the task at hand, and if the teaching is well done, it contributes immediately to productivity. If you capitalize on teaching moments persistently, you will accomplish a great deal of training. Stop apprentices twice a day for two-minute trainings, and over the course of a year you will have given them 500 lessons in basic construction mechanics.

With some employees, spontaneous training is the only kind that is of value. They learn by doing, period. Others will make use of books and other literature that extend their field training. For these guys a gift of a good manual or trade journal is a cost-effective investment. If they pick up a single technique that saves an hour's labor, your investment will be paid for twice over. The likelihood is they will pick up a great deal more than that.

For other workers, what I call "scheduled training"—classes, conferences, seminars—can be effective. Some builders make a significant investment in scheduled training. One Boston builder hires consultants to teach his employees about working with difficult clients and the building science underlying the details in his designs. Other builders cover the tuition costs for college classes or send employees to industry conferences.

Scheduled training has its drawbacks. Hiring good presenters and paying for classes and conferences adds substantially to overhead. Timing the presentation of classes so that they relate directly to work going on in the field can be difficult too. By the time you get to the seminar on difficult clients, they may be history, and the lessons therefore more academic and less impactful. On the other hand, good scheduled training can be a real treat for employees and can strengthen your company. Hire an engaging expert to spend two hours with your crew to discuss an important issue such as interior air quality. Your crew will walk out with intensified awareness of the importance of the work they do in the field every day. They will feel the challenge of additional responsibility. In other words, training not only supports productivity. It fulfills core needs of the people you work with.

Project Leads and Delegation

Good project leads are remarkable people. To do their job, they must draw on extensive trade knowledge, solid craft skills, and an ability to visualize and coordinate the many elements that make up a construction project. Simultaneously with exercising their technical wizardry, they must motivate their crew, fostering in them the sense of being in control, fairly treated, and respected. Leads must do all those things every day amid the turbulence of construction sites, while keeping projects on schedule, within budget, and up to quality standards.

You can spot the presence of a good lead by the look and sound of his job site. The site is well organized, clean, and safe. The work is tight. There's a steady rattle, hum, thud, and whine of tools and material moving into place. Mixed with the sounds of construction is another sound—occasional brief laughter. People are getting along and having a good time, but not wasting time with too much talk.

Levels of leads

Though leads are often lumped together into one category, there are several distinct levels of leads. At the most basic level, lead carpenters—or what we called "foremen" not that many years ago—are given responsibility for laying out and performing the carpentry, either alone or with a helper or two. As leads advance toward the intermediate and then to advanced level, they accept more of the managerial and administrative aspects of the project. They promote and monitor safety practices. They make sure that time cards are filled out accurately. They ensure that materials are ordered on time so that work can proceed smoothly and

COMING UP

Levels of Leaders

The Challenge of Delegation

Handing Off Change Order Writing

Delegation as Teaching

Delegation not Abdication

You can spot the presence of a good lead by the look and sound of his job site.

A top lead like David Lassman is highly versatile. At one moment he's jumping in with his crew to install decking, the next he's laying out centers for the plumbers. Then he moves on to scheduling a materials delivery and taking a call from the client about light fixtures. (Photo by David Gerstel)

Levels of Project Leads

▪ *Basic lead carpenter*—lays out carpentry and works with crew.
▪ *Intermediate lead carpenter*—basic-level responsibilities plus coordination with subs, ordering of material, keeping of time cards. Manages job site safety program.
▪ *Advanced lead carpenter*—basic and intermediate responsibilities plus scheduling of subs and minor change order production.
▪ *Full lead carpenter*—basic through advanced responsibilities plus full change order responsibility.
▪ *Superintendent*—single job production manager. Runs very large projects, such as the construction of "estate homes," office complexes, and apartment buildings. Coordinates carpentry crew (including a lead carpenter) and subs. Handles all project administrative work.
▪ *Production manager*—oversees several projects, small or large, at once.

schedule subs so that bottlenecks in production do not develop.

As your leads reach the advanced level, they take a giant step. They begin assuming responsibility for the production of change orders. Leads struggle with change order responsibility. Builders struggle to hand it off successfully. In the sidebar on p. 218 I've suggested reasons.

Good leads are fairly rare, but that is not because carpenters can't rise to the challenge of project leadership. Rather, it's that they are pushed into the job too rapidly, without training, and become overwhelmed and frustrated. It is a long way from carpenter to full lead. You cannot expect people to cover the whole distance in a single bound, but must recognize that it takes even a fast learner several years to make his way up the ladder of project leadership. If you want your people to make the climb successfully, you must support them by handing off unfamiliar management tasks one digestible chunk at a time.

The challenge of delegation

"It's really hard, delegating," a builder grimly told me. "I've tried over and over. If I don't do a job myself, it does not get done right."

"Yeah," I said, "We all bang up against that. We feel like if we let go of an important responsibility, it will get messed up."

"No," he scolded me. "It's not a *feeling*. I've gotten the factual evidence, over and over. I tell them what to do, and they screw up."

The builder had come to a conclusion that many builders never get past. There's a degree of ego gratification that comes from believing you are the only one who can get the job done. There is also fear and anxiety in giving up control over your old territory to someone else. For those of us who come from the trades, such anxiety can be particularly intense with our first big delegation, handing off responsibility for field production. When we delegate direct control over the hands-on work, we are giving up our accustomed way of making our living. That can feel very threatening.

Letting go is doubly hard because once you have delegated responsibility, you have to leave it delegated, even if efficiency and quality fall off for a time, as they very likely will. If you vacillate between letting go and then grabbing the reins again, you will provoke justified resentment. A lead carpenter, critiquing his boss, draws the picture vividly. "If I'm in charge, I don't want him there. He comes to the site and goes off half-cocked. 'No, no, no,' he's yelling, but we have our systems all worked out. We don't want to be stopped in midprocess."

In other words, when you let go, really let go. If you are handing off project leadership, stay in the background when you go to a job site. Look over the work. Write down your questions. Go over them with the lead and answer his questions. But don't give orders to the lead, his crew, or the subs. Work with and through him. Get in quietly, get out, and leave with an expression of appreciation.

It must be emphasized however, that *delegation is not merely a psychological challenge. It is also an organizational one.* Success requires a well-thought-through procedure for handing off responsibility such as the one I have suggested in the sidebar on p. 219 for handing off change orders, probably the toughest of all delegations except sales.

Delegation as teaching

If you are to succeed at delegation, you must become something construction work does not normally prepare you to be, a teacher. (Of the builders I know, among those who appear to be the very best at delegation are several who were trained as schoolteachers prior to entering construction.) Teaching is a four-step process:

1. Finding out what the student already knows.

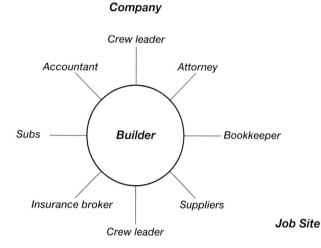

Once you have delegated authority to a crew lead you play a supportive role when you are at his or her job site. You are not the wheel, or even the hub—the lead is. You are a spoke. Act otherwise and you undermine the lead's morale and authority.

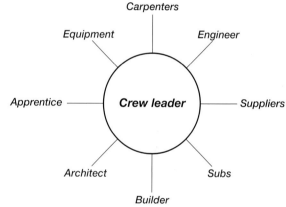

2. Building on his or her prior knowledge.
3. Evaluating the results by asking questions.
4. Building further knowledge and requestioning.

Always begin teaching by giving the student the respect of asking what he already knows about the subject. Then teach from his or her prior knowledge forward. Bear in mind that people learn in different ways, some more via explanations, others more easily via gestures, pictures, demonstrations, even dramatization. Use all ways in showing and telling someone how to do a task. Explain. Draw. Demonstrate. Show an apprentice how to cut a block, don't just

Always begin teaching by giving the student the respect of asking what he already knows about the subject.

Why Change Order Delegation Is So Hard

Even builders who have a hammerlock on other aspects of their business are sometimes stumped by change order delegation. They just can't get their leads to do the job. The reason is that in asking their leads to take on change orders, they are asking them to move from their familiar world of production into the domain of sales, estimating, legal paperwork, and general management. Each change order amounts to a mini-construction project entailing design and/or specification, estimating, a sale to the owner, and a contract as well as the usual job site tasks.

The sales part of change orders is especially hard on a lead. He finds himself having to tell the nice couple for whom he is building an addition that they can forget about taking that trip to Disneyland with their twins. The money they had set aside for it, well, it's going to get swallowed up by the charges for correcting the structural decay and substandard plumbing he's just discovered in the existing walls.

Leads who can successfully handle change orders are three-quarters of the way to being contractors. In other words, taking on change orders is a huge step. If you want your leads to make that big step successfully, you will have to hand the task off in manageable increments such as those suggested in the sidebar on the facing page.

tell him. Take a lead step-by-step through the creation of a materials order. Don't just tell her how to do it. After you have presented the new task to an employee, ask him to run the task back to you, then redemonstrate it to clear up any misunderstandings. Repeat the process until the employee has a firm grip on the task.

Let employees take on tasks at their own speed. You don't necessarily have to complete the delegation in one pass or even one day. In fact, major project management delegations may take months to complete, just like major phases of a carpentry apprenticeship.

You cannot simply give an employee a description of a complex task like change order production and expect him

or her to immediately take hold of it. Many managers, not only builders, make that mistake frequently. They give an employee a complicated verbal explanation, ask "you got that," take "yes" instead of a demonstration for an answer, and then express frustration when the person does the task bass-ackwards. The student did not fail. The teacher did! The students really did think that they had it. The teacher failed to make sure that they did have it.

Sometimes an employee does not get a task because he does not want to do it. In that case, don't try to force it on him. You cannot force a person into successfully handling a task he is not ready for. If it is essential that he takes it on as part of his job, but nevertheless resists, try to help him past his resistance by breaking the task into small steps. If he still digs in his heels, give the task to someone else, even if it means moving the first employee over or down within your company. You cannot leave a vital company responsibility in the hands of someone who refuses to accept it. Not only your own well-being but that of your other employees and your clients is at risk.

Delegation, not abdication

It can happen that your employees will resist delegation more than you, and not only because they are averse to a particular task. They will fight your "letting go." They are accustomed to calling on you to make the significant and even the minor decisions. Now you are asking them to go it alone. What do you do? One builder resorted to simply tossing the ball to his employees and driving away from the gym. He took a lengthy vacation, leaving behind strict orders, "Do not call under any circumstances." Another informed his key employees that he would no longer be carrying his cell phone, which had rung incessantly with calls from project leads asking for guidance. "Make your own decisions," he was instructing them.

Neither of these builders was abandoning his job. They both have controls in place for keeping track of what is going on in their companies. In short, while they delegate tasks, they do not abdicate awareness nor ultimate authority.

Too often, delegation and abdication are not differentiated. Articles in construction industry magazines, intent on exploring the psychological barriers to delegation, underscore the need to "let go," but not to simultaneously "hold on." They don't get around to pointing out that as you step back from personal and direct control you must simultaneously *create controls* for monitoring and managing your company's output. In other words, you may move from player/coach to general manager and take your eye off the ball, but that doesn't mean you ignore the outcome of the games.

As you delegate, you will need to create and maintain controls for both production and financial outcomes. Controls for production need to operate at three levels:

INDIVIDUAL PHASES AND ITEMS OF WORK   Do not give leads unsupervised responsibility for work with which they have little experience. At the start of a job, create checklists of work for which they need support. If a lead has not supervised concrete placement, make sure he has backup from someone who does on pour day.

GENERAL QUALITY   Keep in place a second "eye," whether yourself or an experienced production manager, to double-check work. Large construction companies have greatly reduced building failures and lawsuits by providing

Steps in Handing Off Change Order Responsibility

1. Hand off change order responsibility only to leads willing to take on the challenge.

2. Have the lead take responsibility for spotting extras and reporting them to you.

3. Have the lead observe as you estimate the costs, write up the change orders, and present them to the client.

4. Role-play. Together with the lead, act out presenting change orders for correction of hidden conditions or upgrades to a resistant client.

5. Provide the lead with an estimating checklist and change order forms, and have him practice estimating, marking up, and writing up change orders.

6. Show the lead that failure to charge for extras can destroy the company's profitability (and his chance to share in profits via your profit-sharing program).

7. Delegate processing of small change orders to the lead.

8. Monitor the lead's change order work; do additional training to correct for weaknesses.

9. Increase responsibility in steps until the lead is writing even large change orders.

10. Reward increasing responsibility for change orders. Reward with merit raises. Reward with titles. Make a sharp distinction in your company between basic leads and full leads who handle change orders. People are motivated by status at least as much as by money.

11. Never abdicate responsibility for change orders. Make discussion of change orders a major feature of your regular meetings with your leads, and monitor change order production on your projects.

a second eye—namely, independent inspectors—to back up their supervisors.

HIGH-LIABILITY PRODUCTION
Be especially attentive to high-liability items such as waterproofing. Create

A Case of Abdication

Jerome Waldorf was a savvy and normally vigilant businessman with several decades of experience as a builder when he relaxed his controls and took his big hit. After winning a contract to remodel a civic club, Waldorf hired a highly recommended new man to run the job, and along with the plans and specifications gave him instructions to make sure he had requests for any extra work "in writing" before doing it.

The project moved smoothly under the new lead's supervision. When it was nearing substantial completion, Waldorf noted that it included significantly more work than called for in the plans. He looked forward to submitting a juicy bill for extras. Then, reviewing his lead's paperwork for the first time, he discovered that the man had conscientiously, in accordance with his understanding of his instructions, described the extras in writing. The writing, however, was simply a log. None of it was on company change order forms. None of it had been signed for by the club's officials.

When asked to pay for the extras, the officials declined to do so, then after a lengthy wrangle, finally agreed to settle up for 50¢ on the dollar, leaving Waldorf with a loss of around $50,000. His experience underscores the importance of using feedback, as good teachers do, to make sure the person to whom you delegate a task understands it, and of *never* taking our eye off those crucial delegated tasks that can have a major impact on your company's well-being.

---

f you are able to accomplish delegation without abdication, give yourself a pat on the back.

---

checklists for inspections of high-liability items. Have your lead fill them out for each job. Have the second eye check the checklists against the work.

Controls for financial performance include:

CALLBACKS   Monitor them. How many callbacks does a given lead generate per project? If they amount to more than a few minor adjustments on average, you need to provide additional training, improve your quality controls, change leads, or all three.

CHANGE ORDERS   After delegating, monitor. Is a lead generating an unusually low percentage of changer orders for the type of project being built? Are there change orders in place for all work that

has been done but that is not included in the plans and contract? If the answer to the first question is yes or to the second no, find out why and act fast.

JOB COSTING   Some companies have project leads do it. To me that seems unwise. Leads want their job costs to look good. Consciously or unconsciously, they may delay entering costs in the books. As a result, you find out too late when a job is turning into a financial bust. Job costing for a project should be done by someone other than the person responsible for production, or you have no control in place.

CUSTOMER SATISFACTION   Call customers during and after their projects are completed. Send customers evaluation forms. Ask about the leads. Share those results with your leads. Celebrate compliments and expect receptivity to any fair criticisms. Satisfied customers are your company's lifeblood.

EMPLOYEE SATISFACTION   Keep your ear to the ground. Are your leads providing their crews with the respect they need? If not, encourage and teach them to do so. If they can't get the hang of it, try to move them to a job in which they do not have authority over others.

If you are able to accomplish delegation without abdication, give yourself a pat on the back. You will have met one of the most difficult challenges in running a construction company. There are plenty of builders who can abandon responsibility to employees for tasks they have grown bored with. There are plenty who obsessively keep a hold on every detail of their company's operation. There are relatively few who are able to step back and support their employees in taking on new responsibilities, yet at the same time maintain the vigilance necessary for their companies' long-term success.

Pay

In the previous chapters we have discussed the intangibles like respect and predictability that workers want from a job. We have mentioned studies that indicate workers rank the intangibles higher than pay. But that is a long way from saying pay is unimportant, that so long as a builder treats his workers well in other respects he will be able to get away with paying them poorly.

In fact, after seeing their wages stagnate or even fall in terms of real purchasing power for many years, tradespeople began playing catch-up with a vengeance in the later 1990s. They will likely continue to whenever economic conditions allow. Builders will feel pressure like that experienced by one I know. He is a veteran of the construction business with the skills needed to foster long-term relationships with employees. In fact, his crew likes working for him so much that they once held an appreciation day for him, showing up on a Saturday morning to do the long-postponed repairs on his house, and then fete him with a barbecue and all the fixin's. Half a dozen years later it was a different story. He was desperately trying to meet the wage demands of those same workers so as not to lose them to other builders who constantly recruited them at job sites and the lumberyard with promises of higher pay.

How much to pay

Pay matters to workers a whole lot, not only because they have bills to pay but because pay is a sign of respect, fair treatment, appreciation, and is a status symbol. You need to ask yourself, How much must I pay to attract and hold good people? A former executive of L.L. Bean, the long-lived clothing and recreational goods company, suggests a rule of thumb: Pay 20 percent above average to

get a 30 to 40 percent above-average employee. If you pay generously rather than squeeze your employees, he suggests, they in turn will not feel compelled to hold back on you.

The Bean rule is, however, more than a humanistic generality. Apply it to construction and you can see that the numbers work. Take, as an example, a lead carpenter. Say that the going hourly rate for an average lead is $30. You decide you will pay 20 percent more, or $36, about the top end in your area, for a top person—meaning someone with strong craft skills, good leadership ability, and determination to build his projects to a high-quality standard and on schedule. Here, conservatively figured, is how your investment can come back to you:

- *Higher productivity.* Your lead will, at the very most, need about 54 minutes to do what the average guy does in 60. That translates into 10 percent of his wages.

COMING UP

How Much to Pay

Basic Pay and Benefits

Heavier-Duty Benefits

Profit Sharing, a Best Practice Bargain

Bonuses . . . and Counter-Productive Bonuses

A Compensation Ladder

Basic pay
- A competitive wage
- A legitimate paycheck with legally required benefits

Low-cost, high-return benefits
- A well-organized, clean, safe, work environment
- High standards of craftsmanship
- A 4/3 workweek
- Tool and travel allowances
- Paid vacation

Heavy-duty benefits
- Health benefits
- Profit sharing
- Retirement plans
- Bonuses

■ *Callbacks reduced.* If the lead manages about $10,000 a week in volume and reduces your callback ratio by 1 percent of volume, that saves you $100 a week, or about 7 percent of his wage.

■ *Client appreciation intensified.* An excellent lead who is good with people and is able to keep projects on schedule will promote client trust. It's hard to quantify the value of that contribution to dispute prevention and marketing, but it surely is worth 5 percent.

■ *Thorough change order processing.* Good leads make sure extras are approved before building them. Their thoroughness can easily save you half their wage, but to be conservative peg the savings at 10 percent.

■ *Reduced turnover.* Capable leads inspire the loyalty of their crew and reduce turnover. According to personnel experts, each time an employee leaves and has to be replaced, the cost to the employer runs from 20 to 100 percent of the employee's wage. Using the rock-bottom percentage, you can figure that if your highly paid lead saves you one turnover of a journey-level carpenter a year, that will amount to about 15 percent of his wages.

Already, even with very conservative calculations, we have come up with 47 percent in savings for the 20 percent increase in wages, and we have not even gotten to additional benefits such as the top lead's superior reliability, ability to attract new clients, and affect on your own morale. In my operation, I adhere to the Bean 20 percent rule, and in return, I get high productivity, virtual elimination of callbacks, intensified client loyalty, and close to zero turnover

in my permanent crew. When the Bean executive said 30 to 40 percent, he was not just talking through his woolen watch cap. The guy's got a grip on his numbers.

The legitimate paycheck

Together with a competitive wage, the most basic of benefits is a legitimate paycheck. In the construction industry, where so many people are paid "under the table," or as "subcontractors" when they are really employees, the legitimate paycheck is by no means a certainty for workers. But a legitimate paycheck, as the top sidebar on the facing page shows, is actually a mega-benefit encompassing several discreet ones.

In round numbers, a legitimate paycheck confers on workers a package of benefits typically worth one-third of their wage. Nevertheless, some workers may resist the move to legitimate employee from phony subcontractor status for the simple reason that they are so accustomed to working for cash and evading taxes. If so, you need to get rid of them and move up to employees who are not inclined to be tax cheats. As we will discuss shortly, the risks of paying employees as subs is just too great.

Even if your employees are eager for a legitimate paycheck, you may hesitate to take the step yourself. The additional paperwork and the cost of social security and other employer taxes may seem intimidating, especially if you are just getting on your feet as an independent contractor. But if that is the position you are in, you need to overcome your resistance and go straight as soon as possible. You are unlikely to attract first-class employees if you do not. And you are in serious danger from the IRS.

The IRS is crystal clear about the difference between an employee and a subcontractor. If you are in doubt, request a pamphlet. But frankly, it is not hard to discriminate between employees—the people who work under your direction and steadily for you and no one else—and subcontractors—people who are set up in business for themselves, contract with you for specific tasks and accomplish them in their own way, and work for a variety of clients. Builders know when they are trying to weasel their way around the distinction between employee and sub and so do the IRS auditors who visit their offices.

Ferreting out illegitimate subcontractor arrangements is an IRS priority. Should the IRS discover you are treating employees as subcontractors for tax-avoidance purposes, they can hit you with crushing penalties. The chances of their finding out are good—if not from an audit, then from a bitter former employee or a competitor you have been able to outbid because your tax cheating allows you to charge less for labor.

On the other hand, you *can* succeed as a builder while shouldering the costs of a legitimate payroll. Builders all over the country do. I know a lot of successful builders, and I can say almost with certainty none of them work the employee-as-subcontractor-scheme. They see a legitimate payroll as a necessary benefit for their employees and a necessary protection for their companies.

Farther up the compensation ladder: space and time benefits

Next up the ladder are benefits you can provide at minimal cost or even at a net savings. The first of these is a quality workplace—one that is safe, clean, well organized, and where good work is produced—where, as one builder puts it, carpenters get a chance to "really practice the craft." Providing a quality workplace

The Benefits of a Legitimate Paycheck

Some builders pass out to their employees a summary of the benefits of a legitimate paycheck.

- Employer's contribution to social security: 8% of wages
- Unemployment insurance: 5% of wages
- Disability insurance: 2% of wages
- Workers' compensation coverage: between 10% and 20% of wages
- Liability insurance: 5% of wages
- Tax deposits handled by the employer

The Benefits of the Four-Day Workweek

For years my crews have worked four days a week. The benefits in increased efficiency, morale, and reduced turnover are so great, the 4/3 gives me a significant competitive advantage.

- *Twenty percent reduction* in time for daily setup, roll-up, and end-of-day cleanup.
- *Less time is lost to holidays.* Holidays are less likely to land on a workday. Also, the 4/3 can be shifted around holidays. If your four days of work are usually Tuesday through Friday, and a holiday falls on a Friday, you can shift work to Monday through Thursday.
- *Client appreciation.* Clients endure construction one day less each week.
- *Subcontractor support.* Trusted subs can have the site to themselves for a day a week, enabling them to work more efficiently.
- *Project management load consolidated.* One day a week with no crews on projects.
- *Increased worker satisfaction.* The 4/3 is enormously appealing to many workers. They will stick with a company to hold on to it.

pays off in lower workers' comp costs, reduced callbacks, higher crew morale and—no small point—allows you to feel pride in your operation.

Along with the benefit of a quality work space, you can provide a benefit in the time dimension. I first learned about

Additional High-Impact, Low-Cost Benefits

■ *Travel allowances.* If your crew is driving greater than normal distances to a job site, include a mileage charge in your estimate, and pass the income on to your employees.

■ *Tool allowances.* Pay your crew a stipend in return for use of their personal tools on company projects and/or repair, and replace their tools as they wear out.

■ *Paid vacations.* Pay for vacation days is not burdened with consumables and insurance costs. Therefore, a week's paid vacation for full-time workers costs only about 1.33 percent of their total annual wages.

These benefits involve tax considerations, so before you establish the benefits, check on the current rulings with your accountant or the tax authorities.

the possibilities when I was responsible for reorganizing a corporation from the traditional 5/2 workweek—i.e., five days of work at 8 hours a day, then two days off—to a variety of on/off arrangements, including the 4/3 (four 10-hour workdays followed by three days off). The people who moved to the four-day workweek loved their new schedule and were clearly motivated to hang onto it by succeeding at their jobs. When I set up my company, I went immediately to the 4/3 and realized many benefits, as the bottom sidebar on p. 223 indicates.

Though my own experience with the 4/3 workweek has been almost entirely positive, there may be some drawbacks to it. Occasionally, employees shy away from it. Some have young children and do not like getting home to their kids a couple of hours later in the day. A few are afraid they would not know what to do with themselves over the longer weekend. The 4/3 does impose the cost of artificial lighting at the beginning and end of short, winter days. Some builders fear the 4/3 nega-

tively impacts productivity—they wonder whether crews can work effectively for 10 hours a day (or even 9.5, as they do in my company), especially at such strenuous work as forming foundations and framing. One cabinetmaker who uses the 4/3 reports that his workers tire toward the end of the last day and that their output slackens.

The concern about productivity may, however, be overblown. While it may be true that workers sag a bit at the end of the fourth day, it is also true that they sag toward the end of the fifth day of a five-day week. With the 4/3 what happens is "Thank God it's Friday" turns into "Thank God it's Thursday." Likewise, the notion that a carpenter can be in shape to go five 8-hour days but not four 10s is dubious. You need to be in excellent shape for either. In fact, my crews have formed and framed on the 4/3 schedule. Their productivity has been highly competitive with other builders. Even if some productivity were lost, the loss would be outweighed by other cost considerations. Because the 4/3 is such a precious benefit to employees, it contributes enormously to keeping down turnover and all the costs entailed. Employees don't want to give it up so they don't leave. Thus, the cabinetmaker who thinks his use of the 4/3 may cut output, nevertheless also says emphatically, "We'll never go back."

If you are intrigued by the possibilities of the 4/3 but hesitant, try it out in steps. Assuming your crews give the go-ahead, switch to a 4/3 first for every fourth week, then for every other week. Make clear to your crews that if they want to hold onto it, their productivity must stay up. If it doesn't, go back to the 5/2. If you are reaping benefits go all the way to the 4/3. I doubt you will ever go back either.

Heavier-duty benefits

Like the low-cost benefits described in the sidebar, the traditional heavy-duty benefits—health plans and retirement plans—involve tax considerations. But here tax rulings tend to work in favor of both your employees and yourself. If you provide a dental care benefit worth $100, for example, it will cost you only $100—not $100 plus 30 percent or so in tax and insurance burden as would a $100 wage increase. At the same time, the employee receives the full $100 instead of seeing it reduced to $70 by income, social security, and other taxes.

Because of the tax situation, as tradespeople climb the wage scale, they tend to prefer increased benefits to increased wages. If that is the case with your employees, the first heavy-duty benefit you'll provide is likely to be a medical plan. Cost and quality of medical plans and the laws governing them vary so much state to state that recommending one or another here is not practicable. To learn about possibilities in your area, network with the usual suspects—other builders, suppliers, your insurance broker, even knowledgeable clients. Ask them what your main considerations should be when shopping for insurance. Ask for recommendations as to where to shop. Contact your state department of consumer affairs, contractor's license board, or other government agency and request pamphlets on selecting insurance.

One approach that may work (it works for me) is to sidestep creating a company plan. Instead, let each of your employees select their own policy, then write a monthly company check to the plan to pay all or part of the cost. You'll save paperwork. Your employees will enjoy complete "portability." If they need to leave, they will be able to take their plan with them.

When you reach the point that you are ready to offer retirement plans, you will encounter several options, though they may be different from what's available at this writing. Retirement plans come in a sort of alphabet soup in which the letters are remixed ever so often. As of this writing the combinations that make most sense for small businesses include those listed in the sidebar below. Builders tend to prefer one or the other, depending on their attitude toward their employees, the size and shape of their operations, and their sense of the cost benefits. Thus,

Retirement Plan Options

A key feature of the following plans is that contributions are pretax. Once inside the account, the contributions can be invested in stocks or bonds or other instruments until retirement, growing for decades, again without being taxed. Only when money is pulled from the account do taxes finally kick in.

■ *Qualified Retirement Plans (QRP).* These allow up to $35,000 annually to be put into retirement plans both for owner and employees. They are funded by employers only. No contribution by employees from their wages is allowed. They involve a fair amount of paperwork and carry some costs for setup and annual tax reporting. They can be setup so that employees have to stick around a while to gain full ownership of the money in their QRPs (i.e., vesting does not have to be immediate).

■ *Simple Independent Retirement Accounts (Simple IRA).* These allow employees to contribute up to $6,500 annually of their wages, with employers adding 1 to 3 percent of wages. You can have a Simple IRA along with your employees, but if you make a contribution into your own account, you must make a contribution for your employees' also. Vesting is immediate.

■ *Simplified Employee Pension/Independent Retirement Accounts (SEP/IRA).* These allow up to 15 percent of wages to be contributed. They are funded by employers only—no employee contribution. You can have an account along with your employees. If you contribute to your own account, you must contribute to accounts for employees who have been with you three out of the last five years or more. Vesting is immediate.

The SEP/IRA: My Choice of Retirement Plans

The SEP/IRA is flexible. In good years, when your company earns a profit, you can make contributions to employees' accounts and your own. In a tough year with little or no profit, contributions can be ratcheted down to a nominal amount.

So long as you have relatively few eligible employees, the SEP/IRA can be a real bargain. You may be able to offer SEP/IRA contributions without any immediate burden to your cash flow. You'll need to pencil out the numbers for your own company, but you are likely to find what I did. The immediate tax savings generated by making SEP/IRA contributions to both your own and your employees' accounts roughly equal the contributions for several highly paid leads! In other words, you can make hefty contributions, but because of the tax savings, you end up with about the same after-tax cash balance in your accounts that you would have had you simply taken your guys out for end of year pizza and beer instead of fattening their retirement accounts (and your own) by thousands of dollars. Most carpenters seem to prefer the thousands, though some find it a tough call (we have good pizza around here).

to set up an IRA account, which they can do by filling out a form with the financial service provider of their choice (mutual fund company, brokerage house, bank). At the end of each year, I write a check to their accounts and to my own, with the size of the checks dependent on company profitability for the year. As I have amplified in the sidebar at left, the plan is both highly flexible and cheap, a bargain really. Since contributions are based on profitability, the SEP/IRA does double duty as a retirement-plan benefit and a profit-sharing mechanism. As such, it is the best kind of bonus system.

Bonuses

In construction, bonuses break out into two basic types, one counterproductive and one constructive. They are: *individual performance bonuses,* paid out to individual crew members as a reward for beating a labor cost estimate on a particular project, and *company-wide bonuses,* given out to everyone in the company when their collective effort has earned it a profit—in a phrase "profit sharing."

Individual performance bonuses might seem sensible and beneficial. In fact, they are likely to be destructive of a company's cohesion, the quality of its work, and its reputation. I first became dubious about them when I heard a builder tout his individual bonus system during a seminar on construction personnel policies. He explained that he motivated his leads to push jobs by offering them a cut of the savings if they came in below his estimate for a project. I questioned him, "Doesn't the system tend to encourage corner cutting?" Oh no, he responded confidently, his company had so many quality controls in place the leads were channeled toward producing excellent work even as the chance for the bonus fueled their pro-

When builders attempt to put an individual performance bonus system into place, they not only run into quality-control problems, but into other management issues as well.

one builder likes the qualified retirement plan (QRP) because he feels it gives his employees an incentive to stick around. If they leave before they are vested, they will leave behind a chunk of their retirement account. He figures the additional hold on his employees the QRP gives him makes enduring its extra paper work and costs worthwhile. Another builder opts for the Simple-IRA. He employs a couple of dozen people. Under the Simple-IRA, with its relatively low requirement for employer contributions, he can afford to give something to all his employees, and they are free to make a substantial additional pretax contributions out of their wages.

For my own more compact operation, I have found the SEP/IRA best. It lives up to its name. It is very simple to use. All I need do is ask my employees

ductivity. Wanting to test the truth of his claim, I stopped by one of his job sites and then another and another to marvel at the drunken irregularity of the foundation forms, shear walls with undersides looking like a porcupine belly because so many nails had missed the framing members, and a swamp of tripping hazards and garbage strewn across the sites. His work was as bad as any I have ever seen.

When builders attempt to put an individual performance bonus system into place, they not only run into quality-control problems, but into other management issues as well, including:

RESENTMENT A crew feels they have worked hard and deserve a bonus while the books show costs are over the estimate. How do you know whether the cause is crew inefficiency, an estimating error on your part, or the production manager getting lumber to the job late so that the crew was repeatedly spinning its wheels?

UNFAIR DISTRIBUTION OF OPPORTUNITY Jobs fall into place in such a way that the biggest, juiciest ones with the best bonus opportunities happen to go to one crew for a lengthy period. What do you do to make up the lost opportunities to your other people?

NONFIELD STAFF FEELING EXCLUDED If you have grown your company to the point you employ an office manager, bookkeeper, and/or estimator, how do you include them in a bonus system set up for field personnel?

Such commonsense doubts about individual performance bonuses are reinforced by scholarly studies. A fabulous article in the *Harvard Business Review,* "Six Myths About Pay" (see Resources on p. 258) summarizes the results of extensive research into the relationship of pay and worker motivation. The article reports that over and over individual bonuses have been shown to "undermine performance, of both the individual and the organization...[to] undermine teamwork [and] encourage employees to focus on the short term."

A project manager for a well-regarded construction company noted yet another downside to individual bonuses. They can be demeaning. "They feel like a tip," he said. "The money is nice, but they are embarrassing; they are a handout." He did not want a tip. He wanted to feel like he was part of a team that worked together to achieve long-term profitability and shared in the fruits of the effort. While individual performance bonuses negate that team feeling, even turn people in a company against one another by inciting jealousy and blaming, company-wide profit sharing as bonuses can foster it.

SEP/IRA profit sharing, as described in the sidebar on the facing page, is a company-wide, cohesion-building bonus system that works well even for very small construction companies. It is an incentive for people to work together effectively and can contribute to superior company performance. The evidence indicates, says "Six Myths," that companies using collective rewards such as profit sharing tend to outperform those that do not. An SEP/IRA program will not do the job alone. But along with other benefits such as a legitimate and competitive paycheck, a safe work site where workers are treated with respect, the 4/3 week, and a health plan, an SEP/IRA (or one of the similar plans) can help fulfill workers' needs for fair treatment. It will foster the employee loyalty and commitment that is necessary to a construction company succeeding over the long term.

> While individual performance bonuses negate that team feeling, even turn people in a company against one another by inciting jealousy and blaming, company-wide profit sharing as bonuses can foster it.

The Birth of a Specialty Trade

When I was first learning framing in the late 1960s, we built almost exclusively with a half dozen kinds of nails—mostly 8d and 16d, box and galvanized (sinkers were not yet invented)—with three varieties of plywood, a dozen lumber sizes in two or three species, and a few items of hardware. We hardly used power tools other than the Skil 77 and drills. Almost all of our hand tools fit easily in two small pouches strung on a web belt.

Now framers draw on a shelf's worth of nails for a range of manual and power hammers. They use not only solid lumber but a slew of engineered wood and steel products. While we once installed the odd run of joist hangers or bolts, today's framers are versatile with whole catalogs of hardware. Their power tools include laser and digital devices. Their tool bags are nearly the size of briefcases and are so laden with equipment they must be supported by wide, stiff leather belts and hung from the shoulders with suspenders. No wonder framing has become a specialty trade many builders prefer to sub out rather than handle in-house.

COMING UP

When to Subcontract Work

A Crowd of Suppliers

Finding Subs and Suppliers

Evaluating Subs and Suppliers

Serving the Needs of Your Subs and Suppliers

What You Can Expect in Return

Ever Vigilant

Subcontractors and Suppliers

Every builder needs suppliers, and virtually every builder works with subcontractors. Even independent artisans, like Fred Blodgett—one of my former lead carpenters who now has his own company but whose main interest has become fine cabinetmaking and woodwork—rely heavily on subcontractors. The customers for Fred's woodwork need spaces to put it in—a study, kitchen, or den. His approach is to contract for the construction of those spaces, sub out rough carpentry and specialty work, such as plumbing and drywall, and produce casework and other finish work personally.

Builders who move from the independent-artisan level to employing leads or project managers typically subcontract a great deal of their work. In fact, if your are at that point and you analyze your charges on a job, you are likely to see that relatively little is for the labor of your carpenters and the rough and finished lumber and hardware they build with. The great bulk will be for subcontractors, for premanufactured goods like windows and cabinets and stair systems, and for the labor of coordinating the work of suppliers and subcontractors. Increasingly, builders are in the business of providing management for the installation of work built by other companies. The trend is likely to intensify.

Why subcontractors

As builders we work with an increasing array of subcontractors. Old trades subdivide into specialized new trades. Whole new trades spring up. A few decades ago, for example, foundation, frame, and finish were the province of general contractors. Now, we have specialty contractors in all three areas. Similarly, where we once just had plasterers, we now have stucco, veneer plaster, and drywall specialists. We used to automatically call the tile guy for a kitchen countertop. Now he competes with stone fabricators, cast concrete specialists, plastic laminate shops, and installers of a slew of other synthetic products. Meanwhile, the older trades have been joined by new specialties, including insulating contractors, waterproofing specialists, hydronic heating contractors, security specialists, information technology installers, and solar-power guys, with more sure to come.

This proliferation of trades has been driven by the explosion of construction technology over the last several decades. The old trades and the new trades each encompass a growing array of products and installation tools, all requiring knowledge of when and how to use them. For the builder, the rapid and

The operator of this beast placed 200 cu. yd. of drain rock behind our retaining walls in a morning. Though his hourly charge was stratospheric, he saved us so much labor and time that his services were a bargain. Similarly with many subcontractors, while there rates may seem high, they will lower your costs. (Photo by David Gerstel)

continuing change has posed a severe challenge. How can you keep on top of everything? The answer has been to sub-contract to reliable specialists to control several key factors:

ESTIMATING RISK Estimating direct costs for just the basic carpentry tasks is challenging enough. Doing it for a whole smorgasbord of other trades as well would be overwhelming. Therefore, you parcel the risk out to subcontractors.

COST A crew of tradesmen who are primarily carpenters, and who do a sub trade only occasionally, cannot compete in productivity with a specialist who does the work every day and is fully geared up for it. It may be painful to pay a plumber $75 an hour. But when you realize he does the work two to three times as fast as your lead who costs you $55 an hour in wages and burden, the plumber looks like a good deal.

QUALITY AND LIABILITY A good carpenter might leave behind what looks like good plumbing or wiring or roofing. But beneath the surface it will incorporate judgment calls and details that are second rate compared with the work of a well-trained specialist and will be more likely to fail.

None of this is to say that you can never handle any of the specialty trades between yourself and your crew if you have the skills. There are projects for which doing the work in-house makes sense. If there is a small amount of tile or drywall or other specialty trade work and it is straightforward, you'll be able to estimate its cost accurately and install it. You may even save money. You'll save the labor of managing a sub and the sub's setup costs. The savings may even outweigh your lower productivity on the work.

My experience suggests, however, that the balance very quickly shifts in

The Real Cost of a Cheap Sub

You know a plumber. He is a good craftsman but has lousy management skills. He gives you a bid that is low by 25 percent. It's too tempting. You take it. A month before he is supposed to rough in your job, both his employees get an opportunity to work for a better-run outfit, and they grab it.

Now working alone, he rapidly falls behind schedule, gets to your project three weeks late, and even then puts in only partial days as he scrambles to keep all of his clients satisfied. Meanwhile, as you wait for him to complete rough-in, you have to repeatedly reschedule your drywallers and you run out of work for your carpenters.

When the plumber finally finishes his work, the drywallers are busy filling other commitments. It will be two weeks before they can get to you. Then the cabinets arrive from the manufacturer. You have no place to store them except on site. The drywallers arrive to find the cabinets in their way. That's the last straw. They become enraged and refuse to work. By the time you have them mollified and get them back to the job, one of your carpenters, tired of surviving on unemployment checks and side jobs, has accepted an offer from a competitor.

At this point, you tally your costs in lost time, extra overhead incurred while the job sits still, crew morale and turnover, diminished client trust, damaged reputation, and frustration. You rue the day you went for the low bid. The losses add up to a lot more than the 2 percent savings in overall job costs that the plumber's bid equates to.

favor of subcontracting. My carpenters can handle a few sheets of drywall effectively. A small kitchen's worth, and I'm going to lose money if I don't subcontract. Of course, you don't always make the call strictly by the numbers—you may need to give the drywall to your crew to keep them employed. And sometimes you may want to take on the plumbing because it's *fun*. Personally, I get a kick out of lugging my plumbing tools out to the job, slipping on my overalls, and putting in a pedestal sink, even if I do have to refer to my friend Pete's incredibly good instructional manual (see Resources on p. 258) about four times an hour.

Suppliers

As subcontractors have proliferated, a parallel development has taken place in the world of suppliers. When I was an apprentice, my boss purchased almost all the materials we installed from a single professional lumberyard. Today, it's a lucky builder who has a professional yard nearby that can satisfy all of his needs. Effective construction company management now requires that you be aware of a whole range of suppliers and know when and how to use each of them.

PROFESSIONAL YARD   If you have a really good professional yard in your area, using it will be cost-effective. For a few percent extra cost, you will get far superior and more knowledgeable service that will more than pay for itself.

SPECIALTY YARDS   Construction materials and tools now have proliferated to the point that even the so-called "big box" home improvement stores, with their inventory of 100,000 items, carry only a fraction of what is available. For other items you need accounts at specialty outlets and fabricators, including those handling hardware, windows, waterproofing and drainage products, masonry, and steel.

NEIGHBORHOOD HARDWARE STORES
For each of your projects locate the nearest hardware store. Use it for odds and ends that your crew needs *right now*. The savings in time will outweigh the higher cost of purchases.

BIG BOX STORES   Quality of service varies enormously from store to store and within each store. Search out the competent sales reps at your nearby location and build a relationship with them. Alternately, take up meditation. In the absence of good connections, you will need the patience of the Dalai Lama to do business at some of these places.

WEB-BASED SUPPLIERS Some builders swear by certain Internet tool vendors, citing great service and rock-bottom prices. Personally, I would rather pay 5 percent more to a good local shop that provides knowledgeable guidance in tool selection, reliable warranty backup, and repair service.

EQUIPMENT RENTAL YARDS Better a renter than an owner be—usually. For any piece of equipment costing more that a few hundred dollars that you would only use occasionally, renting typically costs less than purchasing, insuring, storing, repairing, and eventually, replacing your own tool.

FABRICATORS OF STRUCTURAL COMPONENTS Just as cabinets and stairs are now likely to come from manufacturers rather than be fabricated on site or by small shops, structural systems are more cost-effectively produced at plants than at our projects. Increasingly, to be cost-competitive, builders will need to know how to work with manufacturers of trusses and of panelized wall, floor, and roof systems.

A final group of suppliers bears special watching. Those are the suppliers of "green" building products, including salvaged items, those made from recycled materials, and those harvested and manufactured in such a way as to reduce damage to our planet. Builders are learning to use such materials—fly ash concrete, drain rock from crushed concrete, tiles from waste glass, roofing from industrial waste, flooring from bamboo, low VOC paints and caulks, and many others—not only because it is the environmentally considerate thing to do, but because it saves money and gives builders a competitive edge. By using green products, you can create habitable space that does not poison its occupants, as much of the current construction does. And by emphasizing your environmentally considerate practices in your marketing program, you can increase client loyalty (for catalogs of green materials, see Resources on p. 258).

Finding subcontractors and suppliers

In his superb book, *Estimating for the General Contractor,* Paul Cook (see Resources), urges us to remember that having a bid accepted "is not to win the race, but only to qualify for the real contest that lies ahead—the construction." You do not have much chance of winning that contest, he continues, if you are bringing in subcontractors of the "weak, low-bidding variety."

To win out, you must acquire a reliable team of subs and suppliers, not just a first string, but backups as well in every trade. From time to time, in the effort to field a strong team, you'll get lucky. You'll pick up a terrific "walk-on." A good sub or supplier will ask to work with you. The plumber I have called on for almost every job for years buttonholed me at a contractor's meeting. But for the most part, to hook up with good subcontractors you have to look for them. Sources include:

BUILDERS AND SUBS YOU RESPECT Good builders tend to find their way to the same subs and suppliers. Good subs and suppliers get to know one another at the projects of good builders.

THE STREET As you drive around town, look out for job sites that have the telltale signs of the well-run project—safe, organized, swept up, recycling bins instead of a trash heap, work moving

Evaluating Subcontractors and Suppliers

Both subs and suppliers
- Quality of product
- Reliability of scheduling
- Respectful and considerate
- Flexibility in dealing with problems
- Client relations
- Speed, accuracy, and level of detail in billing
- Responsiveness on defects, corrections, and failures
- Cost

Additional subcontractor issues
- Change orders: responsiveness, accuracy, fairness

For larger companies
- Capabilities of individual representatives and/or lead people in the company

general opinions, but also go into detail about key issues including:

QUALITY With subs, quality of materials used and workmanship is paramount. With suppliers, focus on quality of materials and products sold and on service. Does the supplier offer helpful information on material selections, take your orders accurately, and then deliver exactly what you have ordered? Suppliers who regularly make errors loading their trucks will waste a lot of your time.

SCHEDULE With suppliers, find out whether they can be counted on to get materials to a job site when promised. With subs, learn whether they arrive to begin work as scheduled, reach substantial completion in timely fashion, and take care of punch list items promptly.

RESPECT With suppliers, you are looking for consideration for the value of your time. They shouldn't put you on hold to give attention to a larger-volume customer. With subs, you want assurance they will abide by your job site policies. You don't play loud music, they shouldn't either. You recycle; they should, too.

FAILURES Do suppliers promptly and without argument replace defective material? Do subs take care of callbacks and warranty work *immediately?*

CLIENT RELATIONS If a client visits a supplier to see samples, will he be served promptly and with patience? Do subs refrain *absolutely* from discussing quality and scope of work, schedule, and change orders with customers but instead refer all questions to the builder?

In general, smaller subs and suppliers with low employee turnover provide the best service and value. But from time to

ahead steadily. When you see one, mine it for the names and numbers of good subcontractors and suppliers.

CREW MEMBERS, ESPECIALLY NEW HIRES When you hire good carpenters, find out if they know of any good subs and suppliers you have not yet run across.

BUILDING INSPECTORS If you get a tough inspector, meaning one who actually checks your work thoroughly, you have scored! This is a guy who cares that work be done right. Ask him for names of subcontractors who consistently pass inspections with flying colors.

Qualifying subcontractors and suppliers

Before contracting with new subs or suppliers, evaluate them as thoroughly as you would prospective clients or employees. Talk with other builders who have worked with them. Get

time it's necessary to consider a larger outfit. When that's the case, find out who the top employees are. A large subcontractor may have a dozen leads of whom one or two do particularly good work. At a large supplier, one rep may be particularly knowledgeable and helpful. Find out who the top guys are and ask for them. From a certain heating and sheet metal contractor, I get consistently outstanding service. I have found and ask for their best lead. Other builders who take whomever they get complain about uneven performance.

Building relationships

Good subcontractors, and to some extent suppliers, don't really need builders except when we don't need them— during slow times. When business is booming, they have plenty of customers. If you want top subs and suppliers to work with you through good times and bad, don't only ask them to meet your needs. Work to meet theirs as well. When first working with a sub or supplier, allow for a wearing-in period, appreciating that it will take time to dial into one another's style, practices, and preferences. Always, with subcontractors, abide by these four cardinal rules:

NEVER BID PEDDLE   Do not ask a subcontractor for a bid and then use his or her bid to lever a lower bid out of a competitor. "If I ever find that someone peddled one of my bids," a sought-after sheet metal subcontractor told me, "that will be the last bid he will ever get." If you bid peddle, subs will find out because they talk to one another, and one of their favorite topics is general contractors who've screwed them over.

SCHEDULE CAREFULLY   Notify each sub well in advance of when you will need him on a project, then notify him

Scheduling Subs Properly

An electrical subcontractor described the experience of being called out to a project before it was ready for his crew to do their work. "I've wasted a good part of my day, and I'm out hours of wages getting my crew out to the job. Then I have to move to a second job. But because we can't get it done (in what is left of the day), we have to return a second day, incurring more mobilization and travel time, all due to the contractor on the first job telling us he was ready when he wasn't."

The electrician's experience is too typical. Subs complain that they frequently are called to projects prematurely. To compensate for builders' poor scheduling, some subcontractors have taken to checking a site before they schedule themselves and/or their crews to work at it. But such checking is a burden, too. To spare your subs the burden and earn their loyalty, bear down on the scheduling and get it right. Call subs to the job only when you are ready for them.

repeatedly as his start day nears. Make certain to be ready for subs when they arrive. Spare yourself the ill will you will generate by putting a sub in the kind of predicament described above.

ACCEPT FAIR AND REASONABLE CHANGE ORDERS   Don't grind a sub for free extras. One sub explained why he no longer accepted invitations to bid the work of a certain builder: "The guy was always whining. He was always asking for extras and concessions. He killed my profit on every job."

PAY PROMPTLY   One contractor has built sub loyalty by paying within five days at the most and often within a single day of receiving a bill.

Don't underestimate the importance of the intangibles in your relationships with subs. Like you and your crew, they need appreciation, respect, and predictability. You can't be going off on them if something goes wrong. "Stay calm about mistakes," cabinetmaker Steve Nicholls suggests. Trust that they "will be worked out." At the same time, let your subs know you value them. "We all need encouragement for what we do," Steve points out. "I love working with people who like us. I love it. I will bend over backward to take care of those people who appreciate what we do."

If a subcontractor has a good track record with you but you are encountering a few rough patches, work with him or her. A painter once told me about an experience he had with a highly regarded builder in our area. The painter was having family and personal problems, and they were translating into loss of focus on the job. The builder sat down with the painter, asked him what the trouble was, and then told him kindly but firmly that he needed to pull off the job, that his work was so far below his usual high level that it was destroying the clients' trust in the builder's company. Some time later, when the painter had righted his ship, the builder welcomed him back for new projects.

A remodeling contractor found that many of her valued smaller subs were lagging in their installation of office technology. As a result, she was having problems communicating with them efficiently. Rather than berating the subs, she bought them fax machines and cell phones, and even taught them how to use the devices.

Another builder takes time to coach subs who struggle with management. He teaches them how to handle such procedures as change order production and billing. Some builders have even bought copies of this book for their subs—though that's probably going a bit far!

On the other hand, while it can be worth stretching yourself to support subs or suppliers, you need to know when to end a relationship. Watch out for subcontractors expanding rapidly or experiencing heavy employee turnover. Their performance on your projects is likely to nose-dive. If it does, ride close herd on them for any current projects and give them no more until they have their house back in order.

You owe it to your clients, crew, and yourself to hold subcontractors to as high a standard as you hold yourself. Do it and you will earn their respect and loyalty. That's the highest accolade you can earn as a builder. Subs *know*. Far better than the architects or the historical society and magazine award committees, subs know who the good builders are. When good subs want to work with you and speak well of you to other subcontractors, when they say you are one of the builders they would trust to build their own houses, you've got confirmation that you are at the top of your game.

> Some builders have even bought copies of this book for their subs—though that's probably going a bit far!

CHAPTER 8

Project Management

Safety First

SAFETY FIRST! The old adage applies in spades to building. Neglect safety and you put at risk the rewards, both emotional and financial, that can come from running a construction company. I know from personal experience. Early in my career, an apprentice carpenter hurt his back so badly on one of my projects he had to abandon construction work, which he loved. Fifteen years later I still flinch when I drive by the site where he was injured, for had I known then what I know now about job site safety management, there's a good chance he would never have been hurt. We would have saved the career of a good man. We would, also, have avoided the ratcheting up of our workers' comp insurance rates, which cost us tens of thousands of dollars in premiums over the ensuing years.

Battling the odds

Achieving safety is a challenge. Construction is exceedingly dangerous work, killing hundreds of people and severely injuring thousands every year. Even so,

workers are often indifferent to safety. They get careless with themselves—young workers because they are naive, veterans out of arrogance. Never having been hurt, young workers do not understand how horrible it is to be in constant pain and unable to do your job. A young electrician rips his shoulder apart braking a fall off a 40-ft. ladder. From his fellow apprentices

High-quality safety equipment pays for itself over and over. Industrial-grade ladders, such as those shown here, protect my crew from injury. At the same time, they provide the stable platform needed for efficient work.

COMING UP

Safety First

Battling the Odds

Safety Training

Safety Management

Getting Tough

The Safety Management Pyramid

Job site inspection

Safety awareness training

General company management

Worker carelessness and neglect of good safety practices, not equipment break-downs or other factors, are responsible for four out of five job site accidents.

he hears how lucky he is to be kicking back and living off workers' comp payments. He tells them he would give anything to have his shoulder back and be working again. But they don't get it.

Older and experienced workers get cocky. After avoiding injury for a long time, they think they know how to manage job site risk, and they cut their margin of safety too thin. Ten years ago, a top lead carpenter I know, a man with exceptional knowledge of safety procedures gained from mountaineering, elected to walk damp and slippery deck joists rather than set a plank. He fell between the joists onto exposed rebar stubs. He was lucky; he came out of the accident with only a badly bruised butt. Had he landed a few inches over, he would have rammed the rebar into the base of his spine. The most highly skilled plumber I have ever worked with was not so lucky. Believing that he could secure himself with one powerful hand while he set a roof jack with the other atop a steep roof, he skipped the precaution of setting a safety harness or toe board. He lost his grip, slipped, slid and fell 35 ft. to the ground, surviving, but with severe injuries.

If workers are negligent about safety, builders too often dismiss safety management as hopeless. "You can't make a job site safe," says one. The last time I looked, his job site featured exposed rebar stubs, nail-embedded lumber strewn about, uncovered trenches, and flimsy staging swaying 10 to 15 ft. above the ground. Maybe he cannot make a job site perfectly safe, but he could make his site much safer than it is.

You have to battle for safety. You have to overcome the resistance in yourself and in your workers. The emotional and financial risks are too great to ignore. And if those don't motivate you, this one should: You can go to jail for neglecting

safety. Managers whose workers have died as a result of job site hazards have been charged with negligent manslaughter. And they have been convicted. A strong safety program can make a huge difference. You won't eliminate every hazard, but you have a good chance of reducing accidents and injuries. In the years following that tragic back injury to my apprentice, I got serious about safety. Though there have been some close calls, and though we have needed some luck to go along with our effort, no one has suffered a serious injury on one of my job sites since.

Safety training

The bedrock of job site safety is the kind of strong management values and systems we have discussed in previous chapters and which we will discuss in the upcoming section on running jobs. Good company and project management supports strong crew morale, which, in turn, fosters alertness and attentiveness to safety concerns. Bad management fosters frustration and discouragement, which leads to sloppiness.

Atop strong general management, to achieve safety you need persistent, regular safety training, especially programs that promote awareness of safety. According to studies by the United States Department of Labor, worker carelessness and neglect of good safety practices, not equipment breakdowns or other factors, are responsible for four out of five job site accidents.

To keep workers alert to safety, hold brief weekly "tailgate meetings." To achieve maximum effect at a tailgate meeting, focus on a safety issue that relates to work actually going on at the site. Start off with a hook that gets everyone's attention. Is your crew forming foundation walls? Tell them the story about the 26-year-old lead carpenter who fell through an opening in the subfloor onto uncapped reinforcing steel and died of internal bleeding an hour later. Are you about to nail off wall sheathing? Tell about the guy who accidentally tapped a coworker in the head with a nail gun while he was depressing the trigger, and fired an eight penny into his buddy's skull. Stories like those will kindle discussion. That is what you are after. You don't want to lecture. You want people pumping up their awareness by relating their experiences and ideas, then getting right back to work with their safety consciousness heightened.

Tailgate meetings are a variation on the "spontaneous" approach to training discussed in "Crew" on p. 214. They are instantly relevant, short, and cost-effective. I have used them as the core of my own safety program.

Other contractors lean more toward "scheduled training" for safety, making use of classes and seminars. One reports that he has sharply reduced injuries, especially back strain, by having a physical therapist who specializes in sports medicine conduct classes for his employees on how to use their bodies. Some builders invite professional safety inspectors—available without charge through workers' compensation insurance providers—to look over their sites. The inspectors may spot bad practices that you are so used to you have grown blind to them. (And no, they will not report you for an infraction, thereby jacking up your insurance rates.)

A project management routine

Along with safety training to support good practices you need a routine for making sure that good practices are in force and that job sites are free of hazards. Job sites should be checked regularly, and if hazards are noted they should be eliminated right away. If you are starting out as a builder, you will be responsible for the checks and corrections. When (and if) you reach the point of delegating job site leadership, you may hand off primary safety responsibility to your lead carpenters and/or production manager. Even then, however, you must maintain controls to make sure your safety program does not get shelved as the project leads focus on bringing jobs in on time, within budget, and up to quality standards

SAMPLE LETTERS AND FORMS
Job Site Injury Prevention Checklist

FALLING
- Holes covered
- Only heavy-duty ladders in use
- No standing on top rungs of ladders
- Toe boards and harnesses set up on roofs
- OSHA-quality scaffolding with stable towers, safety rails, and wide platforms

TRIPPING
- Debris swept up daily at a minimum
- Protruding pipes and lumber eliminated

TRAUMA
- Rebar capped
- Excavations supported
- Work boots being worn; no sneakers
- Hard hats in use
- Safety glasses in use

CUMULATIVE
- Kneepads worn
- Ear protection used
- Respirators used

EQUIPMENT
- No dull blades
- Worn out tools recycled
- Ground fault interrupters on power cords
- Cords in good repair
- Apprentices trained to handle tools they are using

FIRST AID AND EMERGENCIES
- First-aid kit stocked
- At least one crew member CPR certified
- Phone number of nearest ambulance service posted
- Address of nearest trauma center posted

TOXICS
- Eliminated from job sites as much as possible
- Crew educated to dangers of and handling of any toxic materials present (lead, asbestos, mold, epoxies, paints, waterproofing, cement, pressure treated lumber, others)

(see pp. 215–220 for more on effective delegation and controls).

One efficient control is a checklist, such as the one illustrated on p. 237. If you have delegated safety responsibility, have your leads or production managers inspect their sites regularly, fill out the checklist, and turn it in to you with other end-of-the-week paperwork, such as time cards. If you are acting as your own production manager, use the checklist yourself. Even on a large project, covering the whole list requires only a couple of minutes, because with a good safety program in place there will be very few hazards to note and correct. The checklist is very much like the one I use when acting as production manager. I refer to it as I make a systematic inspection of the site, moving from one end to the other, from roof ridge to foundation, or from inside to outside—whatever pattern suits the job best. I write down any safety hazard that I spot, then report it to the job lead with the request that he have one of his crew correct it immediately.

Over the years, using safety meetings and systematic site inspections, I have had fairly good luck eliminating job site hazards and making sure protections were in place. The biggest problem has been in getting my employees to use personal-safety equipment, and judging from what I see at the job sites of other successful companies, it looks like my experience is quite typical. My crew resists putting on hard hats even when working directly beneath someone else. They fight wearing kneepads, respirators, or ear protection, complaining that they are uncomfortable. They regularly stand on the top rungs of ladders rather than taking a minute to go for a taller ladder. To gain their compliance, I rely on encouragement. But that has not been enough. I have come to realize that to achieve success at safety it's sometimes necessary to go further.

Worker violation of good safety practice must be treated as seriously as any other violation of company policy. Workers who resist it should be reminded, in a respectful way, that they are not only endangering themselves but their fellow workers and the company as a whole. If they do not respond, they should be subject to rapid progressive discipline, all the way to termination, if necessary. That may seem harsh. But as the decades go by, I see that virtually every one of my builder friends has been seriously injured. Some have escaped traumatic injury. They have all their fingers. They don't limp as a result of falling from a ladder. But they invariably have cumulative injuries—bad backs, ruined knees, damaged hearing, respiratory problems—that take a lot of the fun out of their lives. Once you see the consequences of easing back on safety discipline, you realize that it's not only costly, but it's plain unfair to the people you work with.

Job Setup

Good general management—knowing your numbers, nailing your estimates, writing thorough contracts—is the foundation of successful projects. Well-organized job setup—what larger-volume builders speak of as the "hand-off from sales to production"—ties that foundation to the actual building of the project. If setup is done well, the project has a much better chance of going steadily upward toward completion. Job setup is a three-part process: the readying of paper, people, and project site.

Documents ready

If you have followed the recommendations in "Gathering Information" in chapter 5, almost all document prepara-

COMING UP

The Importance of Job Setup

Creating Project Binders

Orienting the Lead

Preparing the Client

Setting Up the Site

A Job Site Hardware Storage System

tion will have been accomplished during the estimating and bidding stages of a project. The documents needed are stored in a tabbed, three-ring binder or on a laptop computer. All that remains now is to make copies for the project lead and for the clients and to organize the copies in their own tabbed binders.

Just what you include in the lead's binder will depend on who will be using it. If your project lead is at the basic level, include only the most basic documents. If the lead is at the advanced or production-manager level, set up a more complete binder. Divisions of a project binder for basic-level lead include:

- *Phone numbers.* For designer, sub-contractors, suppliers, clients, and building department.
- *Plans.* Give the lead the estimating set with structural hardware, un-usual details, and areas of potential change orders highlighted. Alternatively, have him make a high-lighted copy of his own as a way of getting acquainted with the project plans.
- *Specifications.* Again, hand over to the lead your highlighted set or have him make a copy.
- *Assumptions.* The lead needs to have a copy of the assumptions you have made during estimating and included in the contract. Those assumptions, together with the plans and specs, dictate what he will build.
- *Questions.* For larger projects, the questions division should be sub-divided so that there is a separate section for the designer, owner, subcontractors, suppliers, and yourself. For smaller jobs, a page for each person will be adequate.
- *Material needs.* A page for each supplier should be fine.

Moving to Production

V. Build (at last)!

IV. Ready the site
Install exterior protection.
Install interior protection.
Set up hardware storage.

III. Prepare clients
Give binder.
Go over to-do list.
Review schedule.
Prepare for 90% blues.
Describe initial work.
Introduce subcontractors to clients.

II. Orient lead
Give binder with plans and specs.
Walk through job site.
Discuss plans and specifications.
Review flow chart and notifications calendar.
Introduce lead to owner.

I. Create project binders for lead and clients

Divisions of Lead's Project Binder

Basic
- Phone numbers
- Plans
- Specs
- Assumptions
- Questions
- Material needs lists
- Signed change orders
- Safety inspection checklist

Advanced
- Flowchart
- Notifications calendar
- Blank change order forms
- Time cards

▪ *Change orders.* The lead will need a copy of each change order as soon as it is signed so that he knows what to build.

Additional binder divisions for advanced lead or production manager include:

▪ *Flowchart and notification calendar* (to be discussed in the next section)
▪ *Time cards*
▪ *Safety-inspection checklist.* If the lead is responsible for safety, he should be filling out the checklist at least weekly and submitting it to you.
▪ *Blank change order forms*
▪ *Estimating checklist.* A checklist will help the lead identify costs when figuring change order charges.

There is nothing sacred about the sequence in which you organize documents in your binder. What's important is that the organization be logical and consistent job to job so that leads become familiar with it and are able to find their way to needed paperwork quickly. Once you have created a well-organized binder with tabbed sections for a lead, he can use it on project after project. For each new one, you merely provide the lead with phone numbers, plans, specs, and assumptions and with blank time cards, change order forms, and safety checklists. Getting all that together takes a quarter of an hour if you have a computer and a copier in your office. Having it all available to the lead in an organized binder saves many hours of labor during a project.

Project lead ready

Just as you will find it helpful to organize job binders according to a consistent format, you will benefit from establishing a consistent procedure for handing off projects to leads. There is a lot of talk in

our industry about the importance of establishing SOPs (standard operating procedures). They are valuable. Once an SOP is in place it is hard to break out of, just as it is hard to break any habit. You know and feel uncomfortable if you have left out a step in a procedure.

One possible SOP for handing off projects includes:

▪ *Lead review of project binder.* Give the lead time—during his regular work hours and for his regular pay, of course—to get acquainted with his project documents.
▪ *Walk-through.* Go through the project with the lead, preferably at the site, pointing out the areas of special concern highlighted on the plans and specs.
▪ *Lead study of documents.* Give the lead time to closely study the plans, specs, and job site conditions and develop questions.
▪ *Discuss questions.* Talk over the lead's questions and ideas and also those you have come up with during estimating and stored in the Building Notes section of your own binder (see p. 152).
▪ *Review flowchart and notification calendar* (to be discussed in the next section)

Orienting your lead to a new project is a really important step. It is your chance to pass on the deep knowledge of the project you have acquired during planning and estimating. It is your chance, likewise, to prepare the lead for the clients—whose preferences, aptitudes, and quirks you have also come to know. Are the clients easily frustrated and prone to tantrums? Are the clients so intent on being "nice" that they hate to bother you with questions and, therefore, need to be encouraged to express their concerns? Or are they comfortable with the give and take of the construction process? Give your lead the lowdown on the clients and then introduce the lead to them.

Clients ready

If you have done your job well during preconstruction, by the time you are setting up a project, the clients know what to expect and have been told in writing what their responsibilities will be during its construction. At setup time, you want to help them get organized to attend to those responsibilities. You will find it beneficial—especially with clients who have a tendency to get a bit scattered—to give them their own tabbed binder with sections for:

- *Your phone and Fax numbers*, including an emergency number.
- *Questions.* Encourage the clients to write down questions for you, your lead, and the designer as soon as they think of them.
- *Responsibilities.* Although client responsibilities are included in the contract, it's helpful for clients to have a separate copy set up in checklist form, which can be periodically updated and referred to during the job.
- *Addresses, phone numbers, and Web sites of suppliers and/or showrooms* they will need to visit to make the decisions included in their responsibility list.
- *Plans.* If too large to hole-punch, they can be folded in the back of the binder or rolled alongside it.
- *Specifications*
- *Contract*
- *Change orders*

For my projects, I set up a brief preproject meeting with the client to introduce them to the lead, provide them with their binder, and go over their

Santa's Flood

When disaster strikes at one of your projects after midnight, it won't be at the project of clients' who deserve to be bounced around a bit. No. The accident will happen to some of your most considerate and valued clients. And it will happen at the worst possible moment.

Barbara and Steve, two of our favorite clients, were right below the top floor space we were remodeling for them, and their little boy was in the room next to theirs. The whole family was sleeping blissfully, dreaming of Santa slipping into the living room with a soundless sprinkling of snow from his boots (not, most definitely not, being preceded by a thud, slurp, and gush), for it was not just any night of the year. It was Christmas Eve.

At about 2 o'clock in the morning, the ceiling above Steve and Barbara's bed gave out in a deluge of soggy plaster and water that had leaked from the new supply lines installed by the charming, cut-rate, and incompetent plumber I had hired for the job in a misplaced burst of frugality. Steve and Barbara spent the early hours of Christmas morning hunting down their water shut-off, then mopping up, scraping plaster off their rugs and bed clothing, calming their child, and trying to find a plumber to restore their water service.

Had I known of the events, I would have rushed over to help them out, but they could not reach me. I had not yet learned the importance of leaving clients an emergency number.

responsibilities list, calling their attention to any responsibilities with near due dates. Some builders take this meeting further than I. They ask the main subcontractors to attend and use the meeting to make sure that everyone has all of his or her concerns addressed. I have never found such meetings necessary, perhaps because my subcontractors typically meet the clients during the planning and estimating phase of the project. But at the job setup meeting with the clients, I do reemphasize one important agreement pertaining to subcontractors: *To avoid confusion, all communication with subcontractors must go through either my project lead or me.*

I like to close out my client meetings with a touch of dark humor. "You know," I'll say when I think the timing is just

Psychiatric Evaluation of a Construction Project

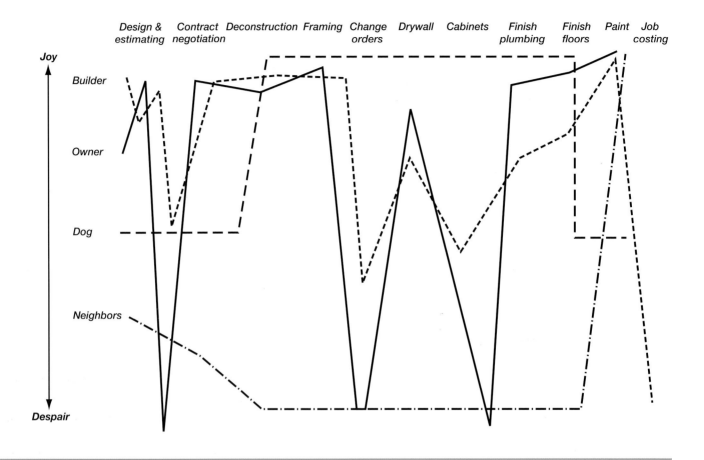

right, "being an owner on a project is really hard. What we are heading into here could very well be the worst experience of your life." Typically, the clients laugh and vent a little anxiety; they have heard what it is like to go through construction. Then I can talk to them seriously about the "90 percent blues." Through deconstruction and other rough work, owners often feel like work is going fast. Afterward, they feel like it is going really, really slowly. The first 90 percent of the work feels like it takes 10 percent of the time and the last 10 percent feels like it takes 90 percent of the time.

I forewarn owners of the letdown. I want them to be aware that the emotional cycle they will go through is typical and to be prepared for it. Several

clients have thanked me for the 90 percent warning when they hit the wall. Others seem to have been encouraged by my telling them builders get the 90 percent blues too, that as we near the end of a project, we become as eager as they are to see it wrapped up, that we have no desire to let it drag out.

At the conclusion of the meeting, I make an agreement as to where to drop off change orders and other documents or samples of finish items. Typically, for remodels during which the clients will continue to occupy the building, the delivery spot will be a shelf or cabinet drawer. For other projects, it is generally their mailbox. Because I like to head into the project on a positive note, I complete the meeting with a preview of the dramatic events that will happen at the outset of the project, beginning with site setup.

Site ready

Setting up a job site is a five-step process:

CREATE A COMMUNICATION AND CONTROLS CENTER   Even for a small project, it is important to set up a clean and quiet corner where the lead can keep the project binder, references such as the building code, a Fax, and a phone. For a bathroom remodel, that might be only a small table in an adjacent hallway. For a major reconstruction of an entire building, the center might be in a corner behind temporary plywood partitions. For larger, new projects, renting a trailer can be worthwhile.

INSTALL EXTERIOR PROTECTION

Shrubs, buildings, pedestrians, vehicles, etc., need to be covered or shielded.

INSTALL INTERIOR PROTECTION

Traditionally, builders have used plastic sheeting, corrugated cardboard, rosin paper, and cheap door skins taped in place to seal off rooms and protect existing finishes. Recently, high-tech systems that use lightweight fabrics and quick erection poles have come onto the market.

SET UP A STAGING AREA   Every project needs a secure area for materials and tool storage. For remodels, existing spaces can usually be cleared. For new work, steel storage containers can be rented at reasonable cost (and can do double duty as communications and controls centers).

INSTALL HARDWARE STORAGE SYSTEM   I have long utilized what I call my "buckets and bins system" for on-site storage of hardware. (A photo of the buckets and bins appears on p. 29.) I have one set of bins and buckets—about a dozen of each—and quick-assembly shelving for each crew. The bins hold containers of larger items such as shims, tubes of caulk, glue, tape of various kinds, and an assortment of rough and finish hardware. The buckets, which are divided with wooden partitions or contain sectioned and stacked trays, are for small items—nails, washers, screws. While the sets required a significant investment of time and money to put together, they pay for themselves over and over.

The system can be speedily broken down at a project, loaded onto a truck, and then installed at the next project. When one of the many items stored in the buckets or bins is running low, the lead notes it in the material needs section of his binder for ordering with the next delivery from the supplier. The buckets and bins help reduce supply runs to a minimum. When a crew member needs an item, it is usually right at hand in a bin or bucket. My crews average less than an hour a week making supply runs, even on large and complex projects. Builders without such a system often go to the supply yard daily.

On top of increasing efficiency, the system boosts morale. It is a drag for carpenters to have to stop what they are doing for lack of half a dozen nails and four shims and trek over to the hardware store or lumberyard to buy them. It is great to be able to find the items in an organized bucket-and-bin system and keep working.

With buckets and bins in place, a job is ready to go. You've got organized paperwork, a lead who understands the project, clients equipped with a binder and checklist to support them in handling their end of things, and a site that

The buckets and bins help reduce supply runs to a minimum. When a crew member needs an item, it is usually right at hand in a bin or bucket. My crews average less than an hour a week making supply runs, even on large and complex projects.

is prepped for action. Now, you are ready to go to work producing on-time, on-budget, quality construction.

COMING UP

Project Management Tools

Flowchart

Notifications Calendar

Shirt Pocket Binders

Detail Sequence Lists

A Project Management Routine

Working with Inspectors

The Construction Triangle

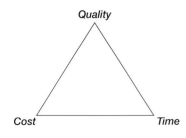

Running Projects

Some years back, my company built an addition to the home of a man who, at the time, was managing the reconstruction of the Kuwait infrastructure destroyed during the U.S.–Iraq war. When my client was in town, he'd come around to the rear of his house where we were working and regale us with tales of his encounters with the Kuwaiti aristocracy. (Sorry your Highness, we just can't install solid gold faucets in your private bathroom at the new airport. They might deform or melt when you turn on the hot water. We just don't do solid-gold fixtures, sir. It would not be professional. I hope you understand our position.) Then he would sit back, light up a cigar, watch the crew work, and encourage the carpenters, "You're ringing that triangle, boys. Keep it up. Keep on ringing it."

He meant that we were meeting his expectations with respect to quality, cost, and schedule, and he hoped we would continue. We did. Quality was achieved because of the dedication and skills of the crew and subs. Costs came within a couple of percent of the estimate because the estimate was thorough. The project was completed right on schedule because we had good management tools to make sure that no bottlenecks developed and that the project did not stand still while we waited for materials or subcontractors. They are the tools I use on every project to make sure it stays on schedule. The tools are dead simple, cheap, and easy to use. They are of two types: *broad scope*, including a

flowchart and a notifications calendar, for managing the overall flow of the project and *narrow scope*, for making sure all the details are nailed down.

The flowchart

The flowchart gives a picture of when each phase of work is scheduled to occur and who will be doing it. You may see project flowcharts called by other names— "project time line charts," "critical path management (CPM) charts," "Gantt charts," and various software names like "Project." I call them flowcharts for simplicity and because they show how a project flows if it is run right.

You can buy software for producing such charts, but from what I have seen, it is questionable whether the productivity benefits outweigh the cost, at least for small-volume companies handling projects of less than a year's duration. The flowchart illustrated on the facing page was created on a simple word-processed form. You can make the form on your computer, edit it to suit individual projects, and fill it out with a pencil. Once you are good at it, you will be able to create such a flowchart in half an hour, even for quite sizable projects, and typically be able to adjust it for change orders in a few 10-minute passes during a project. Here are the elements of a flowchart:

TIME LINE   The time line runs across the top of the chart, with weeks numbered in sequence from "1," the start of the first week, to "16," the beginning of the sixteenth week. (For longer jobs, add a sheet.)

DATES   Dates are filled in above the time line once the starting date of the project is pinned down. Thus, "3/10" is written in above "1" when it's certain the job will start March 10.

PHASES OF PROJECT The phases of work are listed down the left side. They are listed in the order in which they typically take place—setup before deconstruction, concrete before frame, mechanical before plumbing, and so on.

WORK FORCE FOR EACH PHASE On a line next to a phase the people responsible for doing it are named. Here, site earthwork, foundation excavation, concrete, framing and finish carpentry will be done by the crew. Other work such as plumbing by Lunt/Marymor and roofing by D. Haight is subcontracted.

SIZE OF CREW The size of the crew is given in parentheses. A three-person crew—lead, journeyman, apprentice—is shown as (3) for framing. At finish carpentry, we're down to a two-person crew, shown as (2).

LENGTH OF TIME FOR EACH PHASE
The length of time allotted for each phase of work is shown by a line drawn opposite the phase. Framing is shown as taking two and a half weeks, from 4/6 to 4/28. Drywall is shown as taking a week and a half from 5/15 to about 5/25. The length of time for crew work comes from the estimate. If an estimate shows 88 hours of framing for a lead, carpenter, and apprentice, the line for framing on the flowchart would span two weeks plus a day for a crew of three. The length of

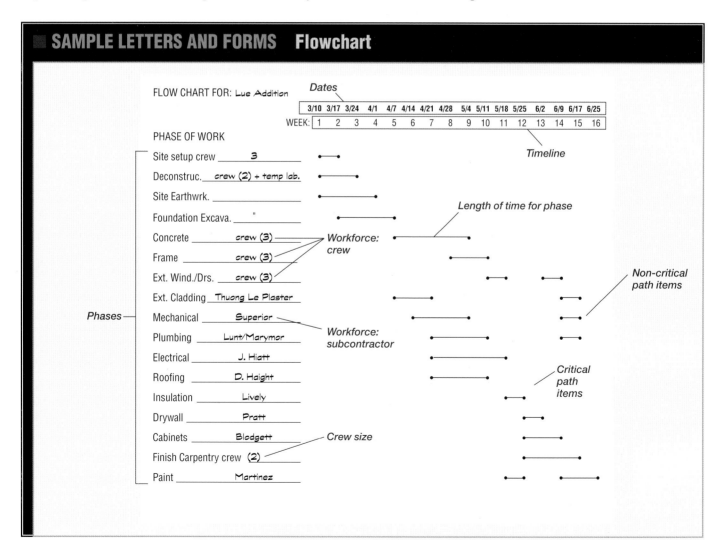

SAMPLE LETTERS AND FORMS Flowchart

time for subcontracted work comes from the subs' bids. If the plumber says he needs a week and a half for rough-in and a few days for finish, a line representing a week and a half and another representing three days are drawn on the chart.

CRITICAL PATH   Certain phases of work (on this job most phases) are "critical" in the sense that they must be completed before other phases can proceed. Thus, framing must take place before mechanical can be done, mechanical must be substantially complete before plumbing can begin, and so on. The time lines for the critical tasks step down the chart from the upper left corner to the bottom right corner in a roughly diagonal pattern. This diagonal is known as the "critical path."

NONCRITICAL ITEMS   The few tasks that are not critical—finish plumbing, electrical, and mechanical—are shown with short time lines off to the right side of the chart.

Flowcharts can be used for more than monitoring overall schedule. If you fill in both the length of the time lines for crew work and the crew sizes accurately, you can use the flowchart for one aspect of job costing labor—namely, to keep track of just how close your labor costs are running to your estimates during a project. For example, your chart shows two weeks for framing by your crew. They have been framing for a week. You look around the site and figure about 50 percent of the framing is done. You know the crew is pretty much on schedule.

Rough though it may be, job costing labor with a flowchart is likely to give you more up-to-date information than your accounting records back in the office. Typically, since not all accrued payroll has been included in them, the job costs recorded in your books run

behind what is going on in the field. In other words, because the crew will normally have worked at least a few more days than they have been paid for, your records will show you as having spent less than you actually have. If your crew has been framing a week and your last payroll period ended two days into framing, you can look at the recorded costs for framing and think you are doing much better than you really are. You may think to yourself, "Great, we've spent hardly anything on framing labor, and we're already halfway through." Using the flowchart, you are less likely to make that mistake.

Take care when scheduling your jobs and making your flowcharts to avoid "sub stacking"—crowding too many subs onto the job at one time. Do you see where sub-stacking is a danger in the flowchart illustrated here? It might be happening from roughly 4/16 to 5/4. During that period, the job may have the carpentry crew and the mechanical, plumbing, electrical, and roofing subs on site all at once. For a spacious work site, that might be okay. On a smaller job, the workers would be in one another's way. In either case, it would take a very good project lead to keep work flowing and give everyone the support they need. Avoiding sub-stacking but staying with a tight construction schedule at the same time is sometimes a fine line to walk.

The notifications calendar

For maximum benefit, the flowchart should be used with another project-management tool that I call a "notifications calendar." It enables you make sure you've got all your ducks in a row. All subs are scheduled to come to the job when needed. Special materials and fixtures are on order well in advance. Inspections are all lined up. With proper use of the notifications calendar, you do not forget to notify a sub until the day before he is needed, only to learn he's booked solid for the next month and a half. You get in your order for that specially engineered beam with a 6-week lead time well in advance, not 10 days before the crew will be ready to install it. As with the flowchart, a notifications calendar form can be created on your computer. The notifications calendar shown at right includes the following features:

SUBDIVISIONS For ease of reference, it is divided into sections for subcontractors, special orders, and inspections. An additional section for labor is helpful for projects on which the regular crew will be supplemented by temporary help.

SHORTHAND RECORDING OF NOTIFICATIONS For recording notifications on my calendar, I use a sort of shorthand that I call "double dating." It may look a bit weird at first, but it is very efficient. Double dating means that when I make a notification, I write down two dates—the date on which the notification is being made and the date the sub or supplier is being told he will needed at the job site, ready to begin work or delivering material. In the illustration, I am letting Superior, my heating and sheet metal sub, know on February 1 that I will need him on April 1. I write "2/1 for 4/1." By the time the job is under way on March 17, I realize that I was a bit optimistic, so I call Superior back and ask to bump the start date to April 7. On the notifications calendar, I write "3/17 for 4/7." As you can see on the calendar, I don't usually write out the word "for"—I replace it with a dash. Thus, when I notify the plumber on 3/17, I just write 3/17- 4/14, meaning that on March 17 I have let him know he should come to the job on April 14.

SAMPLE LETTERS AND FORMS
Notifications Calendar

NOTIFICATIONS CALENDAR FOR: Lue Addition

SUBCONTRACTOR

Mechanical: Superior 2/1 for 4/1 +/-; 3/17 for 4/7
Plumbing: L/M 2/1 - 4/7; 3/17 - 4/14
Electrical: Hiatt 2/1 - 4/28
Roofing: DH 2/1 - 4/14
Ext. Cladding: Thuong 2/1 - 4/28
Insulation: Lively 2/1 - 5/11
Drywall: Pratt 2/1 - 5/15
Cabinets: Blodgett 2/1 - 5/20
Paint: Martinez 2/1 - 6/2

SPECIAL ORDERS

Windows: Blomberg 2/1 for 4/21; confirmed 3/14 for 4/21
Doors: T&W Exterior 41 for 4/21 Interior:
Other:
Other:
Sub special order: L/M - kitchen sink - 8 wk lead time - L/M to order by 4/21 + submit purchase order

INSPECTIONS

Building: rough -
Special: concrete placement - 3/15 for 3/20; 3/18-3/21

PROGRESSIVE NOTIFICATION OF SUBCONTRACTORS Notify subs repeatedly as the job progresses. Let them know their planned start date when the contract for the job is signed. Update the original notification periodically. Give them a call when the job begins. Notify them when your schedule changes due to change orders, weather, or other factors. With new subs whose reliability you cannot yet fully assess, fax the notifications and have them fax it back with a signature. (As former President Reagan said, "Trust, but verify, too.")

RECORDING OF SPECIAL ORDERS Special-order items such as structural steel, windows, and special fixtures will

To keep track of all the meetings, questions, and miscellaneous tasks and information that come up on my projects, I rely on my "shirt pocket office"—a-week-at-a-glance calendar and a mini-loose-leaf binder. (Photo by Metro Image Group)

bottleneck a project severely if they do not arrive on time. Use your notifications calendar as a checklist to make sure all special orders have been made and confirmed by your suppliers—and that means confirmed *in writing*.

RECORDING SUBS' SPECIAL ORDERS

To go the extra mile, track your subcontractors' special orders by requiring them to submit purchase orders and written supplier confirmations of their orders. (I once had a project delayed because a plumber I was trying out for the first—and last—time neglected to order a custom bathtub.)

NOTIFYING INSPECTORS Record notifications to inspectors with a double date—when notified and when needed—just as with subcontractors.

The two broad-scope tools—flowchart and notifications calendar—will improve your project management tremendously. Assuming you're working with reliable people and are conscientious yourself, hassles with subs about servicing your jobs adequately will dry up. They will be at your jobs when you need them. Delays due to special materials getting stuck in the pipeline will end. You will have arranged for them to be delivered with plenty of time to spare. I have used these tools for years, and with the exception of a couple of subs I was trying out for the first time, I have never had subs or materials not show up when I needed them.

Tools: narrow scope

The flowchart and notifications calendar govern the overall flow of a project. But to stay atop the myriad details, you need narrow scope tools as well. For my projects, I have two primary narrow scope tools—what I fondly refer to as my "shirt pocket office" and the "detailed sequence list."

The shirt pocket office has two parts—a week-at-a-glance calendar and a mini-size loose-leaf binder, both of which fit snugly in the pocket of a shirt. The calendar comes into play as a project management tool to schedule job site visits, project meetings, or special project duties—such as backing up a lead when he is using a crane to place structural steel for the first time. (The tasks for which I use the shirt pocket office can be handled with a PDA—Personal Digital Assistant. PDAs, while definitely more stylish, seem less efficient, more costly, and far more prone to breaking down and wearing out. As the technology develops, however, the balance could shift, and PDAs become the narrow scope management tool of choice.)

The pocket-size, loose-leaf binder is a simple yet powerful tool for tracking project information. It holds tabbed divisions for each project and within the project divisions has sections for the lead person, designer, owner, and subcontractors. I use the binder to record all questions I have about the project, answers to the questions, and information I must convey to someone else. When looking over a project, if I have a question about the way an item is built, I write that down in the lead's section. If the lead tells me he can't determine from the plans how a certain detail is supposed to work, I make a note to discuss it with the designer. If the designer's answer requires extra work by a sub, I make a note to phone the sub and ask for a change order.

I keep my shirt pocket office with me always, writing questions and information as soon as they occur to me. I am at the lumberyard. I write down for a client, "See new sustainably harvested decking at our yard." I am elbowing through a crawl space. I note for the lead, "Insulation contractor missed end bay." I am prowling around on a rooftop, and I write down for the roofer, "Need cricket for chimney backside?"

By noting questions and ideas systematically in the shirt pocket office, I reap significant benefits. Whenever I talk with a person associated with a project, I ask him every question I need to ask and give all the information I need to give. I don't find myself completing a phone call with an architect, then having to follow-up with an E-mail about the item I forgot. I get marketing mileage, too. When clients and designers ask a question or give me information, they don't hear me say, "piece of cake" or "no problem." They see their concerns recorded in the mini-loose-leaf binder, and since they also see the binder being used when I am asking them questions, they know the concerns are going to be followed up on. The shirt pocket office creates an impression of reliability, not a bad image for a builder to cultivate.

Over the years, I have encouraged my leads to set up their own shirt pocket offices. Generally, they have preferred to use their project binders for tracking information and questions. That's fine so long as they do three things. Write down information for me, the owners, subs, suppliers, and the designers *immediately* upon thinking of it. Write down questions *immediately* upon thinking of them. Make a note of a material need *as soon as it is spotted.* I want them to avoid falling into the habit of assuming they will remember all the questions and details that come up. They won't, just as I wouldn't. There are just too many of them. Construction is too complex and variable. By and large, my leads have gone along with my insistence on immediacy, and that is a good part of why our jobs run efficiently, with few trips to the lumberyard and details rarely overlooked.

It was one of my veteran leads who developed our other narrow scope tool, the detailed sequence list, illustrated below. The list is particularly helpful for managing information and work flow at the end of a project, when there is typically a tangle of loose ends to tie up. By dividing tasks among crew members and sequencing the tasks, you can effectively allocate labor for wrap-up.

■ SAMPLE LETTERS AND FORMS   Crew Leader's Sequence List

When action at the job site gets too thick to track with a flow chart, the lead makes up a detailed schedule of tasks in the sequence they are to be performed:

MONDAY	TUESDAY	WEDNESDAY	THURSDAY	FRIDAY
Electric Finish	<u>Me</u>	<u>Me</u>	<u>Me</u>	<u>Me</u>
	• Staircase	• Newel caps	• Complete balusters	• install wine rack
	• Guard rail	• Balusters	• Tune-up doors	• Take-off for deck
	• Inspect electrical work		• Window latches	• Order deck
	and call with punch list	<u>Leslie -</u>		material
	<u>Leslie -</u>	• Cove mold for	<u>Leslie -</u>	
	• Window stool	stair treads	• Complete shelves	<u>Leslie -</u>
	• Window casing	• Install vanity tops	• Closet poles	• Cabinet knobs
	• Complete baseboard	• Closet shelves	• Phone	• Caulk & sand
			• Patch hole in plaster	miter joints
	Sheet metal fin.	Electrician's		Plumbing finish
		punch list		Notify painter

My Project Management Procedure

1. Say hello to workers at job site.

2. Inspect for safety.

3. Inspect waterproofing details.

4. Inspect for quality trade by trade.

5. Survey for change orders.

6. Meet with project lead.

7. Write change orders.

8. Contact clients, subcontractors, designer.

Putting It All Together

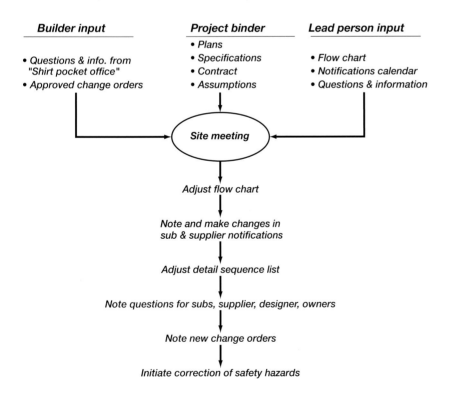

Builder input

• Questions & info. from "Shirt pocket office"
• Approved change orders

Project binder
• Plans
• Specifications
• Contract
• Assumptions

Lead person input

• Flow chart
• Notifications calendar
• Questions & information

Site meeting

Adjust flow chart

Note and make changes in sub & supplier notifications

Adjust detail sequence list

Note questions for subs, supplier, designer, owners

Note new change orders

Initiate correction of safety hazards

At our job site meeting, the lead and I pool our information and questions, adjust our flowchart and notifications calendar as necessary, and note questions and information for others involved with the project.

A project management routine

To get the full benefits of the broad and narrow scope tools you need to use them within a consistent project management procedure—just as a carpenter needs to work out an efficient way of hanging a door and employ it every time if he is to make best use of his tools. I know builders who have all sorts of project management devices, including snazzy computer software. But they are not used within systematic procedures, and the result is that the builders' jobs are often in chaos and riddled with mistakes and inefficiency.

My project management procedure, described in skeletal form at left, assumes the use of lead carpenters. If you are at the start-up phase of your career, you may be acting as your own lead, working at your job site most of the day. Even so, you would do well to occasionally step back from the work and look over your job as if you were a production manager seeing it for the first time that week. Check it over for safety hazards, quality of workmanship, and change orders. Note all concerns systematically in your flowchart, notifications calendar, and detailed sequence list.

With a good project management procedure you will gain increased control over your jobs. Should you decide to enlarge your company and hand off lead responsibilities, you will have trained yourself to move up to production manager. Once at that level, you will be able to accomplish project management for each site in one or two visits weekly, with each visit consuming roughly two to four hours, depending on the complexity of the project, skill of the lead, and number of change orders to be produced.

Begin a site visit by making several passes through the project. The first pass is to say hello to all of the workers. The second is to inspect for safety hazards, as described on p. 237. The next is to inspect the quality of the work—including compliance with the code, plans, and specs. In order to not overlook items, do the quality inspections trade by trade for the whole project—or an area at a time on a big project. During a few appropriate site visits, make a special pass to check moisture control—flashings, drainage, gutters, roofing, and other waterproofing. When moisture control is done poorly, it leads to premature deteri-oration of buildings. When the buildings get in trouble, so do the construction companies that put them up.

Usually you will pick up on extra work requiring change orders during other passes through the project. On remodeling jobs, however, particularly those for which plans are sketchy or the buildings are old and seriously deterio-rated, make a separate and final run, looking for work beyond the scope pro-vided for in the construction contract.

During my job site visits, as I look over the project, my little loose-leaf

Working with Building Inspectors

The arrival of the building inspector causes even veteran builders to tense up. For startup builders, inspection time can be unnerving. You worry, Will I pass? Will I get nailed for a violation of some code I did not even know existed? Will I have to take apart work and do it over?

Knowing a few facts can take the edge off the anxi-ety. Here are the facts: Building inspectors' powers are defined and limited. Their job is to check for compliance with specific codes having to do with health and safety, and that is all. The codes they enforce are arrived at by democratic processes, and if you don't like a code you can join in the process and work to have it changed.

Building inspectors have limited power. They have bosses and their bosses are beholden to elected officials who are beholden to you, the citizen. If you do run into an inspector whose requirements seem arbitrary or irrational, ask him to show you in black and white the code that he claims you violated. If you are reasonably in compliance, and he doesn't bend when you point that out, one option is to tell him politely that you understand his position and wonder whether the best thing to do would be to appeal to his boss on the issue. I have used that approach with an inspector who wanted to cite us for venting a hood a few inches too close to a window, though strict compliance with the code would have required rerouting the duct along a winding path through upstairs bedrooms, at great expense to the owner. The inspector is known as a bully and apparently did not want yet another contractor complaining to his boss. He decided our placement of the vent was okay after all.

In my experience, only a small percentage of inspec-tors are bullies, and only a small percentage are bums who do sloppy inspections. Most are reasonable, well-trained professionals bent on doing their job. To work successfully with them you need only:

■ *Get a permit* and build to the permit plans and specs.
■ *Know the code* and build to it.
■ *Ask for advice sparingly.* Inspectors can't assume responsibility for your work.
■ *Treat your inspectors with respect.* One inspector told me that inspectors are tough people who do not care whether you are friendly to them or not. Baloney!

Inspectors are our allies, not our enemies. I appreciate inspectors who check my work thoroughly and spot viola-tions of the code. Every time they do, they save me a poten-tial callback or lawsuit. Inspectors serve a critical public function. They stop bad construction. That is good, because bad buildings injure and kill people, including children. When I see contractors doing jobs without permits I ask them to get one. If they do not, I report them to the building department. To do otherwise would be like turning my back on a mug-ging. *Bad buildings hurt people.* As builders we have an obli-gation to support the laws which uphold standards and control the renegades in our industry.

binder goes in and out of my pocket as I note questions and information for the other people involved with the project. When I have completed my run, I ask the lead what would be a good time for us to meet. Usually, he can break away within a few minutes. If not, I busy myself until he is ready. After all, at the site he is boss. I am just the support guy. When he is ready, we move to the lead's job site communications center, pool our information and questions, and update our flowchart and notifications calendar. Finally, we discuss any change orders that must be written up for the clients. Next I move on to communicating with them.

COMING UP

Communication

Change Order Follow-Through

Wrap Up

Followup

What It's All About

Working with Clients

By aligning your expectations and the clients' during the contract negotiation stages of a project, you have set the stage for a successful relationship during construction. Both you and the clients know the script. Now, with construction under way, it is time to move onto the stage and play out your agreed-upon roles. In enacting your role, your goals will be to honor your commitment to the clients, building in accordance with the plans and conditions, producing work in which you, your employees and subs can take pride, and getting fairly paid for it. To accomplish your goals, you must take care that the clients are up to date with developments on their project and have the information they need to play their role.

Communication

"It's all about communication." This phrase is repeated over and over in construction circles. There's no denying its truth. But it leads to another question,

"What is communication all about?" Too often the answer stops with a pronouncement of the psychological goal— maintaining "trust." It neglects the operational. That is not to say that the psychological is unimportant. Maintaining trust is crucial to the success of a construction project. But what can be overlooked is that the operational supports the psychological. Communicate with your clients persistently, in a consistent and predictable pattern, and you nourish trust.

Here, in the 21st century we have numerous ways of communicating with clients from so called "snail mail" (the postal service) to instant messaging via cell phones. Each way has its uses and misuses. Instant messaging is best used for urgent matters. Frequent use is too disruptive of the ongoing day's work, and it can encourage reaction rather than thoughtful response.

Voice mail and E-mail are excellent for handling minor details—reminders to clients to take care of one of their responsibilities, answers to client questions about the job. Voice mail and E-mail are much more efficient than face-to-face or over-the-phone conversations, which tend to result in time lost to schmoozing and in which it can be difficult to achieve closure with gabby clients. These days clients may be so busy, that they prefer to limit communication to E-mail. Recently, in fact, I heard about a client who refused to communicate any other way.

For my projects, I do like some phone conversation, and better yet, face-to-face conversation as part of the mix of communications. Though conversation takes time, I am able to get a more accurate read on where the clients are coming from and form a stronger connection with them. I try to talk personally with clients at least once a week.

A communication format

Some builders handle their discussions with clients informally, letting them go where they will. There is a lot to be said for that loose, conversational approach; it will surface information you might miss in a more structured exchange. But there are also advantages to establishing a format for discussions with clients and constantly coming back to it, even if you freelance a bit as well. As it becomes familiar to them, the format helps clients keep their bearings in what, for them, is a complex and unfamiliar process. For you, it serves as a checklist of the crucial subjects that must be covered.

One five-step format is suggested toward the end of the sidebar at right. Beginning with a request to clients to raise any questions or concerns they might have is a nice opening gesture of respect. If the clients do have questions, respond to them thoroughly if you are ready to do so. Otherwise, write the question down, promising to get back as soon as you know the answer. Resist going off half-cocked in response to a question that catches you by surprise and to which you do not have a knowledgeable answer. It is very easy for that to happen, especially when clients are pressing you hard. But if you allow yourself to be panicked into an erroneous answer and the clients find you out, you will only have dug yourself a deeper hole.

After responding to questions, systematically go through your own, referring to the question list you keep in your shirt pocket looseleaf (or other device). Once questions have been covered, you've come to a good moment to present the clients with their bill for work completed. I feel strongly that the bills for construction projects are so large that it is not wise to handle them strictly as an accounting function. It is not okay to simply stick an invoice for $3,000 or $10,000 or $24,000 in the mail. With invoices involving such

Communicating with Clients

- Maintain a respectful tone.
- Communicate on a regular and predictable basis.
- Use voice mail and E-mail for efficient communication about details.
- Talk in person regularly.
- Open the door to questions, concerns, and complaints.
- Treat billing as a communication opportunity, not only an accounting function.
- Present solutions together with problems.
- Communicate in a standard, repetitive format such as:
  —Their questions
  —Your questions
  —Bill presentation
  —Problems and solutions
  —Change orders
- Drop down the glass wall when necessary.
- Say "Let me think about it" when necessary.

large amounts, I like to pay the clients the consideration of hand-delivering them so that I can answer any questions they have on the spot. Simply mailing a bill sets you up for risk of delayed payment. That is very dangerous. Once clients have been allowed to lag too far behind in making their payments for work completed, they have gained enormous leverage in the event of a dispute.

Bill presentation is an opportunity to summarize just what has been built for the huge sum of money the clients are about to fork over and to describe to them what they can expect to see happen with the project in the coming weeks. Mention items of work that you are particularly happy about. If you have just pulled the forms off the perimeter grade beam, checked for square, and found the diagonals varying by only a quarter inch, share your delight with the clients. Explain that "finish work begins at the foundation," that the square foundation will lead to a square frame, which will,

Make bill presentation a bit of a ceremony or even a celebration of good work accomplished for good money paid.

254 ■ Chapter Eight

One of my teachers of the method describes "disengagement" as dropping an imaginary glass wall between yourself and the client and gazing at him or her as if you were observing the behavior of a fascinating animal at the zoo.

in turn, help the crew achieve good-looking, tight trim. In other words, make bill presentation a bit of a ceremony—or even a celebration of good work accomplished for good money paid.

If there are problems as well as good news, try to present the problems together with solutions for the clients to consider. The discussion of problems and solutions serves as a natural prelude to the last item in the format—change orders. They are not the happiest subject with which to end the conversation; you might prefer dealing with them first or second. But one way or the other, they must be dealt with, and fortunately the most painful kinds of change orders—those for correction of hidden conditions—tend to come at the beginning of a project. Toward the end, change orders are more likely to be for client-initiated upgrades in finishes and finish detail. They, not you, will be introducing the change orders, and you can play the more pleasant role of coming back with ideas for achieving the upgrades in the most cost-effective way.

Communicating with difficult clients

Try as you might to eliminate "grinders" and volatile people during the evaluation stage of a project (see p. 116), occasionally one will get through. You will find yourself under contract to a person who wants to squeeze and manipulate you for everything he can get. Even fair-minded clients have bad moments. Already tired from work and family duties, they stop by the job to hear that they are facing considerable extra costs for drilling foundation piers because boulders have been encountered 6 ft. below grade. Or they get word that a factory has fallen way behind schedule on delivery of a custom item and that substantial completion of their project will be delayed nearly a month. At

such times, even the best clients might "go off" or make irrational demands.

Several strategies work with a difficult client. They all involve the principle of "disengagement"—easy to describe but requiring great self-discipline to practice. One of my teachers of the method describes "disengagement" as dropping an imaginary glass wall between yourself and the client and gazing at him or her as if you were observing the behavior of a fascinating animal at the zoo. Once the client's anger has subsided, effective next steps are requesting to continue the conversation later, when the client is more relaxed, or responding with a question: "I see. How would you like us to handle that?" My favored response, because it is not manipulative and expresses respect for the client's concern, while disengaging from the abusive behavior, is to say "Let me think about that " and to not budge from the position.

"Let me think about that," may, in fact, be the most useful phrase in the English language for builders. It gives you the room you need to solve a client's problem and the problem the client has become. When you are done thinking, you can go one of two ways. Call the client and commit to taking care of his or her concern if that is what the contract requires. Otherwise, ask if the client would like you to write up a change order for the extra in which he or she has expressed an interest.

Whatever way of dealing with difficult clients you prefer, make doubly sure to document your exchanges with them. Write down their answers to your questions. Write down their questions and your answers. Send them summaries of significant discussions and agreements. "Get real heavy with the paperwork," one builder says when asked how he deals with an excessively demanding customer.

Change Order Guidelines

- Never do substantial amounts of change order work without a signed change order from your clients.
- Do not let change order charges pile up. Collect for change order work immediately or at your next regular billing.
- Do even small extras only upon receiving verbal approval and a commitment to promptly sign a written change order from the clients.
- Stay alert for change order work, both for hidden conditions and for extras requested by clients. If leads are handling change orders, monitor their performance.
- When pricing change orders use your estimating checklists. Make sure to charge for all direct costs including general conditions. Mark up per your contract for overhead and profit.
- Present clients with change orders immediately after preparing them.
- Require timely, prompt client processing and approval.
- Write up any extras done without charge as "courtesy" extras.

Above all, adhere to strict change order procedures.

Writing and executing change orders

By now, you may be sick of reading about change orders. We have mentioned them often and have gone into them in detail several times. But there is good reason to go at them this one final time. All the preparation for change orders, all the education you've provided clients as to why and when they occur and how they are handled—all that is wasted effort if you don't actually execute them during jobs. You must write them up. You must have owners sign for them. You must collect for them promptly.

I meet builders who know about change orders, provide for them in their contracts, have a pretty good change order form, and yet repeatedly get beat up financially because they back down from taking care of them during projects. The consequences are devastating. The value of the change orders often exceeds the profit margins. If you do not write up

and charge for change orders, you not only will forgo profit. You will have precious little left at the end of a job to pay yourself. There is nowhere other than your pay for the cost of the change orders to come from. All other money in the job will be absorbed by direct costs and by your fixed overhead.

A set of guidelines for handling change orders is suggested in the sidebar above. For the most part, these guidelines are self-explanatory. Adhere to the first two items with the strictness you nor-

The Change Order Track

1. Change order projections during planning (see "Cost Planning")

2. Change order clauses in construction contract (see "The Conditions")

3. List of not included items in construction contract (see "The Conditions")

4. Change order form (see "Two Critical Conditions")

5. Change order production (this chapter)

The value of change orders often exceeds the profit margins.

mally would reserve for the most venerable of religious duties. Be nearly as militant about the next five. The final one is optional. I have found doing small extras at no charge, but writing them up for client signatures, to be a worthwhile practice. It seems to reassure clients that I am not committing "change order artistry," gouging them for every nickel I can get. A builder I respect takes a different tact. He does small extras without charge also but mentions them to the clients only casually. He fears that by writing them up he might make his designers look bad, a legitimate concern. Whichever guidelines you settle on, it is critical to never become afraid to charge for extra work, even in the face of strong resentment from your clients. Stick with fair-minded and consistent procedures and you can work through change orders successfully, preserving solid relationships with your clients in the end, though sometimes in the rather distant end— as in the case of a client who needed four years to settle down from our change order experience before he could bring himself to write a note thanking myself and my crew for our work.

Wrap-up

At the conclusion of each project, you must create a punch list with the client of whatever small items of work remain— tuning up cabinet doors, installing missing electrical trim, replacing a defective bulb, paint touch-up. Begin by listing all the items you know to be in need of attention. Then give the clients a copy of your list and ask them to supplement it with any items they noted.

You can ask the clients to add to your list on either an "open" or a "closed" basis. If you elect open, you will be asking the clients to simply note their items in any way they like on a blank sheet of paper. If you elect "closed," instead of

a blank sheet you will give them a form, which you can create on your computer, that breaks out the project into areas and lists all categories of work—siding, doors, windows, fixtures, trim, drywall, paint, and so on—in each area. The closed approach has certain advantages. Because it guides clients through their inspection, they are less likely to miss something and, therefore, the chance for a callback is reduced. Also, the clients' information comes back to you in an organized fashion, which makes it easier to deal with if their list is lengthy.

On the other hand, if you hold off on making punch lists until there is very little work left and do a thorough job of listing what there is, the clients will find hardly anything additional to write on the list. In that case an open list is fine. And, of course, such thoroughness will inspire client confidence and appreciation (and, therefore, references), whereas having to go over the many items on a closed list will only irritate them. They have had enough of this construction project and your detailed communications. They value it but they want it over! All in all, the best punch list is the open one to which clients will find almost nothing to add.

As discussed in "The Agreement," when the punch list is done, the job is done. You pull off and collect your final payment. You must resist excessively fussy owners who want to make out another punch list (and another and another...) all the while withholding your money. If they have reasonable extra requests to make after you complete the first punch list, you handle them on a callback basis, once you have been paid in full.

What it's all about

Callbacks are sometimes referred to as the "back end of the business." They are not. As we stressed earlier in "Marketing," they bring you around to the front end. They are a great opportunity to stimulate references to new clients. One builder is so attuned to the value of callbacks that he phones clients a year after finishing their project and asks if he can come over to check it out. If they have no complaints, he looks hard for something that needs doing, even if it's just to buff the floor, and he takes care of it. When he talks about his extra measure of service to his clients, he frames it as smart marketing. He says the investment comes back to him many times over in references.

I'm sure it does, but I have come to suspect that with this particular builder (or for that matter, most good builders) there is something other than money motivating him. He returns to the jobs for an emotional reward. I realized that as I was nearing completion of this book and was working with the photographer, visiting projects I had built 5, 10, even 20 years ago. As the photographer set up his shots, I talked with my old clients or got acquainted with new owners.

"Did you design this home?" asked one woman whose friend had purchased it from my original client. "A lot of people contributed," I said. "We worked with a good architect, and the carpenters and subs came up with many of the ideas for finishes and details." She smiled at me, "You all did a wonderful job. It's so beautiful. It is so nice to be in this place."

During another stop, while the photographer labored over a difficult shot of a stairway, I helped the lady of the house core apples for one of her famous pies. We reminisced about how she used to bake treats for the crew every day, how much her husband, who had recently passed away, had loved being involved in the process of design and construction, and how delighted he was with what we had built together.

Your work as a builder gives others shelter, comfort, security, and even joy. (Photo by Ken Gutmaker)

At the home of the the man who'd needed four years to get over his change order experience, I asked his wife if her kids liked their house. "Oh, they love it," came the answer. "We all do. It's a *privilege* to live here."

And so it went, one stop after another. I heard from the clients how much their places mattered to them. I came away thinking about the rewards of being a builder. The money is nice. The friendships with crew and subcontractors are great. The freedom's wonderful. Creating a strong company is satisfying. Then, in the end there is this—the clients living their lives in the buildings you've made for them. It's like what my builder friend Ann Hollingsworth says. You come up with a plan and work out a contract. Then you get with your people and you stand the structure up and finish it out. Years later you come back by and it's still there, still doing its job, sheltering families and their friends and making them feel good to be home. Maybe, as the saying goes, "You can't take it with you," but as a builder you can leave something behind.

Resources

Here I have listed only books, magazines, and other resources that are top quality or at least the best thing I know of on an important subject. Though some of the books are bargains, others are relatively expensive. The value of the time you put into reading a book, however, soon adds up to much more than the cost of even an expensive one. Spending extra dollars to move up to excellent books, thereby leveraging the time you have available for study, is a good investment.

BOOKS AND MAGAZINES

Bookstore

Builder's Booksource
1817 Fourth Street
Berkeley, CA 94710
(800) 843-2028
www.buildersbooksite.com

If you want resources beyond those I have listed in this book, contact Builder's Booksource. The staff is knowledgeable. If they cannot help you, they will put you through to the owner, George Kiskaddon, who knows construction literature inside out. Excepting the few titles for which I have suggested other vendors, Builders Booksource is also a convenient source for the books listed below.

Books

GENERAL

• *Small time Operator* by Bernard Kamaroff. Bell Springs Publishing. An incomparably clear general guide to business basics, including two subjects I do not cover—reconciling your checkbook and paying taxes.

• *Construction Contractors' Survival Guide* by Thomas C.Schliefer. John Wiley and Sons. A short, tough-minded book on the major reasons builders fail. One of the most knowledgeable and successful builders I know says he starts off every year by rereading Schliefer.

• *Natural Capitalism* by Armory Lovins, Hunter Lovins and Paul Hawken. Little, Brown. An inspiring guide to the creation of a nonpolluting yet robust, free-enterprise economy. Though not in the "must read" category if you are focused on the nuts and bolts of running a construction company, *Natural Capitalism* does contain fascinating chapters on green design and construction. It will help you develop language to sell environmentally considerate construction to your clients.

The Essential Start-up Library

If you are new to the building business, I recommend you purchase the following resources as a starter library. Between these resources and my book, you should be able to find answers to the questions that you will have regarding business management and construction technology issues.

- Small Time Operator
- Marketing Without Advertising
- The Contractor's Legal Kit
- Wood: Detailing for Performance
- The Builder's Encyclopedia
- Building Green in a Black and White World
- The Wealthy Barber

ACQUIRING PROJECTS

• *Marketing Without Advertising* by Michael Phillips and Salli Raspberry. Nolo Press. An excellent guide to low-cost, effective, ethical marketing.

• *Mastering the Business of Design/Build Remodeling* by Linda Case, Victoria Downing, and Wendy Jordan. Order from Remodelersadvantage.com. Knowing two of the authors and having read Linda Case's earlier book on design/build, I would expect this one (which I have not had a chance to read as of this writing) to be clear, practical, and very helpful.

• *The Not So Big House* by Sarah Susanka. The Taunton Press. A passionate pitch to owners urging them to hire architects to design their homes, *The Not So Big House* is also a terrific introduction to architectural design. It will give you language for explaining the importance of design to your clients.

• *Low Cost, High Impact Marketing*. Tape of talk by Devon Hartman at 1997 CBTC West. Cambridge Transcriptions. (617) 547-5690.

LEGAL

• *Contractor's Legal Kit* by Gary Ransone. Journal of Light Construction. The best source of starter contracts I have seen.

• AIA Contracts. Call the American Institute of Architects' office nearest you for information on purchasing AIA contracts for small and large projects.

• *Getting to Yes* by Roger Fisher and William Ury. Viking/Penguin. An inexpensive, compact book, *Getting to Yes* can help you learn how to convert destructive conflict into productive agreement.

ACCOUNTING AND ESTIMATING

• *Estimating for the General Contractor* by Paul J. Cook. R.S. Means & Company. Read Cook's book and you will understand what it means to do professional-quality estimating.

• *Contractor's Guide to QuickBooks Pro* by Karen Mitchell, Craig Savage, and Jim Erwin. Craftsman Book Company. Updated each year, QBPro is comprehensive and a challenging read. It can help you get up to speed with a generic small-business accounting program widely used by builders.

TAXES

• *Tax Guide for Small Business*, Internal Revenue Service. See your phone book for an IRS number. I recommend getting the paper version; it's well-organized, clearly written, and really helpful. I did not find that to be the case for the online version.

CONSTRUCTION TECHNOLOGY AND TRADES

• *Wood: Detailing for Performance* by William Dost and Elmer Botsai. GRDA Publications. This marvelously clear book will change the way you install beams and posts, decking, siding, windows, and other exterior details and will greatly improve the reliability and durability of your buildings. It should be required reading for every architect, engineer, and builder who works with wooden structures.

• *Building Green in a Black and White World* by David Johnston. Home Builder Press. Despite poor production by his publisher Johnston offers a helpful guide to moving from the visionary to the practical in green building.

• *No Regrets Remodeling. Home Energy Magazine*. A treasure of information on creating healthy and efficient homes.

• *The Very Efficient Carpenter* by Larry Haun (book and related videos). The Taunton Press. Haun is an old-time union production framer who knows all the moves, and the videos of him at work are both a powerful lesson in job site efficiency and a lot of fun to watch.

• *Plumbing a House* and *Installing and Repairing Plumbing Fixtures* by Peter Hemp. The Taunton Press. Hemp worked on his books for years. The effort shows. They are superb. They can teach you what you need to know about one of the most important sub trades, enable you to do respectable plumbing yourself, and inspire you with Hemp's passion for quality.

INVESTMENT

• *The Wealthy Barber* by David Chilton. Prima. If you prosper at the construction business, you will have money to invest. Chilton's book is a simple and entertaining introduction to the basics.

• *Bogle on Mutual Funds* by John Bogle. Dell. A challenging but compelling book that clears away the fog around mutual fund investing and gives you a disciplined and sensible program for investing over the long haul.

• *The Intelligent Investor* by Ben Graham. Harper and Row. Graham is the teacher and hero of Warren Buffett, and his books are likely the most important ever written on investing. *The Intelligent Investor* is a challenging read, but if you take it on, you will find its perspectives on "value" investing great lessons in the allocation of business resources as well as a prudent guide to putting your money into stocks.

Magazines and conferences

• *Fine Homebuilding*. The Taunton Press, 63 South Main Street, P.O. Box 5506, Newtown, CT 06470-5506. (800) 283-7252. Maybe I am prejudiced because Taunton is my publisher. After 20 years as a reader, I continue to be inspired by *Fine Homebuilding*. Each issue contains detailed information on trade techniques and tools, fascinating narratives about individual projects, and a sprinkling of intriguing information on economic and business concerns.

• *The Builder's Encyclopedia. The Journal of Light Construction*. (802) 879-3335. Updated every year, the *Encyclopedia* is a CD containing all of JLC's articles since 1983. Want to learn more about flashing details, earning a profit, or hiring? On this CD, you will find numerous articles on these and many other technical and business subjects.

• *JLC Live*. Sponsored by *The Journal of Light Construction*. (802) 879-3335. When your company is financially sound enough so that you can afford it, treat yourself to one of JLC's conferences. Cram in seminars by seasoned contractors on a range of business subjects. Cruise the showroom floor and pick up a ton of construction-technology information. Make friends with other builders you can call upon when you need advice.

WEB SITES

Builders and Publications

• The Conrado Company (www.conrado.com). Builder Paul Conrado was an early adopter of my cost-planning approach to acquiring jobs and has made it an integral part of his home-building business. His Web site includes a detailed presentation of his services (which he calls "price planning," the name I originally used). It may help you develop your own cost planning services.

• Winans construction (www.winconinc.com) Paul and Nina Winans run a tightly organized construction company that has achieved a reputation for quality workmanship and management. It offers a wealth of information to both homeowners and builders.

• The Not So Big House (www.notsobighouse.com). The site features links to a many other interesting sites—including a number focused on sustainable (green) building issues.

• Fine Homebuilding (www.taunton.com). Via the Taunton site, you can join an on-line forum and trade tips with other builders.

Vendors of accounting and estimating products

I do not endorse the products listed below but list them only because they have gained wide acceptance in the construction industry. Just which product, if any, might be appropriate for a specific construction business is a decision that can be made only by the owner.

• McBee (www.mcbeesystems.com). McBee provides manual one-write systems for small businesses.

• Intuit (www.intuit.com). Intuit's QuickBooksPro is a generic, small-business computer program used by many contractors.

• Peachtree (www.peachtree.com). Peachtree provides several small-business programs that are favored by some contractors.

• Turtle Creek (www.turtlesoft.com). Turtle Creek provides a relatively low-cost computer program designed specifically for contractors. Its programs operate on both Apple computers and on PCs.

• American Contractor (www.amercon.com). American Contractor sells construction management software.

• Masterbuilder (www.construction.intuit.com). Masterbuilder sells construction management software.

• WinEstimator (www.winest.com). WinEstimator sells estimating software.

Glossary

Note to the reader: The meanings offered here are not intended to be technical definitions but rather informal explanations to help you understand words as they are used in the text.

Account codes—Numbers used to label or code the categories of income, liabilities, and expenses listed in a chart of accounts.

Accounting—Accounting is more than the clerical work of recording income and expenses. That's bookkeeping. The real guts of accounting is setting up your bookkeeping so that it provides information useful for analyzing and managing your business.

The accounting equation—Assets equal liability plus equity (A=L+E). The accounting equation is derived from the more common sense equation, assets minus liabilities equals equity (A−L=E). If your business has an asset, such as a building, worth $100,000 with a $50,000 loan (liability) on it, then your equity in the building is $50,000. In other words, A(100,000)=L(50,000)+E(50,000).

Accrual accounting—One of two basic methods of accounting—cash and accrual. With accrual accounting you record earnings and expenses when they are incurred rather than when you actually make the collections or payments.

Adjustment—An accounting term for moving money from one account to another. If you charged an expense to the wrong account, you can make an adjustment by subtracting it from that account and placing it in the correct

account. An adjustment can also be used to fix a tiny error in your bookkeeping that results in your books (or checking account) not quite balancing.

Assets—Anything of value owned by your business including such resources as office equipment, construction tools, cash in your operating account or real estate. For accounting purposes, a resource is considered an asset whether or not you own it free and clear.

Balance—The amount left over in a checking account after all checks have been deducted from the total of all deposits. Also, your books are said to "balance" when the accounting equation (see Accounting equation) is satisfied.

Balance sheet—A statement showing your assets, liabilities, and equity.

Bookkeeping—Keeping records of your income and expenses.

Break-even point—The point at which a business has earned enough to pay all its expenses (including a salary for the owner), but has not yet earned enough to make a profit.

Business information technology (BIT)—A broad term for all the high-technology tools such as computers and software, Fax machines, and cell phones used by businesses to manage and communicate information.

Callback—A call from clients asking you to come back to their project and repair or correct a defect or failure.

Cash accounting—One of two basic methods of accounting—cash and accrual (see Accrual accounting). With cash accounting you record income or expenses in

your books only after you actually collect the income or pay the expenses.

Cash flow analysis—Projecting your income and expenses over some period of time—a week or a month or even longer—to determine what your cash needs will be.

Cash flow fallacy—A positive checkbook balance suggesting you are in good shape financially when, in fact, once all of your outstanding bills are paid you will be in trouble.

Change order—Authorization by a client to a builder to change the scope of work agreed to in their construction contract. Typically, change orders are written by builders on a special form and presented to clients for their approval and signature.

Chart of accounts—A list of the categories in which you record your collections of income and payments of expenses.

Check register—A log showing the checks you have written and the running balance in your account.

Contact management software—A computerized listing of all your "contacts," the people with whom you do business.

Control—Any management tool, especially an accounting tool, for monitoring your company's performance.

Cost planning—Services a builder provides during the preconstruction phase of a project to help optimize its quality while keeping it within budget.

Cost plan/build—An arrangement by which a builder provides clients with both cost planning services and construction services.

Cost codes—Numbers used to label or code the categories of job costs.

Consumables—All the supplies such as chalk, pencils, tape blades, and saw blades that your employees use up during projects.

Construction management software—Software that has been specifically created for construction estimating, job costing, accounting, scheduling, and related management tasks.

Design/Build—An arrangement by which a company provides clients with all the services needed for their project from design through construction.

Design completion—Completion by a builder of plans drawn up by an independent design firm so that the plans are adequate to support construction.

Direct costs—The costs for labor, material, subcontractors, and services of constructing projects.

Disbursement—A payment to an employee, the owner, a subcontractor, a supplier, etc., from company funds.

Draw—A payment an owner makes to himself from company funds.

Elevations—Exterior or interior vertical views of a building shown on a set of plans.

Equity—Ownership, or the portion of your assets that you own. If your business has a building worth $100,000 with a bank loan on it for $50,000, then your equity in the building is $50,000 (see Accounting equation).

Experience modification factor—A percentage based on your safety record that is used to modify your workers' compensation insurance rate.

Expense—A cost. Usually considered as the opposite of income.

Fixed out-of-pocket-overhead—A term I use to describe the irreducible overhead expenses—such as license fees, liability insurance, and vehicle expenses—that you must pay to keep your business in existence (see Standing still overhead).

Fixed overhead—See Overhead, fixed.

Flowchart—A chart showing the phases of work in a project and the sequence in which they should occur.

Foreman—The person who leads production at a job site. These days the foreman is often called the lead carpenter, lead person, or simply lead.

Functionality—The capabilities of a computer program.

General expenses—One of the three major components of fixed overhead (along with administrative and marketing expenses).

General ledger—The accounting record that breaks all income and expenses of a business into the accounts (categories) shown on the chart of accounts.

Gross profit margin (GPM)—Gross profit margin is the percentage of a construction business' total income left over after the business has paid all the direct costs of building its projects. Thus, gross profit includes both overhead and profit.

Information technology—See Business information technology.

Invoice—A form for billing a client.

Job costs—The direct costs of building projects (labor, material, etc.) as opposed to the indirect costs (general, sales, administrative, also known as overhead) of running a company (see Direct costs).

Job costing—Tracking the various individual costs (for framing labor, framing material, finish carpentry labor, finish material, plumbing, etc.) of building projects.

Labor burden—The costs (such as workers' compensation insurance, health insurance, and taxes) above and beyond wages of employing a person. Labor burden is usually expressed as a percentage of wages and typically runs from 50 to 100 percent of wages.

Labor productivity rate—The quantity of a specific item of work—such as subfloor, rafters, or window casing—a tradesperson can install in a given unit of time, typically per hour.

Lead carpenter—The terms lead carpenter, lead person, and foreman are basically synonymous (see Foreman).

Liabilities—For accounting purposes, the amounts owed by a business; more generally, the risks that go with running a construction company and building projects.

Lost opportunity costs—The lost opportunities to build other projects that you incur to hold a place in your schedule for a client's project.

Markup—A percentage or amount added to the direct costs of building a project to recover overhead or make a profit.

Net pay (net wages)—The amount paid to a worker after all deductions for taxes and benefits have been removed from his or her paycheck.

Net after tax profit—The amount left to a company after all direct expenses, all overhead expenses, and all taxes, have been deducted from revenue.

Net profit—The amount that is left after all direct expenses and all overhead expenses have been deducted from revenue.

Operating capital—The money a builder keeps in a highly liquid account such as a checking account or a money market account to pay the ongoing expenses of building projects and running the company; also called working capital.

Overhead, fixed—The portion of general, administrative, and marketing expenses that tend to remain quite stable from one month to another even though the volume of work a company is doing may vary sharply.

Overhead, variable—General, administrative, and marketing expenses that tend to fluctuate along with the volume of work a company is handling.

Owner's draw—See Draw.

Payables—Bills that a business is obligated to pay but has not yet paid.

Payables journal—A listing of the bills a business is obligated to pay but has not yet paid.

Payroll—A list of employees and the amount of wages or salary due each.

Preconstruction services—Design, preparation of working drawings, specification writing, estimating, value engineering, and other work that must be done to ready a project for construction.

Premium—A charge for an insurance policy.

Profit—See Net profit.

Profit and loss statement (P&L statement)—An accounting record that displays a company's revenue, costs, and resulting profit over a specific period of time; also called an income statement.

Project lead—A term used to cover the whole range of lead people from lead carpenters to project managers.

Proof—In accounting, a mathematical check to make sure that totals shown in the records are correct.

Ratios—A percentage or fraction showing the relationship of one amount of money to another. Select ratios, such as overhead to revenue, help builders analyze their companies' financial performance and make management decisions.

Receivable—An amount of money a business has coming to it.

Receivables journal—A listing of the amounts of money due a company. Usually included is other identifying information such as the customer's name, invoice number, and date of invoice.

Receipt—A written statement of the amount paid for an item or a service. The plural of the term, "receipts," is also used to mean the money collected for work done.

Reconcile—Matching your checkbook and bank balances to make sure that both are correctly taking into account all deposits and payments.

Revenue—Income.

Spreadsheet—A sheet of paper (or a computer screen) divided into columns and rows in which you can categorize, record, and total income and expenses in order to obtain useful financial information.

Standing still overhead—A term I use to describe the irreducible overhead a construction company must endure to stay in business when work is so slow as to be nearly at a standstill (see Fixed out-of-pocket overhead).

Sub-stacking—The practice of scheduling so many subcontractors for the same time slot at a project they get in one another's way and cannot work efficiently.

Take-offs—Quantities of work figured from or "taken off" a set of plans for a project in preparation for creating an estimate of construction cost or ordering materials.

Tie-ins—The areas of a remodel project where new work ties into existing work.

Variable overhead—See overhead, variable.

Wages—The pay that employees receive.

Withholding—The taxes that employers withhold from their employees' paychecks for transfer to the government.

Working capital—See Operating capital.

Index

Note: page references in italics indicate a photograph; references in bold indicate a drawing or chart.

A

Accounting:
  accounting equation, **58**, 59–60
  accounting literacy, terms and concepts of, 90, 91
  accrual accounting, 60, 68
  administrative expenses, 54
  advanced accounting tools and concepts, 58–60
  average job size, comparisons of, 97
  avoiding the cash flow fallacy, 66–68
  avoiding responsibility of, 51–52
  balance sheet, 59
  balance sheet ratios, 98–99
  basic accounting tools and concepts, 56–58
  benefits of, 52–53
  builder's earnings, further study of, 97–99
  callbacks, 75, 220, 256–57, *257*
  chart of accounts, 57
  consumables, 75
  for direct construction costs, 55–56
  direct job costs and gross profit margin (GPM), 97
  equity, **58**, 59
  essential accounting responsibilities, 53, **54**
  establishing an accountant, 19
  for expenses, 54–55
  "free cash," 98–99
  general expenses, 54
  general ledger, 57, **64–65**
  "gross pile," method of, 60–61
  gross profit margin, **58**, 59
  invoices, 58, **62**
  job costing in, 56, 57, **77**
  job cost records, 57, 77–83
  keeping the books, 57, 74
  labor, 74
  labor productivity records, **55**, 56, 57–58
  ladder of accounting systems, **59**, 60
  liability insurance, 74–75
  marketing expenses, 54–55
  net profit, 59
  net worth, 59
  one-write system, 69–77
  overhead and direct job costs, 57, 97
  overhead expenses, 54–55, 57, 97, **97**
  payables and receivables journals, 60
  payment to manager of the company, 55
  payroll, 83–87
  petty cash expenditure, 73, 76
  producing accurate estimates, 56
  profit and loss statement, 58–59, **63**, 66
  proofing income from a project, 61
  revenue comparisons, 97, **97**
  security and control measures, 75
  shoebox system: income and expenses, 60–69
  software for, 35, 36
  spreadsheet, 57, 63–64, **64**, 65, **65**, 66
  tracking income, 53–54
  tracking key ratios, **95**, 96, **96**, 97, **97**, 98
  See also Computer accounting
Alternate dispute resolution (ADR):
  arbitration, 197
  discussing misunderstanding, 196
  nonbinding mediation, 196
  small claims court, 196–97

Alternative methods in estimating and bidding:
  adjusting and standing by the bid, 176
  attaching all markup to labor costs, 172–73
  gross profit margin method, 174–75
  marketing to markup, 173–74
American Institute of Architects (AIA), 179, 188
Arbitration, 197
Association of General Contractors, 118
Attorneys, establishing relationship with, 19

B

Basic Bond Book, The, 43
Blodgett, Fred, 228
Builder, career as:
  acquiring skills in small steps, 12
  arithmetic, competence in, 6–7
  builders resisting operation of own company, 8
  business cycle, ups and downs of, 14–15
  capabilities for, 5–6, **6**
  clarity of purpose, 5, **6**
  communication skills, 5, **6**
  connecting with the community, 13
  construction skills and knowledge, 5, **6**
  creating a mission statement, 6
  defining your market, 18
  developing standard operating procedures (SOPs), 10–11
  developing the company, 22
  entrepreneurial instincts, 9
  establishing controls, 5, 6, 21
  financial discipline, 9, **9**, 10
  going out of business, 13–14
  keeping a time log, 9
  learning trade skills and knowledge, 7–8
  making a plan, 17–22
  marketing for projects, 21–22
  marketplace for quality over quantity, 16–17
  opening a business account, 18
  opportunities and challenges in, 12–13
  patience for the job, 11
  reading, competence in, 6–7
  reevaluating and adjusting the plan, 22
  rewards for a job well done, 13
  selecting form of business, 18–20
  setting up headquarters, 20–21
  standards and reputations of contractors, 15–16
  starting a construction library, 21
  start-up plan, sample of, **18–19**
  taking off the tool belt, 8–9
  time management, 9, **9**, 10
  writing, competence in, 6–7
Builders' associations, membership in, 21
Building inspectors, working with, 251
Building well and doing a good job, 13, 106–107, 256–57
Burger, Warren, 196
Business, forms of, 18–20
Business cards, **21**
Byrnes, Bryant, 196

C

Calculating direct costs:
  allowances, 159
  calculating labor costs, 160
  checking cost calculations, 162–63
  constructing a labor productivity rate, 160
  labor burden, 161–62
  subcontractor costs and material costs, 158–59, **159**
Callbacks, 75, 220, 256–57, *257*
Carpenters, project leads and delegation, 215–20
Cash reserves. *See* Operating capital
"C" corporation, 19
Cell phones, 30, 31, 35
Cleanup, 146, **147**
Clients, working with:
  communication format, 253–54
  communication with, 252, 253
  defining the relationship in policy statement, 38
  difficult clients, communicating with, 254
  wrapping up the project, 256
  writing and executing change orders, **186**, 193–96, 255–56
Competitive bidding:
  appeal to owners and designers, 123
  limits of, 126
  process of, 122, **122**, 123
  reasons for builders using, 123–24
  success at, 124–26
Computer accounting:
  accounting literacy, terms and concepts of, 89, 90
  bookkeeping efficiency of, 89
  charts of accounts, **90–91**
  choosing the accounting program, 92–93
  controls in accounting, 88
  cost effectiveness for accounting, 88
  demonstration versions, trial of, 92
  gaining insight of business performance, 89
  job cost monitoring with, **93**, 95
  payables journal, **93**
  preparing for, 90–92
  tracking key ratios, **95**, 96, **96**, 97, **97**, 98
  types of computer accounting programs, 92
  using an accounting program, 93, 95
Computers:
  backing up information in, 36
  computerized estimating and bidding, 149–51, **151**
  converting to a computer accounting program, 87–95
  costs of information technology, 33–34
  E-mail and Internet, 30, 31–32, 92
  hardware and software options, 31
  learning to use, 20, 21
  organizing an office without, 20–21
  quality in computer-generated forms, 36
  return on investment in, 33–34
  strategies for adopting computers and IT, 34, **34**, 35, **35**, 36
  tracking costs of, 73–74
  using information technology (IT), 30–32

Construction contracts:
 Agreement, the, 183–89
 alternate dispute resolution (ADR), 196–97
 Builder's Obligations in Conditions, 191–92
 change orders and charging for extras and deletions, **186**, 193–96, 255–56
 Conditions, the, 189–93
 describing the work and defining the schedule, 183–84, **184**, 185
 kinds of construction contracts, 180–81
 legal notifications, including requirements for, 189
 lump sum contracts, 180, 186
 Owners' Obligations in Conditions, 190–91
 provisions for payment and payment retentions, 185, **185**, 186, **186**, 187, **187**, 188
 reciprocal obligations in, 192–93
 sources of contracts, 179–80
 staying in control with, 177
 structure and contents of, 178, **178**
 subcontracts, 197–98, **198**, 199
 time and materials (T&M) contracts, 180–83, 186
 using and modifying the AIA contract, 179, 188
Construction Standards Industry (CSI) Masterformat, 149
Contractor's Guide to Quick Books Pro, 90
Contractor's Legal Kit, The (Ransone), 178, 179
Contractor's Survival Guide, The (Schleifer), 74
Contractor's Survival Manual (Mitchell), 44
Contracts. *See* Construction contracts; Subcontracts
Cook, Paul, 231
Cost planning:
 charging for and rewards of, 140–41
 checklist of, 134, **134**, 135, **135**, 136–37
 conceptual estimates in, 136–37
 cost planning agreement, sample of, **135**
 cost planning services, 121–22, **122**
 final estimates in, 136, 137
 four levels of cost estimating, 136–37
 guidelines and safeguards for, 137–39
 marketing of, 139–40
 preliminary alternatives in, 136, 137
 truth and profit in, 138
Crew:
 costs of turnover, 213–14
 crew size, 210–11
 meeting the needs of the crew, 212–13
 one-person crew, 210
 training opportunities, 214, **214**, 215
 two-person crew, 210, 211
 workers' need for predictability, 212

D
Daily setup and roll-up, 146, **147**
Delegation. *See* Project leads and delegation
Design/build, 121, **122**
 appeal and path of, 129–30, **130**
 benefits of, 130–31
 challenges and hazards of, 127–29
 change order artistry, 131
 elements of, 127
 "errors and omissions" coverage, 129
 limits of, 133
 marketing of, 130–31
 phases of a project in, 128
 protection from risks with, 131–32
 using virtual showrooms, 132
Design professionals, working with:
 building with, 114–15
 financial benefit of, 110
 finding, qualifying, and succeeding with, 113–14
 hazards of, 111–12
Developer model of company organization, 202–203
Digital cameras, 30, 31, 32
Discipline and termination:
 policy of discipline and termination, 38, 40
 progressive discipline process, 209–210
 relationship in policy statement, 38

E
E-mail and Internet, 30, 31–32, 92
Employees. *See* Hiring and firing
Environmental concerns, in policy statement, 38
Estimating and bidding:
 alternative methods, 172–76
 calculating direct costs, 158–63
 charging for, 22
 checklists and forms for, 144–45, **145**, 146
 computerized estimating and bidding, 149–51, **151**
 concepts of, 143
 definitions of, 143–44
 figuring overhead, **163**, 164–68
 figuring profit, 169–72
 gathering information, 152–58
 general conditions in, 146–47, *147*
 process of, 143–44
 producing accurate estimates with accounting, 56
 professional estimating, 149
 selling price, 144
 slippery items in rough and finish work, 147–48, *148*, 149
 using the Construction Standards Industry (CSI) Masterformat, 149
 See also Competitive bidding
Estimating for the General Contractor (Cook), 231
Evaluating projects:
 dealing with grinders, 116
 glamour projects and, 119–21
 owners as co-contractors, 117
 owner's credit and financial reliability, 118–19
 projects with a good fit, 119–20, *121*
 realism and fairness, 116–17
 respect and appreciation of builder's management, 117–18

F
Fax machines, 30, 31, 35
Federal Building Company, 108
Figuring overhead in estimating and bidding:
 capacity-based markup method, 166, 167–68
 charging at three levels, **163**, 164
 figuring charges for overhead, 166–67
 identifying overhead costs, 164–66
 uniform percentage-based method, 166, 167
Figuring profit in estimating and bidding:
 figuring charges for profit, 170–71
 market-based markup, 171–72
 risks and rewards of the construction business, 169–70
Financial discipline, 9, **9**, 10
 building and managing operating capital, 44
 line of credit as an asset, 44
 opening a business account, 18
 projecting needs for operating capital, 18
 See also Accounting
Fine Homebuilding, 15, 111, 114
Firing. *See* Hiring and firing
Forbes, 16
"Foremen." *See* Project leads and delegation

G
Gathering information in estimating and bidding:
 checklist for, **153**
 preparing plans and figuring quantities, 153–54, **154**, 155, **155**
 project specifications from the designer, 153
 setting up a project binder, 152–53
 site visit and subcontractor quotes, 156, **156**, 157, **157**, 158
 take-off form for, **156**
"General Conditions." *See* Construction contracts, Conditions, the
"Green" construction practices, 12–13

H
Hartman, Devon, 108
Hayden, Larry, 12, 108
Hiring and firing:
 cost of an apprentice, 206
 costs of turnover, 213–14
 employees, attributes to look for, 205, **207**
 fair and respectful employer practices, 205
 finding and keeping good employees, 204, 205, **207**
 firing an employee, 209
 hiring the right employees, 203–204
 hiring to strength or weakness, 11
 job site interviews, 208–209, **209**
 larger-volume models of company organization, 202–203
 legal concerns of, 203
 models of construction company organization, 201–203
 in policy statement, 38
 procedure of hiring, 205–207, **207**
 progressive discipline process, 209–210
 selecting new employees, 207–208, **208**
 small-volume models, 201–202
 training opportunities, 214, **214**, 215
Hollingsworth, Ann, 13

I
Independent Artisan model, 201, 202
Information technology (IT), 30–36
 See also Computers
In-house contractor model of company organization, 202–203
Insurance:
 business and "nonowned" vehicles, 47
 claims made versus occurrence coverage policies, 46–47
 commercial general liability (CGL) policy, 46–47
 employee insurance, 48–50
 establishing an insurance broker, 19
 exclusions in, 47–48
 finding and selecting a broker, 45–46
 insurance policies for contractors, 46
 legal requirement of, 44
 liability insurance, 46–47
 in policy statement, 38
 setting limits and controlling costs of, 48–49
 tool theft coverage, 47
 tracking costs of, 73
 workers' compensation, 49–50
Internet, 30, 31–32, 92, 132

J
Job cost records in accounting:
 canned costs, 79
 creating cost records, 80–81
 developing and maintaining records, 79–80
 filing cost records for completed projects, 79
 labor productivity, units of, 79–80
 monitoring costs on ongoing jobs, 80–81
 narrative labor productivity record, **81**, 81–83
 three levels of, 78–80
Job setup in project management:
 document preparation, 238–39, **239**, 240
 handing off projects to leads, 240–41
 moving into production, **239**
 project binder, divisions in, 239–40
 project meeting and binders for clients, 241–42, **242**, 243
Job site appearance and behavior in policy statement, 38

L
Labor, materials, and subcontractors:
 crew, 210–14, **214**, 215
 legal concerns in hiring and firing, 203
 pay, 221–27
 project leads and designation, 215–17, **217**, 218–20
 subcontractors and suppliers, 228–29, *229*, 230–34
 See also Hiring and firing